THE LAST GUNFIGHT

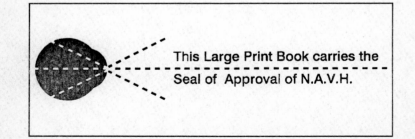

THE LAST GUNFIGHT

THE REAL STORY OF THE SHOOTOUT AT THE O.K. CORRAL — AND HOW IT CHANGED THE AMERICAN WEST

JEFF GUINN

THORNDIKE PRESS
A part of Gale, Cengage Learning

GALE
CENGAGE Learning

Detroit • New York • San Francisco • New Haven, Conn • Waterville, Maine • London

GALE
CENGAGE Learning

LIBRARY OF CONGRESS CATALOGING-IN-PUBLICATION DATA

Guinn, Jeff.
    The last gunfight : the real story of the shootout at the O.K.
Corral—and how it changed the American West / by Jeff
Guinn. — Large print ed.
    p. cm.
    Includes bibliographical references.
    ISBN-13: 978-1-4104-4022-8 (hardcover : large print)
    ISBN-10: 1-4104-4022-2 (hardcove : large print)
    1. Tombstone (Ariz.)—History—19th century. 2.
Violence—Arizona—Tombstone—History—19th century. 3.
Outlaws—Arizona—Tombstone—History—19th century. 4.
Frontier and pioneer life—Arizona—Tombstone. 5. Large type
books. I. Title.
    F819.T6G85 2011b
    979.1'53—dc23   2011018948

Published in 2011 by arrangement with Simon & Schuster, Inc.

Printed in Mexico
3 4 5 6 7 15 14 13 12

For Andrea Ahles Koos:
Let no opinion go unexpressed.

CONTENTS

8

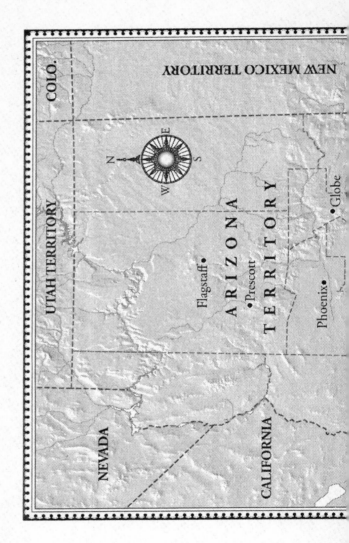

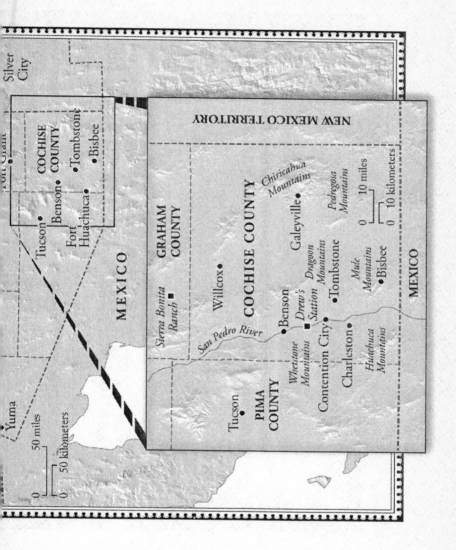

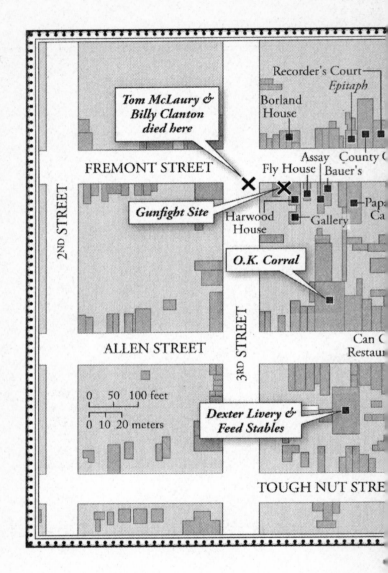

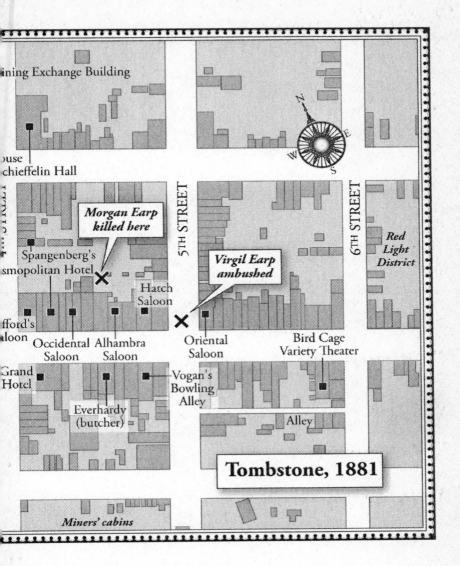

ining Exchange Building

ouse
chieffelin Hall

5TH STREET

6TH STREET

N
E
W
S

Red Light District

Morgan Earp killed here

Virgil Earp ambushed

Spangenberg's
smopolitan Hotel

✗

Hatch
Saloon

✗

fford's
loon

Occidental
Saloon

Alhambra
Saloon

Oriental
Saloon

Bird Cage
Variety Theater

Grand
Hotel

Everhardy
(butcher)

Vogan's
Bowling
Alley

Alley

Tombstone, 1881

Miners' cabins

Prologue:
Tombstone That Morning

Virgil Earp was determined to sleep in on Wednesday, October 26, 1881. The Tombstone police chief tumbled into bed around 6 A.M. after participating in an all-night poker game at the Occidental Saloon. Among others, he'd played against Johnny Behan, the county sheriff, and local ranchers Ike Clanton and Tom McLaury. Before sitting down to play cards, Clanton had spent much of the night threatening the chief's brother Wyatt and Wyatt's gambler pal, Doc Holliday. At one point he and Holliday had to be separated. Holliday eventually headed home to his room in a boardinghouse, but Clanton kept drinking and getting more worked up.

As chief of police, even off-duty and playing in a card game, Virgil Earp always remained alert to possible trouble. But empty threats were common in Western saloons. Men had a few drinks too many, promised to commit mayhem on somebody else, and forgot all about it the next day when they sobered up. Ike Clanton had a reputation in Tombstone as a loudmouth who fired off hot air, not hot lead. Virgil didn't take him too seriously. When the marathon poker game finally concluded — afterward, nobody seemed to remember who won or lost, so no huge sums could have changed hands — Clanton swore again to Virgil that he was going to get his guns and then settle things with Holliday the next time he saw him. He added that it seemed Virgil was part of a group conspiring against him. The Earps and Doc Holliday, Clanton warned, had better get ready to fight. The police chief replied that he was going to get some sleep, Ike should do the same, and he better not cause any problems while Virgil was in bed.

Dawn on that Wednesday morning broke bitterly cold in southeastern Arizona Territory, so it was a good time to stay warm under the covers. A storm was on the way; Thursday would bring sleet and snow. Extremes in weather had been common all year in the region. The blazing heat of summer was a given, but April through early July had been the hottest and driest in memory. When rain finally did come in July and intermittently thereafter, it frequently arrived as a deluge. Just weeks earlier, much of sprawling Cochise County — roughly the size of the states of Connecticut and Rhode Island combined — had been drenched. The desert soil, baked rock-hard by the sun under a coating of sand, didn't absorb moisture well, and roads throughout the county flooded. Now biting winds whipped down from the north, causing the temperature to plummet. It was not a comfortable morning to be outdoors.

Yet as Virgil Earp fell asleep, the main streets of Tombstone still bustled with people. It was always that way, every hour of every day. Tombstone was a mining town, built over a warren of underground tunnels and surrounded by a bristling ring of hoists, smelters, and other structures manned nonstop in a frenzied communal effort to wring as much profit from the earth as possible. The mines operated in shifts, never closing, so neither did many of the town's dazzling array of shops, restaurants, and saloons. Weather, like the time of day, made no difference. Broiling, freezing, day, night, Tombstone pulsated with frantic energy. In some form or another, everyone there was on the make.

For the better part of twenty years, Virgil Earp and his brothers, James, Wyatt, and Morgan, had roamed the American frontier, trying to make the great fortune and secure the leading places in a community that their family had coveted, and failed to achieve, for generations. Tombstone, they hoped, was where their dreams would finally come true. Virgil was police chief and a United States deputy marshal, James had a "sampling

17

room" saloon, Wyatt and Morgan sometimes worked for Wells Fargo, and all four brothers owned shares of mine property in and around town. Wyatt had hopes of being elected county sheriff in another year, a job with the potential to pay him as much as $40,000 a year — the kind of wealth that might gain the Earps admittance to Tombstone's highest social circles. Finally, they would be *somebody*.

Tombstone was a place where such things could happen. Thirty miles from the Mexican border, seventy miles from Tucson, the town was well known throughout the country, mentioned frequently in the business sections of major newspapers from New York City to San Francisco. Its silver mines were said to be the richest since the legendary Comstock Lode was discovered in Nevada Territory in 1859. Legitimate investors, less savory speculators, prospectors in search of strikes that would make their fortunes, and experienced miners looking for work constantly flooded into town, along with those hopeful of siphoning off some of the rumored riches into their own pockets — lawyers, merchants, gamblers, saloonkeepers, prostitutes. In that way, Tombstone was typical of any mining boomtown.

Yet it was also unique. By design as much as by accident, Tombstone was a cultural contradiction, one where the usual mining

18

camp demimonde delights of fixed card games, brothels, and cheap rotgut coexisted amicably with swank hotels and restaurants, world-class stage entertainment, and pricey blended whiskies of the sort sipped in the finest East Coast metropolitan watering holes. Civic leaders were about to debate the advisability of installing sewer lines, and telephones linked the major mines and the busy Mining Exchange Building, as well as a few of Tombstone's glitziest hotels. The town was an addictive hybrid of elegance and decadence, a place soon to be described in one prominent travel magazine as "a spasm of modernism." Tombstone deserved the description. In many ways the town was the logical culmination of what, in just over a century, the American West had come to represent: Limitless opportunities for any man to achieve any ambition, no matter how lofty or unlikely. On this chilly morning, there was no other place like Tombstone in all of Arizona Territory, or in much of America.

Thanks to stringent ordinances prohibiting guns to be carried within city limits, Tombstone was mostly a safe place, too. It was inevitable, in any community with so many saloons patronized by prideful, hard-drinking men, that alcohol-fueled testosterone over-flow periodically resulted in fist-fights or drunken attempts at gunplay. More often, bellowed threats like Ike Clanton's against the Earps and Doc Holliday were never carried out. The efficient town police force sent prospective combatants home to sleep it off, or else locked them up for the night and took them to court to be fined the next morning for disturbing the peace. As the sun rose on October 26, the vast majority of Tombstone residents had never witnessed, much less participated in, physical violence or gunplay within town limits. Billy Breakenridge, who served several years as a Cochise County deputy sheriff, later claimed that "I never heard of a house [in Tombstone] being robbed, or anyone being held up in the city, and it was perfectly safe for any lady or gentleman to pass along the streets, day or night, without being molested." The most substantive proof came in August 1881, when Chief Earp informed the city council that things were so quiet, the town police force could be reduced to three men — himself and two officers, though he reserved the right to appoint civilians as "special deputies" if necessary. (When he testified in a trial in Tucson in mid-October, Chief Earp named his brothers Wyatt and Morgan to serve as special deputies while he was away.) In town, Virgil Earp had a well-deserved reputation as an impartial enforcer of the law; during the broiling heat of summer 1881, he even arrested Wyatt for disturbing the peace and fighting. Wyatt had to pay a $20 fine.

But there was ongoing concern among town leaders about a group they believed not only threatened local tranquillity, but Tombstone's future prosperity. In the surrounding area, particularly in the smaller settlements of San Simon, Charleston, and Galeyville, a loosely knit band of desperadoes collectively known as "cowboys" engaged in raucous lifestyles that frequently crossed over into lawbreaking. The cowboys rustled openly; because of beef shortages in Cochise County, butchers and consumers didn't much care where cattle were purloined, so long as the majority of them were stolen from Mexican rather than American herds. In exchange for a cut of the profits, small ranchers in the area such as the Clantons and McLaurys gladly grazed the rustled stock on their property until it was fattened enough for sale. The cowboys were also suspected — it was never proven — of attacking Mexican pack trains bringing goods across the border to trade, and of raiding Mexican settlements in much the same manner as renegade Apaches. International tension resulted. Members of President Chester A. Arthur's cabinet were consulting with territorial officials about it.

Clashing opinions about the cowboys ramped up an already bitter political feud in Cochise County and Tombstone, the county seat. The town's rival newspapers were engaged in all-out editorial war. The *Nugget*

21

was unabashedly Democrat in its leanings, favoring minimal government intervention in territorial and local issues, and claiming that "cowboy depredations" were grossly exaggerated by area leaders who wanted to enrich themselves at the expense of individual freedoms. The Republican *Epitaph* took the opposite view: The cowboys were menaces not only to local safety, but to Tombstone's reputation. There had been several area stage robberies in the last seven months, surely carried out by cowboys. The *Epitaph* demanded federal intervention, currently forbidden by congressional edict; meanwhile, John Clum, the newspaper's publisher and mayor of Tombstone, joined other civic leaders to form the Tombstone Citizens Safety Committee, ready when needed to mete out swift vigilante justice. In an August 1881 editorial, Clum wrote, "When the civil authorities are insufficient or unwilling to protect a community, the people are justified in taking the law into their own hands and ridding themselves of the dangerous characters who make murder and robbery their business." It was a slap at county sheriff Behan, who rarely arrested cowboys and occasionally managed to let them escape jail when he did, and an equally blunt warning to Tombstone police chief Earp: If he ever failed to keep the cowboys under control while they were in town, his bosses would do it for him.

The last thing Virgil Earp wanted was armed, trigger-happy civilians stalking cowboys on Tombstone's streets. It took the judgment of an experienced lawman like the town police chief to know when to act decisively, and when to let situations fizzle out of their own accord. Ike Clanton's babbled threats to "fix" Doc Holliday and the police chief and his brothers were good examples. Virgil could have arrested him, but guessed that Ike would cool down. As the sun came up on Tombstone that Wednesday, Clanton was probably snoring in a drunken stupor in a town hotel. When Ike woke up with a hellacious hangover, he'd stumble back to his ranch. It was nothing to lose sleep over, and Virgil didn't intend to.

But around nine in the morning, policeman A. G. Bronk roused Virgil after just a few hours of slumber to tell him that Ike Clanton was staggering around town, now armed and still drunk, threatening to kill all the Earp brothers and their friend Doc Holliday on sight. The chief told Bronk not to worry about it, then rolled over and went back to sleep.

About six hours after that, three men died, with a fourth soon to be assassinated and a fifth crippled for life. Yet the impact of the bloody events in and just outside a cramped Tombstone vacant lot extended far beyond the fates of the eight men directly involved.

23

What has come to be called "The Gunfight at the O.K. Corral" became a pivotal moment in American annals because misunderstandings, exaggerations, and outright lies about it provided impetus for future generations to form a skewed, one-dimensional view of frontier history. In fact, it represented an unintentional, if inevitable, clash between evolving social, political, and economic forces, though the Earps and the Clantons and the McLaurys and Doc Holliday had no notion of that when they began pulling triggers. The real story of Tombstone, and of the American West, is far more complex than a cartoonish confrontation between good guys and bad guys. Much of the subsequent misinterpretation can be directly traced back to that critical moment on a freezing October morning in 1881 when sleepy, well-meaning Virgil Earp guessed wrong.

CHAPTER ONE:
THE WEST

If it had been up to Daniel Boone, America's frontier expansion would have begun with the creation of a new state named Transylvania.

In 1775, not long before the first shots of the Revolutionary War, Boone led a small expedition through the Cumberland Gap in the Alleghenies, entering what would eventually become the state of Kentucky. At the time, it was the western flank of the vast British colony called Virginia. Boone had already made several trips to the region since the late 1760s. Now he came as an investor rather than an explorer. Boone worked for the Transylvania Company, a business venture intended by colonial entrepreneur Richard Henderson to enrich himself and his partners by anticipating westward migration and the demand for land there. Boone staked out a site, founded a settlement he immodestly named Boonesborough, and joined Henderson in selling lots to other pioneers. The partners then proposed Boonesborough as the county seat of a colony called Transylvania, but Britain turned them down. After the war, the undaunted duo applied to the Continental Congress to recognize Transylvania as a state. They were rebuffed again; there was some question whether Henderson, Boone, and their partners owned the land at all. They claimed they'd acquired it in an agreement with the Cherokee Indians, but other tribes disputed the legitimacy of Cherokee ownership. Like the state of Transylvania, Boonesborough didn't work out as planned. By the end of the eighteenth century it was a virtual ghost town. Boone himself was gone twenty years before that, moving further west in hopes of acquiring the *right* land that would make him rich and influential. He was among the first Americans with that goal, and, for a while, Boone remained the exception rather than the rule.

In the early years of the new nation, the public perception and the reality of the West were the same. People of limited means yearned to own land, the West was where they could, and that was all there was to it. Most Americans were farmers, or wanted to be if they could acquire sufficient property. Within the settled regions of the original thirteen states, that was a problem. The most desirable farmland was spoken for; much of it was tied up in large private estates. Particularly along the more heavily settled eastern sea-board of the newly minted United States, land was at a premium. The geographic alternatives for landless Americans were limited. To the north, menacing Britain guarded the border of Canada. To the south, the equally powerful Spanish controlled Florida. The only available direction for expansion was westward, beyond the Allegheny Mountains that formed the spines of Pennsylvania, Virginia, and Maryland. Everyone knew there were great sprawling expanses in that direction, and, for those willing to endure hard work and danger it was possible to acquire land of their own and make their living from it. Few hoped for anything more than a subsistence existence, growing enough crops and bagging enough wild game to feed their families and survive in minimal comfort, not luxury. For the earliest frontier settlers, that was enough. While Daniel Boone's namesake town didn't win over many of his fellow pioneers, the trail he blazed into the Western wilderness did. The Cumberland Gap became a popular route in America's expansion to the west.

Congress did what it could to encourage Western settlement. Its goal, until 1890 when the government declared that there was no more American frontier left to settle, was to get as much public land into private hands as possible. The Northwest Ordinance of 1787 declared that the federal government would oversee territorial legislatures — a grandiose concept, since America had yet to acquire any new land to be designated as a national territory. But the fledgling nation was clearly going to expand, and, when it did, rules had to be in place for how much autonomy settlers would have. The basic answer was: Not much. Whenever five thousand eligible voters were present (meaning adult white males), territories could elect assemblies — but the U.S. Congress could veto any laws passed by these assemblies, and territorial governors and judges would be appointed by the national government. Only when a territory's population reached sixty thousand could it petition Congress to become a state. Until then, any territory was essentially a vassal colony, useful to the United States for the space it would add and the contributions it might make to the national economy.

The obvious priority was finding territory to acquire, and America soon butted up against a formidable obstacle to westward expansion. Spain controlled the mouth of the Mississippi River, whose north–south route was critical to American commerce. In 1802, Spain shut down New Orleans to U.S. shipping. President Thomas Jefferson tried to acquire New Orleans and part of Florida from the Spanish, but they ceded their vast "Louisiana" holdings (which extended well up through the continental heartland to the southern border of Canada) to France instead. Here, America stumbled into luck. Napoleon's main concerns were extending his power in Europe and putting down a slave insurrection in France's colony of Haiti. Jefferson acquired the vast Louisiana Territory for $15 million; it added more than 800,000 square miles to the United States, immediately doubling the size of the country. Now there was ample land for the early waves of American settlers. The problem was, no one could be sure just how much. The boundaries between Louisiana and Spanish holdings in the Southwest weren't clear. The Lewis and Clark Expedition had angled northwest to the Pacific coast. Many settlers simply set out in a westward direction, hoping for the best.

These early pioneers were obliged to cooperate rather than compete. Personality conflicts had to be overlooked for the greater good. Everyone had the same goal. They wanted their own land — and welcomed neighbors with the same ambition. The failure of one endangered the chances of the rest. Few farmed exclusively; they had to contribute to the community beyond that. One might have a knack for basic blacksmithing. Another could build and operate a small gristmill. Few of the settlers had much money, or thought that they ever would.

But as American settlement of the West expanded so did the ambitions of some pioneers. Much of the exploring and settling could now be done by boat — with the Louisiana Purchase, America commanded two mighty rivers, the Mississippi and the Missouri. The rivers made it easier to travel, and to ship manufactured goods from east to west, and raw materials from west to east. There had been fur traders in North America since European and British settlers originally reached its shores. They hunted animals with limited success and acquired most of their pelts from Indian tribes. The French dominated the fur trade in mid-continent. In the early 1800s after the Louisiana Purchase, Americans were anxious to do the same. Animal furs brought good prices in East Coast markets, where they could be turned into hats and coat collars and lap robes. The first American "mountain men" made their way west, in the process bringing beaver and sea otter to the brink of extinction in some regions. Westward expansion often destroyed aspects of the wilderness in the process of settling it.

Some of the mountain men blazed new trails, always moving farther west. Jim Bridger was among the first white men to reach the Great Salt Lake. John Colter, who initially came west with Lewis and Clark, described geysers to disbelieving listeners. Kit Carson ranged all the way to what would become California. These mountain men were also businessmen, glad to live wild and free but devoted to making all the money they could while doing it. The process involved competition — most mountain men were affiliated with rival fur trading companies. Each had his preferred hunting grounds and Indian trading partners, and wanted to keep them for himself. Too much cooperation hurt potential profit.

Settlers now coming west to farm were aware of the new financial possibilities. One, with a clear lust for wealth, wrote that he was trying hard "to get the land subdued and the wilde nature out of it. When that is accomplished we can raise our crops to a very large amount and the high prices of everything raised heare will make the cultivation of the soil a very profitable business." Subsistence farming was no longer the main goal for some of these frontier landowners; capitalism — making more money than would have been possible back east — became primary.

The mountain men also initiated another significant change among those migrating west. Families made the trek to farm; a man needed his wife and children to help tend crops and animals. Mountain *men* had a clear gender distinction; when they wanted the company of women, they usually took them from native tribes. During the early years of westward expansion, the ratio of men to women was almost 50-50. Soon, it was a lopsided 80-20.

As more communities were built, overland east–west trade routes were required. Settlers needed manufactured goods; markets back in the East needed raw materials. There were no train lines available in the new territory, and rivers didn't reach everywhere, so wagon routes were established to haul goods across rugged terrain. There was the risk of Indian attack, and because some of the wagons rolled along trails close to disputed borders between the U.S. territories and Mexico, international tension developed.

Back east, westward expansion began contributing more than raw goods and space for pioneers to roam. For any nation, an entertaining mix of actual history and exaggeration provides inspiration to its citizens in the form of folklore — British poet Samuel Taylor Coleridge perfectly described the process as "the willing suspension of disbelief." America had no centuries of history to fall back on, but the Western frontier came to be seen as a magical, near-mythical place. Colorful tales of the West, both fiction and highly exaggerated "fact," began appearing in print and onstage to thrill readers and audiences. In 1823, James Fenimore Cooper published *The Pioneers,* the first of five "Leatherstocking Tales" featuring the adventures of fictional woodsman Natty Bumppo. Though *The Last of the Mohicans* (possibly based on the real-life abduction by Indians of Daniel Boone's daughter) would prove the most lasting installment in terms of popularity, *The Pioneers* depicted the lives of settlers in a Western frontier outpost, and the American public lapped it up. In 1831, James Kirke Paulding's play *The Lion of the West, or, A Trip to Washington* was a smash hit. It was obviously about the real-life David Crockett, a backwoodsman elected to Congress in 1827. Two years later, an unknown author (possibly James Strange French) produced a follow-up "biography," *Life and Adventures of Colonel David Crockett of West Tennessee.* Crockett, no fool regarding the potential political advantages of his newfound fame, wrote an autobiography, *A Narrative of the Life of David Crockett,* which he promoted incessantly. It sold between five thousand and ten thousand copies, a huge number for the time. Many, Crockett included, thought he might ride the crest of celebrity all the way into the White House, but he became embroiled in political wrangles with President Andrew Jackson and soon lost even his seat in Congress. He went to Texas, and laid claim to a permanent place in American history at the Alamo. But the books about him cemented the belief in Americans that the West was a fabulous place, one with unlimited possibilities for adventure, profit, and even fame. To many readers, Natty Bumppo became every bit as real as George Washington, and it was fun to imagine that David Crockett just might be, as he himself roguishly suggested in print, half-horse and half-alligator, with a little touch of snapping turtle. It was no more far-fetched than the general public back in England daydreaming about joining King Arthur and his Knights of the Round Table on a quest for the Holy Grail. Besides, unlike mythical Camelot, the Western frontier was actually *there* — anyone with enough gumption could go and, apparently, prosper.

This growing American belief was captured in print for the world in 1835, when young French aristocrat Alexis de Tocqueville published the first volume of his classic *Democracy in America.* Sent by France to study the U.S. political system and, especially, its penal institutions, Tocqueville observed that in America "millions of men are all marching together toward the same point on the horizon; their languages, religions and mores are different, but they have one common aim. They have been told that fortune is to be found somewhere toward the west, and they hasten to seek it."

As decades passed, the American definition of "West" and "frontier" continually evolved. More vast chunks of land were added to the

U.S. territories — the Louisiana Purchase was followed by the acquisition of Texas as a state, then the Oregon Territory, then the Mexican Cession of the 1840s. It would culminate with the Gadsden Purchase, which was ratified by Congress in 1854. It seemed, for a long time, as though the sprawl of Western land waiting to be settled was limitless. The vastness of the frontier soon lent itself to another reason to move there — it was possible for anyone to leave behind an old identity. A popular territorial folksong inquired, "What was your name in the states?" Men facing criminal charges could and often did easily lose themselves in the territories, where sheer size of jurisdictions thwarted lawmen.

In the territories, Congress established three-pronged law enforcement. A U.S. marshal, based in a territory's capital, enforced federal law. He was allowed to hire a few deputies to work in far-flung, but reasonably well-populated, areas. Counties, established by territorial legislatures with the approval of Congress, elected their own sheriffs, who also could hire deputies. The main duty of most county sheriffs was collecting taxes. Towns elected marshals; they enforced local ordinances. In theory, all three branches cooperated. In practice, this didn't always happen, due to distances involved or poor communication or personal disputes between the lawmen. In worst-case scenarios, such as a brief rebellion in New Mexico when the American governor was assassinated, or in Utah when Mormon militia wiped out a wagon train, the U.S. Army was called in. This marked the beginning of an ambivalent attitude by Westerners toward the federal government. Except in times of physical danger, Westerners generally wanted their government to leave them alone. Laws and taxes represented the kind of impositions that they came west to escape. But they also wanted, and expected, federal arms to protect them from Indians, Mexican raiders, and outlaws that territorial lawmen couldn't control or track down.

One thing the army didn't do very often was swoop in to deflect Indian attacks on wagon trains of settlers — there weren't that many such assaults. Between 1842 and 1859, about thirty thousand Western emigrants died while en route by wagon train, but fewer than four hundred were killed by Indians. The wagon train death rate was 3 percent, compared to the 2.5 percent average among all Americans. Ninety percent of wagon train fatalities came from disease, with cholera the leading cause. As the American territories expanded, in many regions the Indian threat decreased dramatically. There were obvious exceptions — the Sioux in the Midwest and Northwest, the Comanches in Texas, the

Apaches in the Southwest. But many tribes were decimated by illnesses carried by white settlers, or else became dependent on white largesse as game grew less plentiful.

To a large extent until the late 1840s, almost all settlers in the evolving West farmed or hunted. That changed dramatically with the discovery of gold in California. Because of its subsequent explosion in population, California was quickly admitted to the union as a state rather than spending decades conditionally accepted as a territory. Would-be prospectors, many of them too inexperienced to understand much about hunting for gold beyond believing wild tales of boulder-sized nuggets lying on the open ground, surged to California cross-country or by ship, an arduous voyage that could take months from the East Coast. Over the next thirty years, mining camps sprang up in what were or would become the U.S. territories of Idaho, Montana, Colorado, Utah, Nevada, Arizona, New Mexico, and South Dakota. Unlike the farmers who initiated westward expansion some sixty or seventy years earlier, prospectors wanted to come into enormous wealth, and just enough did to encourage the belief in countless others that the same thing might happen to them. One of the most attractive aspects about mining over farming was that, for prospectors but not farmers, it was possible to get started without investing

much. It cost an estimated $1,000 to pur-
chase the tools and seed necessary to start a
farm. A pan and a pick for prospecting cost
only a few dollars, and the potential profit
was much greater. Finding gold or silver or
copper or quartz was the most certain way to
escape what one Forty-niner termed "the
detested sin of being poor." Some still came
west to escape from the constraints of too
civilized Eastern society, from personal
mistakes made in the past, or, in the case of
the Mormons, from perceived religious
persecution. But as gold fever gripped the
nation, just as many or more came to strike it
rich, through honest labor or, far more often
now than previously, chicanery. After the
California Gold Rush the West became, in
the words of historian Cissy Stewart Lale, "a
place for hustlers of all kinds." Unlike inhab-
itants of farming communities, prospectors
and miners often had some form of personal
fortune — gold dust or nuggets if not green-
backs — and any mining town population
was soon increased by an influx of con artists
offering one-sided partnerships, merchants
peddling whiskey, gamblers whose decks of
cards were likely marked, and prostitutes.

The gallant and the greedy traveled west by
wagon, ship, and, increasingly, by rail and
stagecoach. The transcontinental railroad
didn't completely link East and West until
1869, but by the 1850s rail lines poked out

from the East into the Midwest. Because of the railroads, even more raw products from the West could be shipped east — there were virtually no manufacturing plants on the frontier until advancing technology made it possible to transport prefabricated facilities by rail after the Civil War. In 1858, the Butterfield Stage line established a 2,800-mile route between Memphis and San Francisco, a trip that took twenty-four days with no comfort involved. Often, passengers had to climb out and help pull the stage out of mud, or push it up a particularly steep hill. One passenger wrote, "To enjoy such a trip, a man must be able to endure heat like a salamander, mud and water like a muskrat, dust like a toad and labor like a jackass." The stages were usually crowded to the point where several passengers had to perch on the roof or rear baggage compartment. But the stages could go where the railroads didn't. Mineral strikes usually occurred in inconvenient places. Very few settlers made their way to Colorado Territory until 1858, when a gold strike received coverage in the national media; within a year, over 100,000 swarmed in. Nevada Territory was virtually uninhabited until 1859, when the Comstock Lode seized the attention of the world. The name epitomized the new breed of scalawags operating in the West. Canadian fur trader Henry T. P. Comstock acquired much of the massive claim from gullible prospectors Peter O'Riley and Patrick McLaughlin for $40 in cash, a bottle of whiskey, and a blind horse.

The Civil War brought about the next changes in westward expansion. By the conclusion of the internecine struggle, many men emigrating west considered the U.S. government to be an implacable enemy rather than an occasional annoyance. From the early days of American self-rule, residents of Southern states vigorously opposed any form of federal intrusion. In the years leading up to the Civil War, Eastern Republicans, "Yankees," tried to curb the system of slavery that formed the basis for economic prosperity in the South. Southerners were certain, with good reason, that it was the Yankees' intent to eradicate slavery completely. Bitter debate and violence resulted over votes and congressional compromises concerning which territories would be "slave" or "free." At war's end, the Reconstruction era in the South further embittered those living there. Prior to the Civil War, most emigrants to the West came from the North and East. Jobs were scarcer there than in the South. But in the immediate postwar years, young white Southerners, many of them Confederate veterans, wanted nothing more than to escape what they considered to be the intolerable insult of Yankee occupation. These Southerners became Democrats, sworn to hate and actively

40

oppose anything to do with Republicans. As they began making their way west to the territories, they carried their resentment with them.

The arrival of this Southern influx created new tensions in territorial politics. The federal government had always exercised ultimate authority in the territories. It did not escape the notice of arriving Southerners that the men making rules for the frontier were the same Republicans who were overseeing the despised Reconstruction. The Southerners had come west to avoid heavy-handed Yankee authority, not submit to more of it. Their resentment embraced not only the federal government, but anyone in the territories — lawmen, rich investors, rank-and-file emigrants like themselves — they believed represented hated Republican influence. Essentially, the Southerners now coming west wanted to retain their old social values. Northern arrivals, especially investors, focused on modernization and profits. There was no middle ground.

Western products as well as politics changed after the war. Previously, arrivals in the territories mostly farmed or mined. But as the railroad stretched into Kansas, admitted to the Union as a state in 1861, there was a new source of apparently abundant raw material. When emigrants moved into the Midwest plains, they were greeted by huge herds of buffalo. Back east, tanned buffalo hides could be converted into blankets and other products. Buffalo hunting was initially seasonal work — the animals' hides were thickest in the fall and winter. But in the 1860s, manufacturers in the East began using buffalo pelts for industrial applications like machinery belts. The hides became critical to industry. With increased demand came a flood of hunters who worked year-round; the money they could make was irresistible — the average buffalo hide sold for about $3.70 or 15 cents a pound, and a man with accurate aim could take down as many as eighty buffalo on a good day.

Thanks to magazines and dime novels, buffalo hunters became exalted in the East. "Buffalo Bill" Cody, first celebrated in a highly exaggerated *Street and Smith's New York Weekly* story by the writer Edward Judson (using the nom de plume "Ned Buntline"), capitalized on his newfound celebrity by portraying himself in stage plays, then founding a Wild West Show that toured nationally and in Europe for decades to come. Tourists from as far away as Britain began signing up for buffalo hunting excursions. They'd arrive by train, hire a veteran hunter and his crew as guides, and happily blast away. Not surprisingly, by the late 1860s the once innumerable buffalo were already on the way to extinction.

Their decimation threatened more than the buffalo themselves. Towns dependent on Eastern manufacturers' demand for hides had sprung up throughout the Midwest. Without the hunters bringing in their hairy hauls — and spending money while they were there — these towns were in imminent danger of drying up. Many of them were just a few rickety shacks, but some were more than that, with restaurants and laundries and general stores. Then salvation came in the form of other horned animals, the next wave of Western industry.

Texas teemed with longhorn cattle in herds that proliferated while the Civil War shut down traditional markets along the Mississippi. These longhorns weren't the choicest beef on the hoof; they often weighed less than a thousand pounds, much of it bone and gristle besides lean, stringy meat. But longhorns could travel well on very little forage and water. Back east, the demand for beef was incessant. Processing plants were in the East, too. To exploit demand, the cattle needed to be driven north from Texas to towns where railroads connected to the great Eastern cities. Texas had the huge herds required, Kansas had the railroad towns, and in 1866 the first great Texas trail drives to Kansas began. There was an immediate complication. The Texas longhorns brought with them microscopic ticks; the longhorns were immune to the disease — commonly known as Texas tick fever — carried by these mites, but it killed any Midwest cattle that it infected. The Kansas legislature mandated that Texas herds must be driven into the state on the west side of an ever-evolving "tick line." Abilene was the first major railroad town to receive the majority of the herds, then Wichita, then Dodge City. In each instance, the lucky town enjoyed an immediate, massive boost to its economy. Every Kansas railroad community wanted the Texas cattle drives to terminate within its city limits. Competition between the towns was cutthroat. Some sent representatives south to meet the herds on their way north, and they would tout their towns as offering the finest whiskey, tastiest foods, best card games, and most willing women.

Such amenities were prized by the Texans. Herding cattle was a chore involving hard physical labor and near-intolerable boredom. For weeks, drovers spent endless hours on horseback, swallowing dust as they struggled to keep thousands of cattle moving in the same direction, and at night they slept wrapped in thin blankets on hard ground. Food on the trail was basic, often nothing more than beans and bread. Working on a cattle drive proved too tough for America's preeminent frontier hero. When Buffalo Bill Cody invested in a Texas cattle herd, he decided to ride up to Kansas as part of the crew, probably hoping for adventures to incorporate into his Wild West Shows. Instead, he quit along the way, observing, "There is nothing but hard work on these round-ups. [I could not] possibly find out where the fun came in." That's because there wasn't any until the job was over. When the Texans finally arrived in a Kansas town, turned over their cattle, and received their wages, they were eager to enjoy their first real pleasures since leaving home. That was good for the towns, and bad for their lawmen.

The goal of the cow towns was to separate newly arrived Texans from their hard-earned money as soon as possible, and, when they were broke, to see them quickly on their way back home. The drovers might want new clothes, baths, even a visit to church, but their most immediate concerns were getting drunk, gambling, and having sex. The towns had ample saloons and prostitutes available for those purposes, but these were almost always confined to certain blocks. Saloon owners and brothel keepers paid monthly fees to town governments for the privilege of operating. These might range from $35–$50 for liquor licenses to a few dollars for each prostitute working out of a specific bordello. The money was collected by the town police, and some of it was used to pay their salaries. Respectable residents kept their distance. In theory, the Texans would arrive, get paid, spend what they had, and clear out within a few days so there would be room for the next batch to come in and do the same. In practice, it often didn't work out peaceably.

The drovers were a boisterous lot, given to shooting off their guns in celebration if not in anger. Texans in cow towns drank, caroused, and fought — county and town lawmen were in the difficult position of enforcing the law without alienating the lawbreakers. If word spread that Texans having fun ended most of their nights in a Kansas town's jail, then the cattle drives might stop coming there. And, sometimes, blowing off steam escalated into outright violence. In the history of western expansion, there were very few face-to-face gunfights, men calling each other out to see who could draw faster on Main Street while everyone else ducked behind available cover to watch. Instead, shots were either fired in moments of spontaneous, drunken fury or else from ambush. Pistols were notoriously inaccurate. Until the 1890s, they were shipped from factories "sighted in" up to a range of twenty-five yards. Any distance beyond that was problematic. Holsters were mostly used out on the trail. In town, pistols were jammed into waistbands or coat pockets — a nonlawman wearing a gunbelt was such a unique sight that he would cause comment. To curb potential gunplay, officials in most major cow towns — and mining communities, too — passed laws that prohibited carrying guns inside city limits. Outside of town, everyone was responsible for protecting himself. But every cow town had its violent incidents until the cowboys and cattle drives stopped showing up.

The cattle boom petered out as railroads spread into the Southwest, making it unnecessary to drive longhorns hundreds of miles north to Kansas to be sold and shipped. Packs of young Texas drovers no longer arrived in Kansas ready to celebrate after monastic weeks on the trail. And even in the headiest years, most ambitious men who came west to Kansas and settled in the cow towns usually didn't stay. The only people getting rich from cattle drives were the owners of the herds, the brokers who bought and sold the longhorns, and the cow town businessmen who reaped profits from saloons and restaurants. Drifters who wanted to make a fortune for themselves, to become somebody of considerable substance, had to look farther west to where there were fewer limits to what they might achieve. Almost inevitably, that now meant prospecting. The odds weren't great, but the potential was there. Anyone willing to invest the physical effort stood a chance of making a big strike. Most mining boomtowns remained primitive and, if only small amounts of ore were discovered in the vicinity, disappeared within a few years. Many were far removed from the creature comforts of civilization. There were occasional exceptions; Virginia City in Nevada Territory eventually boasted fancy restaurants, saloons, and hotels. But prospectors generally lived in filth, spent most days engaged in hard labor — breaking rock with a pick made herding cows seem easy — and ended up with little to show for their efforts. If they had no luck in one place, they'd move on to another. Tensions ran even higher in mining camps than in cow towns. Each prospector was competing against all the others. The men there had it tough.

But it was worse — much worse — for women in mining camps or anywhere else in the West. A man all by himself in the territories was still respectable; most women on their own were prostitutes. For them, life's choices were reduced to a single goal: Attach themselves to men and get out of the business, or soon grow old and sick and die. In the few fancy territorial towns like Virginia City, some bordellos were high-class, with attractive young females available for high dollar prices, and bouncers on hand to forcibly remove any customer who misbehaved. But in most camps, weary women turned tricks in shabby cribs and regularly endured violence at the hands of their clients. Many turned to drugs. Morphine and laudanum

were the most popular. A sense of despera-
tion was pervasive — the suicide rate among
frontier prostitutes was always high. Their
one advantage was that, in the Western territories, women were so scarce as to almost
always have some value no matter how battered they might be. Men who wanted sex on
a regular, unpaid basis, and who yearned for
someone to wash their clothes, clean their
shacks, cook their meals, and perhaps bear
their children did not have a wide selection
from which to choose. Not all the available
women in the West were practicing prostitutes, but many were. And men looking for
wives in the territories were not always great
bargains themselves.

The results, often, were partnerships rather
than love matches. Few couples were joined
formally in any religious or legal ceremony;
among people of limited means, common-
law marriages were the rule. The woman
involved might take the man's last name, and
sign herself "Mrs." She had some stability
and safety, unless or until her husband tired
of her. Then he could break off the relationship without any legal complications. Courts
would never rule in favor of an abandoned
common-law wife. Ultimately, the advantage
was with the man.

While a man and woman lived together as
common-law husband and wife, no one
questioned their standing as a couple. But in

territorial towns of any consequence, there would always be a small, select upper class of investors and merchants, and these men often did bring wives with them, women who were married in every legal sense. Formally married women might associate in a reasonably friendly fashion with common-law wives, chatting with them on the streets or in shops or in church, but they would rarely invite them into their homes. Men in the West, no matter what their backgrounds, could always aspire to a higher place in society. Women were far more limited in rising above whatever they had been.

As the 1870s advanced, new limits were imposed on virtually everyone in the Western territories. Most critically, the American frontier was dramatically shrinking. The middle of America — Kansas, Nebraska, Missouri, Oklahoma — was generally settled. The California Gold Rush had effectively taken westward expansion all the way up and down the Pacific coast — California itself had evolved into a progressive, well-populated state. Mineral riches in the Colorado and Nevada territories were either played out or, at least, staked out. Territory to the north — Wyoming, Montana, Idaho, the Dakotas — had plenty of room and opportunity, but ferocious winters were a problem. Fortune hunting there, especially prospecting and cattle raising, had to be almost seasonal. In Texas, like California a state rather than a territory, landowners with vast holdings precluded most newcomers from making any sort of economic mark. So for many ambitious men in the West, only the territories of New Mexico and Arizona remained — and in those hard, lovely lands, nothing came easily except sweat.

The Desert Land Act of 1877 recognized that farmers and ranchers in the Southwest needed more than 160 acres of land. In arid country such as Arizona and New Mexico, settlers could acquire up to 640 acres of public land for $1.25 an acre in return for the new owners' agreement to irrigate the property within three years. An initial payment of 25 cents per acre was required immediately, with the other dollar per acre due at the end of the three years. That well-intentioned rule actually limited the options of would-be farmers: It would be practically impossible for anyone to cultivate and sell sufficient crops to pay off the rest of what they owed the government for the land in the time required. Instead, speculators snapped up most of the land made available under the legislation. For only a quarter an acre, they could hang on to the land for three years, hoping a nearby strike would make it vastly increase in value. If that didn't happen, they would be out only a minimal investment. The still unirrigated land could be returned to the government.

Another tweak in existing law would also have unforeseen consequences. Violence in New Mexico Territory, particularly the Lincoln County War of 1878 between competing businessmen and ranchers, resulted in new jurisdictional limits being imposed on the U.S. Army. For a time, the region was placed under martial law, which resulted in considerable public backlash. Congress then revised the long-standing *posse comitatus* statute allowing military intervention when marshals and their deputies were unable to enforce the law. Now the army was required to let civilian authorities thrash things out as best they could.

At least in popular belief, what remained unlimited in the remaining Western frontier, particularly in Arizona and New Mexico territories, was opportunity. Most people came west because they weren't satisfied with who or where they had been. They might want wealth, social status, or just space in which to do as they pleased with minimal interference from the government. In these last remaining territories, nothing was guaranteed, but anything seemed possible. These were still places men could go to in hopes of *becoming*. And so they went.

CHAPTER TWO:
THE EARPS

From their origins to their dreams of wealth and power to their wandering nearly the entire American frontier in search of ultimate success that always eluded them, perhaps no family epitomized the settling of the West more than the Earps. No matter where they were or what they had, they believed there was something better, if only they could find themselves in the right place and circumstances. It was a philosophy that guaranteed constant frustration; thwarted ambition, as much as anything else, earned three of them their eventual places in frontier history.

The first Earps reached the New World in the early eighteenth century, coming from Ireland by way of England. Earps fought the British in the Revolutionary War, and later followed Daniel Boone's path across the Alleghenies to settle for a while in Kentucky. Walter Earp, grandfather of the most famous family members, was typical of settlers on the early frontier in that he practiced several professions at once. Walter farmed, taught school, preached, and served as a notary public. He apparently relished being a man of influence. Some neighbors called him "Judge" Earp. The title notwithstanding, Walter was still no better off than other farmers who'd managed, part-time, to creep just a little higher up the social scale. He hadn't escaped the plow.

In 1845 Walter sold his land in Kentucky and moved to Monmouth, Illinois; several of his grown children moved their families there along with him. This was also typical of the frontier. Any relocation was risky. There was comfort in having relatives with you, people you knew well and trusted. One of the offspring who came to Monmouth with Walter was thirty-two-year-old Nicholas Earp, who inherited his father's ambition as well as his limited talent for elevating himself. This was an uncomfortable combination for Walter; Nicholas found it intolerable.

Nicholas came to Monmouth as the head of his own sizable family. In 1836, he had married Abigail Storm. She bore him two children — Newton in 1837 and Mariah Ann in 1839. Nicholas's daughter died that same year, and so did her mother. Men on the frontier didn't have the luxury of mourning long for lost wives. Eight months later, Nicholas married Virginia Ann Cooksey. She began producing babies, too — James in

1841, Virgil in 1843, and Martha Elizabeth in 1845. Like Mariah, Martha did not survive long.

Nicholas farmed and apparently operated a Monmouth saloon, which would not have required much investment beyond whiskey and glasses. Some researchers believe Nicholas brewed rather than bought the liquor he sold there. Though there seems to be no record of his ever having formally studied law, Nicholas also served as a Monmouth justice of the peace — another "Judge" Earp. Nicholas welcomed any sign of distinction — he was pleased in 1846 when his Monmouth neighbors elected him captain of a group hunt.

That same year, America went to war with Mexico. As soon as Monmouth began organizing a volunteer brigade, Nicholas signed up. He was not placed in command; that honor went to Wyatt Berry Stapp, a local merchant who ranked considerably above Nicholas in the town pecking order. But Stapp appointed Nicholas as third sergeant, a designation that undoubtedly was less than the new noncom hoped — there had to be a first and second sergeant, who also outranked him — but at least rescued Nicholas from the lowly anonymity of private. The Illinois Mounted Volunteers went off to fight in Vera Cruz, and by December 1847 Nicholas was back home, invalided out after being kicked by a mule. Despite that, Nicholas obviously relished his time in the military. When his fourth son was born in March 1848, Nicholas named the boy Wyatt Berry Stapp Earp in honor of his former commander.

When the war concluded in 1848, the U.S. government thanked its veterans with gifts of land. Nicholas was awarded 160 acres in Pella, Iowa. He moved his growing family there — Morgan, Warren, and Adelia were all eventually added to the brood — and ran a harness shop besides working his new property. He must have had some financial success, since he acquired several lots in town and built a two-story home. But Nicholas couldn't settle for that. Six years later, he returned to Monmouth. This time he augmented his farming income by working as a part-time constable. It was another title that provided a certain limited status. Nicholas also tried to further himself in politics, helping to organize a "Fremont Club" named after well-known explorer John C. Frémont, a prominent member of the newly established Republican Party. Nicholas would clearly have admired Frémont, who earned a national reputation as a charismatic, if controversial, explorer of the West, soldier, and businessman.

Nicholas's second sojourn in Monmouth lasted only two years. He may have left town after being fined for bootlegging whiskey. If so, Nicholas would have been outraged rather than ashamed. Earps were never known for gracefully acknowledging mistakes. He packed up his wife and children and returned to Pella, where he went back to farming. Middle-aged, still pursuing grand ambitions that remained unfulfilled, Nicholas was by this time an angry man. His usual expression, captured in occasional photographs, was a scowl. Perhaps from frustration, his temper was volcanic. Like most Earps in succeeding generations, his light blue eyes glared rather than observed. Compromise was not part of his makeup, and that trait was inherited by his sons, particularly Wyatt, Morgan, and Warren. All of Nicholas's boys learned from their father to stand up for their rights, and to maintain fierce self-sufficiency.

The Civil War offered Nicholas's older male offspring the chance to get out on their own, albeit at the risk of their lives in combat. Predictably, the Earps supported Lincoln and his Republican administration. Newton, James, and Virgil all enlisted in the Union army, and thirteen-year-old Wyatt tried to do the same. Nicholas intervened, and Wyatt reluctantly stayed home. Newton and Virgil served out their full enlistments. James suffered a bad wound to his left shoulder and was mustered out early.

When Virgil enlisted, he left behind a wife. Many Pella residents were part of a tightly knit Dutch community, and Ellen Rysdam's parents hadn't been pleased to have their daughter courted by an outsider. So the young couple eloped before Virgil joined the Union army in the summer of 1862. As he and his brothers often demonstrated in years to come, Virgil had a flexible commitment to marriage. His enlistment papers noted he was single. While Virgil was away, and apparently not keeping in touch with his wife, Ellen's father announced that her husband had been killed in combat. The Rysdams, including supposedly widowed Ellen, then pulled up stakes and moved west to Washington Territory. How much Virgil knew about the subterfuge is unclear, but when he mustered out of the army in 1865 he did not try to find Ellen.

For a while during the war, Nicholas served as deputy U.S. provost marshal for Pella, overseeing enlistments and once again finding himself in a position of limited authority. It had to rankle; now in his early fifties, time was running out for Nicholas to become a man of real substance. In Monmouth and Pella he wasn't impoverished, but he wasn't going to do any better in those places than he already had. Fifteen years earlier, gold was discovered in California; men in far worse straits than Nicholas had since made fortunes there. He decided he would go to California, too.

By 1864, wagon trains had been crossing the Western territories for more than twenty years. It was still an arduous trip of two thousand miles or more across all sorts of terrain. Though Indian threats were greatly reduced, the possibility of attack remained. The wagons themselves were uncomfortable to ride in, and everyone involved had to live for five or six months under the most primitive conditions. Nicholas not only accepted danger and discomfort on behalf of his wife and children, he assumed responsibility for all the other families from Pella and the surrounding area who wanted to join the expedition. He was elected wagon master, and took charge of about forty wagons and 150 settlers. They left Council Bluffs, Iowa, on May 12.

For seven months Nicholas was in charge, and by the end of the long journey many of those who'd voted for him as wagon master devoutly wished they hadn't. Nicholas was a stern leader who expected everyone to do exactly as they were told. When other people's children didn't behave to his satisfaction, Nicholas told the parents that if they couldn't make their youngsters behave, he'd spank the kids himself. No sympathy was extended to those who had trouble keeping up. Nicholas scared them into line, liberally salting his commands with profanity. His methods may have been questionable, but when the wagon train arrived in San Bernardino, California, on December 19, not one member of the party had been lost — this despite the predictable harsh weather in the desert and mountains, and two brushes with Indians. These probably weren't desperate life-and-death battles, though later in his life Wyatt Earp, sixteen during the journey, described them that way. Wyatt told biographer Stuart Lake that during one confrontation he took the lead in fighting off a whole band of savages intent on appropriating the wagon train's horses and cattle. But by 1864, a single all-out attack by Indians on a wagon train would have been rare, and it practically defies possibility that the Earp party would have experienced two. It's more likely that on a couple of occasions a few Indians trailed along after the wagons, hoping to pick off a stray horse or cow, and some of the convoy's men and teen-aged boys, including Wyatt, chased them away.

Nicholas Earp didn't come to California to be a prospector. Instead, he acquired some land in San Bernardino and returned to farming, probably waiting to see what other opportunities might emerge. But his father's decision infuriated Wyatt, who hated everything to do with farming except tending to horses. Nicholas demanded total obedience of every household member. He certainly must have been a difficult father for independent-minded sons to live with. That may have been the reason James Earp dropped off the wagon train in Nevada Territory, where he took up saloon-keeping. (Virgil was still in the Union army.) After arriving in California, Wyatt and his father argued, and, given their short tempers, may have come to blows. The result was that Wyatt, still just sixteen, left home. He didn't have to go far to find work. Soon Wyatt was employed by a local freight line, probably caring for horses and doing menial jobs. His professional prospects brightened when Virgil, fresh from the army, showed up as a driver for a stage line between San Bernardino and Los Angeles. With help from his big brother, Wyatt caught on with the same company, and when Virgil was hired by another outfit to drive longer routes, including to Prescott in Arizona Territory, Wyatt worked on those, too.

In 1868, when Nicholas decided he wasn't happy in San Bernardino and moved back to the Midwest, Virgil and Wyatt went some of the way with him. They stopped in Wyoming — James may have gone there, too — and took jobs grading track for the Union Pacific Railroad. The work was hard, and the workers' camps were rough places where brawls were routine. This was where Wyatt must have learned to fight with his fists; he acquired a measured self-confidence from his ability to defend himself, and, when he became a lawman, was always ready to pound a potential troublemaker into submission. Wyatt was slow to trust anyone. Virgil was less confrontational; instead of punching someone, he'd rather drink with him, or diffuse tension with a joke. But when pushed too far, he was just as tough as Wyatt.

The two Earp brothers stayed in the Northwest for about a year before rejoining their parents in the township of Lamar in southwestern Missouri. Newton Earp moved there, too; with the exceptions of James, probably still in Wyoming or Montana, and Morgan, who'd headed off to Kansas, the whole family was back in one place. Besides farming and running a small combination grocery store and restaurant, Nicholas once again gained local status. He was appointed town constable, but resigned soon afterward to serve as justice of the peace. Even as a newcomer to Lamar, Nicholas must have had political influence, because in November 1869, twenty-one-year-old Wyatt was appointed to replace his father as constable. This was Wyatt's first chance to wear a badge, and he evidently liked it. A year later the town held formal elections, and Wyatt ran against three opponents, one of them his half-brother, Newton. Wyatt won by twenty-nine votes.

In 1870, justice of the peace Earp presided over Wyatt's wedding to Aurilla Sutherland, whose family owned and operated the town hotel. The young couple were not together very long. Less than a year after their wedding, Aurilla died, possibly in childbirth or else from typhoid. At some point soon after he became a widower, Wyatt, still town constable, fought in the street with two of Aurilla's brothers. There's no evidence about what started the brawl, but it was the beginning of an extended bad patch in Wyatt's life. A few months later, he bolted from Lamar after being charged with stealing a small sum of public money. Two co-defendants, including Wyatt's uncle Jonathan, stayed in town to stand trial, and were found not guilty. But Wyatt's legal problems didn't end when he left Missouri for Indian territory in Arkansas.

In the spring of 1871, Wyatt Earp, Edward Kennedy, and John Shown were accused of getting William Keys drunk and then stealing two horses from him. Little is known about Kennedy and Shown. All three were arrested and arraigned for trial in Van Buren, Arkansas. The May 9 edition of the *Van Buren Press* explained what happened next:

On Wednesday, between day light and dark, seven of the prisoners confined in the upper part of the jail made their escape, by prying off the rafters at one corner and then crawling round between the roof to the grate in the back of the building where they removed the stone wall sufficiently to admit egress to the body of a man — when they tied their blankets together and lowered themselves down about 20 feet, to the jail yard, and then dug a hole sufficient to crawl under the fence, which they did and made their escape, without the knowledge of the guard. . . . The men that escaped were all desperate characters.

The list of escapees' names included W. S. Earp.

Not all the Van Buren prisoners participated in the jail break. John Shown, one of Wyatt's two partners in the alleged horse theft, fled with him, but Ed Kennedy, the other, chose to stay behind. Kennedy stood trial in June, and was acquitted. For the second time, it seemed that Wyatt had run for no reason. The court verdicts in Lamar and Van Buren suggest, though don't prove, that he had the bad luck to be wrongly accused twice in a row. There's no mention of these incidents in any of his interviews or his memoir. In Wyatt's version of his life, in late 1869 he moved from railroad work in the Northwest to hunting on the Midwest plains, first for an army survey team and then on his own stalking buffalo. He also made brief stops in Monmouth, Peoria, and Beardstown, Illinois. Some of that was true. Part of the time Wyatt must have been a buffalo hunter. It was in

one of their camps that he met and befriended Bat Masterson. But he didn't spend
all of his time out on the range. For about a
year beginning in February 1872, Wyatt did
live in and around Peoria and Beardstown in
Illinois, where he and his younger brother
Morgan worked in bordellos.

Peoria was a bustling town along the Illinois
River, exactly the right location for gamblers
and prostitutes to ply their shady trades —
most men stopping for a night or a few days
were on the prowl for excitement. In many
frontier towns, bordellos were openly acknowledged as vital to the local economy,
and their operators paid city fines to stay in
operation. That wasn't always the case in
Peoria. Periodically, the more conservative
town residents demanded that such sinful
business be curtailed, and police would make
a series of arrests. On February 24, 1872, a
raid on a well-known brothel run by Jane
Haspel netted the Earp brothers. Wyatt and
Morgan were fined $20 each, a nominal sum
indicating that the cops thought they were
customers rather than employees. But in
May, they were arrested again, and this time
their punishment was more severe. Wyatt and
Morgan may have been pimps, luring customers, but it's more likely that they served as
bouncers. The *Peoria Daily Transcript* noted:

Wyat Earp and his brother Morgan Earp

were each fined $44.55 and as they had not the money and would not work, they languish in the cold and silent calaboose.

It was customary for prisoners to work off their fines if they didn't have the money to pay them; it's curious that Wyatt and Morgan chose to serve time rather than perform whatever menial tasks they might have been assigned by the court. As much as anything, this indicates that Wyatt may have been in an emotional tailspin after losing Aurilla. If so, he stayed in it a while longer — and then, apparently, he found comfort in the arms of another woman.

On September 7, a police boat on the Illinois River intercepted a vessel that served as a floating casino and bordello. The *Peoria Daily National Democrat* reported on the seven men and six women taken into custody:

Some of the women are said to be good looking, but all appear to be terribly depraved. John Walton, the skipper of the boat, and Wyatt Earp, the Peoria bummer, were each fined $43.15. . . . Sarah Earp, alias Sally Heckell, calls herself the wife of Wyatt.

Sally Heckell was probably the teen-aged daughter of bordello operator Jane Haspel — the last names are similar, and frontier news-

66

papers were notoriously inaccurate in their identifications. Jane had a child named Sarah, and probably brought the girl into the family business. In the summer and fall of 1872, Wyatt Earp was twenty-three and certainly not ready to give up women despite the loss of his wife a year earlier. Upper-class men, even on the frontier, would not have stooped to any kind of an open relationship with a young prostitute, but Wyatt wasn't in any sense upper-class. Women in the West were scarce. You took what you could get, and since Wyatt was working in brothels it was natural that his possible selections were mostly limited to the women he met there. Some historians theorize that Sally was not in a relationship with Wyatt at all. They might have simply been friends, and after being arrested she claimed to be his wife because wives could not be compelled to testify against their husbands in court. With common-law marriages prevalent on the frontier, Sally would not have been required to produce a marriage license. But based on evidence to come, it's probable that for a time Sally became Wyatt Earp's second wife, joined with him by mutual consent rather than a formal ceremony.

Wyatt had been in Peoria long enough to develop a bad reputation. Being described as a "bummer" in the local press had considerable negative connotations. Bummers were worse than tramps; they were men of poor character who were also chronic lawbreakers. Communities were well rid of them when they moved on. Wyatt did, but it's important to place his problems in Peoria, Van Buren, and Lamar in perspective. Wyatt broke jail in Van Buren and fled from theft charges in Lamar. In Peoria, he not only worked in whorehouses, he kept coming back to the job after being arrested, fined, and even serving a short jail term. But many men on the frontier had youthful brushes with the law. Skimming small sums of public money was almost expected of lawmen and tax collectors in small Western communities. It was an unwritten perk. Horse theft was a serious crime, but rarely to the "string 'em up" extent popularized in dime novels. Though most frontier men didn't work in bordellos, many of them at least visited. One of the attractions of the West was that it was possible to make mistakes, and, in moving on, move beyond them. Evidence against Wyatt in Lamar and Van Buren was so insubstantial that in both cases co-defendants were acquitted or had charges dismissed. In Peoria, Wyatt happened to be earning his living in brothels when the local police force conducted a series of periodic raids to mollify starchy residents. Had his timing there been different, Wyatt might easily have escaped arrest, or even police notice, altogether. None of the Earps were flawless saints, but they also were not shady characters who lucked into heroic places in Western history. What they did do, Wyatt especially, was exaggerate their accomplishments and completely ignore anything in their past that reflected badly on them. In this, they were typical of men of their time — and men today.

With those events in Peoria, the portion of Wyatt Earp's life that has been previously lost to history was essentially over. After Peoria he left a trail to follow, much of it based on stories he later told to would-be collaborators John Flood and Stuart Lake. Others, including Bat Masterson, Wyatt's fourth wife, Josephine, Tombstone mayor John Clum, and Cochise County deputy sheriff Billy Breakenridge, left their own accounts of Wyatt's doings, all one-sided and factually challenged. But working from these materials, and from old newspaper accounts and other documents, we can piece together Wyatt's movements, if not always his motives. He did hunt buffalo. To do that, he needed to go west from Peoria to the plains of western Kansas. Wyatt also gambled. Where he learned a frontier gambler's essential skills at cards — calculating the odds, reading the expressions and gestures of other players, hiding an extra ace somewhere handy — isn't known. Wyatt probably picked up the basics of dealing poker, keno, monte, and faro in the railroad and buffalo hunter camps. After he left Peoria, Sally may have stayed behind for a while; wherever she was, she apparently remained connected to Wyatt, and continued working as a prostitute, based on public records a few years later. Wyatt picked up his own story in the summer of 1873, and the first tale he told would later form the initial basis for the legend of Wyatt Earp, courageous and incorruptible frontier lawman.

Wyatt claimed that in August 1873 he found himself in Ellsworth, Kansas, dealing monte in a local saloon. Ellsworth was in the middle of its brief heyday as a key railroad town in the cattle boom and attracted hard-bitten visitors. Prominent among them that summer were two brothers, Billy and Ben Thompson, native Englishmen who had transplanted themselves to Texas. They made money gambling rather than driving cattle, and, like many frontier card sharps, followed the Texas herds to Kansas towns where the drovers got their end-of-drive pay and eagerly risked it in card games. The Thompsons also had considerable reputations as gunmen. Everyone knew it was dangerous to cross them in any way.

Ellsworth's marshal, Brocky Jack Norton, and several policemen were charged with keeping the peace. County sheriff Chauncey B. Whitney was also in town. An argument erupted in an Ellsworth saloon where the brothers were playing poker. Whitney intervened, Billy Thompson fired his shotgun, and Whitney was badly wounded. He died soon afterward. Covered by his brother and "100 Texas men," Billy left town, riding slowly down its main street to demonstrate that nobody was running him off. Ben Thompson and his Texas cronies challenged anyone else to come and fight. Ellsworth mayor Jim Miller ordered Norton to arrest Thompson, but the marshal, with no desire to face near-certain death, refused. Miller then turned and informed bystander Wyatt Earp that he was now the Ellsworth marshal: "Here's your badge . . . I order you to arrest Ben Thompson." Wyatt buckled on two guns, holsters, and a cartridge belt, then went out into the street and calmly instructed Thompson, "Throw your shotgun into the road, put up your hands, and tell your friends to stay out of this play." Impressed by such courage, the other Texans backed down and Thompson did as he was told. To Wyatt's disgust, his prisoner was only charged with disturbing the peace and fined $25. (Billy, standing trial four years later for Whitney's murder, was acquitted.) Mayor Miller asked Wyatt to stay on as marshal, but Wyatt turned him down, saying he'd just seen proof that Ellsworth valued its lawmen's lives "at twenty-five dollars a head. I don't figure the town's my size."

Then Wyatt went back to hunting buffalo. It's a fine story, but one in which Wyatt greatly exaggerated his role in Ben Thompson's arrest, if he didn't make it up completely.

In late-life interviews, Wyatt said he spent the remainder of 1873 hunting buffalo. But that industry was playing out. There was more money to be made in cow towns than in buffalo camps, and frontier hustlers like Wyatt knew it. In the spring of 1874 he turned up in Wichita, Kansas, a community that made itself the focal point of cattle drives through canny marketing. Wichita extolled itself as "the Magic City." Its magic consisted of making Texans' money disappear. Salesmen touting Wichita's charms rode south on the trail routes to meet Texas crews guiding their herds north. Between 1870 and 1874, Wichita's population exploded from fifty to almost three thousand; a considerable selection of bars and brothels was built across town on the far bank of the Arkansas River. This "sin community" was named Delano Township, and the Texans were funneled there to do their carousing. Wichita police collected licensing fees from Delano's saloon owners and brothel keepers — bordello operators paid $18 a month for the privilege, plus $2 court costs. Individual prostitutes were charged $8 monthly, plus $2 for the courts. When the women complained their profit margins were being ruined, licenses were reduced to $3 and $2 for individuals and $8 and $2 for their bosses. Saloon fees were $25 a month.

Besides dunning shady businesses in Delano, Wichita police also did their best to keep a tight lid on violence there and on the other side of the Arkansas. Wichita was the first major cow town that posted signs forbidding guns to be carried within city limits. A "shotgun brigade" of residents was on call if the police force needed extra hands. Good judgment was required in all aspects of law enforcement. Wichita wanted its citizens to be safe and its Texas visitors to be happy. Lawmen there and in other Kansas cow towns were under constant pressure to maintain that near-impossible balance. Predictably, many of the officers developed permanent prejudices against Texans.

Wyatt came to Wichita with his brother James. James had just married widow Nellie Catchim. She was usually called Bessie, and had a daughter named Hattie. James tended bar in a Wichita saloon, Wyatt picked up a few dollars playing keno, and Bessie opened a bordello in Delano. She soon ran afoul of local law for failing to pay the required license fee — court records indicate that in June 1874 "Betsey Erp" was dragged into court and fined for "set[ting] up and keep[ing] a bawdy house or brothel." She wasn't alone in the dock. "Sallie Erp" — probably Wyatt's common-law prostitute wife from Peoria — was convicted of the same charges and assessed the same fine. Bessie and Sally apparently recruited several girls for their business. Over the next few months, "Kate Earb," "Eva Earp," and "Minnie Earp" were all fined by Wichita courts for conducting unlicensed prostitution. Few prostitutes provided their full legal names to police. It was customary for them to use the last names of their employers. James Earp also came before the courts, and was fined $5 and $2 for unspecified offenses. The Earps seemed to be up to the same unsavory sort of business that Wyatt and Morgan had back in Peoria.

But in Wichita, Wyatt began striving for something more. Playing cards and running whores would never gain him anything more than a minimal living and an ongoing reputation as a bummer. Maybe he had finally worked his way through the loss of Aurilla. Perhaps he was just tired of risking jail. Certainly he still burned, like his father, to be somebody important. In the fall of 1874 he took a first critical step back toward respectability. On October 29, the *Wichita Eagle* reported that "Wiatt Erp" and Johnny Behrens, identified in the article as "officers," chased seventy-five miles after a cattle outfit leaving town and collected $146 owed to Wichita merchants by some of its members.

It was Wyatt's first mention in print since Peoria, and this time it was positive. According to the story, Wyatt and Behrens "fear[ed] nothing and fear[ed] nobody." Wyatt wasn't an official member of the town police force; he was hired on a temporary basis by the merchants to get them their money.

Wyatt's timing was perfect. He made his debt-collecting splash just as city leaders decided that violence in town was too endemic, and the police force needed to expand. That concern dated back to May, when Wichita resident Charley Sanders beat two Texans who harassed his wife. The next day, a crowd of their friends returned and shot Sanders while he was up on a ladder painting his house. Texans had well-deserved reputations for that sort of attack; one or two would feel insulted and then a group of them would retaliate, often from ambush. As much as Wichita wanted Texas drovers to bring their money to town, they were determined to discourage that sort of violent mob mentality. In city elections in April 1875, former marshal Mike Meagher defeated incumbent Bill Smith, and, at the urging of the city council, Meagher immediately hired Wyatt and his debt-collecting partner, John Behrens. Meagher probably didn't know about Wyatt's recent problems with the law in Missouri, Arkansas, and Illinois, but if he did he would not have cared. Few frontier lawmen had clean records; the idea was that men who'd broken laws themselves would understand best how to prevent others from doing the same. Wyatt's salary was $60 a month, plus another dollar or two for each arrest he made. That sounds more lucrative than it really was. Wichita deputies only arrested Texas drovers as a last resort. The drovers couldn't spend their money from a cell.

New deputy Earp spent most of his time performing menial tasks. He functioned as the Wichita Animal Control Department, collecting dead animals from city streets. Deputy Earp enforced building codes, checking chimneys and repairing wooden slat sidewalks. He collected licensing fees, disguised as fines to gratify the town's religious element, from saloonkeepers and whorehouse madams like his sister-in-law Bessie. Despite Wyatt later telling John Flood that he was "in charge of the mounted police in Wichita" — Wichita had no mounted police, unless the marshal or a deputy happened to be on horseback — he was a flunky. But he was a flunky with a badge, and that was a start. And, soon, Wyatt had his own reputation around town. When Texans had to be subdued but not arrested, he cooled them down with whacks on the head with the barrel of his gun. "Buffaloing" was a routine tactic for frontier lawmen, and Wyatt excelled.

In Wichita, Wyatt Earp was a very good lawman, and apparently an honest one. In December 1875 the *Beacon* praised him for arresting a drunk but not relieving his sodden prisoner of a $500 bankroll. Bessie, Sally, and James Earp no longer appeared in court to be fined; the only new stain on the collective Earp family record came in September 1875, when Morgan, apparently passing through town, was fined a dollar for an unspecified, obviously minor, offense. At some point Wyatt and Sally split up; an ambitious policeman could hardly remain with a prostitute common-law wife. Until April 1876, Wichita was well satisfied with Wyatt Earp as a deputy. Then Wyatt's temper and loyalty to family abruptly ruined the good reputation he'd worked so hard to acquire.

It was time for another town election, and Bill Smith wanted to win back his old job as marshal from Mike Meagher. During the campaign, Smith charged that if Meagher was reelected, he'd hire Wyatt's brothers to fill out the police force. A milder man would have ignored Smith — Meagher was a prohibitive favorite to win reelection — but that wasn't Wyatt's way. Wyatt cornered Smith and called on all the fighting skills he'd learned back in the Northwest railroad camps. Marshal Meagher had to pull his enraged deputy off a badly beaten Smith. The *Beacon,* previously so complimentary of Wyatt (even while continuing to misspell his name), expressed editorial wonder that he threw such a violent fit: "The remarks that Smith was said to have made in regard to the marshal sending for Erp's brothers to put them on the police force furnished no just grounds for an attack, and upon ordinary occasions we doubt if Erp would have given them a second thought." Town law was clear — violence was not tolerated, even by Wichita's own policemen. Wyatt was fired and fined $30 for disturbing the peace. In a surprisingly mean-spirited parting shot, the council also ordered that a vagrancy act be carried out against now unemployed Wyatt if he didn't leave town right away. The *Beacon* was kinder, noting, "It is but justice to Erp to say he has made an excellent officer, and hitherto his conduct has been unexceptionable."

Wyatt was done in Wichita, but not in Kansas. One hundred and fifty miles to the west, another cow town had replaced Wichita as the main destination of Texas cattle drives. And where Wichita was a relatively peaceful place, Dodge City was anything but that. Founded in 1872 as a tiny tent community, Dodge exploded in size and population after the railroad expanded to pass through town, and the Kansas legislature moved the tick line west of Wichita. The Atchison, Topeka & Santa Fe Railroad built stockyards in Dodge to facilitate cattle auctions and transferring animals into boxcars. In late 1875, Dodge City was officially incorporated, and town officials determined "stringent" law enforcement would be necessary to control the rowdy cowhands who began arriving in growing numbers. Cattle lost considerable weight on the drives from Texas to western Kansas, so many herds were driven to the area around Dodge and then grazed for months outside town before being driven in to market.

Marshal Larry Deger needed experienced lawmen to help maintain order in a place where, one regional newspaper declared, "the arm of the law is palsied and hangs powerless." Thanks to Wyatt's bad temper, one was available. Just days after losing his job in Wichita, Wyatt was hired in Dodge City. The reason he was fired in Wichita made him attractive to Marshal Deger in Dodge City. A man who'd assault a candidate for sheriff wouldn't back down from Texas drovers. As in Wichita, Wyatt was a junior officer, an assistant city marshal hired to patrol the streets while his boss handled important decisions. At least a raise was involved; Wyatt made $75 a month compared to $60 in Wichita, with another dollar or two added as a bonus for each arrest he made. But essentially Wyatt had to perform the same job in a tougher town.

As envisioned by its leaders, Dodge City was essentially two distinct communities separated by Front Street, better known as the "Dead Line." North of Front Street, rank-and-file citizens lived respectably, going about their daily business. Below the Dead Line, cowhands whooped it up in a predictable series of saloons, dance halls, and brothels, and camped across the Arkansas River. Dodge had a permanent population of about 1,200. Over the course of any year, as many as six thousand cowboys passed through. The odds were against the solid Dodge burghers (most were of German extraction) being constantly able to keep their distance from rowdy visitors.

The atmosphere on Front Street was usually more carnival-like than menacing. Town businessmen were pragmatic; the Texans might be behaviorally challenged, but their continued presence was Dodge City's economic lifeline. So as far as the safety of city residents allowed, the Texans were indulged, even encouraged to have fun in the process of spending their money. One popular Dodge City saloon was even named The Alamo. Vendors sold snacks from trays all along Front Street, and, thanks to an ice house, drinks were served cold. Some of the saloons doubled as theaters and presented live music. Everybody in Dodge City, residents and Texas visitors alike, seemed to love dancing — the town's papers (there were five) constantly reported on "social hops." Except for town officers, no one was allowed to carry guns north of the Dead Line. All the saloons, dance halls, and hotels had prominent racks by their entrances. Texans were expected to leave their guns there, and reclaim them as they left town to return to their camps. Though there were always problems with hotheads and drunks, few of these occurred north of Front Street. In that sense, all parties involved knew their places.

But there was still antipathy between the Texans and the men hired in Dodge to keep them under control. Part of the fun for the Texans was seeing how far they could push things; the lawmen were under constant pressure to keep the visitors in line without discouraging them from coming back again. Town officers had to show restraint, but the Texans didn't. It took more courage to buffalo drunken cowhands than it did to shoot them. The Texans could, and sometimes did, go for their guns. Two years after Wyatt Earp came to Dodge, Bat Masterson's brother Ed was shot and killed there by an inebriated Texan he was trying to arrest. The Texans' lives were rarely at risk. The lives of Dodge lawmen always were.

Wyatt approached his duties in Dodge City the same way that he had in Wichita. Big, strong, and self-confident, he bashed balky Texans across the head with the barrel of his gun frequently enough to earn a bad reputation among them. Wyatt later claimed that some of the Texas trail bosses offered a $1,000 reward to anyone who could "put [him] out of the way." That's unlikely, but it's probable that enough Texans held grudges against Wyatt to keep him constantly alert. He certainly was ready to give up his post as soon as a greater opportunity presented itself. The ranks of Dodge officers were fluid. In part because of the constant pressure, in part because they were opportunists as opposed to career lawmen, marshals and their assistants came and went on a regular basis. At one time or another, Wyatt was joined on the job by three Masterson brothers (Jim, Ed, and Bat) and his own older brother Virgil. Wyatt wanted more from life than keeping law and order along Dodge's Dead Line. In Wichita, becoming a deputy was Wyatt's first step back toward respectability. In Dodge, the assistant marshal's job was a stopgap until he found something better.

It didn't take long. Just four months after he'd pinned on a Dodge assistant marshal's badge, Wyatt resigned and moved to the gold mine town of Deadwood in the Dakota Territory. Earlier in 1876, Deadwood had become famous as the place where Wild Bill Hickok was killed during a card game. Wyatt went there to gamble, and, in the best tradition of his father, Nicholas, branch off into side business. All during the winter he sold firewood, and in the spring of 1877 he rode shotgun for a local stage line. Neither job was going to bring him any substantial wealth. Whatever Wyatt hoped would happen in Deadwood didn't, and by early summer he drifted back to Dodge. One of the local papers noted, "Wyatt Earp, who was on our City police force last summer, is in town again. We hope he will accept a position on the force once more. He had a quiet way of taking the most desperate characters into custody which invariably gave one the impression that the city was able to enforce her mandates and preserve her dignity."

As in Wichita, law enforcement in Dodge City was seasonal work. When herds arrived and Texans came to town, additional officers were added. By the time Wyatt returned to town in the summer of 1877, the town police force was probably already staffed to its limits. So Wyatt spent much of the summer playing cards in Dodge saloons. At some point, he saw his extended family for the first time in several years. Nicholas had decided to try his luck again in San Bernardino, and came through as part of a wagon train. Virgil was along, too, with his new common-law wife, Allie, a waitress he'd met in Nebraska. Virgil and Allie didn't make it all the way to California. They dropped out of the caravan and settled for a while in Prescott, the capital of Arizona Territory.

Soon after the other Earps passed through Dodge, Wyatt found work as a bounty hunter. The railroad hired him to track two train robbers who were supposed to be in Texas. Wyatt trailed them there, following rumors that placed the pair in fort settlements in the western part of the state. He never caught up to the bandits, but in the community of Fort Griffin he first met the man whose name would soon be linked irrevocably with his.

In 1851, John Henry Holliday was born in Georgia to a modestly distinguished family. His father, Henry, a veteran of the Mexican War, had married the daughter of a prominent plantation owner and worked as a druggist. John Henry was taught traditional Southern values, above all an abiding sense of personal honor. He bristled at the slightest perceived insult. Like the rest of their family and friends, the Hollidays were proud when Georgia seceded from the Union and joined other rebel states in fighting the Yankees. Henry received a major's commission and left to fight. John Henry, too young to enlist, stayed home with his mother, Alice Jane. She became seriously ill, possibly with tuberculosis. Henry Holliday also became ill and resigned his commission; by war's end, he and his family found themselves in Valdosta, Georgia. Alice Jane died in 1866, and Henry infuriated John Henry by marrying a very young neighbor just three months later.

Father, stepmother, and son couldn't comfortably coexist. Everyone was relieved in 1870 when John Henry left for Philadelphia to attend the Pennsylvania College of Dental Surgery.

By the summer of 1872, John Henry was back in Georgia and practicing dentistry in Atlanta. It was there that he may have learned he, too, was afflicted with tuberculosis, or, in then current vernacular, "consumption." In those times, it was a death sentence that could perhaps be postponed, but never escaped. Certainly it imbued John Henry with a sense of fatalism. He left Georgia for Texas, stopping for a while in Dallas and forming a dental practice with John Seegar. They demonstrated their professional skills by winning several prizes at the 1873 Texas State Fair, being honored for "the best set of teeth in gold, the best set of teeth in vulcanized rubber, and the best display of artificial teeth and dental ware." John Henry claimed to his family that he'd joined a temperance society and the Methodist Church. If he did, his sobriety didn't last long. Six months after their state fair triumphs, John Henry and Seegar dissolved their practice. John Henry began spending more time drinking and gambling than yanking teeth. Somewhere on the gambling circuit, he acquired the nickname of "Doc" and a reputation for inciting more violence than he could physically

85

handle. In a 1907 edition of *Human Life* magazine, Bat Masterson wrote that Doc "had a mean disposition and an ungovernable temper, and under the influence of liquor was a most dangerous man . . . a weakling who could not have whipped a healthy fifteen-year-old boy in a go-as-you-please fistfight."

Tuberculosis certainly had something to do with Doc's inability to defend himself with bare hands. When cornered, he used guns. In January 1875, Doc was charged with assault with intent to murder after an argument in Dallas escalated into shooting on New Year's Eve. He was acquitted, but after that he began roaming, looking for card games and trouble in such places as Denver and El Paso. Fort Griffin in West Texas became a regular stop. Crowds of itinerants, many of them selling supplies to the military, passed through. Doc was always happy to relieve them of some of their money. By this time he was often traveling in company with Kate Elder, a veteran prostitute who claimed she married Doc in 1876. Theirs was apparently a frontier partnership more than a love match. Doc wanted a woman's company, and Kate needed security. They constantly fought, and periodically split up. But in one way or another, Kate remained part of Doc's life.

Doc and Kate happened to be in Fort Griffin in the fall of 1877 when Wyatt Earp showed up looking for the railroad bandits. She may have reluctantly introduced Doc to Wyatt. When the Earps ran afoul of Wichita law in 1874 for operating an unlicensed bordello, one of the prostitutes hauled into court and fined was "Kate Earb," clearly a typical example of a working girl identifying herself to the law by her employer's last name. Later in Wichita, someone named Kate Elder committed the same offense. She may have left Bessie Earp's bordello and gone to work for someone else. With so few women on the frontier, it's unlikely two different ones with the same name would have crossed Wyatt's path in Kansas and again three years later in Texas.

Kate didn't like Wyatt Earp when they met again in Fort Griffin, or anytime later. She considered Wyatt a terrible influence on Doc, perhaps the only time anyone ever thought of Doc as a victim rather than an instigator. Wyatt told Stuart Lake that he was introduced to Doc in Fort Griffin by Jim Shaughnessy, a man he'd met in Cheyenne. He didn't mention Kate being present, but he didn't like her any more than she did him. Whoever brought them together in Fort Griffin, Wyatt and Doc met. They had perhaps heard a little of each other before that — both were part of the boomtown gambling circuit, and it was a relatively small, insulated community. A warm friendship didn't blossom immediately. Wyatt continued on the trail of the bank robbers, which took him farther into Texas and then on into Missouri. He never caught up with them. Doc moved on, too, drifting from the gambling dens in one town to those in another.

In April 1878, Wyatt was in Joplin, Missouri, still looking for the train robbers, when word reached him that Dodge City marshal Ed Masterson had been killed while trying to arrest two drunken Texas cowboys. Bat Masterson, who'd been elected Ford County sheriff six months earlier, shot the two Texans but couldn't save his brother. Charlie Bassett, a former Ford County sheriff, was named to replace Ed Masterson as town marshal. Wyatt returned to Dodge and was rehired by Bassett as an assistant marshal. It was logical for him to come back, take his old job for a while and regroup — bounty hunting hadn't worked out too well. Wyatt still had no intention of remaining a lawman for the rest of his life. He was thirty now, no longer young by frontier standards. All the Earp brothers were scattered around the West — Wyatt in Kansas, James in Texas, Virgil in Arizona, Morgan in Montana. None of them had yet achieved anything permanent and substantial. If one had, he would have tried to bring the other brothers in on it. They were still searching, still yearning for the one break that could change everything. Then, for Wyatt in Dodge City, something did happen, a series of events that brought him a close friend for life and lent themselves, with benefit of exaggeration, to the building of his eventual reputation.

It began innocently enough in June, when Doc Holliday and Kate Elder came to Dodge. Their arrival had nothing to do with Wyatt. As a frontier gambler, Doc moved around to whatever boomtowns offered fresh chances to fleece less-experienced card players. Dodge City, with its temporarily flush Texans, was perfect. Doc also tried to reestablish himself in a more respectable profession. He took out an ad in the *Dodge City Times:*

John H. Holliday, Dentist, very respectfully offers his professional services to the citizens of Dodge City and surrounding county during the summer. Office at Room No. 24 Dodge House. Where satisfaction is not given, money will be refunded.

Initially, Doc and Kate didn't see Wyatt except in passing — and then, not in any active role as Dodge City's assistant marshal. According to Kate, "Most of the time Wyatt could be seen at a table in a saloon playing cribbage with some rounder or bartender, [or] sometimes taking a hand in a poker game." If he did neglect his day job as a lawman, Wyatt picked a peculiar time to do so. Eighteen seventy-eight was Dodge's busiest cattle drive year yet. An estimated 265,000 longhorns were herded to town from Texas, almost ten times as many as just two years before. As the number of Texans in town escalated, so did the incidents in which Dodge lawmen had to intervene. It was a tense time. Everyone was on edge.

At three in the morning on July 26, a large audience crammed Dodge's Comique Theater, where entertainer Eddie Foy stood on-stage reciting the poem "Kalamazoo in Michigan." Outside, three Texas trail hands rode slowly down the street, heading back to their camp below town after a long night's drinking. They paused outside the Comique, pulled their pistols, and fired several shots through the plank walls. No one was injured — Foy recalled later how impressed he was at the "instantaneous manner" in which the crowd dropped flat to the floor. "I had thought I was pretty agile myself," Foy said, "but those fellows had me beaten by seconds at that trick."

Assistant marshals Wyatt Earp and Jim Masterson were on duty and came running at the sound of gunfire. The Texans spurred their horses and fled, riding across the bridge that spanned the Arkansas River on the outskirts of town. They may have fired a few shots back at Wyatt and Jim Masterson, who certainly pulled their own guns and began firing. A few bystanders added their own shots to the assistant marshals' volley. George Hoy, one of the Texans, was hit in the arm and fell off his horse. The lawmen carried Hoy to a doctor, who checked the wound and announced that amputation wouldn't be required. Hoy gave an interview to a local paper. According to the subsequent story, the young Texan "claims not to have done any shooting; be that as it may he was in bad company and has learned a lesson he won't forget soon."

For the first time as a lawman, Wyatt Earp had drawn his pistol, engaged in gunplay, and wounded and captured a Texan. At least, Wyatt always took credit for firing the shot that took George Hoy down, though he was only one of several men shooting at the fleeing Texans. The *National Police Gazette* mentioned the incident, crediting "Wyatt Erpe, a good fellow and brave officer," with gunning down Hoy. Wyatt, satisfied that he'd faced a crisis and distinguished himself, left Dodge for a few days to attend the state Republican convention in Topeka. When he returned, he learned that Hoy's wound wasn't responding to treatment. Gangrene set in. On August 21, a surgeon amputated the arm, but Hoy died later that day. When he was buried in Dodge City's graveyard, an ominous number of Texans attended the ceremony. Soon afterward, Wyatt told friends that a Texan he couldn't identify tried to shoot him. Wyatt had good reason to be nervous. Texans did not suffer lightly any attacks on their own, even if they were made by lawmen acting in the line of duty.

That certainly factored into Wyatt's dramatic recollection of another immediate near-brush with death. A mob was involved, and, for the only time in Wyatt's version of his life story, he didn't face it down alone. Historians have long wondered how Wyatt Earp and Doc Holliday, polar opposites in every way, came to be such close friends. In Wyatt's unpublished memoir with John Flood, and later in Stuart Lake's full-fledged, if far from factual, biography, there are murky references to Doc saving Wyatt's life in Dodge City. But before Flood attempted to ghostwrite Wyatt's account of his life, he took copious notes while interviewing the old frontiersman about the event. These never made print; perhaps Wyatt believed they gave too much credit to Doc and not enough to himself — after all, it was supposed to be *Wyatt's* story. But Flood's original, handwritten notes still exist in a private collection. Even given Wyatt's constant penchant for late-life exaggeration, they ring true enough to finally offer a plausible explanation for the bond he felt with Doc:

One night, a crowd gathered in Bob Wright's

92

store and declared they were going to take the [town] by storm, and they went out in the streets and commenced shooting in every direction with the intention of intimidating the populace. Upon catching sight of me, they immediately threw their guns on me but I stood my ground right in front of the Long Branch store. They said they were going to get me now.

It happened that Doc Holliday was seated at a monte table at this time, and glancing through the window, he appraised the situation in an instant. Turning to Frank Loving, the dealer, he said, "Have you a six-shooter?" He handed the gun over to Holliday who, without hesitation, sprang through the doorway onto the sidewalk, and, throwing both guns down on the crowd, he said, "Throw up your hands!" This rather startled them and diverted their attention. In an instant, I had drawn my guns and the arrest of the crowd followed. They were confined in jail overnight and fined and released the following day. It was because of this episode that I became the friend of "Doc" Holliday ever after.

Wyatt Earp may not have owed Doc Holliday his life. "A crowd" could have been three or four Texans, still too many for a single assistant marshal to buffalo. Drovers trying to take Dodge "by storm" were much more likely to fire a few shots in the air than to hold a city lawman at gunpoint and announce they were going to get him. For that kind of murderous threat, they would surely not have been assessed a simple fine and released the day after their arrest. Still, with the Hoy incident so recent, and being well aware of the Texans' habitual taste for gang retaliation, Wyatt could be forgiven for discerning more threat in the confrontation than actually existed. Doc Holliday, a casual acquaintance, came to his rescue. It was something Doc didn't have to do; helping Wyatt could have called the Texans' vengeful attention to Doc as well.

Wyatt Earp was not a saint, but because of the pristine reputation he acquired through decades of one-dimensional portrayals in books, movies, and television programs, some of the less savory aspects of his life seem far more damning than they really were. He probably filched a few public dollars while serving as a constable in Lamar. The horse theft charges in Arkansas may have some truth to them, and he certainly broke jail in Van Buren and later worked in Peoria and Beardstown bordellos. Like his father and brothers, his main goals in life were to become wealthy and important. Late in life, making a final attempt to get rich with a memoir, he greatly exaggerated his accomplishments as a frontier lawman. Wyatt was a suspicious man who was reluctant to trust anyone outside his own family. He was unquestionably flawed.

But once Wyatt Earp made a friend, he was loyal to him even at personal cost. For an ambitious man like Wyatt, who was intent on gaining the favor of community leaders then and later, Doc Holliday was the worst possible friend to have, one who would disgust the same people Wyatt wanted so badly to impress. Doc was deservedly renowned as a troublemaker. Just because he became close friends with a lawman, he didn't permanently change his ways. Doc still got drunk, still got into public brawls, and still made a convenient scapegoat if there was anything that could be potentially blamed on him. No allegation against Doc Holliday could seem too far-fetched, and, in the years to come, there were many of them. Wyatt Earp stood by him every time.

Doc Holliday returned that absolute loyalty with his own. Wyatt was mistrustful, but Doc was paranoid. He looked for insults and the chance to respond violently. Some of that had to do with the constant knowledge that he was dying slowly. An inflated sense of Southern honor contributed to his emotional instability. Doc was surely an alcoholic and, as such, subject to extreme mood swings. Wyatt, at least, had his family. Doc had only Kate Elder, and their relationship was tumultuous. Having a friend who accepted him for who and what he was must have meant the world to Doc Holliday. Temporarily, it may even have had a calming effect on him. Doc stayed on in Dodge City for another seven months after he stepped in to protect Wyatt from the armed, rambunctious crowd outside the Long Branch. During those months, and for the only time in his frontier life, there is no public record of his getting into any kind of trouble.

His new friendship with Doc Holliday notwithstanding, Wyatt still believed he was in constant jeopardy from revenge-minded Texans. Editorials in the Dodge City newspapers praised him for his part in shooting down George Hoy; a deputy marshal was supposed to do whatever was necessary to protect the lives of citizens. But that didn't alter the fine balance city leaders wanted their officers to observe in enforcing the law. Counting the two who died after shooting Marshal Ed Masterson in the spring, three men from Texas trail herds had been gunned down by Dodge City lawmen in less than six months. Wyatt and the other Dodge officers may not have been told directly, but surely they must have understood that they were expected to exercise even more discretion than usual in confronting belligerent Texans. It must have weighed heavily on their minds when, about a month after George Hoy died, one of the most famous Texas gunslingers arrived in town, demanding to know what had happened that night outside the Comique Theater.

Unlike Wyatt Earp, whose fame came much later, Clay Allison was legendary on the frontier. How much of his reputation was deserved is impossible to determine, but the clear consensus was that he shot to kill when he was angry, and he was angry much of the time. Allison apparently knew Hoy back in Texas; the youngster may have worked for him at some point. What happened when he showed up in Dodge is problematic. Three versions gained wide notoriety, two of them coming long afterward from Wyatt. The other had Allison arriving with his pistols (or a shotgun) in hand, demanding to see any Dodge lawmen so he could shoot them down. Bat Masterson, well aware of Allison's skill in gunplay, warned all the officers to hide out until Allison got tired of waiting and rode on. They did, and survived.

Wyatt told the story differently, twice. In an 1896 interview with the *San Francisco Examiner,* he related a fairly circumspect account. Clay Allison stalked the streets of Dodge, clearly looking for trouble. Bat Masterson, hovering nearby, covered Allison with a shotgun while Wyatt went to talk to the Texan. Allison said he was looking for "the man that killed my friend Hoyt [sic]", Wyatt said that was he, and then gripped the handle of his six-shooter with his right hand while preparing to grab Allison's pistol with his left. But Allison, wise in the ways of confrontations, spotted Bat with his shotgun and realized he couldn't win. The famous gunfighter backed down, and that was that.

Wyatt's version became far more colorful when he recounted the story to Stuart Lake fifty years after the fact, and thirty years after he told it to the *Examiner*. This time, Wyatt claimed that Clay Allison went for his gun, but Wyatt beat him to the draw, jamming his Buntline Special into the Texan's ribs before Allison's six-gun cleared its holster. Astonished, Allison gave up for the moment, but after fortifying himself with a few drinks in a nearby saloon he got on his horse and shouted threats instead of riding away. Wyatt raised his gun and walked toward the mounted gunslinger, who held his ground for a few seconds, then wheeled and galloped out of Dodge. Two weeks later, Allison came back to Dodge and meekly sent word ahead, asking Wyatt's permission to do some business in town. Wyatt said he could. The two spoke a few times while Allison was in Dodge, and when he rode out he politely waved goodbye to Wyatt.

Wyatt's courageous cowing of Clay Allison became one of the crown jewels of his subsequent glittering reputation. Lake's added detail about Wyatt wielding a long-barreled Buntline Special added just the right touch of color. Long-barreled pistols were occasionally used on the frontier; Wyatt may have owned one. But subsequent tales of how Ned Buntline — Ed Judson, the pulp writer who initially made Buffalo Bill Cody famous — bestowed special weapons bearing his name to Wyatt and four other Dodge lawmen were never verified. There's no record Judson ever came to Dodge while Wyatt was there. In the larger legend of Wyatt Earp, the Buntline Special seems to be American frontier mythology's version of King Arthur's sword, Excalibur. What gun Wyatt used, whether confronting Clay Allison or, three years later, at the edge of a vacant lot in Tombstone, isn't really important. But less than a month after Wyatt claimed he outdrew Allison, he had to use his gun again. This confrontation, in which Wyatt really did distinguish himself, led directly to his leaving Dodge.

James Kenedy was a Dodge lawman's worst nightmare. As the son of Texas cattle baron Mifflin Kenedy, James believed himself to be above the law in any Kansas cattle town that depended on the arrival of his father's herds. Wyatt Earp didn't agree. In July 1878, he arrested Kenedy for carrying a pistol within city limits, and the young Texan had to pay a fine. A month later, another Dodge officer arrested Kenedy for disturbing the peace. That resulted in a second fine, and Kenedy didn't intend to stand for it. He hunted down Dodge mayor James "Dog" Kelley to complain. Kelley, showing some spunk in the face of implied or overt economic blackmail, told Kenedy that, like everyone else, he had to obey town laws. Kenedy apparently threatened Kelley and stormed off.

Dora Hand was a thirty-four-year-old actress who'd earned some acclaim for performances on Dodge City stages. Hand performed all along the frontier town circuit; when her marriage turned sour she moved temporarily to Dodge and filed suit for divorce in the Ford County District Court. The filing took place in October, but the court wasn't scheduled to resume until January. Mayor Kelley of Dodge offered to let Hand and her friend Fannie Garretson stay in his small two-room shack while he was temporarily out of town. Just before dawn on October 4, Kenedy, believing Kelley rather than the two women were inside, rode up beside the house and fired four shots through its walls. Fannie Garretson wasn't hit, but one of the bullets plowed into Dora Hand's right side and killed her. Wyatt and Bat Masterson led a posse in pursuit of Kenedy. When the distance between Kenedy and the posse was about seventy-five yards, they exchanged shots. Wyatt shot Kenedy's horse so the man couldn't ride away. Bat, using a Sharps rifle, shot Kenedy in the shoulder. The wounded horse fell on its rider. Kenedy was pinned underneath; his captors had to pull him free. The young Texan showed no remorse, asking the posse if he'd killed Kelley. Informed that he'd murdered Dora Hand instead, Kenedy snarled to Masterson, "You son of a bitch, you ought to have made a better shot than you did." Bat replied, "Well, you murdering son of a bitch, I did the best I could."

Kenedy was held in the Dodge City jail for two weeks to recover sufficiently from his injury to stand trial. When he did, the judge held the proceedings in the sheriff's office, which was too small to allow spectators. The influence of Kenedy's powerful father was evident; no witnesses came forward to testify against James. Without public comment, the judge dismissed the case. A local paper reported, "We do not know what the evidence was, or upon what grounds [Kenedy] was acquitted. But he is free to go on his way rejoicing whenever he gets ready."

The verdict didn't leave Wyatt in the mood for rejoicing. He was left disenchanted with courts. Clearly, justice in them was not always done. Wyatt broke a few laws himself in his youth, but he had never stooped to violent crime, let alone murder. It didn't help that soon after Kenedy went free, the city council

101

reduced the salaries of Sheriff Charlie Bassett and his assistants Wyatt and Jim Masterson, who were cut from $75 to $50 a month.

Wyatt hadn't come to Dodge City to remain a lawman on a permanent basis. He'd already left twice — to try his luck in Dakota Territory as an entrepreneur, and later in Texas and Missouri as a bounty hunter. Neither attempt worked out as he'd hoped, and Wyatt had returned to Kansas. But earning $50 a month for risking his life with trigger-happy Texans was, apparently, as good as he could do in Dodge. He'd considered trying to acquire some land and build his own herd, but acquiring breeding cattle cost a lot more money than he had, and the alternative of hiring a crew and rounding up free-range longhorns in Texas (or stealing them in Mexico) was also beyond his financial means. Wyatt hadn't stopped wanting to be the boss giving orders, instead of the hired hand carrying them out. In Dodge, that didn't seem likely to happen, despite the fine work he'd done there. He'd shot it out successfully with a gun-waving Texan (George Hoy, probably) and faced down one of the most famous gunfighters on the frontier (Clay Allison, possibly). Even if the culprit hadn't been convicted, he'd tracked and helped capture James Kenedy, who'd attempted to assassinate the mayor and did kill a popular actress. The city council rewarded him by cutting his salary. It was time to move on to a place where the potential for success was greater — but where?

The Earp brothers had kept in touch, sharing their feelings of restlessness. Dodge and Kansas were played out; Wyatt said the town had lost its "snap." James had found no real possibilities in Texas. Morgan was in Montana, but nothing in the Northwest territories engaged him enough to want to stay any longer. Virgil, though, had reason to feel optimistic about prospects in Arizona Territory. For a change, an Earp was apparently getting ahead.

In June 1877, when Virgil and his new wife, Allie, dropped out of the California-bound family wagon train in Prescott, they took over an abandoned sawmill outside town and lived there. Prescott and its surrounding area were booming; mining communities had sprung up throughout the region, and Prescott, the territorial capital, was a stop on the main stage route. The sawmill offered a way for Virgil to make a few dollars and insinuate himself into the local business community. What really established Virgil in Prescott, though, was his role in a shootout that eclipsed anything in which brother Wyatt participated back in Dodge.

In early October 1877, two drifters named Wilson and Tallos arrived in Prescott and began drinking in town saloons. A local man, W. H. H. McCall, recognized Wilson, who was wanted for murder in Texas. McCall summoned constable Frank Murray, and Wilson and Tallos fled on horseback, shooting as they rode away. Virgil happened to be nearby, chatting with U.S. marshal William Standefer and Yavapai County sheriff Ed Bowers. When Standefer and McCall raced after Wilson and Tallos in a carriage, and Murray and Bowers mounted horses and joined in the pursuit, Virgil decided to help out. He didn't have a carriage or horse handy. But he did have his legs, and a Winchester rifle, so he ran after the lawmen. Virgil didn't have to run far. Wilson and Tallos stopped near the edge of town and made a stand. Bullets flew, and in the end the two fugitives were down. Tallos died there, and Wilson expired a few days later. Virgil was given credit in a local paper:

. . . Earp, who appears to have been playing a lone hand with a Winchester rifle was doing good service . . .

Virgil had picked an opportune time to distinguish himself. The lawmen were impressed. So were the owners of Patterson, Caldwell & Levally, a local freight line. They hired Virgil as a driver, and besides hauling freight his duties included transporting various dignitaries around the area. Virgil was a natural for chamber-of-commerce-style activities. Like his brother James, he could chat amicably with anyone, a skill that Wyatt and Morgan Earp pointedly lacked. Soon Virgil was on friendly terms with J. S. Gosper, the secretary of Arizona Territory. The territorial governor was John C. Frémont, Nicholas Earp's old Republican hero. Frémont had made a series of bad investments and needed a job. He was a loyal Republican, so the Rutherford B. Hayes administration appointed him governor of Arizona Territory. Frémont liked the job for the investment opportunities it offered. After being sworn into office in 1878, Frémont spent most of his time away from the territory, haggling with businessmen back east. That left territorial secretary Gosper to handle almost all the administrative duties of the territorial government — and now Gosper knew and liked Virgil Earp. It was the kind of powerful political connection the Earp family had always craved.

By the summer of 1878, Virgil acquired a second influential ally. Crawley Dake was named U.S. marshal for Arizona Territory. The men met and hit it off. Virgil could make almost anyone his friend, if he had the chance to try. Things looked bright for thirty-five-year-old Virgil, especially when the Prescott city council named him the town's night watchman. It paid $75 a month, the same salary Wyatt earned as an assistant marshal in Dodge City. At least it was an official title, Virgil's first. A few months later, he moved up another official rung. Prescott held a November 1878 election for town constable. Virgil was one of two candidates voted into office, and had by far the most votes. His new job paid better. Constables received fees for issuing licenses, collecting fees, and delivering summonses. Prescott was being good to Virgil Earp, but like his father and brothers, wherever he found himself, whatever he was doing, was never quite good enough.

The liveliest, most profitable action in Arizona Territory was now in the south and southeast. Prescott and Yavapai County had their silver mines, but these were suddenly considered lesser operations compared to the tales of staggering mineral deposits recently discovered beyond Tucson, not far from the Mexican border in remote Pima County. Newspapers across America were full of reports. Men were going to the area, digging a bit, and becoming rich overnight. The legendary Comstock Lode in Nevada was a comparative pittance. The Earp brothers were always on the lookout for new opportunities. It would have been impossible for them not to read the stories or hear all the tantalizing rumors. More objective observers might have questioned the odds of everyone rushing to southeast Arizona somehow becoming rich.

The Comstock had become legendary because its riches played out so long. Another silver strike proving even better was virtually impossible. But the Earps, like so many others addicted to the belief of unlimited possibilities on the frontier, weren't about to let common sense or skepticism temper their hopes. Besides, this time in Arizona Territory they had the advantage of Virgil's political connections, something the Earp family had never enjoyed before.

No one is certain which Earp brother took the lead in gathering the clan for a collective move to southeast Arizona. Whichever one did, the others didn't need much prodding. It took a few extra months for Morgan to head down from Montana, but meanwhile in early September 1879 Wyatt resigned as assistant marshal in Dodge City. Before he left town, he told Bat Masterson that he was through working as a frontier lawman. From then on, Wyatt swore, he'd be a businessman, answering only to himself. James and Bessie Earp, with Bessie's teen-aged daughter, Hattie, joined him on his way to Arizona Territory, along with a twenty-one-year-old woman identifying herself as Mattie Earp, Wyatt's latest common-law wife. There's no definitive record of where Wyatt and Mattie Blaylock met, or when they began cohabiting. Some Earpians link them as far back as Wyatt's last days in Wichita. Others believe it didn't happen until Dodge City. Mattie is widely assumed to have been a prostitute like Sally Haspel. At the very least, she turned to that trade later on. What's certain is that, when Wyatt moved on from Dodge City, Mattie was with him.

The party took a short detour through Las Vegas, New Mexico, where Doc Holliday and Kate Elder were living. Doc had fallen back into his old bad habits; in recent months he'd been in all kinds of scrapes, including several shootings where men supposedly died at his hands. Most of these murders attributed to Doc were probably apocryphal. Still, he'd worn out his welcome in Las Vegas. Kate was sorry to see Wyatt Earp again, and even sorrier when he talked Doc into coming with him to Arizona Territory. Kate reluctantly agreed to go, too, though she made no promises about continuing with Doc and the Earps indefinitely.

When they arrived in Prescott, Virgil and Allie joined the expedition, while Doc and Kate decided to stay on for a while. Kate wanted to get Doc away from Wyatt; Doc was predictably intrigued by the gambling possibilities in town. But the three Earp brothers were eager to be going. Their destination was a mining community about sixty-five miles southeast of Tucson and twenty-five miles north of the Mexican border. It was a boomtown still in its early phases of growth, but reportedly one built right over deposits of so much silver that any man arriving there had an excellent chance of striking it rich. Nothing was guaranteed, of course. Risks were involved. In this far corner of southeast Arizona Territory, renegade Apaches still prowled. Their menacing, if mostly unseen, presence was linked to the town's foreboding name. But Indian threats paled against visions of imminent wealth, and in November 1879 the Earps left Prescott and set out for Tombstone.

Chapter Three:
Tombstone

In August 1877, twenty-nine-year-old Ed Schieffelin hit the lowest point in a vastly undistinguished life. It was customary for stores in Tucson to extend limited credit to prospectors in need of supplies. Ed had arrived in town with ore samples gleaned from several months spent wandering the hills of southeastern Arizona Territory. No one was impressed by what he'd found, even though Ed was certain that the bits of rock and "float" — outcropping chunks washed loose by streams and creeks — contained enough silver trace to prove he was on the verge of a major strike. Undaunted, Ed dropped in to the Tully & Ochoa mercantile, where he requested some basic necessities — flour, bacon, probably coffee, sugar, and a work shirt or two — which he'd pay for after he cashed in a little of the silver he felt he'd have soon. Ed had $5 in his pocket, but that was for emergencies. His request to the Tully & Ochoa clerk was routine.

But in Tucson, as in all of Arizona Territory, no one believed an itinerant like Ed could survive long around the Dragoon Mountains and San Pedro Valley. This was the homeland of the Chiricahua Apaches, and enough renegades from that fiercest of native bands still roamed the region that prospecting there was considered suicidal. Besides, Ed looked raggedy even for a down-on-his-luck prospector. Someone around that time described him as "about the queerest specimen of humanity ever seen," citing Ed's "black curly hair that hung several inches below his shoulders. His long untrimmed beard was a mass of unkempt knots and mats. His clothing was worn out and covered with patches of deerskins, corduroy, and flannel, and his old slouch hat, too, was so pieced with rabbit skin that very little of the original felt remained."

The clerk at Tully & Ochoa offended Ed, telling him that he couldn't have any supplies unless he had the cash to pay for them. For a frontier prospector, this was the ultimate insult. Ed was angry and told a friend, "I am going back [to the San Pedro Valley]. It does not matter to me what these fellows say. . . . I have seen enough to show me that there are mines there." Using his last few dollars, Ed bought flour and bacon at another store, then left Tucson, as certain as when he had arrived that he was going to be rich, and very soon. This wasn't unusual for Ed. He felt that way long before he ever came to southeast Arizona.

Since his teens, Ed Schieffelin had roamed the Western territories as a prospector, believing like tens of thousands of others that he was destined to strike it rich if only he didn't stop trying. It was a hard life, fraught with ongoing failure and extreme personal danger. Prospectors like Ed wandered into places most men would never dare go, isolated regions where the varieties of possible death — starvation, illness, accident, attack by animal or human predators — were infinite, and the odds of finding a mother lode of gold or silver were infinitesimal. But Ed was addicted, to the risk as well as to the potential payoff. Arizona Territory was a natural, if especially scary, place for him to come. Since the sixteenth century, explorers had been certain its mountains and hills concealed huge lodes of rich ore. Southeast Arizona had a few settlements — Tucson was founded in 1776 — but it was the land of the Chiricahua, and they preyed on any interlopers. Most of the major towns were established hundreds of miles farther north. The U.S.-Mexican war brought the territory under American ownership, and the Gadsden Purchase in December 1853 tacked on the final extensive acreage. The California Gold Rush a few years before attracted hordes of prospectors into the West, and many of them eventually found their way to Arizona. The earliest silver strikes recorded there were in the north — Prescott with several medium-sized mines, and the larger Silver King Mine in Globe. Mostly, southeast Arizona Territory remained unexplored, though enticing. For even the greediest prospectors, it was one of the few remaining places on the frontier where risk to life outweighed the fortune that might be found there.

There was briefly an exception. In 1856, immigrant German mining engineer Frederick Brunckow arrived in Arizona Territory. Ignoring the risk, he traveled south in early 1857, intrigued by outcroppings on the Huachuca Mountains that ranged past the San Pedro Valley. The vast majority of American prospectors were bumbling amateurs with little or no formal training in geology, but Brunckow knew what to look for. He soon spotted promising deposits of ore on the east side of the San Pedro River. Brunckow and some partners sank a shaft, dug up rock, assayed it (using pulverizing, then heat to reduce the material to its base forms), and confirmed what the German had suspected — this was a rich silver deposit. The newly formed St. Louis Mining Company hired Mexican workers from Sonora and began operations, the Apache threat notwithstanding. There was too much money to be made.

But in 1860, the Mexicans massacred their employers and returned home. No one else had the nerve to prospect and develop mines in the area, though various investors, including frontier businessman-scout Thomas Jeffords, acquired rights to the so-called Brunckow Mine, hoping for the time when the Apaches would be under control and the mine could open again.

In 1863, Arizona was broken off from New Mexico Territory and established as a separate entity of its own. A year later, residents elected their first legislature; its membership came predominantly from mining interests. But territorial mining operations remained mostly in the north. U.S. troops were pulled from the territory by the Civil War. The Apaches were free to terrorize as they pleased; the San Pedro Valley and its surrounding environs seemed more toxic than ever. Bandits from Mexico skulked across the border to raid the ranches of the few settlers brave enough to go there. Eventually a limited number of ranchers like Henry Hooker acquired large tracts of land and had the capital to hire enough men to defend their property. But no one felt remotely safe until the Civil War was over, the army returned, and, in 1872, one-armed General Oliver Otis Howard was able, with the help of Jeffords, to negotiate a peace treaty with the Chiricahua chief Cochise. But the treaty established the Dragoon Mountains, San Pedro Valley, and surrounding region to the Chiricahua as their reservation — Cochise was wily enough to realize he was negotiating from strength, and he insisted on retaining his people's traditional homeland. That meant no one could prospect in the San Pedro Valley, where, less than twenty years earlier, Frederick Brunckow had proven there was silver.

As the West filled up and the boundaries of the remaining frontier continued to shrink, Arizona Territory became known as one of the few areas left where men could still *become.* In 1873, Samuel Woodworth Cozzens's book *The Marvelous Country, or, Three Years in Arizona and New Mexico* was so popular it had to be reprinted twice. The author gave a series of East Coast lectures, extolling the area's beautiful scenery, vast acres available for acquisition, and, of course, its possibilities for making a fortune. All it currently lacked, Cozzens claimed, was "water and good society." One audience member responded, "That's all they lack in hell." But Arizona sounded like heaven to a lot of people.

Prospectors weren't the only arrivals. Parts of Arizona were natural grasslands; ranching was an attractive option. Among the ambitious small-timers to arrive around 1872 and 1873 were Newman "Old Man" Clanton and his brood, which included sons Phin, Ike, and Billy. Like Nicholas Earp, Old Man Clanton had rambled all over the frontier without notable success. He wasn't discouraged enough to stop trying. Soon after he and his family arrived in the Gila Valley about a hundred miles north of Tucson, Clanton followed in the footsteps of Daniel Boone by founding a town named after himself. In June 1874, the Pima County board of supervisors approved his request to recognize a new town and political precinct called Clantonville. The *Arizona Citizen* tried to boost the new settlement with a glowing report:

During the year [Clanton] has been there, himself and three sons have cut a ditch from the Gila River; planted 120 acres with wheat, corn, barley and all kinds of vegetables; and from nothing of consequence to start with, now has a fine farm and plenty about him. . . . The cattle are fat and everything is in fine condition. All parties east or west who desire a place to make a good home easily and cheaply cannot do better.

Things didn't work out as Clanton planned. After three years of waiting for new neighbors to pour in to his eponymous settlement, making him rich in the process, Clanton gave up and moved south to the San Pedro Valley. By

116

then, it was no longer off-limits to would-be ranchers or prospectors.

Until 1874, no one transgressed the boundaries of the Chiricahua reservation. Thomas Jeffords, the trusted friend of Cochise, served as agent and vigorously guarded the rights of the band. But then Cochise died; only the charismatic old chief was capable of keeping his young warriors from chafing under reservation rules and occasionally breaking out to make raids into Mexico, or simply to hunt for game on the too frequent occasions when the government failed to deliver promised food supplies. This was what many observers had been waiting for. Petitions rained down on the territorial and national government, demanding that the Chiricahua be moved hundreds of miles north to the San Carlos Reservation, preserving the safety of white settlers, and, not coincidentally, opening up southeastern Arizona Territory. National outrage over the Custer massacre at the Little Big Horn in late June 1876 may have been the deciding factor. In December 1876 the Chiricahua reservation was closed and the tribe forced to move to San Carlos. Except for San Carlos agent John Clum, who predicted problems, no one seemed aware of, or, at least, to care about, ancient rivalries between the Chiricahua and other Apache bands already living there. Clashes were inevitable, and, almost at once, small groups

117

of Chiricahua warriors led by Juh or Geronimo began periodically breaking out of the reservation to raid in Mexico and hide in the mountains circling the San Pedro Valley until they were rounded up and returned to San Carlos. It happened often enough that in the spring of 1877 the Mexican government put pressure on the United States to station more troops in the San Pedro Valley to cut off traditional Apache raiding routes across the border. The army agreed to build a temporary camp in the Huachuca Mountains just fifteen miles north of Mexico. Ed Schieffelin, who'd been prospecting without any success in upper Arizona Territory, rode down with a company of Indian scouts, "thinking that there was a good opportunity for prospecting by going with them, for they would afford me protection."

For a few days, Ed did his prospecting in a series of day trips away from the new camp. He may have also done some hunting for the post to earn his keep. Ed wrote later that the soldiers at the fort predicted a dire end for him: If he kept tempting fate while searching for silver, what he'd find instead would be his tombstone. "The remarks being made often impressed the [word] on my mind," he noted in his journal. But soon Ed chafed; his preference was to prospect alone, staying away from civilization as long as possible. Leaving Camp Huachuca and its jeering denizens behind, he struck out on his own. Ed didn't minimize the danger. He knew he was risking his life: "I wasn't looking for bullets but I felt if one happened my way it wouldn't make much difference to anyone but me, and I never could figure out that to be dead would be unpleasant." Alone, afraid to make a campfire for fear of attracting Apaches, Ed and his mule Beck worked their cautious way into the San Pedro Valley. Ed carried a rifle and six-shooter, and relied on Beck to warn him of approaching Indians. The mule, he wrote, "was always on the alert, better than a dog."

Ed found himself in a place of exceptional, rugged beauty. The San Pedro Valley is surrounded on all sides by mountain ranges — the Dragoons, the Mule Mountains, the Huachucas, and the Whetstones. Arroyos and hills undulate toward the horizon, making distances difficult to judge and traveling on a straight line virtually impossible. During the day, the bright blue desert sky contrasts with peaks of purple and green and assorted golden tans. The San Pedro River runs through the west part, its banks outlined with cottonwood trees. Wildlife abounds — roadrunners, chirping birds of every description, and enough white-tailed deer to have convinced Ed that, since he was a good shot, he could keep himself reasonably well fed.

Like any experienced prospector, Ed looked for surface outcrops of rock with black lines of potential silver-bearing ore visible. During his first few days in the valley, he didn't find "a color." But he did bump into W. T. Griffith and Alva Smith, who'd been hired by the owners to do some assessment work on the Brunckow Mine site. Griffith and Smith noted Ed's rifle and pistol; they hired him to stand guard for a few days while they worked. Ed was glad for the job. There was safety even in small numbers, and he could make a dollar or two while familiarizing himself with the area. At night, the three men talked. The new Desert Land Act offered 640 acres to any would-be rancher who would irrigate the property. Griffith and Smith were ready to pick out their sites in the valley, and urged Ed to do the same. Ranching had no appeal to Ed — he explained how he believed there had to be rich silver deposits somewhere nearby. They weren't convinced, but Griffith offered Ed a deal. Whenever Ed found a promising location and staked a claim, he should also stake out an adjacent claim in Griffith's name. In return, Griffith would temporarily furnish Ed with whatever supplies he needed. Ed agreed, and a few days later went out to prospect on his own again.

In the hills just a few miles from the Brunckow Mine and the San Pedro River, Ed Schieffelin found promising float. On August 1, 1877, he staked his first claim — 600 by 1,500 feet, according to law. Remembering the sarcastic remarks of soldiers at Camp Huachuca, he named it the Tombstone. A few days later, he made two more claims, one for himself and one, as promised, for Griffith. Sticking with the tombstone theme, he named these Graveyard No. 1 and Graveyard No. 2. The latter was Griffith's. Ed collected float and rock samples from all three, and, with Griffith, left for Tucson to have the samples assayed. But when they arrived, no assayers were available. Ed took the samples to Sydney DeLong, one of the owners of the Brunckow Mine. DeLong took a cursory look at samples from Graveyard No. 2 and declared that whatever Ed had found was "very low grade." He wouldn't look at the other samples Ed had brought. DeLong made it clear that he wasn't interested in going into partnership with Ed and Griffith. He said he already had all the mines he wanted, and that ranching was the way to go.

A growing sense that mining might have dried up was rampant in Arizona Territory and the rest of the Southwest. The Comstock Lode in Nevada Territory had finally petered out. The mines in Prescott were clearly small producers, and except for the Silver King in Globe and the Signal and McCrackin mines in northwestern Arizona, no really significant strikes had been made in the territory for some time. Maybe Arizona wasn't full of hidden treasure after all. DeLong's turndown left Griffith discouraged, but Ed wasn't fazed. They registered their claims — Graveyard No. 2 for Griffith, Graveyard No. 1 and Tombstone for Ed — but Griffith's heart wasn't in the undertaking anymore. He wanted to get on with founding his ranch. He told Ed that he was dissolving their agreement, and no hard feelings. Ed shrugged, got his beloved mule Beck reshod, and returned to the San Pedro Valley. He poked around a few weeks longer and then, down to his last 30 cents, decided to go to Globe and look up his brother Al, who, when last Ed heard, was working at the Silver King. Maybe Al could be convinced to come south to the San Pedro Valley. Ed remained positive that there were massive amounts of silver to be found, if only he could hang on and comb the valley long enough.

It was about two hundred miles to Globe, and when Ed arrived he learned that his brother had been laid off at the Silver King. Al Schieffelin now was working at the Signal Mine, another two hundred miles to the north and west. After a brief stop to earn enough money for food and another set of shoes for his mule, Ed moved on, finally connecting with Al at the Signal. Al Schieffelin wasn't immediately convinced that it was imperative for him to go south with his brother. Instead, he suggested that Ed show his remaining samples to Dick Gird, the highly respected Signal Mine assayer. Unlike Sydney DeLong in Tucson, Gird was impressed by the silver content in the first few bits of float he assayed, and astounded by the quality of the third. He told Ed, "The best thing you can do is to find out where that ore came from, and take me with you and start for the place."

It was February 1878 before the Schieffelin brothers and Gird were outfitted and ready to move south. Nobody working around the Signal Mine took much notice of Ed and Al heading out, but everyone felt certain something big was up if Dick Gird had quit his job to go with them. Several other prospecting parties tried to follow them; one left a day ahead of the Schieffelins and Gird, making Ed fret that he might be beaten to his own hard-won strike. After all, his samples only established that there had to be rich silver veins in a general area of the San Pedro hills. His Tombstone and Graveyard claims notwithstanding, Ed still had to locate more specific sites to make claims and ensure he'd reserved the most lucrative lodes for himself and his new partners.

In late February, the Schieffelins and Gird reached the San Pedro Valley. A few other prospecting teams were working nearby; Ed felt it was a real race now. He and his party made their camp on the old Brunckow site, occupying some cabins there. Gird set up assay works in one, while the Schieffelins went out searching for the sources of the samples and float that impressed Gird so much. Within weeks, they found them: After so many years of wandering, Ed Schieffelin had his major strike. One deposit had a rare, thick line of "horn silver," ore so soft and pure that when Ed pushed a half-dollar into it, the imprint of the coin remained in the silver afterward. Gird said that the sample from that vein was the richest he'd ever assayed. They named the claim there the "Lucky Cuss" because that's what bedraggled Ed Schieffelin finally was. Another fabulous vein took Ed a while longer to trace; that claim became the "Tough Nut" because it had been hard to locate. The bonanza was so overwhelming that Dick Gird found himself encouraging competing prospectors Hank Williams and Oliver Boyer to stay in the region so they, too, could make their own substantial strikes. Gird said he'd assay whatever trace or float they found in return for him and the Schieffelins receiving a share in Williams and Boyer's inevitable claim. A mile from Ed's Tough Nut, they found their own silver, and they named their claim the Grand Central. When Williams and Boyer reneged on their promise to cut him in, Gird protested until they signed over a hundred feet. He and the Schieffelins named their share the Contention, commemorating the temporary disagreement. It always galled Ed Schieffelin that the Grand Central became the richest mine in the Tombstone district. At least the Contention ran a close second.

On April 5, 1878, the Schieffelin brothers and Dick Gird took a step that made general knowledge of their good luck inevitable: They submitted bylaws to the Pima County recorder for the establishment of the Tombstone Mining District in the San Pedro Valley. It was the best way to consolidate their now numerous claims. Word spread fast. Within days, southeast Arizona became a focal point for regional prospectors — and, eventually, for merchants, investors, and speculators eager to share in whatever fortune might be found there.

The prospectors arrived first, some of them grizzled veterans like Ed, others rank amateurs who had no real idea of how to even identify float, let alone follow thin black lines of silver-bearing ore over ridges and underground to wider veins. A few arrived on horseback. Most came on foot, some of them hauling their possessions and mining tools in wheelbarrows. Almost everyone camped in tents; they had no time or inclination to build anything more substantial. Comfort was secondary to the near-hysterical urge to strike it rich fast, before the fellow camping nearby beat you to it. There was nothing particularly sophisticated about the process. You thought you spotted a promising place, took out your pick, dug a short shaft or pit, hacked out some samples, and took them to an assayer. Most of the time, the news wasn't good. You'd wasted your time and sweat on worthless rock. But if your samples tested high enough for silver content, you staked your 1,500-foot-by-600-foot claim, a basic process of setting a mound of stones at one end and some markers on the others. Then it was necessary to go to Tucson and formally file the claim. This very inexact process lent itself to constant squabbling about who had legally claimed what; charges of claim jumping were incessant. Even when you found high-grade deposits, a major strike was rare. Some of the best veins ran out so quickly that their value came to virtually nothing.

It wasn't unusual for packs of prospectors to arrive in an isolated spot on the heels of someone filing several claims there. Copycat prospecting was the norm. In almost every instance, after a few days went by with nobody else "finding color," the crowd drifted away to wait and congregate again when news of another strike somewhere else began to circulate.

The San Pedro Valley proved to be an exception. A broad band of mineral-laden rock ran through it for about thirty miles from the Dragoon Mountains in the east to the Huachucas in the west. For the next several years, enough surface trace continued to be found that the influx of prospectors stayed constant. Somebody was always finding fresh evidence of a possible major lode. Even so, the percentage of deposits extensive enough to merit the construction of a full working mine was minuscule. Although there eventually were more than three thousand mines located in and around the San Pedro Valley, only thirteen had the complete hoisting works necessary for mass extraction.

But the odds still seemed better than anywhere else. Small camps of prospectors sprang up all over the valley. These were not in any sense permanent settlements, just temporary squatting places. But some lasted longer than others, and those that did attracted the next wave of arrivals — small-potatoes merchants who wanted a piece of the action without swinging a pick themselves. Prospectors needed to eat and wanted to drink. They had very little money to spend. Most of the prospectors, like Ed Schieffelin, came to the area with only a few dollars in their pockets. The primitive saloons and restaurants that soon dotted the camps were set up in tents, and catered to the basic appetites of their customers with cheap red-eye whiskey and stew. Everyone involved could pack up and move at any time. The next wave of newcomers began changing that.

In gold mining camps, some prospectors could make small fortunes all by themselves, since gold nuggets and significant traces of gold dust could sometimes be retrieved from streambeds and surface crevices. But gold comprised only about 15 percent of the ore eventually discovered in the San Pedro Valley. More than 80 percent was silver, and every step involved in discovering and processing silver was much more difficult — and expensive.

Prospectors could find the veins of silver, but they could not supply the equipment and manpower necessary to gouge wide tunnels deep into solid earth and rock to extract tons of silver-bearing ore. The ore, once brought to the surface, required complicated stages of processing before silver could be extracted from it. This meant building sampling and assay works, smelters, refineries, and stamping mills. Silver-bearing ore had to be crushed into fine sand, washed in chemical mixes, and the silver finally extracted from the rest of the mineral mix. Then the silver had to be formed into heavy bars for transport and sale. Buying lumber and building waterworks to power machinery required significant investment. Specialists had to be hired to dig the tunnels, and more experts to shore them up. Engineers had to be constantly on hand to supervise. When the tunnels were ready, experienced miners had to be recruited, and paid for weeks or even months before the first silver was extracted, processed, and sold. The cost of opening a single working silver mine could reach a million dollars. For all his fabulous strikes, even Ed Schieffelin was in no position to finance his own mining operations.

So the Schieffelins and Gird next prospected for outside money. They were willing to sell their claims outright, and thanks to Gird's reputation soon had some substantial offers. One they accepted — $50,000 for the Tough Nut and $40,000 for the Lucky Cuss and a few adjoining claims — fell through. That turned out to be fortunate for them. In August 1878 they were invited to form a partnership with a group of businessmen who included A. P. K. Safford, a former governor of Arizona Territory. Safford had contacts with potential investors on the East and West coasts. By October, Ed and Al Schieffelin and Dick Gird were stockholders in the newly established Tombstone Gold and Silver Mill and Mining Company. The operation was capitalized for $5 million, and shares were offered for $10 apiece. Gird traveled to San Francisco, and, using money raised by Safford, ordered mining equipment, a stamp mill (to pulverize the raw ore-bearing rock), and a sawmill. The mills were built in San Francisco and shipped by rail and wagon in pieces to the San Pedro Valley, where they were assembled. Meanwhile, the first dynamite blasts were fired for the underground tunnels of the Tough Nut Mine. Bullion wouldn't begin being processed and shipped until the middle of 1879, but there was no doubt that the San Pedro Valley was in position to become the new national hotbed of mining. Major investors sent inspection teams to the area. Experienced excavators and miners, looking for long-term paydays, arrived to offer their services. The San Pedro Valley in late 1878 was the equivalent of California's Silicon Valley during the high-tech boom era of the 1980s. Ambitious people from all over America gravitated there.

Many of them had no intention of working in the mines. They wanted to sell things to the men who did, and unlike the first few penny-profit merchants who'd arrived, these entrepreneurs offered more sophisticated, and pricey, goods and services. Prospectors had no disposable income, but miners — paid $4 a day — did, and as they came off-duty they were ready to spend their wages. The first prostitutes arrived; workingmen in the West were always eager for their company. Some tents in the San Pedro Valley were utilized as bath houses. Miners grimy from working underground all day were eager to get clean. Gamblers offered participation in card games. Most of all, the miners wanted food, and not just anything on a plate.

Because they spent their ten-hour daily shifts breathing fetid air and, too often, inhaling noxious underground gases, miners' palates were dulled. Like the risk of cave-ins, it was an accepted occupational hazard. When they ate, the miners insisted on distinctive tastes and tangs — historian Joseph R. Conlin describes their preferred meals as including "sweets, acidic pickles, smoked and salty things, high spices that were practically exotic in American cooking at the time." Lunch wagons offered such treats right at the entrances to the mines. Even more highly spiced dishes were available in restaurant tents nearby. Constantly gorging themselves on this combustible fare took its inevitable toll on diners' digestive systems. Conlin notes that the miners of the San Pedro Valley, in common with miners all over the West, were regularly debilitated by "ailments associated with a gamey diet: Bilious fever, constipation, cramps, dyspepsia, diarrhea (excluding cases diagnosed as dysentery), enteritis, gastritis, gastric fever, hemorrhoids, inflammation of the bladder, inflammation of the bowels, kidney and liver disease, and food poisoning."

The constant need for shipments of fresh food meant freight lines were necessary to connect the valley to the outside world. Transportation was needed for businessmen coming to and returning from the area. Two

131

stagecoach lines were established. It was clear that once processed silver began emerging from the new smelters and mills, service would be needed to haul the gleaming bullion safely to Tucson. Wells Fargo, the dominant shipper of valuable goods in the West, took notice. The company sent veteran lawman Bob Paul to "look over the country." When Wells Fargo signed an agreement with one of the valley stage lines to handle bullion shipments, it was an unmistakable sign that, at least for a while, mining and all its attendant economics were in the San Pedro Valley to stay.

With that came the next inevitable step. Speculators began vying to establish town sites. Several — Watervale, Millville, Charleston, Contention — were set up near mining works and the San Pedro River. Richmond was farther away from water, near the hills where Ed Schieffelin made his first amazing strikes. It was much more accessible to the working mines themselves — and, not coincidentally, to the miners eager to spend their money as soon as they emerged from the underground tunnels. But the Richmond location — on a ridge, with arroyos on either side — wasn't ideal. There wasn't enough room. Not far away was a long mesa known locally as Goose Flats. Like Richmond, the spot lacked easy access to water. But it offered space for expansion, and it was close to the mines likely to produce the most silver, and, therefore, employ the most workers with money to spend. Stages could reach it with reasonable ease. It became obvious that this was the place where a dominant San Pedro Valley town could be built. Far less clear was who had the right to own the land, then sell it off to the town settlers.

The land on Goose Flats was public domain, which meant that any individual or group could survey the site and pay the government $1.25 an acre for 320 acres, with the intent of establishing a town by dividing the property up and selling individual sites to settlers for undetermined but "moderate" fees. There were other ways to go about town founding — if, for instance, an incorporated settlement already existed on the property, a patent would be issued to the mayor, who could then dispose of town lots to citizens. The legalese was convoluted. Essentially, if nobody was already controlling distribution of prime public land, speculators could, and would, swoop in and try to hustle their way into fortunes. That happened with Goose Flats. San Franciscans James C. Clark and Joseph C. Palmer, shrewd operators with long experience in shady business dealings, came to Arizona in early 1879 to scope out possibilities in the San Pedro Valley. After adding some area investors, including former territorial governor Safford, Clark and Palmer founded the Tombstone Townsite Company, taking the name from Ed Schieffelin's first mining claim. Safford may have suggested it. They hired a surveyor who laid out a town plan with seven streets named for territorial notables (Fremont and Safford among them) bisected at perfect right angles by numbered thoroughfares (First through Twelfth). Each block was three hundred feet square, divided into twenty-four individual lots. There was nothing particularly imaginative about it. Palmer soon sold his interest in the town site company to Clark. Mike Gray, newly arrived from California, acquired a significant interest in the business from other investors.

The Tombstone Townsite Company began selling lots, but failed to make all its required payments to the government. That led to considerable uncertainty about who owned — and who had the right to sell — which lots in the new community, but arrivals were far more interested in making money than paying attention to that. An eventual complex legal mess was guaranteed — but for the moment, nothing was resolved. It became common for hired gunmen to camp on prime lots, holding them for employers who planned to locate businesses or build houses there.

The biggest news was that Tombstone rather than Richmond was awarded a post office — Dick Gird became the first postmaster, a position of considerable importance in frontier communities. This meant the territorial government conceded Tombstone's primacy among San Pedro Valley settlements, though the Pima County board of supervisors didn't officially incorporate it as a village until November 1879. By then, the whole country was reading and talking about Tombstone. The *Chicago Tribune* noted, "In a few months the discovery of Tombstone put Arizona on the map and caused a rush like that of early Nevada and Colorado."

Not everyone rushing to the area settled in Tombstone itself. Previously, only a few major ranching operations could survive the Apache presence in the area. But with an exploding, hungry population creating an urgent demand for fresh beef, small ranchers began setting up along the San Pedro River and in the deep, grassy arroyos. The Clantons arrived in 1878; they soon made enough profit from peddling their limited amount of stock to local butchers for Ike Clanton to open a restaurant — probably just a lunch wagon or a few tables under a tent — in Millville. It didn't stay in business long, but Ike and his family wouldn't have been especially discouraged. Like everyone else, they had come to the valley to make their fortune as best they could. If one endeavor didn't work, they'd try another. Ranching was always their main focus. Besides silver, beef was perhaps the most vital Tombstone commodity. The Clantons needed to get their hands on as many cattle as they could. It would take too long to raise big enough herds to satisfy Tombstone and valley markets. They had to find another way.

The Clantons weren't the only family hoping to cash in on the local beef shortage. There were dozens of others, including brothers Frank and Tom McLaury, who gravitated to Arizona Territory from Iowa. They first came through Texas, where their brother Will practiced law in Fort Worth. They originally planned to join him there. But Arizona seemed to offer more possibilities. Like the Clantons, the McLaurys weren't embittered Southerners trying to escape Yankee oppression — another McLaury brother had fought for the Union in the Civil War — but they did share the widespread Southern desire to live free of government encumbrance. Life in the still wild frontier of Arizona Territory appealed to them; the confines of a town on a daily basis didn't. Frank and Tom established a small ranch along the Babocomari Creek outside Tombstone and began raising cattle and sheep. The Clantons and McLaurys were natural allies, and soon on friendly terms. They may not have wanted to live in Tombstone themselves, but they hoped that the town would continue to grow explosively and increase the already frantic demand for fresh beef. Both families meant to profit from it.

Tents atop the mesa comprised early Tombstone. The Mohave, its first hotel, opened in April 1879, and it was housed in a tent. But that same month, the first permanent house in town was built. Some of the timber shipped in from the Pacific coast, or purchased from woodcutters fearless enough to risk Apache attack and cut trees in the Huachuca Mountains, began being used for residential building as well as in mine shafts. A social hierarchy requiring more sophisticated housing was starting to arrive — mine and plant managers, lawyers handling the endless series of claim jumping cases, merchants whose shops sold high-quality goods. Unlike roving prospectors, they often came with their families, and none of them were willing to live in tents. It happened very occasionally that a mining camp grew into something finer and more sophisticated. That happened twenty years earlier with Virginia City in Nevada Territory; its town limits eventually included "butchers, bakers, fruiterers, boarding houses and restaurants," along with drugstores and two opera houses. Virginia City flourished because the Comstock Lode attracted elite residents, smart men who founded businesses and stayed in town to run them. Though the breadth of their silver deposits had yet to be determined, the Tombstone mines were already being compared to the Comstock by newspapers all over America. History seemed to be repeating itself.

Eighteen seventy-nine was still too soon to be certain that Tombstone was going to grow into such a special, sophisticated place. But the indications were there. A daily newspaper, the *Nugget,* began publication that fall. A reporter for the *Tucson Star* paid a visit and informed readers that Tombstone's "saloon-keepers are always active, polite and accommodating. The restaurants are models of neatness, and supplied bounteously with the choicest meats and such other dainties as the market affords. Mechanics are employed in erecting buildings in various parts of town." A mayor, William Harwood, was elected in November. Fred White, a thirty-one-year-old from New York, was hired as town marshal at a salary of $125 a month. White had never been a lawman before; he'd been working as a lumberman and carpenter. Tombstone had an urgent need for a marshal because its freshly minted four-member city council had set up a system of property taxes and quarterly business licensing fees. Someone had to collect them — plans for a public school were being discussed, and that project would require money in the town treasury. Tax and fee collection became Marshal White's priority. It was all very organized — too much so for the man who'd inadvertently put it all into motion.

In November 1879, Ed Schieffelin cashed

out his shares in the Tombstone Gold and Silver Mill and Mining Company, netting $600,000, and prepared to move on. Civilization didn't sit well with Ed, and, besides, he and Dick Gird had been quarreling over the kind of complex business matters that held little fascination for Ed. After spending several months prospecting in the Dragoon Mountains, he left Tombstone and the San Pedro Valley, making only occasional returns to the community he'd essentially founded. Ed traveled for a while, spending money in a few big cities, but all he really wanted was to be out prospecting again. Soon he was headed for Alaska, sailing there in a steamship he built with some of his Tombstone fortune, and feeling as certain as ever that another big strike was waiting to be discovered just over the horizon. He left behind a legacy that resonated with other men who never gave up on their dreams. If Ed, as undistinguished a fellow as ever tried to make a fortune, managed to do it in Tombstone, then anyone could. One early resident recalled, "You never heard a hard-luck story in Tombstone. Everyone had great expectations. He might not have a dollar in his pocket — but he had millions in sight!"

The Earp brothers certainly did, and they showed up in Tombstone just a few weeks after Ed Schieffelin decided it was time to move on.

Chapter Four:
The Earps Arrive

The floor of the San Pedro Valley is pocked with hills and arroyos; the undulating terrain permits spectacular long-range views of surrounding mountain ranges, but frequently prevents unobstructed lines of close-up vision. Approaching from the northwest, traveling in three wagons with extra horses tethered behind, the Earps probably didn't see Tombstone on its low-slung mesa until moments after they heard it — a cacophony of tooting mine whistles, braying pack animals, and incessant hammering, all of them sounds indicative of a vibrant, growing community. In fact, Tombstone in December 1879 sounded better than it looked. Though wood and adobe buildings were being added to the ubiquitous tents at a rapid rate, it was clearly a town still in the early stages of development. That suited the Earps perfectly. There was more opportunity to rise in an embryonic community than in towns like Dodge City, Wichita, or Prescott, where social and economic hierarchies were already solidly in place. And, thanks to U.S. marshal Crawley Dake, one of the Earp brothers was arriving in Tombstone as a man of some immediate importance.

Dake had appointed Virgil to be a U.S. deputy marshal, representing law enforcement on behalf of the U.S. government in the booming community of Tombstone and its surrounding region. It was on-call rather than full-time employment. Virgil would mostly have to make himself available to help out territorial, county, and city officials when requested. But it was making use of a connection in high places, and a fine way for Virgil to meet the most influential men in town. If he impressed them, then the deputy job might lead to something better — higher appointive office, or perhaps getting cut in on some can't-miss business deal. During his first weeks in Tombstone, Virgil had plenty to keep him busy.

Wyatt didn't. Like Virgil, he arrived with big plans, but Wyatt's went awry from the start. Before leaving Dodge he'd acquired a wagon with the intent of using it to establish a stage line in Tombstone. But two were already in operation, and there was no need for a third, especially since Wyatt would have been competing with better-financed rivals who conveyed passengers in enclosed coaches. He apparently had no fallback plan beyond joining everyone else in Tombstone in trying to strike silver in the surrounding hills. The three Earp brothers had been in town for only a few days when they and a partner, Bob Winders (probably a friend of James Earp's from back in Texas) began filing claims. Like other area prospectors, they had no intention of building and operating mines themselves. Their hope was to stake one or two claims with enticing assay reports that might make bigger fish want to buy or lease the property — the equivalent of modern-day real estate markets where small investors acquire property at low prices and then try to flip it for a quick profit. In the coming months, they'd have occasional success, but nothing substantial enough to raise themselves above the ranks of other struggling, would-be profiteers.

James found a job in a Tombstone saloon; his sights were always set lower than Virgil's or Wyatt's. The Earp women — Virgil's wife, Allie; Wyatt's wife, Mattie; James's wife, Bessie, and his stepdaughter, Hattie — brought in some money by sewing and mending canvas tents. Wyatt remained at loose ends. The most obvious job to seek would have been as a policeman serving under Tombstone sheriff Fred White, but Wyatt didn't want to be a lawman anymore. While he was in Dodge City, he'd told friends he wanted to own his own ranch, and the San

Pedro Valley provided the perfect opportunity. There was land available, and, like the Clantons and McLaurys, Wyatt could soon have come into possession of some Mexican cattle. He'd proven back in Missouri and Illinois that, when he wasn't enforcing the law, he was willing to circumvent it. But Wyatt wasn't interested in being a small-time rancher, either, scrambling to make a living. The things he wanted — real money, social prominence, *importance* — were far more likely to be found within Tombstone town limits. Other men were succeeding there. E. B. Gage, the newly appointed superintendent of the Grand Central Mine, was treated like a celebrity. Carl Bilicke and his son Albert were upgrading their Cosmopolitan Hotel from a tent to wood and adobe — everyone thought they were special. Then there was John Clum, the former Indian agent who'd quit the San Carlos Reservation in protest of the treatment of Indians there. Clum was about to establish a newspaper called the *Epitaph* to compete with the *Nugget;* as soon as Clum got to town, Gage and the Bilickes and other men of influence accepted him into their ranks. But nobody made any fuss about Wyatt Earp. Perhaps a few people in town had heard of him, a second-tier lawman coming in from Kansas. Tombstone already had a marshal. There was nothing for Wyatt to do but rely on his old, proven way of eking out a living

— playing cards in Tombstone's tent saloons, falling back into the same demimonde he wanted so badly to escape. In between hands of faro and keno and poker, he plodded around the Tombstone hills, staking claims and crossing his fingers — just one more semi-anonymous drifter trying to get rich quick.

At first, all the Earps lived together in a one-room, dirt-floor adobe dwelling. They then built separate shacks — it was a relatively cheap process — but kept close to each other. Family solidarity remained important. Morgan was soon on the way; he resigned as a policeman in Butte, Montana, early in 1880. Morgan came to Tombstone by himself, leaving common-law wife Louisa back with family in California for a while until he felt ready to send for her. To some degree, all the Earp men at least got out and mingled with other Tombstone residents. Their wives, and James's stepdaughter, Hattie, had less social interaction. Allie and Mattie were common-law; Bessie was a former prostitute. They were not socially acceptable to the wives of men Virgil and Wyatt wanted to impress. For the sake of their husbands' ambitions, they kept in the background, and the male Earps probably preferred them there anyway.

Tombstone continued to grow at an explosive rate. There were perhaps nine hundred residents in late 1879 when the Earps arrived.

A census six months later pegged the town's population at 2,100, and that didn't account for all the prospectors, ranchers, and assorted hangers-on camped outside the city limits. Tucson remained the largest town in Arizona Territory with a population of seven thousand. (The census listed Wyatt as "farmer," a generic term for a man without any specific occupation.) Every day on Allen Street, stagecoaches arrived so crammed with passengers that some had to ride on the roof or hang from luggage bins on the back. Tombstone residents established the custom of rushing out to greet the stages — every newcomer was a potential cash cow, and it was important that they receive a warm welcome to town. Far more than in other mining towns, the flood of arrivals featured a higher class of potential citizens. Miners — rough-hewn, often hailing from foreign lands — were the predominant population in other communities. But the silver deposits discovered around Tombstone were closer to the surface than those of other frontier lodes. That meant a single miner there could do the work of three elsewhere. There were never more than about four hundred miners working in Tombstone. Its burgeoning population included a much higher percentage of reputable businessmen — bankers, retailers, lawyers, engineers, accountants — than anywhere else in Arizona Territory. These individuals demanded creature comforts, and, because enough money was being generated by the local mines, they got them.

When the railroad reached Tucson in March 1880, goods of all kinds could be shipped in from around the country, and freight lines were available to convey them to Tombstone. Mercantile stores offering fine lines of clothing, home furnishings, and food opened in rapid succession — and the food no longer needed to be nonperishable. Dick Gird, with some of the hundreds of thousands of dollars he earned after selling his shares in the Tombstone Gold and Silver Mill and Mining Company, built an ice house at Millville, just across the San Pedro River from Charleston. This meant hungry, discerning Tombstone residents could enjoy imported fruit, cold beer — a town brewery opened for business — and even ice cream. The most frequent dining dilemma was what kind of fine food to enjoy for any given meal. Spaghetti with meatballs, chow mein, roast duckling, oysters that were fried or poached or served in a delicate sauce — all these delights and more were available in Tombstone's elegant restaurants, with multiple-course meals offered for 50 cents or less. Many of the new buildings were constructed of wood instead of the ubiquitous adobe. For the first time, Tombstone *looked* sophisticated, at least in comparison to other important Arizona Territory towns. Globe and Tucson were virtually indistinguishable from squat Mexican villages south of the border.

Many eyewitness details of Tombstone history trace back to February 1880, when George Whitwell Parsons arrived. He was a compulsive chronicler of his life and surroundings, and kept diaries that spanned sixty years. Parsons had worked for a bank in San Francisco that failed in 1879. He read about Tombstone in the San Francisco newspapers, which "determined me . . . to go to the Tombstone District and begin as a common miner. Learn the business and stick to it." Parsons wasn't entirely taken by his new home. "One street of shanties some with canvas roofs," he wrote on February 17. He and some friends found a temporary place to stay, "rough house — simply roof and sides with openings all over through which wind came freely." But after walking around a bit, Parsons liked his surroundings better: "Fine broad street. Good square meal four bits. Very reasonable indeed, considering. Business good here and signs very encouraging indeed. Money here." Parsons spent his first few months learning the mining business the hard way, working as a laborer in exchange for small percentages of new claims. None panned out for him, but he remained optimistic for several years. In the meantime, his East and West coast roots allowed him entry at a

147

top level of Tombstone society to which the less cultured Earps could only aspire. For future historians, Parsons's journal would prove a treasure trove of information about Tombstone economics and culture. Though his entries soon included descriptions of elaborate masked balls and candlelight suppers with Tombstone's few *nice* single women, Parsons's first extended commentaries concerned rat infestation, an issue that plagued everyone in town, regardless of their social standing.

Dogs ran wild through the Tombstone streets and relieved themselves indiscriminately. So did horses, and the mules pulling freight wagons; in an attempt to keep the town's busiest thoroughfare less polluted, no hitching posts were allowed on Allen Street. Garbage collection was minimal. Tombstone employed a town scavenger, but there was always more rotting debris than one man could pick up. As a result, packs of rats joined the ubiquitous desert scorpions and spiders in swarming through town in alarming numbers. Even in fine new residences built of adobe and wood, people fell asleep trying to ignore the scrabbling of rodent paws nearby. Men like Parsons, sleeping in the open or something close to it, often woke to feel rats (or tarantulas or scorpions) scuttling over their legs or faces. Just four nights after arriving in Tombstone, Parsons reported in his

148

journal, "Rats and mice [made] a deuce of a racket last night around a fellow's head on the ground. Rolled over on one in the night and killed him — mashed him deader than a doornail."

Cats became prized possessions, and there weren't enough to go around. Finding a stray feline was considered great luck second only to making a significant silver strike. In March, Parsons bragged about nabbing a near-feral cat on his way back from church, hurrying home with it "before I was clawed or bitten to death. Peace tonight among the rats."

Newcomer Clara Spalding Brown described another perpetual Tombstone irritant. The wife of a teamster, she left San Diego to join her husband in Tombstone during the early summer of 1880. While in San Diego, Clara wrote occasional columns for newspapers in Boston and Hartford, describing her life on the Pacific coast. Once in Tombstone, she began sending reports back to the *San Diego Daily Union* about the goings-on in a frontier mining town. She had plenty to tell. Clara knew quite a bit about business, and she crammed her columns with news about which Tombstone mines were producing how much bullion, and estimates of how tax rates there affected average citizens. The columns weren't all facts and figures — Clara became a fixture on the Tombstone social circuit, helping organize drama clubs and sharing with San Diego readers her experiences at all the best parties. But Clara's initial description of Tombstone emphasized its state of constant filth:

> The camp is one of the dirtiest places in the world. When black garments appear to have been laid away in an ash barrel, and one is never sure of having a clean face, despite repeated ablutions, it is time to talk about dirt. The soil [is] loose upon the surface, and is whirled into the air everyday by a wind which almost amounts to a gale; it makes the eyes smart like the cinders from an engine; it penetrates into the houses, and covers everything with dust. I do not believe the famous Nebraska breeze can go ahead of the Tombstone zephyr.

Water and Apaches were more serious concerns. Tombstone got most of its water from barrels hauled in by wagons. Customers paid 3 cents for a gallon. Some prospectors, including the Earps, spent time scouting for springs as well as silver. Residents and the miners working outside town were constantly concerned about the quality of the water they drank. The digestive systems of the entire community were affected. In his diary, George Parsons mentioned "mean water and several kinds. Consequently, diarrhea." Another time, water from a well was laced with thick scum, though people drank it anyway. An investigation turned up a dead man beneath the water's surface.

Everyone worried about the water, but they feared the Chiricahua. Renegade leaders like Juh and Geronimo led occasional San Carlos Reservation breakouts by small bands of mounted warriors. These never attacked Tombstone or even the smaller surrounding towns of Charleston and Contention City. Lacking numbers and weapons to stage any sustained assault on well-armed larger numbers of white men, the renegades skirted the American settlements and made for Mexico instead, where they could raid isolated farms and hamlets. But most Tombstone residents lived in dread of Apache attack anyway. The slightest rumor of renegades nearby sent the town into a panic.

But dirt, rats, bad water, and Indians weren't enough to offset the lure of fortunes to be made — and spent — in Tombstone. One way or another, everyone was there to make money — and, gradually, they were able to live elegantly while trying to do it. The prominent men in town needed fancier places to drink and talk a little business than tent saloons. By the summer of 1880 several swanky establishments had opened, all vying to offer the finest whiskey to be enjoyed in the most luxurious surroundings. These upscale spots had separate music and gaming rooms, the better to relax customers and then relieve them of their money. When visitors came to town to negotiate deals, they stayed in hotels rivaling the best in New York or San Francisco. The Bilickes' Cosmopolitan Hotel completed its transformation from rickety tent to two-story showcase: Its veranda featured potted orange trees, and guests were invited to pick treats off the branches. The rival Grand Hotel advertised walnut furniture and spring mattresses. In July, Tombstone became connected to the outside world with telegraph lines. The Mining Exchange Building was constructed so land deals could be negotiated nonstop, and telephone wires were strung between it and individual mines, as well as to the choicest hotels. Most significant of all, the powerful Wells Fargo Company bestowed an ultimate accolade by opening a branch office in Tombstone. This indicated that Wells Fargo, the preeminent transporter of valuable shipments, believed it would have steady business transporting bullion and payroll cash between the town mines and Tucson. One of the first beneficiaries of that decision was Wyatt Earp.

When Wells Fargo opened an office in a new town, it usually hired a local man to run it. In this case, the company selected Marshall Williams, a native New Yorker who came to Tombstone as an agent for one of its two stage lines and also opened a cigar and stationery store. Williams was a popular, influential man about town; he was elected vice president of the Tombstone Republican Club. Membership in this group was a sign of social standing among town leaders. Williams then had to hire someone to serve as "shotgun messenger," or armed guard, to ride on any Tombstone stages that carried Wells Fargo cash boxes. (Wells Fargo didn't own and operate stage lines; it leased space on local stages for its shipments.) The shotgun messenger position was crucial to the company's operations, because, in the event of a successful robbery, Wells Fargo fully reimbursed its customers. That was good public relations in the business community, but Wells Fargo also wanted it known among the criminal element that the men hired to guard its cargos were all skilled gunmen who would kill without qualms. It made sense that Williams offered the job to Wyatt, who had a background in law enforcement. It made even more sense for Wyatt to accept. Though he'd left Dodge City determined never to work for anyone else again, his first months in Tombstone hadn't resulted in the kind of income necessary for such independence. Besides, Marshall Williams was the sort of town leader that Wyatt wanted to impress. He soon got his chance, and it didn't involve fending off would-be stage robbers.

In July 1880, U.S. Army Lieutenant Joseph H. Hurst came to Tombstone. He reported that six mules had been stolen from Camp Rucker some seventy-five miles east of town. Hurst believed that the rustlers must be hiding the mules nearby, and he asked for help in tracking them down. Deputy U.S. marshal Virgil Earp was delighted to help out. It would be a high-profile opportunity to display his leadership skills.

In all their law enforcement jobs, the Earps relied on informers. They realized the value of monitoring local gossip, and soon Virgil learned that the missing mules might be found on Frank and Tom McLaury's ranch on Babocomari Creek. He put together a small posse consisting of his brothers Wyatt and Morgan and Marshall Williams, the Wells Fargo agent. Virgil trusted his brothers implicitly, and including Williams was a canny way to ensure that the right people in town heard about the Earps' efficiency. Hurst came along, too, though he had no power to make arrests. His job was to identify the mules. Virgil, as the lawman with jurisdiction, certainly believed he would decide how the problem was resolved — perhaps with an arrest or two.

When the posse reached the ranch, Frank and Tom McLaury weren't there, but the stolen animals were. Hurst pointed out the mules. The McLaury ranch hands weren't inclined to give them up. Virgil had the authority to seize the mules and arrest whom he chose, but he didn't get the chance. Lieutenant Hurst negotiated a deal with Frank Patterson, a cowboy who apparently had been placed in charge by Frank and Tom. Hurst and Patterson agreed that no one would be arrested. Instead, the posse would leave, and the mules would be returned to Hurst the next day. The deal allowed the McLaurys and their cowhands to save considerable face, always important in the macho culture of the frontier. Hurst would get his mules back, which was all he cared about. The McLaurys wouldn't appear to have backed down. But the agreement didn't sit well with the Earps. As always, their instincts were to enforce the law. Property had been stolen, and tracked down. At the very least, the six animals should have been immediately retrieved from the ranch. Virgil, Wyatt, and Morgan were undoubtedly gratified when the mules weren't delivered as promised. Probably they were whisked to another location the moment the Earp posse rode out of sight on its way back to Tombstone.

Hurst was furious, but a return trip to the Babocomari would probably have been futile. He'd missed his chance. Instead, on July 27 the lieutenant tacked up posters around Tombstone offering a $25 reward for information resulting in the arrest, trial, and conviction of the mule thieves. The notices stated that the mules had been "secreted at or in the vicinity of the McLowry Brothers' ranch," where "they were . . . branded on the left shoulder over the Government brand." Hurst specifically identified "Frank M'Lowery" as one of the brigands who at the very least "aided in the secretion of the stolen animals."

On August 5, Frank responded with a letter published in the *Nugget.* He chose the *Nugget* over the *Epitaph* because its editorials were clearly sympathetic to small ranchers and the Democrats. (John Clum's *Epitaph* was openly pro-Republican and friendly to the larger local business interests.) Frank protested that he'd personally met with Hurst on the ranch, and told him he knew nothing about the mules. He denied the animals were even there — a point of contention, since Hurst identified them to the Earps — and expressed outrage that the good McLaury name had been so publicly besmirched:

If [Lt.] Hurst was a gentleman, or if I could appeal to the courts for protection, I would proceed differently in this matter, but Hurst is irresponsible and I have but one course to pursue, and that is to publish to the world that J. H. Hurst . . . is a coward, a vagabond, a rascal and a malicious liar. This base and unmanly action is the result of cowardice, for instead of hunting the stock himself he tried to get others to do it, and when they could not find it, in order to cover up for his own wrong acts, he attempted to traduce the character and reputation of honest men. My name is well known in Arizona, and thank God this is the first time in my life the name of dishonesty was ever attached to me. Perhaps when the matter is ventilated it will be found that the Hon. Lt. Hurst has stolen these mules and sold them, for a coward will steal, and a man who can publish the placard that bears his name is a coward. I am willing to let the people of Arizona decide who is right. Frank McLaury, Babacomari, August 2, 1880.

A short (five foot six), feisty man, Frank McLaury may not have confined his outrage to print. Virgil Earp claimed later that Frank confronted him, demanding to know if Virgil had anything to do with the notices posted by Hurst. Virgil swore that he didn't, only to have Frank threaten that "if you again follow us as close as you did, then you will have to fight anyway." Virgil said he replied "that if ever any warrant for [McLaury's] arrest were put into my hands I would endeavor to catch him, and no compromise would be made on my part to let him go. He replied that I would have to fight, and that I would never take him alive." Though Virgil may have exaggerated,

Frank would certainly not have appreciated the Earps riding onto his property looking for rustled stock. It was the kind of animosity that lingered, especially since on the same day Hurst tacked up his accusatory reward posters a second Earp brother pinned on a badge. When he left Dodge City, Wyatt swore he'd never be a lawman again. But in Arizona Territory he was offered an opportunity that he simply couldn't turn down.

U.S. marshals and their deputies in the frontier territories had the unenviable task of trying to enforce federal law in jurisdictions the size of European countries. Town marshals in the West were responsible for controlling mostly male populations under generally primitive conditions that encouraged rather than restricted conflict. Salaries were minimal, though territorial and town officers sometimes had opportunities to enrich themselves in deals with prominent businessmen they'd impressed — Crawley Dake, the U.S. marshal for Arizona Territory who befriended Virgil Earp, was a good example. But county sheriffs were virtually guaranteed to make a lot of money. Their chief function was to collect taxes from the railroads and the working mines and the thriving mercantiles selling expensive wares to rich area residents. In return, the sheriffs kept 10 percent of what they collected, and, in some cases, that take soared as high as $25,000 or more annually, a fortune for the time. Law enforcement and its attendant dangers were also involved, but the sheriffs hired deputies to handle the bulk of those responsibilities. The deputies received salaries and whatever small percentage of tax revenues their boss decided to share with them. Like town marshals, county sheriffs had to stand for election every few years. There was always considerable competition for the lucrative top county jobs.

On July 27, 1880, Pima County sheriff Charlie Shibell appointed Wyatt Earp as a deputy. Tombstone had become a major town, replete with businesses to be taxed and citizens who demonstrated occasional disrespect for the law. In hiring Wyatt, Shibell was adding an officer who apparently had the experience necessary to provide efficient, pragmatic enforcement. He'd collect some taxes, deliver and execute arrest warrants, and, most importantly, pursue lawbreakers who committed their crimes outside town limits but within county boundaries. For Pima County, these stretched hundreds of miles in every direction, but Wyatt would concentrate on the immediate Tombstone area. The job of county deputy carried with it a certain amount of status — Shibell would rarely be in the southeast corner of his jurisdiction, leaving Wyatt as the nominal man in charge. What must have really intrigued Wyatt was the opportunity for more. Shibell was a Democrat. Wyatt was a Republican. If Wyatt distinguished himself in a subordinate role, the time might come when he could run for the top job and its munificent income. Shibell would be seeking reelection in November 1880 — perhaps too soon for Wyatt to gain sufficient reputation to challenge him, and, besides, Shibell was a pleasant fellow who was doing Wyatt a huge favor by making him deputy. But 1882 wasn't that far away. Maybe then Shibell wouldn't choose to run for another two-year term. Besides, there were rumors that the territorial legislature might soon vote to split off the rich southeast portion of Pima County and make it a separate county. A highly visible deputy might be considered a leading candidate to become the new county's first sheriff; with all the rich Tombstone mines to be taxed, it would be the equivalent of the sheriff being able to print his own money. In all likelihood, the new county would be established at some point between elections. The territorial governor would appoint a sheriff to serve until the next scheduled balloting. Arizona governor Frémont was a Republican, just like Wyatt, who had to like his chances.

In the interim, though, Wyatt would have to keep troublemakers in line and, in southeast Pima County, this was a considerable challenge. He had a lot more territory to cover than ever before — Dodge City and Wichita were towns, and in the course of his duties as policeman or deputy marshal, Wyatt had rarely had to venture beyond them unless he was tracking criminals who'd broken laws within city limits. That didn't mean that all his time in his new job would be spent out in the hills and arroyos of the San Pedro Valley. In Tombstone, a county deputy sheriff might be asked to back up the town marshal when necessary. Jurisdiction was occasionally trumped by necessity. Tombstone, like the county, was predominantly male. The same 1880 census that pegged the town's population at 2,100 noted that just 212 residents were adult women. Many of the remaining 1,900 or so were sophisticated businessmen who settled their differences with discussion over port and cigars or, if necessary, through litigation. But others were more rough-hewn, fueling their disagreements with equal doses of whiskey and machismo. Protecting reputations, never backing down or losing face, was paramount. Threats were routine, fights were less frequent, and gunplay was rare. A town ordinance passed on August 12, 1880, forbade carrying concealed weapons, reducing chances of someone unexpectedly yanking a pistol from beneath a coat and opening fire. Violent acts of any nature were almost entirely confined to the working classes — miners, teamsters, ranch hands. Parts of Tomb-

161

stone were built above underground mine tunnels, and unless residents frequented town saloons, they were in far more danger from cave-ins than bullets.

As was the case in any frontier setting, one-on-one, Main Street showdowns in Tombstone were aberrations. When shootings did occur, they were usually the culmination of drunken brawls, or else took place from ambush. Even if death resulted, surviving combatants could often count on the courts for exoneration. Western judges and juries were generally sympathetic to pleas of self-defense in almost any instance of real or perceived threat. A good example occurred in Tombstone about a month before the Earp posse made its way to the McLaury ranch. Mike Killeen, a bartender at the Cosmopolitan Hotel, believed, with some justification, that "Buckskin" Frank Leslie, another Cosmopolitan bartender, was making advances toward Killeen's wife, May. On the night of June 22, May left a dance with Leslie and her enraged husband went looking for them. George Perine, a friend of Leslie's, ran to warn his pal, who was cuddled with May on the porch of the hotel. Killeen found them first. There was scuffling, and shots were fired. Killeen fell wounded, and died on June 27. He lived long enough to claim that Leslie and Perine had started the shooting. The two were charged with murder, and claimed self-defense. In Leslie's case, Tombstone justice of the peace Mike Gray only called Leslie and the newly widowed May Killeen as witnesses, completely ignoring others who certainly would have testified differently. Gray dismissed the case, ruling that Leslie had acted in self-defense. After all, Killeen was clearly an angry man who *could* have fired first. (Murder charges against Perine were also dismissed.) Leslie then married May Killeen, who divorced him a few years later on grounds of adultery.

Violence resulting from perceived insults extended to such trivialities as snide remarks involving fashion. On July 24, Parsons wrote in his diary, "Another man killed night before last. Too much loose pistol practice. Bradshaw killed Waters because Waters resented with his fists being teased about a shirt." If Bradshaw was convicted afterward of murder or even manslaughter, Parsons neglected to record it. Compared to other frontier boom areas, Pima County and Tombstone had a relatively low incidence of gun-related violence — but the potential was always there.

As an ambitious Pima County deputy sheriff determined to make a good record for himself, Wyatt Earp was not about to shy away from confrontation, in town or outside it. Gunplay, for Wyatt, was always a last resort. He wasn't quick to shoot because he didn't have to be. As a genuinely tough man, he almost always could overpower a law-breaker with his fists or by buffaloing him. In that sense, he was a lawman who exercised restraint. But Wyatt was also inflexible. It was not his nature to alter his style to adapt to different circumstances, which meant his experience in Kansas cow towns was absolutely the wrong kind of preparation for law enforcement in Pima County. In Wichita and Dodge City, Wyatt Earp could walk up to a drunken, pistol-waving cowhand, whack him over the head, drag him off to jail, and a day or two later his victim would be on his way back home to Texas. The opportunities for retaliation were short- rather than long-term. When Wyatt did the same thing in or around Tombstone, his victim might stick around indefinitely because he lived there, and hold a considerable grudge besides. He'd tell his friends, who would resent the way their pal had been treated. With any individual arrest, Wyatt might earn dozens of permanent enemies.

Even the suggestion of guilt by Wyatt or any other perceived "government" oppressor could spark festering resentments. When the McLaurys were accused in a few posters of abetting rustlers — not convicted of the crime, or even arrested for it — Frank McLaury felt compelled to defend his honor with the lengthy letter published in the *Nugget,* and, if Virgil Earp was to be believed, with personal threats besides. Certainly the McLaury brothers felt resentful toward the Earps afterward, and so did many of their friends among the other ranchers in the area. In his memoir, John Plesent Gray described his pals Frank and Tom as "plain, good-hearted industrious fellows. They may have harbored passing rustlers at their ranch, but what [Pima County] rancher did not?" The implication was clear — the wrongdoers were not the McLaurys, who were simply conforming to local custom, but the lawmen, who were either boneheads or troublemakers.

But inevitable antagonism between himself and local ranchers was only part of the problem for Wyatt. As Pima County deputy sheriff, he also had to contend with a steady influx of arrivals who were every bit as experienced in breaking the law as Wyatt was in enforcing it. Like his adversaries back in Wichita and Dodge, many hailed from Texas. But these weren't drovers intent on a little wild fun. They dealt in cattle, too, but instead of herding them, they stole them. For that they acquired a generic nickname that eventually evolved into a complimentary description, but one that in 1880 was intended as a slur, a means of identifying men so low and violent that no evil act was considered beneath them:

Cowboys.

CHAPTER FIVE:
THE COMING OF THE COWBOYS

For almost three decades after joining the Union in 1845, Texas had a well-deserved reputation as the most lawless of all states. Keeping order within its borders proved virtually impossible. There were too many places to hide, too much ground for outgunned, outnumbered lawmen to cover. State legislators had to devote most of their available attention and budget to fending off Indian attacks. Texas became a magnet for fugitives from every other part of the country. All across Texas, towns and ranches were terrorized by packs of armed thugs who broke laws with impunity because there was no one to stop them. By April 1874 the situation was intolerable, and state legislators met in Austin to finally do something about it. They had a goal, to take back control of Texas from the Indians and the outlaws. They also had a plan, which involved transforming a small, disreputable rabble into a lethal juggernaut that would sweep offenders out of the state and turn them into somebody else's problem.

The Texas Rangers were the brainchild of original Texas colonist Stephen F. Austin. In 1823, when the first Anglo settlers came into the region, Austin recruited ten "rangers" to fight off Indians. In 1835, the first formal company of fifty-six Rangers was organized. They had to supply their own horses, guns, and food. The Rangers served as scouts for Sam Houston's army in the fight for independence from Mexico and General Santa Anna, as troops in ongoing Indian battles, and as special forces for Zachary Taylor and Winfield Scott in the U.S.-Mexican war. In the process, a few — Bigfoot Wallace, John S. Ford, Henry and Ben McCullough — became well known for combat prowess and daring. But gradually the Rangers' effectiveness and reputation deteriorated. In between major assignments, they were responsible for generally enforcing the law, and many of the Rangers weren't much removed from lawbreaking themselves. When the Civil War broke out, most of the Rangers left state service to join the Confederacy. During Union occupation of Texas as part of postwar Reconstruction, the Rangers essentially ceased to exist as an organization. The U.S. Army was called on to keep order, and it couldn't in any consistent way. More than ever, Texas attracted men who, for one reason or another, wanted to live outside the law.

Ambitious rancher-entrepreneurs, sensing an opportunity to establish or extend empires, hired unprincipled gunmen as mercenaries. Range wars raged. Much of the state was in chaos.

But Reconstruction came to an end, and the Texas state legislature regained authority. In April 1874 it met and reorganized the moribund Texas Rangers. The service was split into two specific units — the Frontier Battalion under Major John B. Jones, ordered to join with the U.S. Cavalry in fighting the Comanches and Kiowas, and the Special Force of Captain Leander H. McNelly, tasked with eliminating the threat of outlaws — murderers, mercenary fighters, rapists, and, most especially, rustlers, who were decimating the herds of honest ranchers. Jones and McNelly were given forces of almost five hundred men each, split into various companies. Lackluster discipline gave way to rigid controls; Ranger officers were obliged to furnish commanders and state officials with regular, written reports detailing specific actions and accomplishments. A Code of Conduct was instituted, with special emphasis on the responsibility of Rangers to obey as well as enforce the law. ("All officers of the law are creatures of it and a creature cannot become bigger than a creator and whenever an officer undertakes to set himself up as superior to the law or superior to the

168

citizens, whose servant he is, his usefulness as an officer ceases.") Pay, if not munificent, was reasonable by the standards of post–Civil War Texas. Privates got $13 a month and keep, plus 50 cents a day toward feeding and maintaining their horses. Top-ranking officers like McNelly made $166.

The new system worked. Jones's Frontier Battalion fought fifteen major Indian battles in 1874, and within another year Indians no longer posed a constant threat in Texas. McNelly's Special Force, soon renowned as "McNelly's Rangers," achieved equally spectacular success in their pursuit of outlaws. His monthly field reports detailed everything from the number of carbines issued to his men to how many sets of binoculars he had in working condition (one); they also note almost casually the fatalities inflicted by his squad on the men they pursued. In separate incidents during a single patrol, Jack Wingate, suspected of murder and theft, was "killed in att'g to escape"; John Mayfield and Jesus Sartuche, also wanted for theft and murder, died "while resisting arrest." In another excursion, McNelly and his men "surrounded camp of thieves . . . who resisted arrest and opened fire on our men; result five [outlaws] killed, one wounded. Fifty head of horses and thirty-two head of work oxen captured, which were turned over to owners." In the border town of Brownsville, rustling ran unchecked. McNelly and his Special Force arrived in 1875, and one Ranger was killed by the outlaws. In response, McNelly's men cornered and killed twelve of the rustlers. Then they stacked the dozen corpses in the town square and left them there to symbolize the inevitable fate of anyone else foolish enough to fight back. Rustling in and around Brownsville fell off significantly.

With the threat of Indians now minimized, Jones's Frontier Battalion was available to join McNelly's forces in hunting down outlaws. From 1874 through roughly the end of the decade as many as three thousand were jailed, killed, or, more frequently as word of the Rangers' lethal prowess spread, fled Texas to try their criminal fortunes somewhere else. This was exactly what the Texas legislature had intended. Its members didn't care where the rustlers and gunslingers went next. They just wanted them out of the state. And, for the outlaws, options of where to run were limited.

Wherever they relocated, several factors were necessary for the lawbreakers to continue a relatively unfettered criminal lifestyle. Above all, they needed space, lots of it, with a very limited number of lawmen trying to maintain order there. No state or territorial troops like the Texas Rangers should be lurking. Cattle had to be part of the equation;

rustlers couldn't make a living without beef to steal and sell. Towns with saloons and card games and prostitutes were necessary. The outlaws might not mind living rough most of the time, but they also wanted to indulge their hedonistic tendencies. What was the use of having ill-gotten gains if they couldn't be spent having riotous fun? Self-indulgence, and above all answering to no one other than themselves in a time when most men were buckling under to bosses and laws and government — these were the attractions of the outlaw life.

But with Texas removed from the mix, few places offered the right combination of geography and opportunity. The most promising were the territories to the immediate west — New Mexico and Arizona. There was plenty of room to roam and hide, mining towns and other settlements where amenities could be found, limited law enforcement, and cattle to steal, with much of that beef within easy reach across the border in Mexico. So, beginning in the mid-1870s, Texas outlaws began drifting west, at first mostly into New Mexico. Many of them gravitated toward the territory's southwestern "boot heel," which jutted against the boundaries of Arizona and northern Mexico. For the most part, the outlaws stole Mexican cattle, cutting deals with small ranchers above the border to graze the stolen animals and fatten them for market in return for a share in the profits. Often the rustlers conducted their illegal arrangements in New Mexico's neighboring territory, where silver strikes in the southeast region had attracted hordes of new arrivals and, in the process, created a growing market desperate for fresh beef. As canny entrepreneurs, the rustlers stepped in with supply to meet demand. They were welcomed there by almost everyone but the authorities.

Outlaws were nothing new in Arizona Territory. In January 1871, more than three years before the Texas legislature re-formed the Rangers, Arizona governor Safford asked his legislature for permission to raise an armed force of twenty men. Wagons carrying freight, vital to the territorial economy, were regularly waylaid by bandits. Ranchers complained about raids by rustlers. The brigands identified by Safford were Mexicans who stole from Arizona settlers and then rode back into their own country to thwart pursuit. A Texas Rangers–like force, Safford believed, could cut off the Mexicans before they reached the sanctuary of their native country, where U.S. lawmen could not follow. The governor was granted permission to raise a temporary force, but it proved ineffective and was soon disbanded.

Silver strikes in the northern part of the territory increased stage traffic, and Wells

Fargo began leasing space on Arizona stage lines for bullion shipments. Stage robberies occurred sporadically. Unlike scenes in later Western movies, these didn't involve long-distance chases. The heavy stagecoaches, crammed with passengers and laden with luggage, had difficulty maneuvering up and down the territory's many gullies and arroyos. Would-be robbers stationed themselves near the steepest slopes where the stages could make only creeping progress and held them up there. Governor Safford recommended that highway robbery be made a capital offense, and punished with the death penalty. Legislators turned him down, in part because Wells Fargo itself opposed the governor. The company believed jurors would never vote to convict a man of stage robbery if they knew he would be executed as a result.

Despite the best efforts of Safford and lawmen in Arizona Territory's counties and towns, thieves from Mexico never stopped coming north to steal cattle and rob freight wagons or occasional stages. Complaints were regularly made to the Mexican government. But by late 1878, Mexico began reciprocating. For the first time, outlaws based in southern Arizona and New Mexico territories were regularly raiding south of the border. They, too, preyed on freight shipments, but mostly they stole cattle, horses, and mules — draft animals were as much or more in demand in southeast Arizona as beef. This angered Mexican authorities, dismayed territorial officials in the United States, and was a godsend for small ranchers in the New Mexico boot heel and southeast Arizona.

For American rustlers, cattle ranches in the northern Mexico state of Sonora and lucrative American markets in southern New Mexico and Arizona were connected by the San Simon and Animas valleys, which served as perfect routes for driving stolen herds. There was plenty of water and grass to nourish the livestock along the way, and the flanking mountains concealed deep canyons where the cattle could be hidden in the event of pursuit. Skeleton Canyon and Guadalupe Canyon were the two most often used for this purpose. The Animas Valley route wound to within sixty miles of Tombstone, the blossoming epicenter of the southeast Arizona silver mining boom. The San Simon Valley came within thirty miles. Between them and Tombstone were dozens of small ranches whose owners, like the Clantons and McLaurys, were always in need of additional income, and who had little love for the authorities. Cooperation between them and the rustlers was natural. The small ranchers, acting as middlemen, would graze stolen Mexican cattle, fatten them for market, drive them into Tombstone and other surrounding communities for sale, and take part of the profit. Tombstone butchers and restaurants weren't especially concerned about where cattle came from, so long as the meat was suitable for resale and consumption.

Stolen Mexican cattle weren't only purchased by civilians. The army was always desperate for beef, both to feed its soldiers and to supply meat to Indians on their reservations. It might be obvious where some of the cattle being purchased had come from, but need trumped principle.

The small ranchers got more than money from the rustlers; much of the time, it was a friendly as well as an economic partnership. The outlaws were in no sense lovable louts. Certainly some of their rancher-partners cooperated because they believed their own stock, if not their lives, might be in jeopardy if they didn't. But the rustlers believed in returning favors. When the outlaws needed fresh horses to make raids into Mexico or to escape pursuit by the law, they borrowed them from the ranchers. In turn, when the ranchers conducted roundups or branded their own small herds, rustlers would often pitch in to help. Everyone involved benefited, except the Mexicans robbed of their stock — and that was hardly a concern. Prejudice against nonwhites was rampant. Only the federal government and territorial leadership were particularly concerned about Mexican outrage. Good relations between the countries were necessary if U.S. troops wanted permission to pursue Apaches past the border.

In their leisure hours, the rustlers began patronizing the saloons in small towns like Galeyville and Charleston. Law enforcement was limited there, usually in the person of a single town policeman or sheriff who realized it was much safer to observe the outlaws at play rather than interfere with their fun. The rustlers in turn were smart enough to generally avoid carousing in Tombstone, with its town marshal and police force, U.S. deputy marshal, and county deputy sheriff. The rustlers disdained lawmen, resented them, did their best to give the appearance of constantly thumbing their noses at them. But in Pima County they had a good thing going and it made no sense to antagonize the authorities there. Reports varied about how many outlaws had loosely settled there and in the New Mexico boot heel, with estimates varying from a few dozen to several hundred. No one knew for certain, including the outlaws themselves. They did not belong to a single, unified gang; instead, they took part in informal affiliations that might find them riding with temporary partners at different times.

Though the outlaws confined their socializing to small settlements and their banditry

— mostly — to Mexico, notice was taken of them in Arizona Territory's larger cities. In Tucson, Prescott, and Tombstone, newspaper editorials deplored the presence of criminals and, frequently, urged federal intervention to drive them away. That was virtually impossible because of the *Posse Comitatus* Act. Other suggestions in print were even more specific. The *Arizona Daily Citizen* declared, "citizens may be forced to combine and offer a bounty for [their] scalps as the people of New Mexico do for Indians." It was also the newspapers that tagged the outlaws with a nickname that reflected their particular interests in rustling.

Cowboy (often written as *cow-boy*) wasn't a new term minted by journalists in Arizona Territory. In America, the word dated back to Revolutionary times, when cow-boys watched over herds of colonial cattle. During the great trail drives between Texas and Kansas railroad towns, "cowboys" were the Texas drovers who couldn't behave themselves. As the frontier contracted and crimes such as rustling began attracting more official notice, "cowboy" became a generic term to describe habitual thugs or lawbreakers.

When territorial officials and newspaper editorial writers in late 1870s Arizona Territory railed against the new influx of lawbreakers, they often called them cowboys. National publications such as *Harper's* magazine adopted the term. A typical headline in the *Arizona Daily Citizen* trumpeted:

THE COWBOYS
Depredations Committed by Organized Thieves
Bad State of Affairs on the Border

As the cowboys settled into the area, some of them began to emerge not necessarily as official leaders, but at least as exerting unusual influence among the loosely knit group. It was difficult to know any of their real names or backgrounds; men on the run in the West were liable to change their names as often as they did their clothes. Many of the Arizona cowboys had committed crimes in other places and arrived in the territory planning more of the same. Two in particular would figure significantly in the lives and eventual reputations of the Earps.

"Curly Bill" Brocius came to Arizona from Texas, where he was probably known as Curly Bill Bresnaham. According to Wyatt Earp, Curly Bill was just under six feet tall and heavily built. His age and place of birth are points of conjecture, and there is a chance his real name was William Graham. Part of the allure of cowboy life was the opportunity to continually reinvent yourself, and Curly Bill took frequent advantage. He only began to appear in a quantifiable way in 1878, when

Texas Ranger and newspaper reports noted that Curly Bill Bresnaham was riding in West Texas with notorious outlaw Bob Martin. While no cowboy was ever an official leader among his outlaw brothers, Martin came very close. Long after the Texas Rangers had mostly eliminated bandit threats in other areas, he robbed and rustled in the far western regions of the state. In May 1878, he and his sidekick Curly Bill ambushed an army payroll wagon just outside El Paso, wounding two soldiers before being driven off. They were captured in Mexico, extradited back to Texas, and held for trial in the small town of Ysleta. Each was sentenced to five years in prison, but lawyers for the defense claimed they could produce a witness who'd seen Martin and Curly Bill in El Paso at the time of the attempted robbery. The extended appeal process prevented them from being immediately shipped off to prison, and on November 2, 1878, they escaped from Ysleta, which certainly had been their intention all along.

Bob Martin and Curly Bill next surfaced in the New Mexico boot heel, where, together and separately, they rustled cattle below the border, perhaps robbed a few stages, and generally took advantage of limited law enforcement. They were joined in the area by several other cowboys who would later make their mark on Tombstone history, among them Pony Deal (or Diehl), Sherman Mc-Masters, Billy Leonard, and Luther King. Apparently, the outlaws made the same kind of mutually beneficial arrangements with small ranchers around Silver City as they would in Tombstone. In November 1880, Martin was part of a group that recovered some stock stolen from local ranches by other cowboys, Leonard and King reportedly among them. As Martin and another man (not Curly Bill, who was occupied elsewhere) drove four horses back to the ranch of their rightful owner, they were ambushed by Leonard, King, and two partners. Martin was shot in the head and killed. Future events proved Curly Bill didn't hold a grudge against the men who murdered his friend and mentor. He, Leonard, and King would be inexorably linked in Tombstone's near future.

In a sense, Martin's death may have been liberating for Curly Bill, who, in Arizona Territory, used the last name of Brocius. No one can be certain why he did. The role of sidekick didn't fit Curly Bill's personality at all. He was a tireless self-promoter who sometimes engaged in outrageous behavior (on one occasion ordering couples in a small town saloon at gunpoint to strip and dance naked for over an hour) to get the attention he craved. With Martin gone, some lawmen believed that Curly Bill had taken control over the outlaw horde infesting the region.

He enjoyed the notoriety and never did anything to correct their wrong impression.

The other best-known cowboy operating in southeast Arizona Territory didn't have to go out of his way to build a reputation as a hard, dangerous man. John Ringo was feared by everyone, and with good reason.

One of the few cowboys whose background is reasonably well documented, John Peters Ringo was born on May 3, 1850, in Greenfork, Indiana. His father, Martin, suffered from tuberculosis, and in 1864 the family joined a wagon train heading west. Martin thought the salubrious Pacific coast climate of California might help him live a few years longer. Ironically, he didn't survive the journey. Along the way in Wyoming, Martin's shotgun accidentally discharged and killed him. Fourteen-year-old John may have seen it happen. It must have been a ghastly sight. According to a local newspaper, "the load entered his eye and came out the top of his head, scattering his brain in all directions." A witness added that "I never saw a more heartrending sight, and to see the distress and agony of [Martin Ringo's] wife and children was painful in the extreme."

Martin's family, now consisting of widow Mary, sons John and Martin, and daughters Fanny, Mary, and Mattie, continued on to California and settled in San Jose. Mary Ringo ran a boardinghouse. John worked on a farm. At some point he began a lifelong habit of drinking heavily. There is conjecture that he also suffered from frequent bouts of severe depression. Sometime around 1869 or 1870 John left San Jose, and his whereabouts are a mystery until Christmas 1874, when the twenty-four-year-old was arrested in Burnet, Texas, for firing shots in the air in the town square. By summer 1875, he'd been arrested twice more for disturbing the peace. The following year John was in trouble with the law again, this time on more serious charges. He and a friend named George Gladden were accused of murdering James Cheyney during a nasty range war in Mason County in central Texas. The killing was particularly cold-blooded. Cheyney, washing up in a basin on his porch, invited Ringo and Gladden to join him there. They shot him while he was drying his face. In March 1876 Ringo and Gladden were convicted on the weird count of "seriously threatening to take the life of a human being." Gladden was sentenced to ninety-nine years in prison. There appears to be no record of Ringo's sentence, but he and Gladden were jailed in the town of Lampasas. They managed to break out on May 4, only to be recaptured by the Texas Rangers in late October after engaging in rustling.

Back in jail, this time in Austin, Ringo appealed his conviction in the Cheyney case, arguing that the jury hadn't been instructed by the judge that they could assess a fine rather than a prison sentence. It worked; the conviction was overturned and Ringo got a new trial. This time, no witnesses were available — or at least willing — to testify against him, and the case was eventually dismissed.

Ringo celebrated regaining his freedom in a curious way. He returned to Mason County, ran for constable in November 1878, and was elected by a comfortable margin. In Texas as in the rest of the West, voters clearly believed that lawbreakers made the best law enforcers. This was Ringo's initial foray into politics, and in another election two years later he would prove he learned a great deal from the experience.

Temporarily, Ringo seemed eager to settle down; he even registered a brand with county government, indicating he planned to raise cattle instead of stealing them. But the tug of the outlaw life was apparently too strong. Within a few months Ringo left Texas on a wagon train heading west. He dropped out in Silver City, New Mexico, and settled in the cowboy camp in the San Simon Valley.

There, John Ringo established himself as a brooding enigma. Perhaps alone among the outlaws, he owned and read books. People remarked about his good manners. But he rode with the rustlers, and gained a reputation as perhaps the best gunman among them. A. M. Franklin, a shopkeeper in the small community of Safford, Arizona, graphically described Ringo's prowess:

> I knew Ringo well. . . . A cheerful good looking fellow with a half eyes cynical smile, and a powerful mind. When he said a thing, he meant it and every one knew it. In that was his strength. Of course, he had his pistols too. He could put two beer bottles, mouths towards him, let his pistols hang from his fingers, then with a dexterous jerk, I don't know just how, He would have them in position and break both bottles at once. His main stunt however, was shooting from the hip.

Ringo was often an affable companion, but his mood could change in an instant. In December 1879, only a month after he arrived in the San Simon Valley, he joined thirty-one-year-old Louis Hancock for a friendly drink in a Safford saloon. Ringo ordered whiskey for both of them. Hancock said he'd rather have beer. Ringo yanked out his pistol, smashed Hancock over the head, and then shot him in the neck. Hancock survived, but Ringo was ordered to appear before a grand jury in Tucson that would consider filing charges against him. He didn't show up, instead sending a note claiming a foot injury prevented him from traveling. It was a gracious note, swearing that "as I wish to live here, I do not wish to put you to any unnecessary trouble," and requesting that Pima County sheriff Charlie Shibell "please let the Dist Atty know why I do not appear, for I am very anxious that there is no forfeiture taken on [my] Bond." The district attorney chose to order the bond forfeited and asked that a warrant be issued for Ringo's arrest, but once again the haphazard courts system of the West bumbled in Ringo's favor. No record exists of the matter being resolved, and he went on as before.

One friend Ringo did acquire and keep was Ike Clanton. He and Ike filed a joint claim for land in the Animas Valley in southwest New Mexico Territory. Along with a third partner, Joe Hill, they sold a herd of cattle, probably rustled in Mexico, to the San Carlos Indian Reservation. These ventures typified the relationship the cowboys wanted to have with the area's small ranchers — mutual cooperation and benefit. The outlaws took pride in occasionally protecting the rights and property of their small-fry friends, even to the extent of rebuking their own. A widespread story at the time had Curly Bill dismayed when one of the rustlers stole a family's milk cow. Curly Bill ordered the fellow to return the cow immediately, declaring "We steal from stages, from the government and from corporations, but not from babies."

Whether or not the tale is apocryphal, it captures a telling attitude among the cowboys. They considered themselves to be lawbreakers but not criminals, an important distinction. *Law* represented everything they resented — government intrusion, with marshals and sheriffs and Texas Rangers telling them what they could and could not do. Disturbing the peace, stealing cattle, even robbing stages were in some sense acts of defiance against oppressors. Though some of the cowboys did not initially hail from the South, they subscribed to Southern resentment of any interference with personal freedom. Many were either from Texas or had spent considerable time there; they brought with them to Arizona Territory the bone-deep nineteenth-century Texan prejudice against Mexicans, former persecutors who had been beaten back by force of arms. Protective as they might be of struggling ranchers in southeast Arizona, the cowboys took delight in stealing from near-impoverished settlements south of the border. To the cowboys, most Mexicans had no rights. They loathed them.

Even more, they loathed American lawmen who meddled in their business. To a certain extent, they were willing to moderate their behavior to avoid confrontations with them. The cowboys, for the most part, stayed out of Tombstone except to conduct occasional brief business. In return, federal, county, and town officials turned a blind eye toward most of the rustling, unless stock was taken from local ranches, or, as in the case of the Camp Rucker mules, from the U.S. military. Stolen Mexican livestock was critical to the local economy. In a pragmatic if not legal sense, the cowboys were providing a valuable public service. Preserving the shady status quo served everyone's best interests. But other issues remained in play, particularly personal honor and political ambition.

Reputation meant everything to the cowboys. Many were in southeast Arizona because the Texas Rangers had proven to be tougher than they were. Men who made it a point of pride never to be pushed around had been forced to flee. It was important to the cowboys that they reestablish themselves as dominant alpha males in their new surroundings. This was undoubtedly why they didn't avoid Tombstone altogether. There was no real reason for Curly Bill or John Ringo to ever go there; their small rancher partners could conduct any necessary "big town" business. But occasionally showing themselves to the largest possible segment of the local population was important to the cowboys' public image, even if it increased their risk of attracting unwanted attention from the lawmen there. It was also a signal to those lawmen that the cowboys wouldn't be intimidated. They would go where they wanted, do what they wanted, and no one was going to stop them. So long as everyone observed certain unspoken limits — the cowboys avoiding crimes that the lawmen couldn't ignore, with the lawmen mostly overlooking their lesser transgressions such as rustling Mexican cattle — a bloodless standoff could endure.

With his appointment as a Pima County deputy sheriff, Wyatt Earp entered the potentially combustible mix. To achieve his goal of succeeding Charlie Shibell as county sheriff, or else being appointed sheriff of a newly formed county that included Tombstone, Wyatt needed some spectacular success in his deputy's role. The important people Wyatt hoped to impress — Tombstone business leaders, territorial officials, newspaper kingpins like John Clum — all were concerned, even obsessed, with the cowboy presence in southeast Arizona. Wyatt surely realized that the best way to ensure his future, to finally gain the financial success and social prominence he and the rest of the Earps had craved for so long, was to successfully confront the cowboys in some highly visible way. John Ringo and his cohorts had reputations as bad men, but they didn't scare Wyatt, who'd taken on plenty of tough guys in Wichita and Dodge City. He had absolute confidence in his ability to control any situation. What

Wyatt needed, in the fall of 1880, was for the cowboys to commit some offense so blatant that it couldn't be ignored, and then be instrumental in bringing them to book for it. At some point, they were bound to — Wyatt believed that such characters couldn't maintain self-control forever. To an extent, though, he underestimated his current antagonists. Wyatt equated the southeast Arizona outlaws with the trail drive kids he'd previously had to wallop into line in Kansas. He was contemptuous rather than wary of them: Texans and cowboys, in his experience, were seldom real threats to any lawman prepared to stand up to them.

The cowboys and Wyatt Earp were on an inevitable collision course. It was a question of when, not if, something dramatic would happen. But just before it did, two final leading players and a young woman who filled a key supporting role arrived on the Tombstone scene. Doc Holliday, Johnny Behan, and Josephine Marcus had nothing to do with how the Earp–cowboy feud began, but each was critical to how subsequent events exploded, and therefore to the way Western history was written.

CHAPTER SIX:
DOC, JOHNNY, AND JOSEPHINE

Doc Holliday never stayed in one place too long. Either his hot temper got him into trouble, or gambling profits dwindled, or he just got bored. It was probably the latter in Prescott. For the nine months or so he resided in the territorial capital, Doc avoided legal problems. He even mingled with prominent citizens; John Gosper, the secretary of Arizona Territory who presided over the legislature during Governor Frémont's frequent absences, lived in the same boardinghouse. But Prescott soon paled for Doc. Clearly, local mining operations were being eclipsed by those in the southeast corner of the territory, and men with money to risk in card games were flocking there. New Prescott city ordinances restricting gambling added to the crimping of his income. Doc never had much money. According to Kate Elder, Doc's thickest bankroll ever was $8,000, which came through a small family inheritance rather than a poker jackpot. When, in the spring of 1880, a letter arrived from Wyatt Earp extolling all Tombstone had to offer for a man with a talent for playing cards, Doc was ready to pack up and go.

Kate wasn't. To Doc, Prescott might have proven to be a dull, temporary stopping point, but for Kate the chance to live there quietly with him was as good as her life was ever likely to get. Tombstone, with its bars and brothels and frenetic atmosphere, was exactly the kind of place where Doc and trouble would inevitably become re-acquainted. Even worse, Wyatt Earp was there. Kate could only imagine what kind of problems his influence on Doc might cause. She tried to talk Doc out of going, but he wouldn't be persuaded. They argued, and Kate made the ultimate threat: If Doc went to Tombstone, she wasn't going with him. He said he was going anyway. Kate packed up and moved to the eastern Arizona Territory mining town of Globe, where she opened a small boardinghouse. She didn't break with Doc completely. On some legal documents, she signed her name as "Kate Holliday," and on a few occasions she went to Tombstone to see him. Years later, she told a journalist that during these visits she would plead with Doc to leave before something terrible happened. He paid no attention.

Doc didn't head south to Tombstone right away. He made a short trip back to Las Vegas,

New Mexico, first, probably to demonstrate to old antagonists there that he was doing fine. Doc apparently felt better than he had for a long time. When he left Dodge City two years earlier, he'd been so sick that he had to be transported in a wagon. But the clean desert air in New Mexico had revived him, at least so far as his gradually debilitating disease would allow, and the climate in Arizona was equally salubrious. Doc's return visit to Las Vegas didn't last long. A June 1880 census indicates he went back to Prescott for a little while, possibly to try to build up a gambling stake before heading off to Tombstone. But he arrived there by late September, when he registered to vote.

It was a heady time in Tombstone. Telegraph poles finally connected the town directly to the outside world; it was a major step. A U.S. court commissioner was appointed with jurisdiction over criminal cases and violations of tax and customs laws, a clear indication that the federal government believed Tombstone was going to be a long-term business hub. Wells Spicer, a lawyer and occasional journalist, got the post, and also became a justice of the peace. On September 20, city streets were formally cleaned for the first time. Two days later, a traveling circus stopped in town. Local leaders organized Tombstone's first volunteer fire department. City councilman Harry B. Jones was named its president, and other prominent members included Milton Joyce, owner of the classy Oriental Saloon, City marshal Fred White, and Wells Fargo representative Marshall Williams. Wyatt Earp, always angling for more civic prominence, was named secretary. But when a drunk interrupted the group's second meeting, it was White and not Wyatt who removed the offender by pitching him through a window. Camillus S. Fly, eventually one of the frontier's most renowned photographers, moved to Tombstone and set up a studio. Prominent people were flocking to Tombstone; they had plenty of money to pay for portraits. Fly and his wife also opened a boardinghouse in the same Fremont Street lot as their photo studio. Doc later took a room there.

Feeling relatively healthy, free of what he certainly must have believed was smothering by Kate, newly immersed in the strutting macho atmosphere of Tombstone's red-light district where men sometimes gambled recklessly, usually drank heavily, and were constantly on the alert for insults requiring violent response, Doc predictably couldn't stay out of trouble long. On the night of October 10, he began arguing in the Oriental Saloon with Johnny Tyler, who'd acquired a reputation around town as a mean-spirited brawler. Neither man was armed. Obeying the town ordinance that banned concealed weapons, Doc had checked his pistol with the bartender when he came into the saloon. Tyler had caused problems in the Oriental before. Wyatt Earp had recently acquired an interest in the saloon's gambling concession in return for preventing Tyler, among others, from disrupting card play there. Before the situation on October 10 could escalate from shouted threats to actual violence, saloon owner Milton Joyce and several onlookers separated the two. Tyler was ordered to leave, and did.

Joyce began berating Doc, who was still angry and in no mood to listen. He talked back, which infuriated Joyce; the saloon-keeper physically threw the frail, feisty dentist out into the street. Doc, now crazed with rage, demanded that his pistol be returned. Joyce, fully aware of Doc's violent tendencies, refused to give it to him. Doc stalked off to his room at Fly's boardinghouse, where he grabbed another pistol and stormed back to the Oriental. In typically overblown fashion, the *Nugget* reported what happened next:

[Doc Holliday] walked toward Joyce, who was just coming from behind the bar, and with a remark that wouldn't look well in print, turned loose with a self-cocker [number of shots]. Joyce was not more than ten feet away and jumped his assailant and struck him over the head with a six-shooter, felling

[Holliday] to the floor and lighting on top of him. [city marshal Fred] White and [assistant marshal] Bennett were near at hand and separated them, taking the pistols from each. Just how many shots were fired none present seem able to tell but in casting up accounts Joyce was found to be shot through the hand, his partner, Mr. Parker . . . shot through the big toe of the left foot, and Holliday [was bruised from] a blow of the pistol in Joyce's hands.

Doc was so dazed and bloodied by Joyce's pistol-whipping that at first White and Bennett thought he was dying. When they realized Doc was only stunned, he was arrested. Joyce filed a complaint, and Doc was released on $200 bond to await trial.

Beyond the obvious slapstick aspects of the brawl — Doc, supposedly a lethal gunman, barely grazed Joyce while shooting at him from point-blank range — the legal implications were daunting. Milton Joyce was one of Tombstone's leading citizens, and Doc Holliday tried to murder him. The elasticity of frontier law might have mitigated that act somewhat: During his earlier diatribe to Doc, Joyce had threatened him, and he'd certainly laid hands on Doc in the act of tossing him out of the Oriental into the street. Doc could claim he feared for his life and was only acting in self-defense. But a judge and jury might not buy that story, since Doc clearly went to fetch another gun and returned to the Oriental seeking a second confrontation. Given Doc's previous record of starting fights, and his stubborn pride — it's hard to imagine him declaring in public court that he was *afraid* of Milton Joyce — the odds in any trial would not have been in his favor. A hefty fine seemed certain, and a prison sentence was not out of the question.

But Doc wriggled out of it. The original charge against him of assault with a deadly weapon was plea-bargained down to simple assault and battery when no witnesses appeared to testify against Doc. Wyatt must have had something to do with it. As Joyce's minority partner in the Oriental's gambling operations, he was in position to plead with Joyce on Doc's behalf. Wyatt could have reminded Joyce of how Johnny Tyler had caused previous problems for the saloon. Whatever favor may have been called in, Joyce agreed to let the charge be reduced, and Doc was released after paying a $20 fine and $11.25 in court costs. But that wasn't the end of it. Doc may have thought the issue was forgotten, but Joyce held a grudge against Doc — and against Wyatt Earp. This didn't manifest itself immediately. Wyatt retained his interest in gambling at the Oriental, and Joyce made certain his rowdier clientele remained aware that the county's deputy sheriff, a man with the authority to make arrests, was part of management. But Milton Joyce was a Democrat, one of the few among Tombstone's controlling elite. His political influence was limited in town but considerable in the territorial capital, where Democrats held a majority of seats in the legislature. At some point in the future, if he had a chance to thwart Wyatt in some way that wouldn't directly affect his own business, Joyce would certainly take advantage. In the meantime, he could remind fellow Tombstone movers and shakers that Pima County deputy sheriff Earp was friends with a real troublemaker, casting doubts on Wyatt's own character. Thanks to Doc's trigger-happy ways, Wyatt now had a powerful, if as yet undeclared, antagonist.

Doc himself went on exactly as before. Even if he felt unwelcome in the Oriental for a time, there were plenty of other snazzy places in Tombstone where a man could take a drink. Among them was the bar at the newly opened Grand Hotel, which ushered in almost unimaginable heights of luxury in accommodations and dining. The *Epitaph* praised its "spring mattresses that would tempt a sybarite, toilet stands and fixtures of the most approved pattern, the walls papered, and to crown all, each room having windows. All are outside rooms thus obviating the many discomforts in close and ill-ventilated

197

apartments" — always a plus in dusty, smelly Tombstone. The paper went on to laud the hotel's dining room, which featured walnut tables, and, for visitors and locals alike who enjoyed their cocktails, "the bar occupies the east half of the main front and is in keeping with the general furnishings." Behind that bar, at least for the first few months the hotel was in operation, was a short, sparkling newcomer to Tombstone who soon would figure prominently in town affairs.

Johnny Behan had a knack for becoming everybody's friend. It was his main skill in life, and he exploited it. He arrived in Tombstone in September 1880, about the same time as Doc, but unlike the irascible dentist, Johnny was determined to make a good first impression. It was a necessary step in his plan to resuscitate a once promising political career.

Born in 1845 in Westport, Missouri, Johnny's family ran a boardinghouse there that sat adjacent to the early miles of the Santa Fe Trail. Famous frontier figures passed through Westport, among them explorer-soldier John C. Frémont and mountain man Jim Bridger, who opened a store in town. They may have whetted Johnny's taste for the West. Tension between his father and grandfather, who strongly disagreed on issues involving religion and slavery, probably encouraged him to strike out on his own. An April 1864 census lists him as a laborer in Arizona Territory, but Johnny had no intention of pursuing menial work for long. In July 1864 territorial residents elected their first nine-member legislative council and eighteen-member House of Representatives, which promptly divided the sprawling territory into four huge counties, each named for an Indian tribe. Somehow, nineteen-year-old Johnny made influential friends. He received an appointment as a clerk for the legislature, bringing him into contact with many of the state's most prominent business leaders (mining interests dominated the council) and lawmen. Johnny made a positive impression on the right people — children raised in confrontational homes often develop the knack of telling people what they want to hear, to avoid conflict and to keep everyone happy. This worked well for Johnny in the territorial capital of Prescott.

In October 1866, Yavapai County sheriff John P. Bourke named Johnny Behan as a deputy. He served in that job for two years and then, still just twenty-three, Johnny was elected county recorder, one of the most important jobs in the county since accurate records were the basis for efficient tax collection. Nine months after that, he married Bourke's stepdaughter Victoria Zaff. Less than six years after having to earn a sweaty living with his hands, Johnny Behan held critical public office and was married into a prominent family. And things kept getting better: In July 1871 Victoria gave birth to a son named Albert, and later that year Johnny succeeded his father-in-law as sheriff of Yavapai County, home to the territorial capital and location of most of the territory's major business and mining interests. About the same time Wyatt Earp was grubbing out a meager living in the whorehouses of Peoria, Illinois, Johnny's annual income in Yavapai County probably reached or slightly exceeded $15,000 to $20,000, enough to support his family in high style. He invested in local mines and a sawmill.

Most young men would have been happy with achieving that much, but Johnny still had bigger things in mind. County sheriffs earned a mere percentage of hefty taxes paid by truly wealthy, influential men. Why settle for scraps instead of trying to become rich and important himself? Johnny took a real risk, giving up his position as sheriff to run on the Democratic ticket for Yavapai County's representative to the Seventh Territorial Legislature, which would convene in Tucson in 1873 (Tucson and Prescott continually vied for the honor of serving as the territory's capital, which switched back and forth at the whim of the legislature). He won, and spent much of the next two years supporting legislation to sink more artesian wells, prohibit sale of liquor to Indians, provide better care and treatment of the insane, and to persuade the U.S. secretary of the interior to build a territorial prison. It was the kind of record that seemed to stamp Johnny Behan as a young man destined for even higher political office — perhaps territorial governor someday, if ever a Democrat rather than a Republican gained the White House.

Then Johnny's fortunes took a sudden turn for the worse. In May 1875, his wife, Victoria, filed for divorce, in itself not a political death knell for politicians in Arizona Territory. Former governor Safford was divorced; territorial secretary John Gosper soon would be. But Victoria Behan was angry enough to seek Johnny's public humiliation, declaring in her divorce petition that he "has within two years last past at diverse times and places openly and notoriously visited houses of prostitution." She even offered a name: Among others, Johnny supposedly cavorted with sixteen-year-old prostitute Sadie Mansfield. It was probably true — Johnny never denied anything alleged in the petition.

So long as the women involved paid their licensing fees, prostitution was not illegal in the territory. Prominent clients were simply expected to be discreet — at some point Johnny apparently wasn't. And, as Victoria undoubtedly became aware, he didn't restrict his philandering to an occasional paid coupling. Throughout his adult life, Johnny dallied with numerous women, sometimes even the wives of friends or business partners. Just a smidgen over five and a half feet tall, with features more cherubic than chiseled, Johnny was anything but an Adonis. Still, in the gritty West, most men were far more concerned with making money than charming the ladies. Johnny used the same persuasive skills to make conquests as he did to win votes.

Victoria's divorce from Johnny was granted in June; her ex-husband was ordered to pay $16.66 a month in child support for their son, Albert. There the matter seemed to end. In April 1876 Johnny was named census marshal for Yavapai County and spent more than a month canvassing residents. That fall, he ran for his old job as county sheriff — and lost by seventy-eight votes. Losing his first race had to sting. Johnny still maintained enough political connections to be named sergeant at arms for the Ninth Territorial Legislature when it met in Tucson in 1877. Afterward, hoping for a fresh start, he relocated to Mohave County in the northwestern region of the territory. Johnny ran a hotel there and made a few mining investments. Though he lost a bid for county sheriff, Johnny made enough new friends to be elected Mohave's representative to the Tenth Territorial Legislature. In mid-1879, Johnny moved back to Prescott, which had regained its status as territorial capital from Tucson. The key political action was there, not in Mohave County. In that year there would be new Yavapai County elections, and Johnny hoped to be returned to office in his old political stomping grounds. That would cap his comeback, and get him back on track for bigger and better things. In the interim, he tried to reestablish his reputation in Prescott and the county as a good citizen. He started a small business to provide services to local mines and joined posses in pursuit of bandits. The strategy would probably have worked except for an incident in October that resulted in more disgrace for Johnny.

According to the *Prescott Miner,* the "Hon. J. H. Behan had occasion to call at the Chinese laundry this p.m., when a controversy arose, leading to some half-dozen of the pig-tail race making an assault on him with clubs." Johnny "tried to defend himself with a revolver, which, unfortunately, failed to work. He received several cuts about the head." In all the prejudiced West, no race was more disdained by the white majority than the Chinese. Originally brought to the frontier as laborers for the railroads, many Chinese settled in the territories and operated small businesses, often vegetable farms, laundries, or restaurants. Still, many whites considered them to be subhuman, or at best

203

mincing second-class citizens obligated to be subservient in every way to their ethnic superiors. To most potential voters in Prescott, particularly those who didn't know Johnny, it didn't matter how the fight might have started — the *Miner* didn't specify — or that Johnny was outnumbered six to one by foes using clubs. A white man, a supposedly tough former county sheriff, was beaten up by some measly Chinese. What kind of an inept buffoon must the "Hon. J. H. Behan" be?

Democrats in Yavapai County took notice. In August 1880, they convened to select candidates for the fall elections. Johnny expected to receive the nomination for county recorder. Another Democrat, William Wilkerson, was the incumbent, but Johnny felt certain his long service to the party would carry more weight. It didn't. Wilkerson was renominated, and even an optimist like Johnny Behan realized that his political career in Yavapai County was over. He felt betrayed. He could have given up any further hopes for public office and settled down in or around Prescott, making a decent living from his various business investments and regretting what might have been. But Johnny had relocated and politically regrouped before. All he needed was another fresh start somewhere vibrant. Johnny's experience was in Arizona Territory; it would have made no sense to move somewhere else and have to completely reestablish himself. Political power flowed to where the economy flourished, and, in Arizona in fall 1880, that meant one place in particular.

In its September 15 edition, the *Epitaph* noted that former territorial legislator and Yavapai County sheriff Johnny Behan and his ten-year-old son, Albert, had moved to Tombstone. Whatever Johnny's considerable failings might have been as a husband, he was always a devoted father. Victoria Behan was about to remarry, and Johnny was happy to have Albert live with him. Father and son arrived in Tombstone with their worldly goods and a sleek horse named Little Nell. Johnny bought the mare for $20, groomed her for racing, and eventually would sell her for $1,000. Public races were a popular form of entertainment in frontier towns. Residents would saddle up or hitch their prized steeds to carriages and compete to the whooping approval of their neighbors. Back in Prescott, Johnny would have heard rumors about the legislature carving out a new county in the southeast portion of the territory sometime in 1881. If that happened — and, according to well-placed sources such as Johnny's, it was a cinch — then the new county seat would inevitably be Tombstone, and county officials would be named by the governor to serve until the next scheduled election cycle in 1882. Who would be more appropriate to appoint to an important post such as county sheriff than experienced public servant and lawman Johnny Behan? An important first step was to impress Tombstone business leaders, who would undoubtedly be consulted by the governor. Johnny had the political savvy and social smarts to do exactly that. Entering Little Nell in town races was one good way to become quickly and favorably known. Another was to have the kind of job that would bring him into regular, convivial contact with the Tombstone elite.

Johnny invested with a partner, John Dunbar, in a livery stable. Most businessmen in Tombstone didn't own their own horses. If they wanted to ride out to look over mining investments or treat their families to a frolic in the country (always a risk, considering renegade Apaches), they would rent horses or a buggy. The stable was a safe investment for Johnny, offering a needed service to his new community. But he also hired on as bar manager of the new Grand Hotel, the perfect job for furthering his political goals. Tombstone's heaviest hitters came there to drink, and to see and be seen. It was the fanciest place in town, one where they could glory in their eminence, and when they ordered their gin fizzes and vintage wines the refreshments were served up by one of the most pleasant fellows they'd ever met. A block away at the

Oriental Saloon, Wyatt Earp was also trying to impress the big shots, but from a far less advantageous position. Wyatt ran card games, and depended on winning a lot more often than he lost. Never overly sociable under the best of circumstances, at the Oriental, Wyatt had to focus on his cards, not socializing. Tombstone movers and shakers were unlikely to form positive impressions of a taciturn fellow who was determined to separate them from considerable amounts of money. At the Grand Hotel bar, smiling Johnny Behan mixed their drinks and shared gossip and jokes. Wyatt was grim. Johnny was fun. In terms of potential popularity, it was no contest.

There was an obvious impediment to Johnny's plan. He was a Democrat. Most of the influential leaders in Tombstone were Republicans. So was Governor Frémont. But the new county would be separated from Pima County, and Pima sheriff Charlie Shibell was a Democrat. Small ranchers, miners, and rank-and-file citizens in the area were overwhelmingly Democratic. So, too, were territorial legislators back in Prescott, and Governor Frémont had to compromise with them on many issues to gain sufficient votes for some of his own programs. If Johnny could get appointed sheriff by the governor in 1881 without too much opposition from Tombstone Republicans, then he could run for reelection in 1882 in a county where the majority of voters were fellow Democrats. For the present, it was a matter of getting along with everybody regardless of political affiliation, and that was something Johnny could surely do.

Johnny also joined the new Tombstone volunteer fire department. As a newcomer, he wasn't going to be named an officer in it like Wyatt, though Wyatt's title of secretary clearly indicated worker bee rather than leadership status. As an experienced territorial legislator, Johnny could be useful in explaining parliamentary procedure, and when attending meetings undoubtedly joined enthusiastically in the ritual backslapping and joshing that made participation in civic endeavors enjoyable as well as demanding. Johnny eclipsed Wyatt in that regard, but, beyond political ambition, he and Wyatt had one other thing in common to the social and political detriment of both.

Johnny had great interpersonal skills and charm, but his marriage to Victoria Zaff was really what propelled him up Yavapai County's political ladder. She was an acceptable spouse to the wives of power brokers, someone worthy of their notice and friendship. In Prescott prior to their scandalous divorce, the Behans were invited to the best parties and mingled socially with those in position to help the career of a promising young man. To cement his political fortunes in Tombstone and a yet unformed new county, Johnny needed the same kind of high-end social access. He would have been wise to marry again to the right kind of woman — a young widow who already had a place among the town's genteel upper faction, perhaps, or the spinster daughter, sister, or cousin of a prominent Tombstone businessman. There were always a few such ladies available. In his Tombstone journal, George Parsons devotes endless pages to descriptions of his own unsuccessful wooing of several of them. A marriage of convenience would not have required Johnny to completely rein in his always raging libido. Tombstone had its share of prostitutes, some expert in discreetly satisfying the sexual excesses of prominent male citizens. Johnny probably did consort with them, and he also continued seducing other women, including the wife of his business partner, John Dunbar. Such shenanigans were foolish, but potentially survivable in terms of social standing.

Common-law wives were not. Even though common-law arrangements were the rule rather than the exception for working-class citizens on the frontier, they were unacceptable among the bluebloods. No common-law wives danced at the Tombstone Social Club's annual New Year's Masquerade Ball, or exchanged friendly gossip with the ladies attending the town's exclusive Thanksgiving

Grand Calico Gala, though they might be hired to cook and serve food to the guests, or else sweep out the ballrooms afterward. Their husbands were allowed some of the trappings of social respectability — membership in the volunteer fire department, or invitations to join the Tombstone chapter of the Independent Order of Odd Fellows, though only after attesting they believed "in the existence of a Supreme Intelligent Being, the Creator and Preserver of the Universe." But even the husbands of common-law wives were limited in matters of social access.

Wyatt Earp, unschooled and clumsy in the arts of skillful backroom politicking and social climbing, probably had no concept of this. He did keep Mattie Blaylock cooped up in their house most of the time, but more from his beliefs in the proper, subservient role of women than in any attempt to hide her existence from disapproving eyes. Being saddled with Mattie meant that no matter how hard Wyatt Earp tried, Tombstone leaders like *Epitaph* publisher John Clum, mine director E. B. Gage, and the hotel-building Bilickes were never going to fully admit him to their august circles if only because their wives wouldn't stand for it. They might tolerate Wyatt's company so long as he was useful to them in some way, but nothing more than that. Wyatt was oblivious to this fact.

Johnny Behan understood it perfectly, yet

during his first months in Tombstone when he was striving to make the best possible impression on the right people he still took a common-law wife. It flew in the face of everything Johnny wanted to achieve, but the lure of the woman involved overwhelmed his ambition and common sense. She seemed that unique, that special.

Josephine Sarah Marcus was probably born in 1861, and died in 1944. She spent most of her later years concocting G-rated fables to conceal her R-rated escapades as a young woman, and to prettify her long, tempestuous relationship with Wyatt Earp. Josephine's web of half-truths and outright lies is so skillfully woven that it's impossible to be absolutely certain regarding almost anything about her. In particular, facts regarding how she got to Tombstone and what she did after she arrived are hard to come by. But get there she did, in large part because Gilbert & Sullivan collaborated on a comic opera about the daughter of a ship's captain who defied her father to marry a member of his crew. Much of history results from apparently unrelated dominoes tumbling one over another.

From the moment it was first performed in England on May 28, 1878, *H.M.S. Pinafore* was a smash hit. Its popularity extended across the Atlantic; within months, *Pinafore* was being staged in major American cities, including New York, Chicago, Boston, and San Francisco. The San Francisco performances entranced teen-aged Josephine Marcus, whose father, a baker, had moved his family there from New York some years earlier. Josephine was a high-spirited girl with a yen for adventure and romance. Though no photographs of a young Josephine have ever been fully authenticated, she was undoubtedly attractive. Bat Masterson, who didn't like her personally, described Josephine as "the prettiest dame" in Tombstone. When a friend urged her to audition for a *Pinafore* touring troupe sometime in summer or early fall of 1879, Josephine earned a small supporting role. It was an opportunity to prance in costume onstage and see some of the country — at least, the Southwest frontier portion of it.

Josephine's *Pinafore* company was headlined by veteran actress Pauline Markham. For performers like Markham who were well known but a level removed from the truly famous, the Southwest territories were lucrative locations for staging a tour. Sophisticated residents trying to bring culture to relatively isolated boomtowns were willing to pay hefty fees to any stars able to endure rough, lengthy travel. The Markham troupe made its way to Arizona Territory by train and then stagecoach. Where they performed once they arrived is a matter of conjecture, but one place must have been Tucson — in his memoir, John Clum (who lived there prior to relocating to Tombstone in early 1880) recalls that he and some other civic leaders "brought in a professional opera troupe, which presented the comic opera, *Pinafore.*" It had to be Markham's company. Another stop they made was in Prescott. It was probably there or in the wild outskirts of town that Josephine first met Johnny Behan. The *Pinafore* tour coincided with Johnny's return to Prescott from Mohave County. As Josephine related the story decades later, dashing Johnny was part of a posse assigned to protect the troupe from a band of renegade Apaches. More likely, the touring company ran into the posse while it was pursuing Mexican bandits. In any event, Josephine was dazzled by Johnny and he was equally smitten. The attraction predictably evolved into temporary romance. Markham's company performed *Pinafore* and moved on. Johnny stayed in Prescott, working to rebuild his reputation and political career. He may have professed undying love. Johnny was expert in telling people what they wanted to hear. Not long afterward Josephine became ill and her parents arranged for her transportation from Arizona Territory back home to San Francisco. From Johnny's perspective, that should have been the perfect ending. He'd made another conquest, this one an exotic-looking young actress, and by getting sick and going home she'd provided a clean break so he could move on.

But Johnny didn't. There was something about Josephine — certainly her looks, probably her determination to *do* things, to experience all the excitement she possibly could — that kept him intrigued. Possibly Josephine was smart enough to suggest she loved Johnny, too, without taking the immediate step of becoming one more notch on the Behan bedpost. Whatever the reason, Johnny pursued her after she left, with letters and possibly even a trip to San Francisco to see her. Josephine claimed that Johnny asked her to marry him, but she wasn't certain that she loved him enough to accept the proposal. He kept in touch, badgering her with missives declaring his eternal devotion and, once he moved to Tombstone in mid-September 1880, telling all about the grand new town where he lived and his certainty about the kind of financial and political success he was going to achieve there. Johnny wrote that all he lacked to make his life perfect was Josephine Sarah Marcus as his bride. She simply had to come out to Tombstone and marry him. At least, that was how Josephine told the story. Johnny never recorded his own version for posterity.

Around the end of September 1880, Josephine acquiesced. She said she was persuaded by a visit in San Francisco from Kitty Jones, the wife of a Tombstone lawyer. Kitty raved about how wonderfully well Johnny was doing in Tombstone, and how much he wanted Josephine to join him there. She decided to go, and arrived in Arizona Territory sometime in October. Morgan Earp may have been riding shotgun guard on the stage that carried Josephine from Tucson to Tombstone. Josephine liked looking at men as much as they enjoyed ogling her, and she thought Morgan was particularly handsome.

Of all her efforts to eliminate scandal from the story of her life, Josephine never scrubbed so hard as she did in presenting the account of her first months in Tombstone. Determined to preserve a *proper* love story for the future readers, in her old age Josephine wrote in an attempted memoir that, as a very moral girl, she stayed in the home of Kitty Jones and her husband under strictly chaperoned conditions while waiting for Johnny to marry her as promised. In fact, she moved in with him right away, and at some point began signing her name as "Josephine Behan," an affectation of common-law wives eager to establish in some public way that they were part of a formal couple. Ten-year-old Albert was still with his dad; Johnny and Josephine may have tried to explain her presence by identifying her as the child's governess. It wouldn't have fooled anyone. Frontier governesses were seldom so alluring. In any event, she was in Tombstone and living with Johnny. Unlike Mattie Blaylock Earp and the other Earp common-law wives who stayed out of sight and remained relatively anonymous, everybody in town undoubtedly knew Josephine had arrived. It wasn't in her nature to stay demurely indoors. She was flashy and seductive and few people in Tombstone had ever seen anyone like her.

But any formal marriage plans soon went awry. In her memoir, Josephine recalls her impatience as Johnny kept putting off matrimony. Certainly Josephine came to Tombstone with the expectation of getting married. Living temporarily as the common-law wife of a frontier lothario was deliciously risqué adventure. Being shacked up long term without the assurance of a legal marriage license was something any intelligent young woman with other options would not find appealing, and no one ever denied that Josephine was both smart and well aware of her considerable charms. If he'd really promised to formally wed Josephine, Johnny reneged.

Once he'd been with Josephine in Tombstone long enough for initial physical attraction to be satisfied and subside, Johnny had ample reason to rethink any promises of permanent commitment. Pragmatism could have had something to do with it. The social handicap of having a common-law wife remained, and even if Johnny formally married Josephine it would not have rendered her acceptable in the eyes of elite Tombstone women. For one thing, Josephine was Jewish. There were plenty of successful Jewish families living in Arizona Territory, but they were mostly expected to socially interact with their own kind and not with good, practicing Christians. (Religion played little or no part in business dealings; faith was considerably less important than profit.) For another, Josephine had been a *showgirl,* which, to nice women in Tombstone and everywhere else in the 1880s West, was the equivalent of *whore.* Being with Josephine was a social millstone Johnny would never be able to completely escape.

More likely, Johnny soon figured out that the advantages of living with Josephine — sex, certainly, but also the thrill of parading a trophy playmate around in front of other men in an environment where females of almost any age and appearance were scarce and much sought after — were outweighed by her difficult personality. Then and forever, Josephine Sarah Marcus was what future generations would term high maintenance, and in the extreme. She wanted her own way in everything and was willing to flirt, weep, plead, threaten, or aggressively badger to get it. Instead of remaining smitten, Johnny may have felt stuck.

By the last week of October 1880, all the key figures in eventual Tombstone mythology were in place. Wyatt Earp went about his duties as Pima County deputy sheriff, trying to impress local leaders with his diligence and efficiency. Virgil Earp roamed the area in his role as a U.S. deputy marshal, and Morgan Earp continued working for Wells Fargo as a shotgun guard. Doc Holliday caroused far more than he should have. Johnny Behan was beginning his ill-fated relationship with Josephine Marcus while simultaneously ingratiating himself with the town and county elite. The Clanton and McLaury brothers fenced stolen cattle and enjoyed their new partnerships with Curly Bill Brocius, John Ringo, and the rest of the cowboys.

None of them realized that they were experiencing Tombstone's last few days of relative calm, which were irrevocably shattered one fall night when some of the cowboys, in the mood for a little fun, rode into town. On October 27, deadly dominoes began tumbling.

CHAPTER SEVEN:
IT BEGINS

County law enforcement didn't occupy all of Wyatt Earp's attention in late October 1880, though he continued to carry out the duties of deputy sheriff, usually by serving warrants. On October 23, he arrested Pete Spencer (also known locally as Pete Spence) for selling two stolen Mexican mules. Spencer, who ran a wood-cutting business, openly associated with the cowboys. They undoubtedly stole the mules, brought them to Spencer, and paid him a brokering fee for handling the sale. Spencer eventually beat the charge — it was impossible to prove he knew that the mules had been stolen. Between his arrest and court hearing, Spencer was free on bond. He spent part of the time assaying ore with U.S. deputy marshal Virgil Earp. Tombstone continued to foster unlikely business partnerships.

Wyatt continued working as a gambler; after ten months in Tombstone he was still scuffling financially. He had his quarter-interest in the games at the Oriental Saloon, but that didn't mean he was there every night dealing cards himself. Wyatt would fund faro "banks," giving dealers in his employ cash to finance games, and return at the end of the evening to close the games, pay the dealers, and keep any remaining winnings for himself. Wyatt might play a hand or two at the Oriental, then drift to some other Tombstone saloon and gamble there. He felt comfortable in card games, much more so than spending an evening at home with Mattie. Faro and poker weren't idle recreation for Wyatt — he was trying to make money. But even if he already had all the income he needed or wanted, Wyatt Earp would still have sought out card games in saloons. Far more than scouring the Arizona desert for wrongdoers, smoky bars were his preferred milieu.

Sometimes his job as deputy sheriff took precedence, and Wyatt's gambling nights were interrupted when he was required to act in his capacity as a lawman. That was the case just after midnight on October 28. Wyatt was playing at the Bank Exchange Saloon when he heard shots fired nearby. Wyatt threw down his cards and hustled outside to investigate. He met his brother Morgan and a gambler named Fred Dodge. They went with him.

Earlier that evening, Curly Bill Brocius and a few friends had gathered in Tombstone. The group included Frank Patterson, who had been involved with Lieutenant Hurst and the search for stolen Army mules, James Johnson, who sometimes worked in the local mines, Edward Collins, and Richard Lloyd. They had drinks in several saloons, and at some point met and began chatting with miners Andrew McCauley and Andrew Ames. It was a pleasant evening. Everyone was having law-abiding fun. It may have been Curly Bill's first visit to Tombstone. No concerned citizen scuttled off to find Marshal Fred White or any other lawman to warn that cowboys were in town. If anything, at this point in late 1880 many Tombstone business owners were probably pleased whenever the supposed desperadoes made one of their rare visits. They always had money to spend and usually behaved themselves as well as or better than the town's rowdier bar-hopping residents. When the cowboys got into mischief, it was most often in their regular hangouts of Galeyville and Charleston.

As October 27 faded into October 28, the cowboys and their new miner friends drifted onto Allen Street. Everyone felt relaxed, some of them too much so. Whooping it up is rarely a silent pursuit. One or more of the cowboys began firing aimless shots into the sky. It wasn't illegal to carry guns on the Tombstone streets, only to have them concealed, so the possession of weapons wasn't a crime. But disturbing the peace was, and Curly Bill knew it. He tried to get his cowboy pals to stop, allegedly saying, "This won't do, boys," but they kept shooting at the stars. A crowd began to gather. Lawmen wouldn't be far behind. Anxious to avoid arrest, Curly Bill, McCauley, and James Johnson sprinted away, taking refuge behind a cabin between Allen and Toughnut streets. They hadn't broken the law, and didn't want to be considered guilty by association with those who just had.

Hearing the shots, Marshal White ran toward Allen Street. He saw Curly Bill, McCauley, and Johnson and assumed they were the shooters. McCauley and Johnson moved a little away. Curly Bill stood his ground, probably intending to explain that he had nothing to do with the ruckus. But White thought he had his man and called out, "I am an officer, give me your pistol."

Wyatt, hurrying up with Morgan and Fred Dodge, saw White approach Curly Bill and heard him bark his order. Wyatt wasn't carrying a gun. He asked Morgan for his, but Morgan didn't have a pistol either. Fred Dodge did, and handed the weapon to Wyatt. A dozen yards ahead, Curly Bill reached down to take his gun from his holster, probably obeying White's command, but not quickly enough to satisfy the Tombstone town marshal. White's experience as a lawman was limited. A year earlier, he'd been selling wood and doing carpentry. White snatched at Curly Bill's gun, grasping the barrel like the handle of a hammer. Wyatt came at Curly Bill from behind, throwing his arms around the cowboy. White shouted, "Now, you goddamn son-of-a-bitch, give up that pistol," yanked at the gun, and it went off. The bullet ripped through White's groin and probably tore off one of his testicles. He shrieked, "I am shot," and collapsed. The blast came at such close quarters that White's clothing caught on fire.

Whether he'd meant to or not, Curly Bill Brocius had just shot the Tombstone town marshal. Wyatt had Fred Dodge's pistol in his hand and would have been well within his rights as a lawman to gun Curly Bill down on the spot. But it had never been Wyatt's custom to shoot at suspects when there were other means of subduing them. Now he reverted to his preferred method in Wichita and Dodge City and slammed his gun against the side of Curly Bill's head. Wyatt's skill at buffaloing remained intact. Metal squarely met skull and the force of the blow knocked the cowboy to the ground. Morgan and Fred Dodge tried to beat out the flames on Fred White's clothes. It wasn't easy. The fallen marshal was writhing in agony. Wyatt grabbed Curly Bill's collar and hauled him to his feet. Dazed, Curly Bill protested, "What have I done? I have not done anything to be arrested for." But Wyatt took him into custody, hauling him off to the Tombstone jail. Then he and some others rounded up the rest of the cowboys and miner Andrew Ames. Andrew McCauley wasn't arrested.

Fred White was taken to a doctor; his wound was severe. The bleeding could be staunched, but with only primitive medical facilities available, infection was inevitable. He lingered for several days, but it was plain he would not survive. On October 30, White, just thirty-one, died. His reputation in Tombstone was such that, during his funeral on November 1, all gambling operations ceased and every business closed. It was the ultimate town accolade.

Meanwhile, there was the matter of what to do with the popular marshal's killer. Curly Bill continued to profess his innocence. He hadn't fired any shots in the air, he was trying his best to get away from the men who were doing the shooting, he'd been grabbed by White and Wyatt, and his gun went off by accident when White pulled at it. His protestations meant very little to the Tombstone populace, whose collective fury was fueled by the *Epitaph*. John Clum's main marketing strategy for his newspaper was to regularly identify some menace to the public good and rally support for its suppression, if not its outright eradication. His earliest target was Tombstone's small Chinese population, but Clum soon recognized that the cowboys could be demonized on a far grander scale. The *Epitaph*'s next-day coverage of the White shooting blamed everything on "a lot of Texan cowboys, as they are called, [who] began firing at the moon and stars." Plucky Marshal White "was ruthlessly shot by one of the number. . . . Too much praise cannot be given to the Marshal for his gallant attempt to arrest the violators." Wyatt, Virgil, and Morgan were lauded "for the energy displayed in bringing the murderers to arrest." It was one thing for drunks or gamblers to occasionally take potshots at each other outside saloons and whorehouses. But a lawman gunned down while performing his civic duty was an affront to law-abiding citizens.

Rumor spread that a mob might form, haul Curly Bill out of his jail cell, and lynch him. Wyatt and Virgil stood guard and discouraged the cowboy's potential attackers. George Parsons predicted in his diary that "vigilantes will probably take care of the next assassins." The tragedy resulted in some good news for the Earps. Meeting in emergency session, the Tombstone council appointed Virgil to be "temporary assistant city marshal," filling in for Fred White at a salary of $100 per month until a special election could be held on November 12. This meant that between them, at least for a few weeks, the two Earp brothers controlled all three levels of law enforcement in and around Tombstone —

Virgil representing the federal government and the town, Wyatt serving as the county deputy. Virgil had planned to run for local constable, a minor post, in hopes of supplementing his meager, erratic income as a U.S. deputy marshal. But after his temporary appointment by the council, he backed out of the constable's race and announced he would seek the full-time position of Tombstone marshal.

Mike Gray, though embroiled in controversy for his role in town lot disputes as co-owner of the Tombstone Townsite Company, had secured an appointed position in Tombstone as a justice of the peace. The Brocius case came before his court. Gray fined Ames $40 for carrying a concealed weapon and discharging it in the street. Collins, Johnson, and Lloyd were assessed fines of $10 each. Charges against Frank Patterson were dismissed; witnesses testified he had tried to make the others stop shooting. So had Curly Bill, but he also shot Fred White.

Gray ruled that the case against Curly Bill should be transferred to Tucson courts because there was so much local animosity toward him. Wyatt, Virgil, and Morgan took the prisoner to Benson by buggy and then on to Tucson by train. On the way, Curly Bill asked Wyatt to recommend a good defense attorney. Wyatt suggested a lawyer named James Zabriskie, but Curly Bill said that

Zabriskie had previously prosecuted him in a Texas court. Curly Bill languished in a Tucson jail cell while Wyatt returned to Tombstone, where a county election immediately supplanted Fred White's death as the news of the day. Once again, the cowboys were in the middle of it. They'd previously stolen cattle. Now they were going to steal the election.

Politics were taken seriously in the territories. Everybody there was striving to get ahead, and having influence with the right legislators and lawmen was a tremendous advantage. Ballot box tampering was part of almost every election. Tension between Republicans — usually established businessmen who often originally hailed from the North and East — and Democrats — most often farmers, ranchers, and hustlers with Southern leanings who wanted as little government oversight and control as possible — ramped up every time elections were scheduled. In southeast Arizona Territory, home to plenty of both pro-government, profit-minded Republican businessmen and anti-authority, independent-spirited Democrats, the election in early November 1880 for Pima County sheriff was crucial. The enforcement philosophy of whoever was elected sheriff would directly affect the fortunes of the cowboys. Incumbent Charlie Shibell was the quintessential Democrat. He liked everybody to be happy, and though he enforced most laws he apparently had no plans of interfering with the rustling that helped feed much of the San Pedro Valley. Republican challenger Bob Paul, who'd previously been a lawman in California before working for Wells Fargo, was reputedly a stickler for by-the-book law enforcement. A stiff-necked county sheriff was the last thing rustlers like John Ringo and their rancher partners like the Clantons wanted. They were all Democrats anyway, and the prospect of Paul replacing Shibell and putting a crimp in their illicit operations goaded them into action.

John Ringo was in no sense a political naïf. He'd already been elected to public office in Texas. He knew how the process worked. In August 1880 he attended the Pima County Democratic convention in Tucson and managed to get himself selected as a delegate for the San Simon/Cienega district. His reputation as a gunslinger-rustler was overlooked even though James Hayes, a member of the Committee on Credentials, was the brother-in-law of Louis Hancock, whom Ringo had shot just eight months earlier. In the territories, political partners were willing to forgive each other for the most egregious personal sins.

Once he became an official delegate for the Democrats, Ringo politicked successfully to have the Pima County board of supervisors designate the house of his old rustling partner Joe Hill as the polling place for Precinct 27, which included most of the cowboys' favorite stomping grounds in the San Simon Valley. Ringo and his pal Ike Clanton were appointed as two of three election officials for the precinct, charged with overseeing the honest casting of ballots. When it was learned that Joe Hill had moved away, Pima County supervisors changed the polling place and removed Ringo and Clanton as poll officials, but it really didn't matter. The cowboys had taken political control of the precinct. In Tombstone, avowed Republican George Parsons worried that his party was being outmaneuvered. "Republicans haven't much show in the territory," he wrote in his diary, also noting that "the old issues are not forgotten."

On November 2, 1880, Pima County voters cast their ballots for sheriff. Results weren't immediately known. Each precinct had to have its results certified, with a deadline of November 17. Nobody waited that long. By November 7 it appeared that the close contest had been narrowly decided in favor of Democratic incumbent Charlie Shibell, who was declared the winner by forty-two votes. He had the voters of John Ringo's Precinct 27 most to thank. Of 104 ballots cast there and certified by an election judge named Henry Johnson, Shibell was the choice for sheriff on 103. The problem was that Precinct 27 had only about fifty eligible voters. Bob Paul protested, arguing that all 104 ballots should be disqualified. That would leave him the winner. Paul filed a formal civil suit in the territorial courts. An investigation was launched. With the election returns in limbo, Charlie Shibell continued to serve as Pima County sheriff.

In early November, Wyatt Earp resigned as Shibell's deputy and began working on behalf of Bob Paul to overturn the election results. Depending on the outcome, Wyatt had made a canny or exceptionally foolish move. If the Republican candidate prevailed, he would undoubtedly reappoint Wyatt as deputy sheriff. Then, when the legislature created the new county that included Tombstone, Wyatt could expect Paul to back him in his bid to be appointed sheriff there. Perhaps even more importantly, Wyatt was sending a message to the powerful Republican leaders in Tombstone that he was a loyal party man. Of course, if Charlie Shibell was reelected as sheriff after all, Wyatt would be permanently out of a job he used as a showcase of his ability to serve as a county sheriff in his own right. But Wyatt hadn't resigned as a gesture of faith that justice would prevail in the Pima County sheriff's race. He had a plan to make certain that it did. But before it could be implemented, the collective political fortunes of the Earps suffered a staggering blow.

Virgil Earp entered the special election for marshal of Tombstone with considerable confidence. For one thing, he was the incumbent, if only on a temporary basis. He was already a U.S. deputy marshal, so clearly he was well qualified for a town job. Virgil's opponent was Ben Sippy, a part-time policeman who had served under Fred White. Sippy's campaign took the form of political ads in the *Nugget.* Accordingly, Virgil might have expected editorial support from John Clum's *Epitaph,* but he didn't get it. John Clum's wife was heavily pregnant and approaching full term; perhaps the publisher was distracted. But on November 12, Tombstone voters chose Ben Sippy over Virgil Earp for sheriff by the comfortable margin of 311–259. In the space of four days, Virgil and Wyatt lost two-thirds of the collective family clout as lawmen. Virgil retained his job as U.S. deputy marshal, but that had less local status than a county or town office. Meanwhile, Charlie Shibell appointed Johnny Behan to replace Wyatt as Pima County deputy sheriff. For Shibell, it was a politically astute move. Johnny was an enthusiastic Democrat. There was no way he would desert Charlie in his time of need in the manner of Republican

Wyatt Earp. Like Wyatt, Johnny was a veteran lawman. Shibell's critics couldn't claim Johnny got the job based solely on party loyalty. And, for Johnny, the job of deputy sheriff offered him the same advantage that it had to Wyatt — a chance to showcase his skills as a lawman to Tombstone power brokers and local voters.

Wyatt probably took little notice of Johnny Behan's appointment to replace him. He was preoccupied with making sure Bob Paul became the next Pima County sheriff. The key to Wyatt's plan had spent all of November and most of December languishing in a Tucson jail cell. Curly Bill Brocius was due in court there on December 27, where during a preliminary hearing a judge would decide whether there was sufficient evidence to bring him to trial for the murder of Fred White. As an eyewitness to the shooting, as well as being the lawman who ultimately subdued and arrested Curly Bill, Wyatt would be the chief witness. Whether he went free or languished in prison depended almost solely on what Wyatt testified. Curly Bill and his cowboy allies expected the worst. On December 9, the *Arizona Daily Star* reported that "Rumor reaches us that the 'cow boy' friends of 'Curly' the 'cow boy' who shot and killed Marshal White, at Tombstone, some time ago, say, in case he is tried and not acquitted they will come to Tucson in force and take him from the jail. This may not be an idle threat."

Wyatt met with Curly Bill and, perhaps, some of the other cowboys. He made it clear that, under the right circumstances, no jailbreak attempt would be necessary. Wyatt was prepared to testify that the shooting of Fred White was accidental, caused mostly by White's impatient grab at Curly Bill's gun. What Wyatt wanted in return was for the cowboys to admit that they'd fixed the ballot box in Precinct 27, which would give the disputed election to Bob Paul. Wyatt thought his attempted blackmail was admirably pragmatic rather than shameful. He proudly related the story to John Flood, his original biographer, and then later to Stuart Lake. Lake summarized what he was told:

Wyatt . . . met with Curly Bill's followers, saw chance to face them, to tell truth about election. San Simon 104 votes cast, less than 50 voters in precinct. All election officials outlaws. Curly Bill acquitted.

On December 27, Wyatt testified that Fred White gave Curly Bill's gun "a quick jerk and the pistol went off." Other expert testimony established that Curly Bill's gun was damaged, and cocked in a certain way that made it liable to fire under such chaotic circumstances whether the cowboy intended it to or

233

not. The judge then ruled that there was insufficient evidence to prove White's death was anything other than accidental. Thanks in very large part to Wyatt Earp, Curly Bill was set free. But he felt no gratitude toward the man whose testimony had done so much to exonerate him. Rather, he carried a permanent grudge. Wyatt said later it was because he had pistol-whipped Curly Bill in front of his cowboy friends. It's far more likely that Curly Bill resented being blackmailed. It proved to him that, if it suited his purposes, Wyatt Earp flouted the law just as flagrantly as any rustler.

One day later on December 28, James Johnson, who'd been with Curly Bill on the night of the Fred White shooting, testified in a Tucson court that he was the mysterious "Henry Johnson" who certified Precinct 27's 104 votes. According to Johnson, he had been ordered to do this by Ike Clanton, John Ringo's pal and business partner. The judicial process would take longer, extended mostly by legal appeals by Charlie Shibell. But from that moment it was clear that Wyatt's scheme had worked and Bob Paul would become sheriff of Pima County. While Paul awaited the official verdict, he went back to work for Wells Fargo, riding shotgun on some routes when stages were transporting company treasure boxes.

Five months earlier, Wyatt had angered the

McLaurys in the matter of the stolen army mules. Now he'd crossed Curly Bill, Johnny Ringo, and Ike Clanton. The list of his enemies was growing. Wyatt probably had no idea and, even if he did, wouldn't have cared. Wyatt understood cards much better than people. He was expert in calculating the odds in poker games, but had little comprehension of the infinite number of ways in which human beings try to get even.

Johnny Behan's tenure as Pima County deputy sheriff got off to an uneven start. He arrested a suspect who broke into a miner's cabin, and ran down another after a long chase through the desert. But while off-duty, Johnny also overturned his buggy while racing Little Nell at an unacceptable speed. Buggies tearing recklessly down Tombstone streets were an ongoing problem; just recently, one had struck a small boy, who luckily wasn't seriously injured. The incident didn't do much for Johnny's reputation in town. And, in late December, Johnny also had a run-in with Wyatt Earp.

Later, each would offer a different version of what happened. According to Johnny, he went looking for Ike Clanton to serve a subpoena requiring Ike to testify in the Bob Paul–Charlie Shibell election case. He asked Virgil Earp where to find Ike, and Virgil directed Johnny to Charleston. Johnny rode there after dark, and on the way was passed by a galloping horseman heading in the same direction. Johnny believed the rider was Virgil. A second rider sped by — Johnny thought he recognized Doc Holliday. When Johnny got to Charleston, he found Wyatt and Doc, but not Ike. They told Johnny they were in town looking for a horse of Wyatt's that had been stolen. Ike was nowhere to be found, and Johnny left the subpoena with a man who said he was heading out to the Clanton ranch. Johnny never explained why he didn't go on to the ranch and serve the subpoena himself. When he saw Ike later, Johnny recalled, Clanton told him "that [Wyatt] Earp said I had sent a posse of nine men down there to arrest him and take him to Tucson." Though Johnny never said so directly, his implication was clear: For whatever reason, Wyatt Earp had alerted Ike to the subpoena delivery, giving him time to clear out of Charleston and avoid having it served. That made absolutely no sense. Ike's testimony, if truthful, would only have helped Bob Paul's cause. But Wyatt's version was just as doubtful. He claimed that someone stole his horse named Dick Naylor, a steed Wyatt prized because he was a fine racer. Cowboy Sherman McMasters, who sometimes served Wyatt as an informer, told him that Billy Clanton had the horse in Charleston. Wyatt and Doc rode over and found Dick Naylor in a corral there.

They confronted Billy, who essentially admitted he'd stolen the horse and dared them to do something about it. Wyatt could have pistol-whipped the eighteen-year-old or had him arrested, but decided to just take his horse, warn Billy of dire consequences if he did it again, and ride with Doc back to Tombstone. Wyatt added that at some point during Dick Naylor's theft, one of Johnny Behan's friends rode the animal — suggesting that the deputy sheriff was in league with horse thieves.

No matter what really happened between Johnny and Wyatt during the incident, it became a critical point of contention less than a year later. In the meantime, a precedent was established. Johnny Behan and Wyatt Earp were never going to agree on anything.

While Virgil and Wyatt had their rocky moments, late 1880 and early 1881 were good times for several other family members. Youngest Earp brother Warren drifted in and out of Tombstone. Warren Earp struggled all his life with drinking, and got into lots of scrapes with the law. But during his visits to Tombstone, his brothers sometimes found him temporary employment, even occasionally as a special deputy. James Earp opened his own "sampling room," another term for a barebones bar. James didn't have the financial wherewithal to operate a pleasure palace like the Oriental, but there were plenty of dedicated drinkers in Tombstone who just wanted to drink lots of whiskey and could care less about opulent surroundings while they did. Hattie, James's stepdaughter, became engaged to local businessman Thaddeus Harris. They married in early 1881 on her eighteenth birthday. Perhaps the happiest Earp of all was Louisa, Morgan's common-law wife. For almost a year after he arrived in Tombstone, Morgan insisted that Louisa stay with her family back in California. In January 1881 he finally allowed her to join him in Arizona. After arriving, she sent a series of letters back to her sister Agnes describing the wonders — and rigors — of her new home: "We have had a little snow shower, it layed on the ground about 2 hours. We have had no rain and it is very dry and dusty and the wind blows very hard for the past two weeks except for a few days which was so warm we nearly melted with the doors and windows open." Like other Earp wives Mattie, Allie, and Bessie, Louisa was expected to stay out of sight and concentrate on household chores. But in one letter to her sister, she described a thrill longed for by all common-law wives — Morgan wanted her to use his last name. "He wishes me to have my letters directed to Louisa Earp," she gushed to Agnes, "so you can direct the next one as so — Louisa Houston,

Mrs. Morgan Earp."

With political tension running high in Tombstone, the town still did its best to celebrate the 1880 holiday season with special events. Horse races were held on Thanksgiving, and there was a well-attended contest in which thirteen competitors vied to be crowned the best rifle shot in Tombstone. Wyatt apparently didn't enter. The winner was someone named H. A. Plate. Virgil Earp placed fourth, Johnny Behan was eighth, and Doc Holliday wallowed in a tie for tenth place. Various elaborate balls concluded the annual festivities — none of the Earp brothers and their common-law wives were invited to attend — and then it was time for town elections on January 4. The race for mayor was by far the most critical, and its key issue was the ongoing controversy about town lot control and ownership. By the end of 1880, the question of who owned what in Tombstone had deteriorated into a tangled legal morass that had everyone on edge.

Viewed from a modern perspective, the Tombstone town site controversy may seem less compelling than rustling and stolen elections and gunfights. But it was a major contributing factor to the mounting tension in Tombstone that led to inevitable bloodshed — on the frontier, the property you owned defined who you were. And because of a shady partnership between the Tombstone Townsite Company and mayor Alder Randall, the property of most residents and business owners was in jeopardy.

In 1879, the Townsite Company made an attempt to survey land, lay out plans for a town to be named Tombstone, and sell lots in it, all according to federal law for unincorporated public property. But even when the company failed to make required payments to the government and lost its right to sell the lots, people kept moving in and building homes and opening businesses. In the interim Tombstone became incorporated. At that point, the town mayor was required to sell lots to residents and businesses for nominal fees, which in Tombstone's case essentially meant confirming the ownership of people already living and doing business there. But in November 1880, Mayor Randall quietly deeded most town lots to the Townsite Company. He undoubtedly got a fat payoff in return. Townsite owners Mike Gray and James Clark immediately began demanding payment from current occupants, threatening to throw them off the property by force if they didn't cooperate. Led by John Clum, town spokesmen went to court and won an injunction barring Clark and Gray from reselling lots until the legalities could be sorted out. They ignored the injunction and kept trying to evict anyone they classified as squatters.

The problem festered. Alder Randall wisely chose not to seek reelection. Voters would gleefully have turned him out of office, and rumors abounded that Randall was going to be lynched any day. (Five months later, Randall was brought up on charges of malfeasance while in office, only to escape punishment on a technicality. The courts ruled an action such as betraying the property rights of Tombstone citizens wasn't specified as a felony in territorial law.) Whoever was elected as the new mayor of Tombstone on January 4 would inherit a mess that he would be expected to act upon promptly. After a false start, town Republicans believed they had the perfect candidate.

John Clum already wielded considerable power in Tombstone. Besides publishing the *Epitaph,* he also served as town postmaster. Opinionated and outspoken, Clum was the kind of leader who elicited extreme reactions from supporters and opponents. He was politically ambitious. As an avowed Republican and determined foe of the Tombstone Townsite Company, Clum's goal in the January 4 election was to win the office of mayor for his party and then settle the matter of town lots in Tombstone once and for all. Clum and other leading Republicans formed the Tombstone Citizens League and prepared a slate of contenders for local office. To emphasize their commitment to law and order, they called it the Citizens Protective Ticket. Clum headed the list as its candidate for mayor. Besides his reputation as a crusader, Clum also had the potential to attract sympathy votes. His wife, Mary, had just died in childbirth on December 18.

On January 4, 1881, Clum was elected mayor of Tombstone, swamping Democrat Mark Shaffer by a vote of 532–165. He took office and immediately began issuing mayor's deeds for disputed property, assuring recipients that these were the real ones. Clark and Gray, who had been legally forbidden to sell the lots they believed were theirs, promptly went to court and won an injunction prohibiting Clum, too, from assigning lots. It would obviously be some time before the courts rendered a final decision in favor of one side over the other. The issue that Clum swore he'd resolve if elected mayor was more convoluted than ever, and in Tombstone it would be only a matter of time before more violence broke out over property ownership. Meanwhile, Clum was in office, and, if he couldn't immediately steamroll Clark and Gray as Tombstone voters had been promised, then he had to retain the support of frustrated citizens by battling some other menace to the town. The obvious target was the Texas cowboys, whom Clum had already been assailing on the pages of the *Epitaph* for months. Within two weeks of his taking office, they handed Clum several new, convenient opportunities to rail against them in his dual roles of mayor and newspaper publisher. Two incidents took place in neighboring communities. The third began somewhere else and culminated in Tombstone itself.

After his narrow escape from a potential prison term or even the noose, the cowboy cause would have been better served by Curly Bill Brocius lying low for a while, but that wasn't in his nature. Perhaps he wanted to prove that he wasn't intimidated by the local law. On January 9, five days after John Clum was elected mayor, Curly Bill and some of the other cowboys showed up in Charleston, just ten miles from Tombstone. Parsons noted in his diary that they "played the devil generally — breaking up a religious meeting by chasing the minister out of the house — putting out lights with pistol balls and going through the town." Nine days later, he was at it again, this time in Contention City. There, according to the *Arizona Star,* Curly Bill and his comrades were guilty of "shooting at a peaceable citizen, of robbing a till of $50, and other offenses equally unpardonable." But when a town deputy tried to arrest them, the well-armed cowboys backed him down. From Contention City ten miles west of

Tombstone they rode on to nearby Watervale, where they lingered for two days. Curly Bill spent the time taunting local lawmen to come and get him. Recently appointed Pima County deputy sheriff Johnny Behan would have been the logical choice, but he didn't intervene. Probably the newspaper reports exaggerated the cowboys' Contention City spree. Shooting at a citizen rather than at the sky would have been classified as attempted murder, and "robbing a till" was larceny. Pragmatic lawmen could and did overlook rustling Mexican cattle and a bit of noisy horseplay that didn't endanger lives, but they would not have ignored such blatant criminality.

Curly Bill had nothing to do with the most shattering incident, which occurred in Charleston on January 14 and spilled over into Tombstone. Eighteen-year-old gambler Michael O'Rourke, better known as Johnny Behind-the-Deuce, shot and killed W. P. Schneider, a machinist and blacksmith. Several of Schneider's friends — who were apparently legion in Charleston — swore that O'Rourke murdered Schneider in cold blood after O'Rourke bumped him in the street and the engineer told him to watch where he was going. A second version had the men arguing in a saloon after Schneider complained to a companion that the weather was cool. O'Rourke overheard, made some remark, was insulted when Schneider informed him that he wasn't part of the conversation, and promised to gun Schneider down whenever he came back outside. With little interest in objectivity and a political stake in stoking the flames of public outrage, Clum claimed in the *Epitaph* that "true to his promise, the lurking fiend . . . with hell in his heart and death in his mind, drew deadly aim and dropped his victim dead in his tracks."

No matter what the original circumstances were, an angry crowd began to gather. Local constable George McKelvey, fearing for O'Rourke's safety, took him into custody, loaded him onto a wagon, and rattled away to deliver the prisoner to Tombstone, where there were more lawmen to protect him. Some members of the Charleston crowd saddled their horses and rode in pursuit. Mob lynchings were often rumored in and around Tombstone — former mayor Alder Randall and Curly Bill having been most recently identified as potential victims — but this time it was a very real possibility.

Some claimed later that Virgil Earp met McKelvey outside of town and personally escorted O'Rourke to Tombstone ahead of the mob. Others gave the credit to Tombstone sheriff Ben Sippy. Whoever was responsible, O'Rourke was brought inside Vogan's Bowling Alley. Some of the pursuers from Charleston rode into Tombstone soon afterward, and word spread in town that a cold-blooded killer was available for stringing up. The timing for spontaneous vigilante justice was right. Everyone still remembered Fred White's death — his killer had gone free. The *Epitaph* was full of stories about violent crimes committed by savage cowboys against honest citizens. Here was an opportunity to demonstrate that in Tombstone at least, murderers got what they had coming. Even though he wasn't one of them, Johnny Behind-the-Deuce dangling from the end of a rope would send an unmistakable message to cowboy brigands. A new mob formed in the street outside Vogan's. Inside, local lawmen gathered, including Virgil, Ben Sippy, and Johnny Behan. They summoned friends to help them stave off trouble. Wyatt was undoubtedly among them. Strolling around town with a business acquaintance he identified only as "Mr. Stanley," George Parsons described in his diary what happened next:

Many of the miners armed themselves and tried to get at the murderer. Several times, yes a number of times, rushes were made and rifles leveled, causing Mr. Stanley and me to get behind the most available shelter. Terrible excitement, but the officers got through finally and out of town with their man bound for Tucson.

It was touch-and-go for a while, but O'Rourke was safely extradited that night to Tucson, where he was placed in jail and held for trial on a charge of murder. O'Rourke escaped soon afterward and was never recaptured.

But the mob incident in Tombstone had two long-term consequences. One affected Wyatt Earp's eventual reputation. Clum's *Epitaph* credited Ben Sippy, Virgil Earp, and Johnny Behan with backing down the crowd outside Vogan's. Sippy came in for the most praise: "No one who was witness of yesterday's proceedings can doubt that [without] his presence, blood would have flow[ed] freely." Wyatt wasn't mentioned at all. His name doesn't appear in George Parsons's journal account. The *Citizen* declared that "to Deputy United States Marshal Virgil Earp and his companions the credit of saving the young man from the fury of the miners is due." But in an interview twenty years later Parsons recalled "the day that saw the Earps" — who would have included Wyatt and Morgan, and maybe James or Warren — "and Doc Holliday standing off the crowd." Wyatt gave himself even more dramatic credit, telling a writer that Virgil "turned [O'Rourke] over to me, and miners came swarming in, and I faced five hundred of 'em and just didn't let them get him. That's all." As with his tales of arresting Ben Thompson in Ellsworth and

247

facing down Clay Allison in Dodge, Wyatt always liked to conjure up scenarios where, alone and steadfast, he backed down a mob. It's impossible to know exactly what happened in Tombstone that night. But many years later Wyatt received widespread credit for single-handedly standing off a lynch mob, even though he almost certainly did not.

The other consequence was more immediate, and had much more impact on events in Tombstone in the months ahead. Miners may have led the surge on the night of January 14 to snatch Michael O'Rourke from the law and hang him high, but their fury was shared by many of the town's prominent citizens. The same leaders who prided themselves on bringing social and cultural sophistication to Tombstone now began to explore the possibilities of raw vigilante justice. George Parsons declared in his diary entry for January 14 that O'Rourke, still only accused and not found guilty of any crime, "should have been killed in his tracks. Too much of this kind of business is going on. I believe in killing such men as one would a wild animal. The law must be carried out by the citizens, or should be, when it fails in its performance as it has lately done." Even as Michael O'Rourke was escorted out of Tombstone on his way to a Tucson cell that night, Parsons was "requested to attend a strictly private gathering" where town leaders formed what

Parsons later described as "a Vigilance Committee . . . which numbered about 100 men with a council of ten of which I was a member." The group met again three nights later, and Parsons noted "an interesting talk tonight and sense taken in a matter." The sense taken, and certainly made plain to the Earps, Johnny Behan, and other current or aspiring town and county lawmen, was that from then on in Tombstone due process would be considered far less desirable than satisfactory results. Local officers would either enforce the law the way that the committee wanted or the committee would rally private citizens to step in and do whatever it deemed necessary.

What Tombstone's leaders expected of their town and county lawmen became even more critical during the first two days of February. On the first of the month, the Eleventh Territorial Legislature in Prescott voted to carve seven thousand square miles from southeast Pima County and create a new entity called Cochise County. On February 2, the legislature selected Tombstone as the Cochise County seat. There was tempered rejoicing in Tombstone. In its new role, the town would gain a courthouse and considerably more political clout in the capital. Because regular territorial elections were not scheduled until November 1882, Governor Frémont had to appoint temporary officials. He waited until

February 10 to announce his choices, including the first Cochise County sheriff. Wyatt Earp and Johnny Behan were considered to be leading candidates. One of them expected to be selected by the governor. The other knew he would be.

CHAPTER EIGHT:
COCHISE COUNTY SHERIFF

Except for the money involved, whoever was named the first sheriff of Cochise County would be saddled with a difficult, thankless job. The most obvious drawback was the sheer size of the area for which he'd be responsible — seven thousand square miles of towering mountains, precipitous canyons, and trackless, arroyo-bisected desert. No sheriff, no matter how dedicated, could patrol it all on a regular basis. Outlaws trying to elude pursuit could choose among thousands of places to hide; posses led by even the most skilled trackers were likely to be baffled. Proximity to the border compounded the problem; American fugitives with the sheriff hot on their trail could cross into Mexico, beyond his reach and jurisdiction. Mexican *bandidos* often came north on raids, striking quickly, and then escaping back home with their loot.

The potential for violence was always present. Beyond overt criminals, many county residents had dubious pasts. Even if they'd come to southeast Arizona with the intent of going straight, they were on the run from the law somewhere else. Outside town limits, everyone carried guns; with the Apaches lurking, they would have been fools if they hadn't. The Cochise County sheriff would never be able to relax. At any moment he might be attacked in the course of performing his duties.

And the sheriff couldn't expect appreciation, let alone cooperation, from many of the citizens he was charged with protecting. Political factionalism was partly to blame. With Republicans and Democrats at war for political dominance, whichever party the new sheriff didn't belong to would constantly criticize his performance, focusing on problems and ignoring any achievements. Small ranchers like the Clantons and McLaurys did not want their rustler business partners arrested or even hampered. As a general rule, outside of wealthy business leaders in Tombstone, most Cochise County residents fiercely resented virtually any form of government. In the territories, political "rings" routinely dominated county offices, favoring friends and functioning to generate personal profit rather than deliver quality public services. This caused rank-and-file citizens, often with justification, to associate public officeholders with incompetence and corruption. Fairly or not, many of the Cochise County sheriff's constituents would automatically assume that he was a crook, particularly since he was becoming wealthy through tax money — *their* money.

Taxes were at the heart of the creation of the new county. Cochise County was immense, but it had formed less than a third of original Pima County. Even more than law enforcement, the primary duty of a county sheriff was to collect taxes, and it had proven impossible for Pima County's sheriff to effectively locate and assess small ranchers and individuals in the far southeastern reaches of the area. Consequently, many of them had been able to avoid any taxation at all — in their minds there was nothing wrong with that. Why voluntarily pay for the government intrusion that they hated so much? The first task of the Cochise County sheriff would be to track down every taxable entity and citizen, arbitrarily determine property values, assess taxes, then collect them from people ready to squabble over every cent. They could choose to challenge his valuations. A county board of supervisors was in place to consider protests. The sheriff was required to attend and testify in time-consuming hearings. The same supervisors kept a close eye on the sheriff's accounts to make certain he was not skimming additional income beyond a monthly stipend of $150 for room and board, plus the 10 percent of collected taxes to which he was legally entitled.

But that 10 percent was an irresistible lure. A grumbling antigovernment citizen raising goats on a few isolated, rocky acres might mean only a dollar or two to the sheriff each year, but the Cochise County tax base rested primarily on working mines and ore treatment plants and the railroad, businesses worth fortunes and taxed accordingly. They were the reason that candidates for Cochise County sheriff in 1881 could anticipate a substantial income of anywhere from $25,000 to $40,000, or $500,000 to $900,000 in modern-day dollars. Not all of it was personal profit; routine office expenses and deputies' salaries had to be paid for, but even after those deductions there was enough left over to automatically make the sheriff an important man, someone to be reckoned with by political and business power brokers. They would still consider him an employee, a useful tool for generating revenue and controlling undesirable elements, but at least he would be an extremely well-paid one. To Wyatt Earp and Johnny Behan, that possibility trumped all the inherent headaches that came with the office. They both wanted the job badly, and meant to get it.

On paper, Wyatt was well qualified to be named sheriff of Cochise County by territorial governor John C. Frémont. Party affiliation was paramount, at least in Wyatt's eyes. Like Frémont, he was a Republican, and one so dedicated that he had resigned as Pima County deputy sheriff to help his party's candidate there overturn stolen election results. As the governor was making his decision regarding Cochise County sheriff in February 1881, the Bob Paul–Charlie Shibell contest for Pima County sheriff was still held up in the courts. After a judge disallowed the disputed Precinct 27 votes and declared Paul the winner, Shibell filed an appeal and, in the interim, remained in office. But Paul was going to eventually triumph — even Shibell's supporters realized that this final appeal was a delaying tactic rather than a strategy for victory. Wyatt, with his blackmail of Curly Bill and the cowboys, could and undoubtedly did feel personally responsible. Perhaps Frémont and other Republican leaders didn't know the specifics, but Wyatt had openly worked on Bob Paul's behalf and he expected them to remember it. In Wyatt's mind, he had *earned* the Cochise County sheriff's job.

Beyond party obligations, the governor could appoint Wyatt based on law enforcement experience. He'd never been the man in overall charge before, having served as a policeman in Wichita and as an assistant marshal in Dodge City, but at least he'd previously worn a badge in places where lawmen faced constant challenges from hard-nosed drifters who often sought out rather than avoided confrontations. During his brief tenure as Pima County deputy sheriff under Charlie Shibell, Wyatt had performed competently and, in the case of Curly Bill's arrest, even with distinction by clubbing the cowboy into submission rather than shooting him.

Two factors worked against Wyatt. He was a gambler who associated with questionable types, especially the notorious Doc Holliday. And he was not a glad-hander, someone who made all the right social connections and could be counted on to win votes through force of personality as well as job performance. Whoever the governor appointed as sheriff would have to run for reelection in November 1882. It was hard to imagine Wyatt Earp out stumping for support at the polls. Wyatt expected the system to work without understanding how to make it work in his favor. Because of his testy dealings with Frank McLaury, Curly Bill, and the Clantons, a solid rancher-cowboy bloc was always going to be against him. Tombstone Republicans might back him, but Democrat and Oriental Saloon owner Milton Joyce still held a grudge against Wyatt after his fracas with Doc and Wyatt's intercession on his pal's behalf. Joyce had little political power in Tombstone where Republican businessmen held sway, but he had considerable clout with a territorial legislature dominated by Democrats. Because of it, Joyce received an appointment to the Cochise County board of supervisors. A more astute candidate than Wyatt would have tried to mend fences with Joyce. The notion didn't occur to Wyatt, and Joyce undoubtedly did his best to spread the word in the legislature that this fellow Earp would not do as county sheriff. Governor Frémont had to take Democratic opposition into consideration. By 1881, the federal government allowed territorial governors very little discretionary power. As much as possible, they were expected to keep their territories quiet. Controversy of any kind put a governor's job in jeopardy. He could be replaced at the whim of the president or important members of the administration. John Frémont had no love for Arizona Territory. He wanted to be its governor because of the business opportunities available to him while in office. Remaining governor by getting along with the Democratic majority in the territorial legislature was in Frémont's best political and financial interest. The leading Democratic candidate for appointment as Cochise County sheriff was a man who understood that, and was in position to exploit it.

Johnny Behan had no intention of letting the sheriff's job slip through his fingers. He came to Tombstone in the fall of 1880 fully aware that soon the town would become the center of a newly formed county. He understood the delicate political balance in the territorial capital, where Republican Frémont had to peacefully coexist with Johnny's fellow Democrats. In Tombstone, Johnny was diligent in getting to know the right people and encouraging them to like him. Nobody important among Tombstone's Republicans would object too much, at least initially, if Governor Frémont chose Democrat Johnny to be sheriff.

In some ways, Johnny's law enforcement credentials exceeded Wyatt's. Johnny had already been Yavapai County sheriff. He left office voluntarily rather than being voted out, and then went on to serve as county representative in the Seventh Territorial Legislature. Later, Mohave County had sent Johnny back to the capital as its representative to the Tenth Legislature. In between, he served the Ninth Legislature as sergeant-at-arms. He had firsthand experience with government bureaucracy. It was true that Johnny was no fighter — he hadn't been able to lick even a few Chinese in a Prescott laundry. But as a county sheriff he didn't have to be. In Arizona Territory chief law enforcement officers hired deputies — sometimes known as "undersheriffs" — to perform routine law enforcement duties, make deliveries of warrants, and generally keep things under control. Though there had been scandal in his private life, to date Johnny's public service was generally above reproach. Given the governor's need to keep Democratic legislators happy and Johnny's experience in the job, it became obvious to everyone involved, except Wyatt, who Frémont's eventual choice would be.

But Johnny also had the career politician's instinct to try and turn opponents into allies. Wyatt Earp lacked the political connections and outgoing personality to beat Johnny out for the appointment, but his toughness could be an asset in Johnny's efforts to keep the cowboys and other rough-and-tumble Cochise County residents in line. At some point, Johnny offered Wyatt a deal. Johnny told Wyatt he felt certain Frémont would give him the job. When he became sheriff, Johnny proposed naming Wyatt as his undersheriff. He would assign some of the tax duties to Wyatt, who could keep the departmental 10 percent of whatever he collected. Obviously Johnny was going to reserve collection of big accounts for himself and let Wyatt struggle with small-potato, obstreperous taxpayers in the far reaches of the county. It was an exceptionally pragmatic offer. For a pittance of his $25,000 to $40,000 per annum fortune, Johnny would gain an intimidating assistant whose talent for knocking heads more than offset Johnny's lack of fighting skills.

Johnny was so confident of his own chances that he urged Wyatt to keep trying to get the Frémont appointment. If Wyatt did get the governor's nod, Johnny promised, he'd expect nothing from Wyatt in return. That was good, Wyatt told him, because if the governor picked him Wyatt would name his brothers as undersheriffs — he had them "to provide for." He accepted Johnny's offer, not realizing that the promises of politicians often have very short shelf lives. This meant that when Frémont made his announcement in February, Wyatt suffered not one but two nasty surprises. Johnny Behan became the first sheriff of Cochise County by gubernatorial appointment, and the undersheriff he soon named to share in his new responsibilities and income was Harry Woods. Wyatt, who always kept his word, felt betrayed.

Johnny reneged on his promise to Wyatt out of political necessity, which, to Johnny's way of thinking, was in no sense a dishonorable act. To him, it was Wyatt's own fault. When he quit as Democrat Charlie Shibell's deputy to work for the election of Republican Bob Paul as Pima County sheriff in early November 1880, Wyatt was openly enlisting in the all-out, no-quarter war being waged in Arizona Territory between the two parties. If he'd stayed out of the controversy and remained Shibell's deputy, he would not have earned the enmity of Johnny's fellow Democrats. Then Johnny could have appointed him to be Cochise County undersheriff as promised. But Wyatt took up the Republican cause in a very public way, and whatever gratitude he won among his fellow party members paled against the partisan fury his actions induced among the Democrats. Johnny was not about to let an inconsequential promise to Wyatt Earp jeopardize his new, reinvigorated standing with Democratic leaders who could, if they chose, put up a candidate other than Johnny for Cochise County sheriff in the November 1882 elections.

Harry Woods as undersheriff was the perfect choice to solidify Johnny's standing within his party. As a member of the territorial House of Representatives, Woods, an avowed Democrat, was a key player in the creation of Cochise County. He even suggested its name. Having Woods on his team guaranteed Johnny another huge advantage. The new county sheriff would receive nothing but positive coverage in one of Tombstone's two influential daily newspapers because Woods wrote for the *Nugget.* Sometime in April of 1881 Woods bought the newspaper. That gave John Clum and his Republican *Epitaph* one more reason to consistently oppose everything county sheriff Behan did, but by the time Johnny took office Tombstone politics were so heatedly partisan that Clum would have maligned him in print anyway on general political principles.

Johnny filled out his staff with an ever-evolving series of deputies hired more for convenience than any specific background in law enforcement. Billy Breakenridge had been a freighter and served as an army scout. William Bell sold liquor in Charleston. Frank Stilwell previously owned and operated a saloon with Pete Spencer, whom Wyatt had arrested for selling stolen mules just a few months earlier. Stilwell was known locally for his habit of referring to money as "sugar." He was also rumored to have been involved in a murder at the old Brunckow Mine in November 1879. Given the political realities, Johnny couldn't hire any Earps; even if he had approached Morgan, a logical choice for county deputy given his experience as a lawman in Montana, family loyalty would have precluded Morgan accepting the job. As far as the Earps were concerned, Johnny Behan had lied to Wyatt, and an insult to one brother was taken as an attack on them all. They never forgot or forgave.

Even as Johnny took his oath of office and opened his sheriff's office in the back of the Dunbar Corral in Tombstone, the legislature in Prescott debated new ways to combat the increasing spread of crime, especially in the territory's newest southeast county. Governor

Frémont delayed his latest excursion to the East long enough to formally request that legislators turn their "earnest attention" to crime along the border by emulating Texas and its Rangers with a hundred-man force that would spend three months in the field pursuing outlaws. Besides rustlers, Frémont emphasized, there was a growing number of stage robberies. In just ninety days a tough squad of experienced gunmen might effectively drive the undesirables to other states or territories where they would become someone else's problem. It wasn't a bad strategy; the cowboys congregated in southeast Arizona because there were no Ranger-like nemeses to harass them there. But the legislature turned the governor's proposal down, insisting that federal troops should take on the cowboys. Congress and its *Posse Comitatus* Act prohibited army involvement in civilian law enforcement, so once again it was left to local lawmen to somehow keep the cowboys under control. In Cochise County, Johnny Behan and his mostly inexperienced deputies hardly seemed up to the task. But Johnny, who always preferred negotiation to confrontation, devised a strategy that at least temporarily made one of the key cowboys an integral part of his team.

Billy Breakenridge had a tough time during his early months as Cochise County deputy sheriff. Predictably, his boss focused on tax collection rather than law enforcement, and Deputy Breakenridge was ordered to ride out into the area around Tombstone, assessing values on property that often had escaped the notice of the previous Pima County sheriff and his deputies. Breakenridge went about his thorny business with limited success until he finally reached Galeyville, where, he wrote, "no taxes had ever been collected, and where the rustlers held full sway." The rustlers were among the Cochise County citizens Breakenridge was expected to dun for tax payments. Acting on Johnny's instructions, the deputy asked someone to introduce him formally to Curly Bill Brocius. In his Tombstone memoir, Breakenridge recorded the startling request he made of the cowboy, and Curly Bill's response:

I told him who I was and what I was, and said I wanted to hire him to go with me as a deputy assessor and help me collect the taxes, as I was afraid I might be held up and my tax money taken from me if I went alone. The idea of my asking the chief of all the cattle rustlers in that part of the country to help me collect taxes from them struck him as a good joke. He thought it over for a few moments and then, laughing, said "Yes, and we will make every one of those blank blank cow thieves pay his taxes."

It was the perfect approach, one that played to the cowboy's vanity by asking for his protection and not-so-subtly acknowledging that Curly Bill and his pals were perfectly capable of overpowering the deputy and pilfering the taxes he collected anytime they felt like it. And to his amazement Breakenridge discovered that Curly Bill meant what he said. The cowboy made all his friends pay up, telling them that if they were ever arrested things would go better for them if they were on record as paying their taxes on time and in full. "I [also] learned one thing about him, and that was that he would not lie to me," Breakenridge wrote later. "His word to me was better than the oaths of some of whom were known as good citizens." Thanks to Curly Bill, Breakenridge returned to Tombstone with nearly $1,000 collected from the cowboys. Nothing epitomized Johnny Behan's commonsense approach to law enforcement more than this. Rather than risk ongoing confrontation, he cannily turned a potential adversary into an ally, and everyone benefited. Besides beef for local consumption, rustling now provided tax dollars for Cochise County improvements.

Newly designated as the county seat, Tombstone continued to grow. Its official population peaked at just over four thousand, and visitors — dry goods salesmen, Mexican traders, transients of every description — added several hundred more on a daily basis. Sanitation remained a problem. Periodic outbreaks of typhoid and diphtheria resulted. But the town itself blossomed in many ways. Though there were already several fine, small theaters, in early 1881 Albert Schieffelin decided to create a "dramatic shrine" in his own honor and began building a magnificent two-story adobe showplace to be named Schieffelin Hall. Its stage was the largest to be found anywhere between Denver and San Francisco. The building's magnificence was such that elaborate balls were held there months before construction was completed. A town library opened in the back of a tobacco shop. Well-to-do ladies in town organized the Home Dramatic Association. Parties hosted and attended by prominent citizens approximated the social circuits of major cities on the East and West coasts — Tombstone's bluebloods, *San Diego Daily Union* correspondent Clara Brown assured her readers, were enjoying their socializing on a sophisticated scale: "To give tone to [one] affair, refreshments were served by darkies, in imitation of metropolitan style." The grandest soiree of all was held on Washington's Birthday, and Brown observed that "the most conspicuous feature of the evening [was] the stately minuet performed by sixteen courtly dames and gallants." Entertainment at various events was provided by the Tombstone Brass Band, comprised primarily of Welsh and Cornish miners.

Education and religion were not overlooked. Built for the staggering sum of $1,500, the Sacred Heart Catholic Church opened in spring 1881 with space for two hundred worshippers. Presbyterians and Methodists already had houses of worship. The Tombstone public school was attended by 135 students, and enrollment would double within two years. Town improvements were paid for with revenue from newly imposed quarterly city licenses: $10 for bakers, $15 for butchers, $10 for individual prostitutes (and anywhere from $20 to $60 from their madams, depending on the number of women working in their brothels), $250 for anyone selling "wine, malt or spirituous liquors." It was all quite organized and upscale, with a nagging exception. Most of the town was peaceful, but in the saloon district people kept getting shot.

Try as its leaders might, Tombstone could not entirely escape the violence endemic to mining towns. Cultural opportunities and culinary delights meant little to men who were only interested in drinking and gambling. That combination guaranteed occasional trouble no matter how diligently town lawmen patrolled saloons, whorehouses, and back alleys. In one week early in 1881 two incidents shook the community, and both occurred at the Oriental, where Wyatt Earp now depended on his one-quarter ownership of the gambling concessions to make a living.

By reputation and in fact, the Oriental was one of the ritziest saloons operating in Tombstone. It attracted high rollers of every stripe — not only experienced gamblers, but also neophytes who'd just come into money from a mineral strike or property sale and figured their good luck would carry over to the card tables. In fact, luck had very little to do with it. Professional gamblers almost inevitably prevailed because they understood the odds involved in every hand dealt, and if that didn't work to their advantage they could rig the game in any number of virtually undetectable ways. Few career gamblers, including Wyatt Earp and Doc Holliday, ever completely escaped charges that they were cheating. Even when games were honest and players were evenly matched, losers who'd been drinking heavily were prone to believe they somehow must have been rooked. Resulting rows frequently turned violent, even in the fanciest establishments.

On February 25, veteran gamblers Luke Short and Bat Masterson ran games at the Oriental. Neither had come to Tombstone with the intent of settling in. Their intention was to play awhile as dealers, win some money, and move on. Certainly Wyatt was glad to see them there. As part-owner of the gambling concession, he would share in whatever they won — and, as veteran card sharps, they were going to win on a consistent basis.

Charley Storms, another veteran of the frontier gambling circuit, had a bad night in the Oriental playing faro. It put Storms in a bad mood. He began drinking heavily, and lost enough control to slap around the smallest faro dealer he could find in the saloon. Luke Short was diminutive, but he was also an experienced street fighter and gunman. He stood up to Storms, who was in terrible danger and too drunk to realize it. Bat Masterson, experienced in diffusing tense situations, separated the pair and walked Storms back to the hotel where he was staying. He suggested that Storms turn in. Then Masterson returned to the Oriental, where he reminded Short that Storms was really a decent fellow who, when sober, would have known better than to act the way he did. Short was ready to forget the whole thing. It wasn't the first time he'd been accosted by a sore loser. He and some of the other dealers were outside the saloon taking a break when Storms reappeared waving a gun. Short drew his own pistol, shots were fired, and Storms fell dead with a bullet through his heart. George Parsons noted in his diary that Short seemed "very unconcerned after shooting."

For him, it was simply an unpleasant consequence of his profession. Short was cleared of murder charges and soon left Tombstone, as did Bat Masterson. It wasn't the sort of incident that town leaders could pretend hadn't happened; Clara Brown, herself an established member of the town's swankiest social set, tartly reported to her San Diego readers that it must have "seemed to be about time for another murder."

On March 1, the same day that Brown wrote her report, violence visited the Oriental again. This time a man known as One-Armed Kelly was gunned down by someone named McAllister. Parsons wrote in his diary, "Another man shot this A.M. about four o'clock and will probably die. . . . Oriental a regular slaughter house now. Much bad blood today." Appalled at the reputation his establishment was acquiring, Milton Joyce closed down gambling there, though the bar itself remained open for business. Joyce lost considerable revenue until he reopened the Oriental's gaming operations in October. But Joyce was a comparatively wealthy man who could weather a period of reduced income. His decision was a staggering financial blow to Wyatt Earp.

When he resigned as Charlie Shibell's deputy sheriff in Pima County, Wyatt voluntarily gave up a monthly salary and stipends for delivering warrants. He did this confident that he'd soon have the same job back with Bob Paul, but court appeals stymied his expectations there. Even so, that was insignificant compared to Wyatt's certainty that he'd shortly have a magnificent income as Cochise County sheriff. That didn't happen, either. There were still potential land deals to be made, with Wyatt and his brothers acquiring and selling mining claims, but they were relatively small fry in the Tombstone property mix. After losing the sheriff's job to Johnny Behan, Wyatt had to count on his gambling interests at the Oriental for most of his regular income, and Milton Joyce's decision to shut the saloon's gaming tables down essentially left Wyatt broke. He could and did continue gambling himself, and running games for a percentage of winnings at other saloons, but that meant Wyatt was just one more card-playing hustler and far removed from the grand destiny he still envisioned for himself. Wyatt had been in Tombstone for about fifteen months, and after these political and business setbacks he was no better off than when he had arrived. Given his history of moving on when his dreams went unfulfilled in Lamar and Wichita and Deadwood and Dodge City, Wyatt might have been expected to pack up a wagon again and try his luck somewhere else. But he was committed to Tombstone. On March 19, 1881, Wyatt turned thirty-three. He'd been a frontier itinerant since he left his father's California farm seventeen years earlier, and he'd scuffled enough.

There were, in Tombstone, three ways other than lucking into a significant silver strike for a man of limited means to gain personal power and fortune. The first was to be elected or appointed to a position of considerable public influence and personal income. So far, Wyatt had no luck there. The second was to have a friend or relative in an important position — the territorial legislature, perhaps, or the new Cochise County board of supervisors — who could grant favors. Wyatt had no one like that. The third way was to impress town business and political leaders by denouncing local law enforcement and advocating vigilante justice. Wyatt couldn't go that far. John Clum and some hundred other civic leaders Wyatt wanted badly to impress had formed the Citizens Safety Committee on the night when an angry mob was thwarted as it tried to lynch Johnny Behind-the-Deuce outside Vogan's Bowling Alley. Wyatt had helped save the fugitive from its wrath. But this third option still held potential for Wyatt. Though he couldn't support citizens taking the law into their own hands — he'd been a lawman, wanted to be again, and his brother Virgil was currently a U.S. deputy marshal, after all — even a political primitive like Wyatt

272

sensed an opportunity. Citizens Safety Committee members convinced themselves that they were advocating a moral and cultural crusade rather than primitive vigilantism. George Parsons, one of the leaders, wrote on February 8, 1881, in his journal that "peculiar organizations of a certain character are very necessary at times under certain circumstances for the maintenance of right and paving the way to the highest order of civilization."

Wyatt still wanted to be county sheriff, almost as much for the prestige as for the dazzling income. Every generation of Earp men sought titles or badges, signs that they were leading members of their communities. After years of serving as a constable, policeman, assistant marshal, and deputy sheriff, he was back to being plain Mr. Earp. Wyatt had realized ever since he became Charlie Shibell's deputy sheriff that a certain means of winning the approval of Tombstone's power brokers was to crack down on the cowboys. If Wyatt could make the right people believe that he shared their concern about slack law enforcement, and that Wyatt was capable of ridding the area of the troublesome cowboys, then he would have their wholehearted support — and an excellent chance of unseating Johnny Behan in the November 1882 elections.

Enlisting Curly Bill to help with county tax

collection was just one way during the early months of 1881 in which Johnny Behan gave the anti-cowboy forces in Tombstone something fresh to criticize. What was important to the Citizens Safety Committee, and therefore to Wyatt, was that the new county sheriff was openly consorting with known criminals and, at least in their eyes, doing little or nothing to keep the cowboys under control. The *Epitaph* made Johnny a frequent target of scorn, questioning not only his judgment but his potentially dark motives for aligning himself with lawbreakers. The rival *Nugget,* owned and published by Johnny's undersheriff, Harry Woods, was just as editorially vehement that his critics were misguided, or else deliberately exaggerating to further their own pro-government, anti–individual rights agenda.

The controversy was constant. More from instinct than thoughtful analysis, Wyatt recognized the outraged elitist constituency that could form the core of his support in a campaign against Johnny. What he needed was another cowboy-precipitated incident, a flash point that would give him the opportunity to demonstrate his own hard-hitting law enforcement skills and Johnny's lack of them. Sooner or later, the cowboys could be counted on to do something outrageous enough to arouse all law-abiding Cochise County citizens.

It turned out to be sooner.

Chapter Nine:
The Benson Stage Robbery

No one would have blamed Bob Paul for being in a terrible mood on the evening of March 15, 1881. He should have been spending the cold night indoors, perhaps counting tax dollars he'd collected that day as sheriff of Pima County and calculating his 10 percent take. It was almost four months since John Ringo and the other cowboys tried to steal the election for incumbent Charlie Shibell, and six weeks since a county judge overturned the tainted results and declared Paul to be the winner. It was over and everybody knew it, but Shibell challenged the verdict in the Arizona Territorial Supreme Court. He remained in office while his obviously futile appeal was pending; every day cost his erstwhile opponent a considerable fortune, which Shibell could keep for himself so long as he still served as sheriff. Bob Paul was reduced to riding shotgun on stages for Wells Fargo for $125 a month while awaiting permission to assume the lofty office and income he'd won fair and square back on November 2. (The court would deny Shibell's appeal and Paul would be finally sworn in as Pima County sheriff at the end of April.)

On March 15, Paul worked the thirty-mile Tombstone-to-Benson route. Being jolted around on the hard open bench of a stagecoach was unpleasant in the finest weather, but it had snowed lightly during the day. Now in late afternoon the wind was biting cold, and stops along the way to pick up passengers in Watervale and Contention City meant that the frigid trip stretched out longer. Paul's job was to stay alert for robbers. The stage carried one of Wells Fargo's famous "treasure boxes," a twenty-inch-by-twelve-inch-by-ten-inch wood and iron container painted a dull green. Locked inside was about $26,000 in coins and bills. Cash money was vital to commerce in the territories. Only the very rich had checking accounts in banks. Everybody else needed cash for their transactions.

Guarding a treasure box was wearying anytime, and particularly traveling from Tombstone to Benson. The route was rugged, with plenty of deep draws that required the driver to skid the stage down one side and painstakingly inch it up the other. Sometimes — hopefully not on this wintry night — not just the shotgun guard but the passengers had to climb down and help drag the stage uphill. Everybody knew that stage robbers usually struck when their wheeled target was slowed on particularly steep slopes. Because of their frequency on this trip, Paul couldn't relax for a minute.

A half-dozen passengers were onboard when the stage left Tombstone, and two more got on in Watervale. Because there was only room for one inside the carriage, Peter Roerig had to squat on top behind Paul and Bud Philpot, the driver. Additional cargo was taken on at Contention City, but no other riders. During the Contention City stop, Paul's bad night got worse. Philpot complained of stomach cramps. He switched places on the bench with Paul, who now had to drive the stage's six-horse team in addition to guarding against bandits.

From Contention City it was two more roller-coaster miles to Drew's Station, a rest stop where passengers could stretch their legs while stage line employees switched teams of horses. It was about 10 P.M. when the stage bound for Benson approached. Up on its bench, buffeted by the icy wind, uncomfortably aware that at any moment the man sitting next to him might involuntarily explode with vomiting or diarrhea, trying to control horses and function as a guard at the same time, Bob Paul was ready for a break. Perhaps he was looking forward to the comfort of a hot cup of coffee while the horse teams were switched out, but he never got it. As Paul slowed the stage on the approach to yet another draw's incline just a few hundred yards before Drew's Station, a masked man stepped out into the road and shouted, "Hold!"

Bob Paul was an experienced lawman who'd cut his fighting teeth back in California's riotous Calaveras County. With his stage at a near-standstill he shouted back, "I hold for no man," and then other armed, masked bandits rushed forward out of the darkness. They shot at the stage and Paul returned fire. It was too dark to tell whether the pellets from Paul's shotgun hit their intended targets but Bud Philpot, sitting next to Paul on the driver's bench, was shot through the heart and tumbled onto the ground. Peter Roerig, seated behind Paul, was also hit. Paul grabbed wildly at the flopping reins and whipped the horses into a sweaty burst. The stage lurched up the draw and sped forward past the rest stop. Men at Drew's Station heard the shots and rushed out to investigate while Paul raced straight on to Benson. They found Philpot lying dead by the side of the road and saw several mounted men, presumably the bandits, riding away. A search of the spot turned up three masks made of braided rope and more than a dozen used cartridge cases. Whoever the robbers were, they did not intend to be recognized, and they were prepared to shoot when they set up their ambush.

A rider from Drew's Station galloped to Contention City and informed Arthur Cowen, the Wells Fargo agent there, about the incident. Cowen had to ride to Tombstone to deliver the news, since Contention City had no telegraph service to the new county seat. Bob Paul completed his manic drive to Benson around 11 P.M. and immediately telegraphed Wells Fargo agent Marshall Williams in Tombstone. Williams got Paul's telegram just before Cowen arrived from Contention City. In Benson, Peter Roerig was discovered to be mortally wounded. The Wells Fargo treasure box was delivered intact, but the attempted robbery claimed two lives. Back in Tombstone, lawmen and citizens alike were galvanized into furious action. "Men and horses were flying about in different directions," George Parsons wrote.

There had been stage robberies in the area before, but never any like this one. Typically, bandits waylayed stages at points where they slowed along the road and then stripped passengers of wallets and jewelry — mostly penny-ante stuff that amounted to takes of a few hundred dollars at best. The indignity of being held up was often worse than the losses suffered — outside Cheyenne in 1876, even Doc Holliday was relieved of his watch by a smirking highwayman. In 1879, not long before the Earps arrived in Tombstone, acting territorial governor John Gosper issued a proclamation authorizing payment of $500 "to anyone who shall kill a highway robber while in the act of robbing the stage, and $300 for arrest and conviction." Gosper's chief concern wasn't protecting the valuables of stage passengers. Stages carried U.S. mail, including letters of credit between banks and investors. If the delivery of mail was constantly disrupted, the territory's economy would suffer. Investigating mail-related robberies — federal crime by legal definition — was the responsibility of U.S. marshals and their deputies. County sheriffs and town marshals weren't required to get involved.

The first stage robbery near Tombstone occurred in mid-September 1879. Two masked men stole watches and about $100 in cash from passengers, but didn't touch the mail being hauled. There were occasional stage holdups afterward with no deaths or injuries involved. Just three weeks before Bob Paul was attacked outside Drew's Station, there was a stage robbery three and a half miles outside Contention City. George Parsons noted in his journal that there was "only $135 in W F & Co's box, it being [an] off night. Passengers undisturbed." This was, in a sense, an unspoken rule: Stages might be robbed, but drivers and passengers wouldn't be harmed. The thieves outside Drew's Station killed two men. Drunken arguments and ill-tempered fistfights sometimes escalated into killing, but wanton, cold-blooded murder was rare in Cochise County and its surrounding environs. The Benson stage bloodshed was further proof to Tombstone's Citizens Safety Committee that violent crime was rampant. According to Parsons, on the night of the Benson stage robbery armed Safety Committee members led by Mayor Clum took it upon themselves to follow "several desperate characters in town, one known as an ex-stage robber." Much to their disappointment, none of their quarry committed overt illegal acts allowing them to be shot. "Couldn't fix anything," Parsons grumbled.

Lawmen in Tombstone had no time to rein in would-be vigilantes. They were too busy organizing a posse to pursue the bandits. Johnny Behan was in charge. As county sheriff, he was responsible for tracking suspects in murders committed outside city limits in Cochise County. But as a U.S. deputy marshal, Virgil Earp had to be involved too because there were mail sacks on the stagecoach. That made the attempted robbery a federal crime. Johnny told several of his deputies to saddle up — there's no record of which ones he included. Virgil deputized Wyatt and Morgan; he had the authority to do so, and it was natural for him to want his brothers along on such a potentially hazardous manhunt. Bat Masterson was still in town, and the Earps were pleased to invite another experienced lawman along. Marshall Williams, Wells Fargo's agent in Tombstone, also came. The hybrid posse galloped out of town, racing back to Drew's Station to pick up the trail of the brigands there. At some point Bob Paul joined them. Bat Masterson returned to Tombstone early in the chase when his horse gave out.

The fugitives were difficult to track. They knew they'd be pursued, and were canny enough to ride single file whenever possible, guiding their mounts over rocky ground to avoid leaving hoofprints. The few signs the posse could detect indicated their quarry was heading east toward the Dragoon Mountains. Then they apparently swung back toward the San Pedro Valley. An exhausted horse was found abandoned at a small ranch, but his rider, certainly one of the bandits, was nowhere to be found. For three days the men from Tombstone kept on until they lost the trail completely. To find the killers now, they'd have to get lucky, and they did.

Following the San Pedro River as they hoped the fugitives had, about thirty-five miles north of Benson the posse came to a ranch owned by Leonard and Hank Redfield. Like most small ranchers in the area, the Redfields were suspected of occasional collusion with the cowboys. It seemed likely that, if they'd come in that direction, the Benson stage robbers would have stopped at the Redfield ranch, certainly to eat and rest and, perhaps, get fresh horses. As they rode up, the posse spotted someone milking a cow — in itself nothing remarkable, but the man had two guns strapped to his waist and a rifle lying close to hand. He was taken prisoner and interrogated. Wyatt was in charge of the procedure, and whatever coercion he used was effective. The man sang like a proverbial canary. He identified himself as Luther King, and admitted he'd been part of the attempted robbery. The abandoned horse the posse found earlier was his. But King insisted that he hadn't fired any of the shots that killed Bud Philpot and Peter Roerig. Instead, he'd been standing off the road holding the reins of all the horses while Billy Leonard, Jim Crane, and Harry Head donned masks and attacked the stage. King, Leonard, Crane, and Head were all familiar names to the posse — they were part of the cowboy contingent. Just a few months earlier, King and Leonard had been members of the gang that killed Curly Bill Brocius's pal Bob Martin in New Mexico. Now they were marauding in southeast Arizona.

King helpfully told Wyatt that his three confederates in the Benson holdup were making for the boot heel of New Mexico and its warren of cowboy hideouts. If they reached there it would be almost impossible to find them. Johnny Behan took custody of King. The Redfield brothers hovered nearby, and Wyatt warned Johnny not to let either of them talk to the prisoner. He suspected that King would ask them to catch up to Leonard, Crane, and Head and alert them that the posse was hot on their trail and now knew their names. But Johnny allowed the Redfields and King to chat anyway; he may have wanted to demonstrate that Wyatt Earp couldn't tell him what to do. Hank Redfield then rode off. The Earps were certain he was on his way to reach Leonard, Crane, and Head before the posse did. There was little time to lose.

Johnny and his deputies returned to Tombstone with King, while the others continued after the three remaining fugitives. For Johnny, showing up with one of the culprits would be a public relations bonanza — the new county sheriff back from the manhunt with a prisoner. Marshall Williams went with him, anxious to notify Wells Fargo by telegram about how the pursuit had progressed so far. They arrived in Tombstone on March 21, six days after the attempted robbery and murders. King was placed in the county jail. The next day, Johnny set out again, accompanied by Billy Breakenridge and Frank Leslie. The three rejoined the Earps and Bob

Paul and followed the stage robbers into New Mexico before losing their trail. Worn out, with several members on foot because their horses were too exhausted to carry them, the posse straggled back to Tombstone comforted by the thought that at least one confessed perpetrator was in custody there.

Except he wasn't. When he departed on March 22, Johnny left new undersheriff Harry Woods in charge. Woods's main duty was guarding Luther King. Apparently he was a lenient jailor who didn't bother with minor details such as locking cell doors. On the night of March 28, with his boss and the rest of the posse still absent, Woods stepped outside the jail to talk to attorney Harry Jones. Jones was brokering the sale of King's horse to liveryman John Dunbar, Johnny Behan's business partner. While Woods was distracted, King walked out a back door, mounted a horse someone had waiting there for him, and fled from Tombstone and from history. Though there has been considerable speculation about what happened to King afterward, there is no definitive record.

King's escape was the result of either a monumental lapse in judgment or collusion. The anti-cowboy forces immediately assumed the latter. Parsons, ever their spokesperson in the pages of his journal, wrote that "King, the stage robber, escaped tonight early from H. Woods, who had been previously notified of an attempt at release to be made. Some of our officials should be hanged. They're a bad lot."

Johnny Behan, a master of political spin, couldn't disguise King's escape as anything other than a public relations disaster. His best hope was to deflect public suspicion toward someone else, and the Earp faction included an obvious target. Whether Johnny was personally responsible, Tombstone almost immediately buzzed with a new rumor: Doc Holliday was one of the bandits who ambushed the Benson stage and killed Bud Philpot and Peter Roerig. Maybe the Earps were in on it, too.

On March 15, the day of the stage robbery, Doc Holliday had rented a horse from Dunbar's livery in Tombstone and ridden off. Late that night he returned to town, saying he'd planned to join a poker game in Charleston but it had broken up by the time he'd arrived. His rented horse seemed worn out from hard riding. Doc spent the remaining hours until dawn running a faro game at Tombstone's Alhambra Saloon. That left a significant stretch of the night, including the hours of the attempted stage holdup, where Doc's whereabouts could not be confirmed.

In itself, that meant very little. Even if he hadn't gone to Charleston, Doc could have ridden to any of several nearby towns to gamble or drink or dally with a prostitute. The lack of witnesses to corroborate his presence somewhere other than with the bandits outside Drew's Station wasn't especially incriminating. Men focusing on cards, liquor, or women often took little notice of who was or wasn't in the same saloon or whorehouse with them. But it was well known that, back in Las Vegas, New Mexico, Doc Holliday had been friends with Billy Leonard, one of the three alleged killers of Philpot and Roerig. Supposedly Leonard supplemented his gambling income in Las Vegas and, later, in Arizona Territory, by fencing stolen jewelry. Even if true, it wouldn't have mattered to Doc, who chose his few friends without regard to public opinion.

Public opinion kicked in hard against him now. As early as March 21 everyone in Tombstone knew that Billy Leonard, Jimmy Crane, and Harry Head had been identified by Luther King as the men who'd murdered Philpot and Roerig. Marshall Williams told George Parsons, who undoubtedly spread the word to all his Safety Committee friends. After King's escape, the *Nugget* declared that "It was a well-planned job by outsiders to get him away. He was an important witness against Holliday" — this despite the fact that King had only implicated Leonard, Crane, and Head. But the possibility that Doc was part of the gang didn't seem far-fetched.

Given his past eccentric, violent actions, Doc was apparently capable of anything, including criminal acts. The only possible catch was his loyalty to avowed law-and-order disciple Wyatt Earp, and that connection lent itself to the next wave of gossip. Perhaps Doc participated in the ambush because the Earps told him to. Twenty-six thousand dollars was a substantial sum of money, and thanks to their Wells Fargo connections — Morgan currently served as a company guard, and Wyatt had in the past — the Earps could have known ahead of time the amount being transported on the Benson stage that night. Gossip spread that, possibly with the assistance of Marshall Williams, they removed the money from the Wells Fargo treasure box even before the stage left Tombstone. The ambush outside Drew's Station was a feint. Leonard, Crane, Head, King, and perhaps Holliday were supposed to ride off with the box so no one could take possession of it in Benson and discover that it was empty. Writing many years later, cowboy sympathizer John Plesent Gray claimed that Crane told him all about a failed Earp plot with a slightly different twist:

Jim Crane said the whole thing had been planned by the Earps. Morgan Earp was to go out that night as messenger [shotgun guard], and he had given the tip that about twenty thousand dollars was in the Wells

Fargo strongbox. The holdup would have met with no resistance and it looked like easy money. But Bob Paul stepped in as messenger . . . and simply ran away from the robbers.

The rumors and Gray's subsequent claim were ludicrous — after escaping the fatal attack, Bob Paul delivered the treasure box that night with all $26,000 intact, and there was never any indication that Paul replaced Morgan as shotgun guard at the last minute. Wyatt was betting his political future on getting rid of the cowboys, not collaborating with them. Twenty-six thousand dollars was a small fortune, but it paled beside the annual income Wyatt could anticipate as county sheriff. Still, it was juicy conjecture and many people chose to believe some form of it, especially the small ranchers outside Tombstone city limits who were friends with the cowboys and disliked Wyatt anyway. John Clum, trying to whitewash certain Tombstone events in a memoir written decades later, recalled that "Doc announced he would make a sieve out of the next low-down blankety-blank who repeated the gossip. Things quieted down — tale-bearing became a lost art." In fact, the tale bearing intensified in the months ahead.

So did open demonstrations of the bad feelings between Wyatt and Johnny. Previously,

Johnny probably did not like Wyatt but hadn't considered him a rival of any consequence — he easily outmaneuvered him to be appointed county sheriff. It was hardly Johnny's concern if the fellow didn't understand how politics worked. Johnny might have felt relieved when it became clear Wyatt was positioning himself to run against him in the November 1882 election. That would spare Johnny having to face off against a savvier Republican opponent, perhaps John Clum or George Parsons. But Wyatt's role in Luther King's arrest and the political hay he could make from King's escape forced Johnny to reevaluate the situation. He had to feel heartened by the rumors of the Earps' involvement with the Benson stage robbery, probably helping to spread them himself, and he soon took another opportunity to thwart Wyatt. Back home after losing the trail of Leonard, Head, and Crane in New Mexico, Johnny billed Cochise County for about $800 in posse expenses. Besides costs for renting horses and buying supplies, men selected to serve by the sheriff were routinely paid stipends, even if they were already on the county payroll as deputies. Johnny parceled out the money to his own employees, but didn't share a cent with the Earps on the questionable grounds that he had not deputized them. It was U.S. deputy marshal Virgil Earp who invited his brothers along — let the federal government reimburse them for their time and trouble. It was an uncharacteristically mean-spirited gesture on Johnny's part. King's escape and the subsequent political fallout had shaken him badly.

Virgil was particularly annoyed, probably realizing that governmental red tape would delay any posse payment to Wyatt and Morgan for months. The Earp brothers, without a single full-time job between them except James with his "pouring house," were in immediate need of the money. But in the matter of their posse service, a financial happy ending was provided from another source. Virgil said later that "we did not get a cent until Wells Fargo found it out and paid us for our time." Company records show that for "Search of robbers" following the Benson stage incident, V. Earp was paid $32, with WY. Earp and M. Earp each receiving $72. Virgil probably got less because as a U.S. deputy marshal he was already on the government payroll. As a Wells Fargo employee Bob Paul got nothing extra, and since his participation in the posse precluded regular service as a shotgun messenger, his stipend for the entire month of March was just $47. In all ways but one, Wells Fargo was frugal regarding expenditures. But the area in which it was always prepared to dispense generous amounts made certain that the Benson stage robbery wasn't forgotten in Tombstone, and made Wells Fargo a key player in events leading to the famous confrontation there seven months later.

Reputation meant everything to Wells Fargo. The company was founded as a small independent freight business in 1844 by Henry Wells and William G. Fargo, and gradually grew into a dominant giant. It began making overland stage deliveries in 1866, and selling passenger tickets two years later. But passengers provided incidental income. Wells Fargo made most of its money transporting valuable cargo — coins, bills, occasionally jewels and bullion. Despite the presence of desperadoes on the frontier, Wells Fargo customers could feel certain that they would never lose a cent to robbery — not because holdups never occurred or succeeded, but because Wells Fargo self-insured every shipment. If thieves escaped with a client's property, the company reimbursed the customer in full, even if the amount was tens of thousands of dollars. Then Wells Fargo devoted its considerable resources to getting the stolen valuables back, or at least ensuring that the bandits were caught and punished. This was a powerful deterrent to would-be thieves.

Wells Fargo employed a few full-time "special officers" to investigate robberies and, if necessary, coordinate pursuit of the perpetrators. Generally, hands-on authority was left to the local town agent. Special officers only became involved if a situation was so critical that it required corporate control. The company would authorize a generous reward for the capture of the thieves, usually between $200 and $750 depending on the amount stolen from the stage. In an era when rewards paid by the government rarely exceeded $50, law officers were anxious to earn the munificent sums offered by Wells Fargo. The company often preferred that the lawmen not let the general public become aware of how much money was being offered. Trigger-happy civilians blasting away indiscriminately in the hope of earning hundreds of dollars and, perhaps, getting themselves shot up in the process, was not the kind of publicity Wells Fargo wanted under any circumstances.

Following the Benson holdup attempt, Wells Fargo sent special officer James B. Hume to Tombstone to confer with Marshall Williams, its agent there. It was an indication that the company took this holdup attempt seriously. No cargo had been taken, but the driver and a passenger had died. Hume's task was to consult with Williams and Bob Paul, the Wells Fargo employees who were on the scene, and then determine the amount of rewards necessary to keep local lawmen on the hunt for Leonard, Head, and Crane until they were apprehended. Because the crime was so heinous, Hume authorized rewards of $1,200 for each of the three killers. The amount was so astounding that instructions to Bob Paul for alerting local lawmen to the prospective bounty included the admonition, "Don't post, but place in the hands of discreet and reliable persons only." A total pot of $3,600 guaranteed the attention and co-operation of every law officer in Arizona and New Mexico territories. Hume was free to leave Tombstone and look after Wells Fargo business elsewhere, secure in the knowledge that someone would find the rewards irresistible and track the three Cochise County fugitives down. So long as additional civilian lives weren't at risk in the process, Wells Fargo really didn't care who or how.

In the wake of the murders outside of Drew's Station, and in keeping with the town's lofty status as county seat, Mayor Clum and the Tombstone city council met to pass or revise several ordinances. One was cosmetic: Henceforth, the title of the town's head of law enforcement would be chief of police rather than marshal. It sounded more appropriate for such a self-important, sophisticated municipality that was determined never to be mistaken for a rustic frontier shantytown. The chief's new job description, though, was specific and substantial: He would "prevent the breach of peace, suppress riots and disorderly assemblages, arrest and take to the city jail every person found violating any law or ordinance, or any person found committing acts injurious to the quiet and good order of the city." Tombstone policemen must arrest anyone found "brawling, quarreling, using profane or indecent language" and those "found in such a state of intoxication as to violate public decency and all persons . . . found engaged in any disorderly act." Town officers could no longer exercise personal discretion in the performance of their duties. Tombstone was going to be a strict law-and-order city, just the way the Citizens Safety Committee wanted it.

Clum and his allies believed a revamped rule adopted on April 19 concerning weapons would particularly tamp down the potential for violence:

It is hereby declared to be unlawful to carry in the hand or upon the person, or otherwise, any deadly weapon within the limits of said City of Tombstone, without first obtaining a permit in writing for such purpose (and upon good cause shown by affidavit) from the presiding officer, or the Board of Police Commissioners.

Banned weapons included knives as well as every type of firearm. It sounded comprehensive, but closer examination revealed loopholes. Permits could be and were routinely issued, and recipients were often the same heavy-drinking gamblers who engaged in many of the shootouts the council wanted to prevent. Doc Holliday certainly had a permit. People arriving in Tombstone could lug their arsenals along to whatever might be their "primary destinations" — hotels, shops, saloons. They'd check the weapons there. They were also permitted to carry their weapons while leaving town, no matter how extended those departures might be.

The attempted stage robbery, the murders of Philpot and Roerig, the jail break of Luther King, the failed hunt for Leonard, Head, and Crane, the eye-popping Wells Fargo rewards for their capture, the Tombstone council's new edicts regarding arrests and carrying guns: None of these was solely responsible for the confrontation to come, but each was critical. Dominoes kept tumbling.

Chapter Ten:
Plans Go Awry

No matter how hard civic leaders tried, there were certain aspects of life in Tombstone that couldn't be controlled. Progress wasn't inevitable or eternal. The average lifespan of frontier boomtowns was three years, and in 1881 Tombstone had been in existence for two. About the same time that Mayor Clum and the council met to revise gun laws, there was an unexpected local development. As miners in and around Tombstone continued gouging deeper into the earth, water began to seep into underground shafts at about five hundred feet beneath the surface. Tombstone's water supply had always been limited, so public response was ecstatic. Much of the new water wasn't potable, but there was a welcome use for it all the same. Mayor Clum ordered buckets of the precious liquid to be hauled up from the shafts and sprinkled on a regular basis over the town's dirt streets, which somewhat reduced the swirling dust that constantly plagued residents and visitors. Clum and other leaders were so obsessed with the cowboys that they completely missed what the mine water represented — the first real sign that Tombstone's glory days were numbered.

If nobody yet realized that water seepage in deep mine shafts would eventually become a critical problem, there were other indications that the town might be heading for trouble that didn't go unnoticed. The most obvious was that there were no important new silver strikes. Led by Ed Schieffelin, the early prospectors had apparently accounted for the major lodes. There were still occasional "finds," bits of mineral vein that suggested there might be more to be discovered. That kept a constant stream of hopefuls out in the hills around town, clacking away at rock faces with picks and shovels. The mines in operation were thriving, extracting impressive amounts of ore. But even the most massive lodes had limits. If no significant new discoveries were made, Tombstone's silver riches would eventually dwindle, then disappear. So would the town.

Civic and economic competition was also a growing concern. In terms of mining and its related industries, Tombstone was no longer the only hot spot in the sprawling San Pedro Valley. Thirty miles to the southeast, adjacent to the Mexican border, came a series of mineral strikes — mostly copper, and some silver and gold. The copper lodes were enormous, and in 1880 the town of Bisbee was founded. Built up and down the sides of precipitous slopes in the heart of the Mule Mountains, Bisbee looked as spectacular as its surroundings. Wells Fargo soon extended its shipping services there. Major investors now had a plausible alternative to Tombstone. Bisbee didn't rival Tombstone for business or political primacy yet — but at some point it clearly might. Tombstone's best defense was to continue to upgrade its own attractions to outside business interests. Maintaining an image of upscale sophistication was crucial. By the early months of 1881, Tombstone's streets were illuminated by gas lamps. High-end clothing stores did booming business — demand by monied residents for the latest fashions worn in New York and San Francisco was insatiable. To a great extent, town leaders could at least ensure how Tombstone *looked.*

But they couldn't dictate the weather, and in the spring of 1881 it turned against them. Anyone coming to southeast Arizona accepted the inevitability of summertime heat, but in 1881 the broiling temperatures didn't wait until summer to arrive. By late April George Parsons noted in his journal that "hot weather seems to have set in. Sun powerful. Don't care to do much in daytime." Everyone grew irritable in the heat and there was no respite from it, no cooling rain showers or even clouds to temporarily block the sun. Even the wind sizzled. There was the mounting sensation that at any moment Tombstone might combust, and on June 22 it did.

Sometime during that stifling afternoon the owners of Alexander and Thompson's Arcade Saloon discovered that a newly purchased barrel of whiskey was undrinkable, a remarkable conclusion by frontier standards. They began the process of returning the whiskey to the manufacturer by rolling the barrel out into the street. There they prepared to measure how much was left — the barrel's bunghole was popped open so a gauge rod could be stuck down inside. One of the men paused to light a stogie. A spark flew through the bunghole and the resulting explosion splashed burning alcohol in every direction. The wooden walls of Tombstone's downtown business and saloon districts were already blistered dry from the heat. Within seconds four square blocks were in flames.

Mayor John Clum was away on a trip to the East. One of the purposes of his trip was to acquire a fire engine for Tombstone. Meanwhile, the town was unprepared to battle a blaze of such magnitude. In a dispatch to the *San Diego Daily Union,* Clara Brown described the chaotic scene:

A fire under any circumstances is serious

enough, but particularly fearful to contemplate when there is almost nothing to fight it with. People did the best they could, pulling down buildings and wetting others in an attempt to confine the limits of the conflagration. . . . From Fifth to Seventh and from Fremont through to Tough Nut Streets, nearly everything was swept away.

Somehow, there were no fatalities, but an estimated sixty-six of Tombstone's prime businesses and saloons were reduced to smoldering ruins. As night fell, what already seemed like an unmitigated disaster became worse. Lot jumpers, drifters probably hired by the Townsite Company, moved in to take possession of ravaged disputed property. In many instances they set up small round tents on the lots and lounged inside, daring anyone to make them leave. Under the tragic circumstances it was an especially heinous act. Outraged occupants, driven out by flames only hours earlier, demanded immediate official response. Anarchy loomed; order in Tombstone hung in the balance. Town leaders called on their chief of police to step in, and the man they suddenly depended on so desperately wasn't Ben Sippy.

Ben Sippy's brief tenure as Tombstone town marshal, then chief of police, was not distinguished. Elected in November 1880, by January 1881 he already had been reprimanded by the city council for being absent without leave. In May he was called on the council carpet again for "action in regard to releasing certain prisoners." Though he received kudos for helping protect Johnny Behind-the-Deuce and diffusing a lot jumping controversy in December 1880, by late spring it was clear to Clum and the council that Ben Sippy wasn't the tough-minded officer they wanted enforcing the law in Tombstone. On June 6, Sippy requested and was granted a two-week leave of absence. He barely passed beyond town limits when both the *Epitaph* and *Nugget* began reporting that he fled to avoid angry creditors. One man to whom Sippy owed money displayed a framed picture of the departed police chief, with the caption "Though lost to sight, to memory dear. Two hundred dollars worth." In mid-June the council concluded Sippy was gone for good and appointed Virgil Earp as a temporary replacement.

To Wyatt Earp, working as a lawman was a means to other ends. Being an officer meant more than that to Virgil. Losing to Ben Sippy in the November 1880 special election for Tombstone town marshal hurt him deeply. Virgil had won his only previous race for public office two years before that, when Prescott voters chose him as constable. Virgil, with his credentials as a U.S. deputy marshal and all-around good fellow, had expected to win easily in Tombstone, and he hadn't. Now, in the aftermath of the fire, there was opportunity for redemption.

Before he took any action against the lot jumpers, Virgil consulted with members of the council and the Safety Committee. Pleased by the deference he displayed, they instructed the acting chief of police to use his own judgment. Virgil immediately formed a posse comprised of town policemen and several carefully selected volunteers, including his brothers and gambler–Wells Fargo informant Fred Dodge. They visited all the lots in dispute, informing jumpers there that the property was being immediately restored to whoever had possession of it before the fire. The courts would decide who owned what, and meanwhile the jumpers were ordered to leave. The first few Virgil spoke to retreated to their tents and refused to vacate the premises. At Virgil's command, the posse roped the tent poles and yanked the canvases off the lots. The jumpers were left with the choice of leaving on their own or with the help of Virgil and his men. Grumbling, they walked or rode away.

It was Virgil Earp's finest hour. Six days after the fire, the council appointed him to be permanent chief of police with a monthly salary of $150 and 5 percent of all the city taxes that he collected. While not as munificent as the county sheriff's income yearned for by Wyatt, this provided a comfortable living for Virgil and his wife, Allie. Virgil had the job he wanted, and though he didn't give up his part-time position as a U.S. deputy marshal, he devoted most of his attention to the kind of by-the-books town law enforcement that the council and Safety Committee expected. Virgil began by hiring eight police officers, none of them his brothers. Under Virgil's command, they made forty-eight arrests during June and sixty in July. Most were for being drunk and disorderly, but two were for carrying concealed weapons, three for committing a nuisance, one for discharging firearms, and one for fast riding. The council wanted even the most minor transgressions punished with arrests and fines. Virgil wanted to keep his job, and he obliged them.

By August everyone in town had gotten the message, and Tombstone policemen made only twenty-two arrests during the entire month. This enabled Virgil to suggest to Mayor Clum and the council that, with the town finally under control, the police force could be reduced to himself and two officers, James Flynn and A. G. Bronk — law and order and budget cuts, too. They enthusiastically accepted his proposal. If any major problem arose, Virgil was allowed to temporarily appoint special deputies until the crisis was past. The *Epitaph* declared that "Mr.

Sippy, late chief of police, did the public of Tombstone one very great service when he asked for [a] leave of absence." The council and Safety Committee could not have been happier with their current chief of police, or with the way the entire town rebounded from the June 22 fire. Within a month, half of the destroyed business district was rebuilt, demonstrating Tombstone's can-do attitude to potential investors. Now if only something equally impressive could be done about the cowboys, who clearly had no intention of going away.

In their regular hangouts of Galeyville and San Simon, the cowboys couldn't mistake the organized antipathy growing toward them. The governor wanted tougher laws and a Texas Rangers–like territorial force to drive out lawless elements. Tombstone had its Citizens Safety Committee. South of the border, the Mexican government issued official protests about gringo rustlers and raiders, and was rumored to be gearing up to enforce border security if American authorities didn't. The cowboys still did not think of themselves as criminals. They had rowdy fun north of the border, and taking Mexican cattle was pleasant business rather than theft because Mexicans had no rights. Stage robberies were an aberration perpetrated by individuals rather than through collective

306

planning. Governor Frémont, Acting Governor Gosper, Tombstone mayor Clum, and other outraged officials thought of the cowboys as a guerrilla force, one with scheming leaders issuing orders that vagabond minions obediently carried out. In fact, there was no organization among the cowboys. They recognized each other as reasonably like-minded peers. Friendships and alliances were fluid. There were no permanent units. Authorities argued about how many cowboys lurked in Cochise County. Gosper estimated there were about one hundred. A U.S. deputy marshal swore the number was closer to four hundred. Johnny Behan, whose best interests were served by claiming a minimum, insisted there were no more than fifteen to twenty-five. In fact no one knew for certain, including the cowboys.

During the summer of 1881, the cowboys were more entrenched in Cochise County and the southwest boot heel of New Mexico than ever. They didn't spend all their time rustling and terrorizing small towns. Many bought land, trying to establish themselves as small ranchers similar to business partners like the Clantons and McLaurys. Thanks to Johnny Behan's pragmatic recruitment of Curly Bill as a collector, many of the rustlers even paid taxes. The frontier had shrunk dramatically. Unless they wanted to try their luck full-time south of the border, the cowboys really had no other place left to go. So they stayed where they were and kept on doing the things they did, while the Safety Committee in Tombstone yearned for their extinction and denigrated Johnny Behan for befriending rather than opposing them.

Curly Bill's tax collecting was only one bone in the committee's collective throat. The cowboys who'd tried to rob the Benson stage and killed two men in the process were still at large, including the one who'd walked right out of the county jail. This was an issue that wouldn't go away. Its fallout tainted Johnny's chances to remain in his lucrative job. He was uncomfortably aware that rich, politically influential men in Tombstone were planning to put him out of office in the November 1882 elections because they felt certain that he turned a blind eye to cowboy depredations. It was what they had come to believe and they were unlikely to change their minds. If Johnny did attempt to win them over by somehow cracking down on the cowboys, he would alienate what had become almost by default his base constituency in Cochise County — the small ranchers and settlers outside Tombstone who did shady business with the cowboys, and who resented government and pushy big business just as much as the cowboys did. What Johnny desperately needed by mid-1881 was a means of resolving at least part of the Benson stage robbery case that would impress the Safety Committee with his commitment to law and order yet didn't jeopardize the cooperative relationship he'd forged with the cowboys. A scenario delivering those incompatible benefits seemed impossible — and then, there it was.

In early July 1881, Kate Elder made the latest of several trips from Globe to Tombstone to visit Doc Holliday. Doc and Kate had been living apart for over a year, but she hadn't given up trying to convince him to leave Tombstone. On this visit like every other, she pressed him on the subject. Kate had her boardinghouse in Globe, but if life there with her was too humdrum for Doc she would gladly relocate anywhere so long as it was far away from Wyatt Earp. On July 4 or 5 Kate repeated the suggestion once too often and Doc, never the most patient of men, reacted sharply. He certainly belittled her, using the biting tone and colorful vocabulary that made him such a master of insults. Doc may even have hit her. Whatever happened between them, Kate retreated to a saloon where she drank and talked about secrets Doc supposedly revealed to her. Johnny Behan still had friends in town. Someone alerted him to Kate's slurred tales. Johnny recognized heaven-sent opportunity and immediately acted on it. Under the headline *"Important Arrest,"* the pro-cowboy *Nugget* offered a gleeful report on July 6:

A warrant was sworn out yesterday before Judge Spicer for the arrest of Doc Holliday, a well-known character here, charging him with complicity in the murder of Bud Philpot, and the attempted stage robbery near Contention some months ago, and he was arrested by Sheriff Behan. The warrant was issued upon the affidavit of Kate Elder, with whom Holliday had been living for some time past.

Johnny couldn't have crafted a more perfect scenario. Doc Holliday's girlfriend swore that he'd been part of the Benson stage robbery gang. By arresting Doc, Johnny acted swiftly in the cause of justice — let the *Epitaph* and the Safety Committee try to find fault with that. But Doc wasn't a cowboy or in any way affiliated with them, so the cowboys couldn't feel Johnny was persecuting one of their own. Perhaps best of all, everybody knew Doc Holliday and Wyatt Earp were close friends. This would rekindle rumors that the Earps might have been part of the Benson stage attack, too. Wyatt would have a tough time running against Johnny as a strict law-and-order candidate if his best pal was found guilty of participating in the murders of Bud Philpot and Peter Roerig. All Johnny needed was for Doc to be convicted before fall 1882 when the campaign for Cochise County sheriff would begin. Johnny must have felt euphoric by the time he turned in on July 6.

The next day it began falling apart. Kate got drunk again and was arrested by a town policeman. After being fined $12.50, she still didn't leave Tombstone. Instead, she was back in court on July 8, charged with "making threats against life." It's not certain who it was she threatened. This time Kate was jailed. She hired Wells Spicer, the U.S. commissioner who presided over Doc's hearing, to represent her, and Spicer was able to have her released on appeal. Eventually the charge against her was dismissed, but Kate's testimony implicating Doc was tainted by her subsequent actions.

The charges against Doc based on Kate's affidavit were investigated by county district attorney Lyttleton Price, whose subsequent report to Spicer concluded that "there [is] not the slightest evidence to show the guilt of the defendant." Price suggested that the charges against Doc be withdrawn, and Spicer complied. Instead of a political coup, Johnny had another embarrassing mess on his record. Even the usually supportive *Nugget* was forced to conclude, "Thus ended what at the time was supposed to be an important case. . . . Such is the result of a warrant sworn out by an enraged and intoxicated woman." Amazingly, Doc forgave Kate before she returned to Globe. She had undoubtedly forgiven him for horrible transgres-

311

sions in the past, and now it was his turn. Whether their relationship was based on love or convenience or some combination of the two, it survived a while longer — which sometime late that summer or in early fall couldn't be said of the romance between Johnny Behan and Josephine Marcus. Unlike Kate Elder, when Josephine set out to get even with a man she knew how to do it right.

More than half a century later, Josephine confounded two young women helping her to concoct a sanitized memoir by refusing to disclose much of what happened to her in Tombstone. There was apparently just too much misbehavior to neatly cover up, so she didn't try. The last reminiscence she offered before obstinately skipping ahead to her post-Tombstone experiences was how, finally, she got fed up with Johnny's shenanigans. According to Josephine, the last straw came when she discovered Johnny was having an affair with another woman. Though the veracity of anything Josephine ever wrote or said is questionable, that much rings true. Johnny was a lifelong womanizer. By the fall of 1881 Josephine had been living with him in Tombstone for about a year, a long time for Johnny to maintain fidelity. He was undoubtedly tired of Josephine's demanding ways. Perhaps she might have overlooked his philandering if she had a ring on her finger, but Johnny kept finding excuses to postpone matrimony. From Josephine's perspective, becoming his bride was imperative. She'd had her adventures as an actress on the frontier and the spicy delight of living in what dull people would consider sin. The novelty was over. Her dashing lawman beau was mocked by the important people in town and every day seemed likely to lose the job that enabled them to live in high style.

During the summer, Josephine contacted her parents and indicated she was ready to return to San Francisco. They sent $300 to cover travel expenses, a generous amount. According to Josephine, when the money arrived Johnny fooled her by suggesting that instead of buying a train ticket, she could use it to build a new house for them to live in. As soon as the house was ready, there would finally be a wedding. Josephine handed the money over, and that was the last she heard from Johnny about marriage, and soon afterward she broke up with him for good. There was no explanation in her eventual memoir about why she remained in Tombstone for several more months instead of asking her parents for more money to pay her way home. Perhaps she was ashamed to admit to them what had happened, but it's much more likely that she stayed in town because she had her eye on a new man, one whose presence in Josephine's arms would infuriate

Johnny Behan. Romance and revenge always appealed to Josephine.

Tombstone was considerably larger than typical boomtowns, but not so much so that most residents didn't know each other at least slightly. Wyatt Earp was not among its most prominent citizens, but he'd been a county deputy sheriff, was an officer in the volunteer fire department, and as a prospective candidate for county sheriff did what he could to make a name for himself. Wyatt was big and good-looking. John Clum described him as "above six feet in height, well proportioned and neat in his attire. . . . His facial features were strong, positive and pleasing." Bat Masterson added that Wyatt weighed "in the neighborhood of one hundred and sixty pounds, all of it muscle." Wyatt had piercing blue eyes. His fashionable drooping mustache accentuated his sharp cheekbones and prominent chin. Josephine always had an eye for handsome men. Even if she hadn't heard Johnny at home carping about Wyatt Earp, she would eventually have noticed him.

Wyatt could not have helped but notice Josephine, too. She stood out among Tombstone's limited female population. Wyatt was often oblivious to subtlety, but Josephine wasn't subtle. She enjoyed being admired by men and knew how to encourage it. Staying in Tombstone after breaking up with Johnny, she could take her pick among men, and the one she picked was calculated to consternate her former lover the most. It's impossible to know whether Josephine would have been initially attracted to Wyatt if he hadn't been Johnny's rival, or if he was homely. Happily for her, neither was the case.

While Josephine was newly unattached, Wyatt wasn't. Very little is known of Mattie Earp, his common-law wife who stayed home and mostly out of public sight. Like every other woman in a similar arrangement, Mattie's security was at the mercy of her common-law husband. There is no way to be certain what relationship blossomed between Wyatt and Josephine while they were in Tombstone. She left no record of how she spent the months there between breaking up with Johnny sometime in late summer or early fall of 1881 and returning to San Francisco around the end of the year. Wyatt continued living with Mattie until the spring of 1882 when, with the other Earp wives, she was sent to safety in California. But Wyatt and Josephine obviously connected on an emotional level neither ever experienced with anyone else. After publicly becoming a couple in San Francisco in late 1882, they stayed together until Wyatt's death almost forty-seven years later. Even if they weren't lovers in Tombstone, at some point their intense mutual attraction must have been obvious to astute observers. Perhaps Mattie Earp didn't notice, but Johnny Behan certainly did.

If Wyatt didn't immediately lose himself in a love affair with Josephine despite his strong attraction to her, it was because much of his attention and energy were focused elsewhere. Ambition took precedence over romance. During a tumultuous summer when everyone else seemed to be thwarted by miscalculation or misfortune, Wyatt believed he had a foolproof plan to make himself Cochise County sheriff. Its centerpiece was the capture of the Benson stage robbers Johnny Behan had so ingloriously failed to apprehend, and its key component was the betrayal of the fugitives by one of the cowboys' most trusted friends.

Months after the botched robbery of the Benson stage and the murders of Bud Philpot and Peter Roerig, Billy Leonard, Harry Head, and Jim Crane were still at large. Their whereabouts were no secret. They lurked in and around the Animas Valley in New Mexico's boot heel, a favorite gathering place for cowboys on the run from the law. Any pursuit there by lawmen would be futile; by the time they arrived, the killers would have learned of their approach and been long gone. The fugitives were so complacent that they occasionally left their safety zone to visit with their cowboy and small rancher pals back in Arizona Territory. Critics of Cochise County law enforcement constantly carped about the inability of Johnny Behan to bring Leonard, Head, and Crane to justice, though in fairness there seemed to be little Johnny could do. The outlaws were mostly skulking outside his jurisdiction. His budget for pursuit was limited. Time constraints were also an issue. The county sheriff's main responsibility remained the assessment and collection of taxes.

But Wyatt wasn't hampered by the responsibilities of an incumbent. He could devote much more time to showing up Johnny by nabbing the three killers himself. Though Wyatt never mastered the backroom intricacies of politics, he had a natural understanding of one aspect of human nature. Leonard, Head, and Crane had literally gotten away with murder, but they hadn't made any profit from it. Feeling cocky and invulnerable to the law, they could be tempted by news of a sure thing, another stage toting a Wells Fargo treasure box that could be ambushed in some dusty draw. As before, they'd get away afterward, but this time they'd take along the money. Their hubris could be the basis of a successful trap. But the bait had to be dangled before the trio by a confidant of theirs. Wyatt had several candidates in mind. Joe Hill was a cowboy who dealt in rustled cattle, and he'd been involved in John Ringo's attempt to steal the 1880 Pima County sheriff's election — a plot that Wyatt helped to thwart. Frank McLaury had publicly clashed with the Earps over the theft of army mules. Ike Clanton was the sort of loudmouthed bully the Earps routinely whacked around in their stints as lawmen. They were all known to be friends with the alleged killers and Leonard, Head, and Crane would never suspect any of them of being in league with Wyatt, which is why he specifically wanted their help.

In early June, Wyatt asked Hill, McLaury, and Clanton to meet him behind the Oriental Saloon. Wyatt didn't pretend that they were in any sense friends. Instead, he had a business proposition for them, one he described in candid terms. Wells Fargo offered generous rewards of $1,200 each for Leonard, Head, and Crane. Wyatt wasn't interested in the money, though — he explained that he wanted the glory of capturing the notorious killers because it would almost guarantee him being elected Cochise County sheriff. So if Hill, McLaury, and Clanton would help him do it, they could have all $3,600 of the reward money, less whatever it cost Wyatt to rent horses for his posse. Everybody but the three fugitives would come out ahead.

When his listeners didn't immediately decline, Wyatt offered details. The McLaury brothers had just relocated to a new ranch near Soldiers Hole about twenty miles east of Tombstone and thirty miles north of the

Mexican border. Leonard, Head, and Crane would be told that a particularly rich treasure box was to be shipped by stage between Tombstone and Bisbee. They'd be invited to use the McLaury ranch as a launching point for a robbery, but when they arrived Wyatt and some others — undoubtedly Virgil and Morgan, and probably Doc Holliday — would be waiting to take them prisoner. Hill, McLaury, and Clanton shouldn't worry about anyone ever learning about their roles, because Wyatt would take full credit for himself. Leonard, Head, and Crane would never know that they'd been betrayed by their friends. Wyatt would triumphantly turn the notorious killers over to the law (the custody of U.S. deputy marshal Virgil Earp, surely, rather than Cochise County sheriff Johnny Behan), Wells Fargo would pay Wyatt the cumulative $3,600 reward, and after deducting expenses he'd quietly pass it along to them with no one being the wiser. The three potential co-conspirators asked for time to think it over.

Soon Ike was back with an opinion and a question. Leonard, Head, and Crane were tough men who would never be captured alive. Would Wells Fargo pay its rewards for corpses as well as for living bandits? Wyatt asked Marshall Williams, Wells Fargo's agent in Tombstone, to cable the parent company in California and find out. The terse reply stated, "Yes we will pay rewards for them dead or alive," confirming the chilling fact that Wells Fargo considered itself above the constraints of law. To date no judge or jury had convicted the three Benson stage holdup suspects of anything, yet Wells Fargo was willing to finance their executions. Williams passed the telegram along to Wyatt, who showed it to Ike on June 7. Ike said that they had a deal.

Wyatt's motive for making the offer was obvious, but the reasons his new partners accepted it weren't. The money involved was substantial, but not the kind of fortune that they could live on for very long afterward. Clanton and McLaury in particular depended on cooperating with the cowboys for much of their livelihood. Playing key roles in bringing three of them to justice — a substantial blow to the loosely knit Cochise County cowboy congregation in general — seemed in a sense self-defeating. But there was another issue involved. Local lawmen would overlook rustling because mostly Mexican cattle were stolen and beef was urgently needed in area markets. But robbing stages and committing murder in the process were crimes of such magnitude that not only Cochise County but federal authorities were obligated to act. If there were more such incidents, law enforcement response would inevitably result in most of the cowboys either being arrested or, more likely, driven from the region. Then small ranchers like the Clantons and McLaurys couldn't profit from rustling partnerships with them. If Leonard, Head, and Crane were gunned down it would serve as an object lesson to the rest of the cowboys: They had to be smart about the level of their lawbreaking so everyone could keep on benefiting.

This was sophisticated thinking and probably beyond the brainpower of Ike Clanton. But Frank McLaury was an intelligent man who was well aware of the danger to his personal income caused by real as opposed to rumored cowboy depredations. Ike's main reason to cooperate with Wyatt was more pointedly selfish. Once the deal was struck, Ike felt chummy enough with the Earps to confide to Virgil why he'd agreed to sell out his supposed friends. After the attack on the Benson stage, Ike said, he'd driven some cattle onto land in New Mexico owned by Leonard, since if Leonard was on the run he wouldn't be using it. But Leonard found out and objected, informing Ike that he had to either move his stock or buy the property. If Leonard was arrested or killed in Wyatt's ambush, Ike could claim the New Mexico property for his own.

Joe Hill was instructed to ride east to New Mexico, find Leonard, Head, and Crane, and tempt them back to Cochise County with the fictitious report of a rich stage to rob. While he was gone everyone else had to wait, and strained nerves fueled with whiskey always brought out the worst in Ike Clanton. On the same night Hill left, Ike got into a brawl with a fellow named Little Dan Burns. As they were separated, Ike bellowed that the next time he saw Burns he'd use a gun instead of his fists. In the morning they ran into each other on Allen Street in front of the Wells Fargo office. Despite town ordinances Ike carried a pistol and so did Burns. Police Chief Virgil Earp separated them before shooting could commence and sent them on their ways, perhaps sparing Ike a visit to jail because of their new clandestine partnership. As Virgil anticipated, the fracas was soon forgotten. He took it as proof that Ike Clanton was all threat and no follow-through.

No plans in Tombstone that summer seemed to go as anticipated, and Wyatt's was no exception. About ten days after departing for New Mexico, Joe Hill returned with practically the worst news possible — Billy Leonard and Harry Head could no longer be ambushed on the McLaury ranch because they were already dead. Details were sketchy. Someone, possibly Tombstone judge and Townsite Company owner Mike Gray, had hired Leonard and Head to drive brothers Ike and Bill Haslett off some prime property in the Animas Valley. The brothers got wind of the pending attack and killed Leonard and

Head first. That gave the Hasletts the right to claim two-thirds of the cumulative $3,600 Wells Fargo reward, but they didn't live long enough to collect it. The cowboys were not formally organized, but they were always ready to avenge their own. A group that included Benson stage robber Jim Crane and — at least by rumor — John Ringo gunned down both Hasletts.

Wyatt's plan had unraveled. He was left to ponder some other strategy that would highlight his law enforcement skills and Johnny Behan's lack of them. There was still time. The election for county sheriff was seventeen months away. Surely in the interim Wyatt would come up with something else. His co-conspirators were frustrated, too, but it seemed at least initially that they hadn't lost anything. The cowboys remained in the area, still rustling and requiring the help of their small-rancher middlemen to graze and sell the stolen stock.

Then one day during the summer, Marshall Williams got drunk. He encountered Ike Clanton, and in a misguided attempt at boozy fellowship he assured Ike that making deals with Wyatt Earp was always a good idea. Any partner of Wyatt's was a friend of Williams. This was the first time Ike realized someone other than the Earps knew about the ambush plan, further proof that Ike was no great brain. As the company's agent in Tombstone,

Marshall Williams had sent and received the critical Wells Fargo telegrams. Obviously Wyatt had to have informed him of the plan. But his encounter with Williams frightened Ike — who else might Wyatt have told? If word spread, Ike's life was in danger. The cowboys had slaughtered the Haslett brothers in reprisal for the killings of Leonard and Head. As Ike realized all too well, to the cowboys betrayal of trust was an unforgivable transgression. He spent the summer imagining the ways they might punish him for it. Ike frequented bars while he obsessed over the horrifying possibilities. As his fracas with Little Dan Burns indicated, a drunk, nervous Ike Clanton was always prone to act foolishly, and he had never been as constantly inebriated and panic-stricken as he was now.

On July 4, 1881, Cochise County residents gathered in Tombstone to celebrate Independence Day. Traditionally there was a gala program with massive displays of fireworks, but on this occasion organizers dialed down the pomp and expense. Money originally set aside to fund the affair was donated instead to the new Hook and Ladder Society, which boasted fire wagons and hoses purchased immediately after the terrible blaze on June 22. News from the East that President James Garfield had been shot by an assassin and might not survive also made all-out festivities seem inappropriate. But Tombstone was too proud to entirely avoid putting on a show. The portion of the town destroyed in the fire was being rebuilt from the ashes, so in spite of recent tribulations there was much to celebrate. The program on the Fourth consisted of a dramatic reading of the Declaration of Independence, the recitation of an original poem in the town's honor, and a speech by Thomas Fitch, a former member of the U.S. House of Representatives who now practiced law in Tombstone and was widely known as "the Silver-Tongued Orator." The town glee club entertained with several numbers, and the Tombstone Brass Band blared out patriotic tunes.

But the speeches and the music were punctuated by pounding rain and an accompanying cacophony of thunder. Tombstone and Cochise County had spent the previous months parched by burning heat. Now, in moments, there was far too much water for the dry ground to absorb and streets in town and roads outside began to flood. All the fine structures that remained standing or were being rebuilt disappeared under thick coatings of mud. People dressed in holiday finery had to slog home drenched to the bone. The deluge continued almost uninterrupted for weeks. Nature itself seemed to mock the pretensions of Tombstone and everyone who lived there.

CHAPTER ELEVEN: ESCALATION

In the spring of 1881, Galeyville butcher Al McAlister and cowboy George Turner claimed that they'd won a contract to furnish beef to the army camp of Fort Bowie in the Chiricahua Mountains. It was likely a lie meant to keep the law off of their backs; McAlister and Turner ran with the cowboys and were far more likely to rustle stock than to legitimately buy it. During the second week in May, they hired two helpers and rode across the border into Sonora, ostensibly to buy cattle in the town of Fronteras and then drive it back north.

At exactly the same time just outside Fronteras, rustlers struck the ranch of José Juan Vásquez and drove off about five hundred head of cattle. Vásquez rallied ranch hands and friends and raced in pursuit. The Mexicans came upon Turner, McAlister, and their two drovers making camp for the night with a sizable herd and assumed the cattle were the ones stolen from Vásquez. The

Americans were ordered to surrender, refused, and after a volley of ensuing gunfire all four and Vásquez lay dead. On the Mexican side of the border, there was a sense that justice had, for once, been served. American rustlers paid the ultimate price for their crime — the hope was that a message was sent to their villainous *compadres.*

The cowboys did receive a message, but not the one that the gloating Mexican vigilantes intended. So far as the cowboys were concerned, two of their friends went into Mexico and were murdered. Rumors immediately spread that the cowboys were organizing a retaliatory attack on Fronteras. The Mexican government sent troops to the border to repel the anticipated invasion, but there wasn't one. The cowboys had a more effective strategy and it was already in place.

Border crime wasn't one-sided. Mexican brigands took regular advantage of proximity to American ranches and markets. In particular, the Mexican government's high taxes on alcohol and tobacco encouraged smuggling. The smugglers brought gold and silver north and traded for liquor, cigars, and loose tobacco. They sold those items back in Mexico for a tidy profit, with their customers still benefiting from lower prices than they would have paid for heavily taxed, government-approved purchases. The cowboys preyed on the Mexican smugglers, frequently ambushing them before they reached Tombstone and other Cochise County towns. It seemed to be a smart strategy because there was no apparent benefit to the Mexican government in protecting criminals from their own country.

In late July, a particularly well-laden pack train headed north through Sonora, using the Skeleton Canyon route along the Arizona–New Mexico territorial border. Subsequent newspaper accounts estimated there were sixteen Mexican riders hauling $2,500 in bullion and also driving mules intended for sale. The goods and the men transporting them never reached their intended destination. An American rancher passing through the canyon came upon a few of the mules wandering loose, their packs torn open and empty. Four Mexicans were reported dead. In Galeyville, the cowboys proudly showed off their spoils. Even the *Epitaph,* otherwise so condemnatory of anything the cowboys did, seemed perversely pleased with how American rapscallions robbed and routed ne'er-do-well Mexicans:

[The Mexican smugglers] stopped at a curve in the road at Los Animas, near Fronteras, to prepare their frugal breakfast. While busily engaged preparing their tortillas they were saluted with music of twenty rifles fired by cow-boys who lay in ambush awaiting them. The Mexicans took this as an invitation to leave and did not stand on the order of their going but left all their mules and pack saddles. . . . When they stopped running they were at Fronteras and their party was four short.

Four cowboys had died outside Fronteras in May. Two months later, the cowboys killed four Mexicans in roughly the same spot. The cowboys may have considered the McAlister-Turner attack to be canceled out, but the Mexican government was incensed. It lodged formal complaints with Governor Frémont, and the Mexican legation in Washington bombarded the U.S. secretary of state with letters of protest, trying to shame the federal government into intervening. The dead men might have been smugglers, but they were still Mexican citizens. The incident escalated from a regional clash into an international crisis. If Mexico restricted border access, then American troops pursuing Apache raiders fleeing south might not be able to cross freely. Legal trade between the two nations was in jeopardy.

Tombstone business leaders were appalled when stories about Cochise County border tensions appeared in papers around the country. In mid-August, when the cowboys robbed a smaller band coming north to trade in Tombstone, the *Epitaph* made an editorial about-face, no longer considering cowboys routing Mexicans to be a source of ethnocentric pride. Now Clum insisted that "unless immediate steps are taken by the citizens to rid the county of these outlaws there will be no more protections of life and property." If the authorities couldn't get the job done, Clum railed, then outraged citizens would: "It remains to be seen how much longer such damnable acts . . . shall go unpunished."

Clum wasn't the only Tombstone resident in a foul mood. The weather had everyone living there on edge. The constant rain resulted in flooding, and the town was effectively isolated from the outside world for weeks at a time. Businessmen were discomfited because mail delivery was interrupted. Stages couldn't get through, so bank drafts and land contracts couldn't be exchanged with banks and businesses in Benson and Tucson and Prescott. Food shortages added to the general sense of frustration. When all other trappings of sophisticated society failed, at least Tombstone residents could count on epicurean delights. Now even basic sustenance was hard to come by. "We're in a bad way in town," diarist George Parsons wrote on August 25. "Eggs and potatoes gone and flour getting scarce owing to the wash-outs. No mail at all and things generally are in a deplorable condition."

Stages with mail and wagons loaded with

330

foodstuffs couldn't pass along the water-logged roads, but individuals on horses still could, especially to the south and east of Tombstone. Despite tightened security, border rustling and smuggling continued unabated, and the Mexican government determined that drastic measures were appropriate.

Newman "Old Man" Clanton survived to age sixty-five on the frontier by knowing and working every angle. In some ways he and Nicholas, the Earp brothers' father, were soul mates. They were both ambitious, domineering men who expected their sons to do as they were told. The Earp boys escaped their father's control early in life. In 1881, Old Man Clanton still had three of his in thrall — thirty-six-year-old Phin, thirty-four-year-old Ike, and nineteen-year-old Billy. They acted as their father's subordinates, taking orders and obediently carrying them out. By frontier standards the Clantons were pragmatic businessmen. They cooperated with rustlers because there was profit in it. They pursued wealth in legitimate ways, too, buying and selling land, moving around the frontier looking for the big deals that would make their fortunes. They never found any, but in Cochise County they came closest. The shady side of the cattle business thrived, in part because the county sheriff looked the other way. It wasn't just the Clanton sons who were actively involved. Their father sometimes ran with the rustlers, too. He was doing that on the night of August 13, 1881, when a squad of Mexican soldiers decided to hell with border restrictions — an example must be made to impress upon American bandits that they could no longer steal from Mexico with impunity.

Old Man Clanton and several other men who were part of the loosely knit cowboy faction — Dixie Lee Gray (son of Townsite Company owner Mike Gray), Charley Snow, Billy Byers, and New Mexico rancher Billy Lang — bedded down for the night in Guadalupe Canyon, a spot where the Arizona, New Mexico, and Mexico borders intersected approximately one hundred miles east of Tombstone. They had with them cattle that friends later claimed were cut from Lang's personal herd. The group was supposedly driving them to Tombstone to sell there. Others suggested that the stock was stolen in Mexico, and the rustlers stopped for the night just north of the border, secure in the knowledge that Mexican troops could not cross and pursue them there. They were joined by Harry Ernshaw, a milk cow buyer on his way to Tombstone, and later that evening Benson stage robbery fugitive Jim Crane rode into camp. Old Man Clanton's flexible attitude toward the law was evident as he and his companions welcomed a man wanted for double murder. Probably after a bit of companionable drinking, everyone turned in. During the night they were awakened by noises on the camp perimeter. Lang, Clanton, and Ernshaw rose from their bedrolls to investigate. What they believed might be a prowling bear turned out to be Mexican soldiers, who began firing with the intention of annihilating all seven Americans. For the attackers, it was the equivalent of a shooting gallery. They'd caught their victims completely off-guard. Charley Snow, Dixie Lee Gray, Billy Lang, Jim Crane, and Old Man Clanton were all slaughtered. Billy Byers, shot through the abdomen, managed to escape into the desert darkness. He survived and so did Harry Ernshaw, who, according to the *Epitaph,* "ran away amidst a shower of bullets one of which grazed his nose." The Mexicans stripped the bodies before they rode home. Their government never officially acknowledged the attack, which apparently was in response to yet another recent cowboy raid into Sonora that left eight Mexicans dead.

Reactions in Cochise County varied. There were fresh rumors that the cowboys would retaliate with a mob of about two hundred. Dixie Lee Gray's family believed the attackers were not Mexican soldiers but "escaped smugglers" from the earlier Skeleton Canyon shootout, "taking revenge on the first Americans they could find." Tombstone leaders were privately pleased with the news. Maybe the cowboys would take the bloody hint and move on. George Parsons wrote in his journal that "this killing business by the Mexicans, in my mind, was perfectly justifiable as it was in retaliation for [the] killing of several of them and their robbery by cowboys recently, this [Jim] Crane being one of the number. Am glad they killed him, as for the others — if not guilty of cattle stealing — they had no business to be found in such bad company."

Wyatt Earp had no public comment, but unlike Parsons he didn't revel in the death of Jim Crane. With Crane's demise and the earlier shootings in New Mexico of Billy Leonard and Harry Head, all three alleged killers involved in the Benson stage robbery were permanently beyond Wyatt's reach. There would be no parading of captured suspects to embarrass Johnny Behan and ensure Wyatt's election as county sheriff in November 1882. Now Wyatt had to find some completely different means of emphasizing his law-and-order credentials.

There was another critical consequence to the massacre in Guadalupe Canyon. The death of Old Man Clanton relieved his son Ike of any restraining influence. Trading in rustled Mexican cattle, working behind the scenes with John Ringo to fix a county sheriff's election, getting a little drunk and

334

disorderly in Tombstone — these were illegal acts on Ike's part, but by Cochise County standards they were not major crimes and his father had no objection. But the canny Clanton patriarch knew better than to attract too much attention from lawmen. Ike never openly defied an officer or challenged one to fight, not because he had enough self-discipline to control his own worst instincts but because his father wouldn't have stood for it. With Old Man Clanton in the grave, Ike was finally free to act however he pleased without worrying about how his father might respond afterward. It was now a matter of which foolish, potentially lethal, thing Ike might do first.

In the wake of so much violence and controversy outside the city limits, many Tombstone residents tried to carry on as usual. In town, at least, things were generally peaceful. Police Chief Virgil Earp seemed to have everything under control. When the floods abated, mail service was restored and regular food shipments resumed. Well-to-do citizens stepped up their dabbling in the arts. A series of literary nights kicked off with Mrs. Charles Hudson reciting William Cullen Bryant's "Thanatopsis" to an appreciative crowd. Her husband ran a Tombstone bank. Clara Brown helped organize the Tombstone Dramatic Relief Association, which planned to "[place] its services at the disposal of the public for any worthy [cause]." Its amateur thespians immediately began rehearsing for a benefit performance of *The Ticket of Leave Man,* a drama selected after much debate over the venerable *H.M.S. Pinafore.* But the poetry recitation and preparations for the play couldn't distract residents from the danger that seemed to loom all around, and on the afternoon of September 5 a town meeting was convened at Schieffelin Hall. Its purpose was to discuss ways of protecting the community, and not only from the depredations of the cowboys. A hundred miles to the north, Apache renegades once again were reportedly breaking out of the San Carlos Reservation. They usually fled south to Mexico, and their route took them close to Tombstone. Citizens there were concerned about the cowboys, but they were terrified of the Indians.

Mayor Clum presided at the meeting. It was a rowdy affair. Everyone wanted something done to keep the Apaches at bay. There was more squabbling than any attempt to achieve consensus until Tom Fitch, the lawyer who'd been the main speaker at the town's rain-drenched Fourth of July celebration, rose to remind everyone of how much Tombstone's economy depended on good national press. No one would benefit, Fitch cautioned his squirming audience, "if this scare got abroad." He suggested that the crowd pass a resolution "reposing faith in the Government's ability to cope with the present [Indian] emergency." It was an obvious public relations gesture and only approved after Fitch noted that in any real emergency "sufficient force could be gathered in a short time without aid of meetings." A committee was formed to explore this option. Tombstone leaders were ready to move from an advisory Citizens Safety Committee to a full-fledged armed militia that would be instantly available to gun down renegade Indians, cowboys, or anyone else suspected of being a danger to the public. The working name for the new group was the Tombstone Rangers. Officers were elected — none of them Earps — and recruitment began. Within days, eighty townsmen signed up.

Less than a week later, John Gosper arrived in Tombstone. The acting territorial governor supposedly came to personally investigate cowboy depredations and renegade activity in the area. As much as anything, he was hustling local political support for his overt, ongoing campaign to replace Frémont as governor. Endorsing the Tombstone Rangers was useful to Gosper in two ways. Having a civilian militia in Cochise County might deter outlaw activity, and becoming an outspoken booster of the newly organized group would ensure his good standing with local Republicans. Gosper even promised to supply the Rangers with horses and weapons. Many Tombstone residents had no mounts or guns of their own — as town dwellers with easy access to stages and police protection, they didn't have need of them on a daily basis. That was for rural folk out in the decidedly uncivilized countryside.

It also served Gosper's political ambition to update key Washington administrators on a supposed rift between the Cochise County sheriff and the U.S. deputy marshal who also served as Tombstone's chief of police. Gosper hoped that growing concern in Washington over border tensions caused by the cowboys would convince Secretary of State James G. Blaine — acting on behalf of President Chester A. Arthur, who succeeded James Garfield after his death on September 19 from wounds suffered in the assassination attempt — to name him governor in place of Frémont, who spent more time traveling outside the territory than he did presiding over the legislature in it. After separate meetings with Johnny Behan and Virgil Earp, Gosper, identifying Virgil by the wrong town title, wrote that the Behan-Earp situation was hopeless:

[Mr. Behan] represented to me that the Deputy U.S. Marshal, resident of Tombstone, and the City Marshal for the same,

and those who aided him seemed unwilling
to heartily cooperate with him in capturing
and bringing to justice these out-laws. . . .
In conversation with the deputy U.S. Marshal, Mr. Earp, I found precisely the same
spirit of complaint against Mr. Behan [the
Sheriff] and his deputies.

The upshot, Gosper explained, was that
either a strong territorial governor would ad-
dress the border tensions or else indiscrimi-
nate vigilante justice might be imposed by
civilian militia fed up with inadequate local
law enforcement. That Gosper was simultaneously endorsing such a militia group in
Tombstone was something the acting governor apparently did not feel compelled to
share. His letter exaggerated the differences
between Johnny and Virgil. They weren't
friends. The Earp brothers always stuck
together, and Virgil believed Johnny had
betrayed Wyatt by not appointing him undersheriff as promised. But Virgil took pride in
his professionalism, even if this sometimes
obligated him to cooperate with other lawmen he didn't personally like. He may have
indicated to Gosper that he found Johnny's
performance lacking, but Virgil would never
have said he wouldn't work with Behan when
necessary. Wyatt was the Earp with whom
Johnny shared so much mutual antipathy that
they could never work together.

Tombstone's original Safety Committee and its hard-line objectives had not been widely discussed outside gatherings of town leaders. But public recruitment for the Tombstone Rangers made the existence of the new militia common knowledge throughout Cochise County. The cowboys and their allies assumed that, despite all the Indian talk, they were the group's real targets. Frank McLaury felt threatened enough to confront Virgil, not realizing that, as an experienced lawman, Virgil hated the idea of civilian vigilantes just as much as the cowboys did. Virgil couldn't publicly oppose the formation of the Rangers because his bosses in the Tombstone city hierarchy so strongly supported it, but he was uncomfortable with the plan all the same. According to Virgil, in September outside Tombstone's Grand Hotel, Frank accused him of "raising a vigilance committee to hang us boys," whom McLaury identified as "the Clantons . . . Ringo, and in fact all us cowboys." If he used those specific words, then for the first time Frank McLaury was identifying himself, his brother, and the Clantons as full-fledged cowboys themselves rather than their friends and occasional business partners — and, so far as the Earps were concerned, the Clantons and McLaurys were now just as much a part of the cowboys as Curly Bill or John Ringo. Virgil denied the accusation and reminded Frank that it was the Earps who had protected Curly Bill from angry citizens after the shooting of Fred White. But Frank persisted, warning that if Virgil ever came for him "I will never surrender my arms to you. I had rather die a-fighting than to be [hanged.]" Frank and many of the cowboys apparently believed that the Earps were ringleaders among those plotting for their destruction. That impression was bolstered by incidents in early and mid-September.

On September 9, Virgil received a telegram from Pima County sheriff Bob Paul. In February, a stage robbery had occurred outside Globe, and cowboys Pony Deal and Sherman McMasters were the primary suspects. Paul wanted to arrest and question Deal first, probably hoping to elicit a confession that implicated McMasters, too. He asked Virgil not to arrest McMasters, who routinely came to Tombstone, until Deal was in custody and had been interrogated. The September 9 telegram notified Virgil that Paul had just taken Deal into custody. McMasters happened to be in Tombstone. Virgil saw him on the street there. He wired Paul back, asking if he should now take McMasters into custody.

While Virgil waited at Tombstone's main telegraph office for Paul's reply, John Ringo raced into town, lashing an exhausted horse.

It was odd that Ringo should make such an ostentatious public entrance into town, since, at the moment, he was a wanted man himself. A month earlier he and Dave Estes, another cowboy, had been accused of stealing the pot of a Galeyville poker game in which they'd been the big losers. Estes was arrested soon afterward, and the case against him was dismissed. Rather than risk a different verdict, Ringo remained at large. Now someone found Virgil at the telegraph office and informed him that Ringo was in town looking for Sherman McMasters. It seemed obvious that Ringo had learned of Pony Deal's apprehension and the imminent arrest of McMasters. He was risking his own capture to warn his fellow cowboy.

Just as he was informed of Ringo's arrival, Virgil finally got a return message from Bob Paul asking him to take McMasters into custody. Virgil borrowed a gun — he didn't carry a weapon while on duty unless some special situation made it necessary — and recruited his brother James to help with the arrest. The Earp brothers looked for McMasters in several saloons and then went on to the O.K. Corral where he kept his horse. But by then Ringo had warned McMasters, and the two made their getaway after stealing horses from the nearby Contention Mine. Allowing the fugitives to get away didn't look good on Virgil's record, particularly with the heightened sense of vigilantism in town.

This was one of the few times James Earp ever acted as a temporary officer. Virgil had asked his older brother for help because Wyatt and Morgan were busy pursuing two other cowboys accused of stage robbery. On the night of September 8, the Tombstone-to-Bisbee stage was waylaid in the Mule Mountains by several masked men — afterward driver Levi McDaniels and his passengers couldn't agree whether there were two or four. McDaniels was ordered to toss down the Wells Fargo treasure box and mail sacks. The passengers were collectively relieved of about $600, and one lost his gold watch. It was a professional ambush, with threats kept to a minimum. When they had been frisked the passengers were ordered back into the stage and McDaniels told to drive on. Just as he took the reins, one of the masked bandits shouted, "Hold on there," and checked McDaniels's pockets, commenting, "Maybe you have got some sugar." McDaniels didn't, and he was allowed to continue on to Bisbee.

Word of the robbery reached Tombstone the next morning and Wells Fargo agent Marshall Williams organized a posse. Besides himself it included county deputies Billy Breakenridge and Dave Neagle, Fred Dodge, and Wyatt and Morgan Earp. They found some tracks at the scene of the crime. The boot heel of one of the robbers left a distinct narrow mark, and one of the horses used in the getaway was unshod. The posse was able to follow the trail into Bisbee, where a shoemaker told them he had just replaced a very narrow boot heel for Frank Stilwell, Johnny Behan's former county deputy. Another clue fell into place: One of the robbers had searched McDaniels for "sugar," Stilwell's slang expression for money. It was well known that Stilwell and Pete Spencer, whom Wyatt had previously arrested for selling stolen stock, were currently riding together. The posse found and arrested Stilwell and Spencer and brought them back to Tombstone.

Frank Stilwell's arrest was a political godsend for Wyatt. For months, anti-Behan forces had suggested the sheriff and his deputies were somehow directly involved with cowboy crime. This didn't prove it — Stilwell only occasionally served as a deputy sheriff, and at the time of the Bisbee stage robbery he may not have been on the county payroll. But his arrest was the basis for a fresh wave of anti-Behan innuendo — the *Epitaph* identified "Deputy Sheriff Stilwell" in its stories — and Wyatt now had a fine new campaign issue. Wyatt's elation lasted about a week, when U.S. commissioner Spicer held a hearing and dismissed the charges against Stilwell and Spencer. Their defense attorney produced several witnesses who testified that the alleged thieves were elsewhere at the time of the robbery. The witnesses may have been lying, but there was no way to prove it. The other evidence was largely circumstantial: Stilwell wasn't the only man in Cochise County who sometimes wore narrow-heeled boots, and the word "sugar" wasn't unique to his vocabulary.

The Earps didn't give up. A few weeks after Stilwell and Spencer triumphantly left Spicer's courtroom, Virgil arrested them on federal mail robbery charges. They were taken to Tucson, arraigned in court there, and again released on bond. New preliminary hearings were set for the third week in October. Virgil's action was taken by the cowboys as further evidence that the Earps would never stop harassing them. Wyatt claimed that Frank McLaury and several other cowboys subsequently surrounded and threatened Morgan Earp. According to Wyatt, Frank told Morgan, "I have threatened you boys' lives, and a few days later I had taken it back, but since this arrest it now goes." Normally mild-mannered Virgil was spooked. He warned Billy Breakenridge that the McLaurys had threatened to kill everyone involved in the arrests of Stilwell and Spencer, so if Billy met Frank or Tom he should shoot first before they could attack him. Breakenridge wrote in his memoir that "I laughed at [Virgil], as I knew about the feud between them." In fact,

Breakenridge added, he spoke to Tom McLaury a few days after being cautioned about him by Virgil, and the younger McLaury brother assured Breakenridge that "he was sorry for [Stilwell and Spencer], but it was none of his fight and he would have nothing to do with it, as he had troubles enough of his own." The Earps were becoming as paranoid as the cowboys.

The first week in October brought a temporary truce. A band of Apache warriors led by Geronimo and Cochise's son Naiche fled the San Carlos Reservation and skirmished with the U.S. Cavalry in the Dragoon Pass north of Tombstone. After breaking off the engagement, the Indians began raiding area ranches, probably to secure fresh horses to ride down into Mexico through the Sulphur Springs Valley east of town. Citizens of Tombstone were always ready to panic at the slightest possibility of Indian attack. The Tombstone Rangers were still in organizational stages, but about three dozen men quickly formed a volunteer company to find and fight the renegades. They were a mixed lot, with some like George Parsons complete amateurs in Indian warfare. Mayor John Clum had experience as an Indian agent. Johnny Behan and some of his deputies joined the party, and Virgil and Wyatt Earp rode with them. Indian threats took precedence over political and personal feuds.

If the ensuing adventures of the Tombstone militia had been made into one of the ubiquitous Western movies of the 1940s and 1950s, it would properly have starred the Three Stooges rather than John Wayne. From start to finish it was an exercise in near-slapstick futility. Almost as soon as the party rode out of town, the skies unleashed a torrential rainstorm that turned the dusty ground into deep, gluey mud. Several previously intrepid members promptly turned around and rode home. Those who remained had trouble keeping together as their horses wallowed through what Parsons described as "ground . . . so soft and boggy" that the animals sank in it up to their knees. Hostiles were definitely in the area — they stole horses from the McLaurys and also from the ranch of John Randolph Frink, then disappeared into the storm. Frink assured the soggy riders from Tombstone that the renegades could be found some twenty miles farther on. Before continuing the pursuit they rested for a few hours on Frink's property, vainly trying to dry off and checking that their waterlogged guns would still fire. Everyone wanted hot coffee, but during the brewing process somebody's boot fell into the pot. They drank the stuff anyway. About 3 A.M. they resumed the hunt with Frink guiding them. Parsons wrote

347

that the full moon "shed a ghastly light over the line of determined men riding over that vast prairie, as it seemed to be; through the long wet grass and across the soggy country." In their exhausted state and with reduced numbers it was obvious that even if they found the Apaches they couldn't fight them effectively. But pride wouldn't let them quit until they reached the remote spot where Frink promised they'd encounter hostiles. In a culture where reputation meant everything, it was considered better to make a foolish fight and die rather than to give any impression of weakness or, worse, cowardice. But there was no fight with Geronimo and his renegades. Parsons noted bleakly in his journal, "Scouted thoroughly, but with [the] exception [of] some pretty fresh scattering trails, there was no signs and none of a large force, such as we had expected to find." Though none of them would have admitted it, they were probably relieved.

In all, the posse traveled some 125 miles in forty-eight hours, a tribute to grit if not common sense. The long ride home took them close to the McLaury ranch near Soldiers Hole, and they stopped there for breakfast. The McLaurys and the Earps may have been at odds, but frontier hospitality dictated that everyone in the posse be welcomed and fed. Frank and Tom may not even have been present, but some of their cowboy friends

were, including Curly Bill Brocius. Wyatt and
Curly Bill simply nodded at each other,
tacitly acknowledging the tension between
them by observing only the most basic courtesy. Virgil upset George Parsons by shaking
Curly Bill's hand and engaging him in conversation. This was Virgil at his pragmatic
best. The cowboy was going to continue his
lawbreaking ways. Virgil didn't want Curly
Bill coming into Tombstone and raising hell,
so it made more sense to be friendly rather
than antagonistic. It didn't guarantee that
Curly Bill would commit his misdeeds somewhere else, but it might make him a little less
inclined to cause problems for Virgil.

The Apache scare subsided — it turned out
that rumors of numerous killings of white
settlers by the hostiles were just that — but
the Cochise County crime wave continued
with another stage robbery outside Charleston on October 8. On October 11, John Frémont finally resigned as governor of Arizona
Territory. John Gosper was disappointed
when he was not immediately appointed to
the office. Instead, he had to continue serving as acting governor while the Arthur
administration decided on Frémont's successor. A preliminary hearing on the federal mail
robbery charges against Frank Stilwell and
Pete Spencer began in mid-October in Tucson. Deputy U.S. marshal Virgil Earp and

Cochise County sheriff Johnny Behan were both called to testify. They made the trip together, proof that Gosper had exaggerated the problems between them. Before Virgil left, he appointed his brothers Morgan and Wyatt as special deputies to help keep the peace in Tombstone while he was away. Virgil and Johnny returned to Tombstone just in time to join in the hunt for three fugitives who broke out of the county jail on October 24. Other posse members included county deputies Billy Breakenridge and Frank Leslie as well as Wyatt and Morgan Earp. But the fugitives eluded them that night, and the next day Virgil, Johnny, Leslie, and Dave Neagle went out again without success. They returned to Tombstone late on October 25 feeling worn out.

Wyatt was fed up with an ongoing problem of his own. Ike Clanton continued accusing Wyatt of breaking his promise to keep Ike's role in the plot to capture Billy Leonard, Harry Head, and Jim Crane secret. Ike was convinced that if Curly Bill, John Ringo, and the other cowboys found out what he'd tried to do they'd come for him. What Ike didn't understand was that Wyatt had his own reasons for wanting their failed deal to remain secret. If Wyatt had bribed Ike Clanton to betray three trusting friends, that would be worse in the eyes of many Cochise County voters than Ike's willingness to do it. Because so many small ranchers and rural county residents would automatically support Johnny Behan anyway, Wyatt couldn't afford to lose any potential votes — and he would if word of his deal with Ike became common knowledge. The longer Ike kept whining to Wyatt, the greater the possibility that Ike would be the one to let the secret out to the detriment of them both. It was time to finally convince Ike he was wrong about Wyatt revealing their plan, or at least to make him shut up about it.

Lately, Ike had accused Wyatt of revealing the failed plot to Doc Holliday. At some point in October, Wyatt told Ike that he'd had enough. Doc was away from Tombstone, but when he returned Wyatt would have him tell Ike that it wasn't true. Wyatt was not a patient man under the best of circumstances, and for months he'd been frustrated in his attempts to gain a political advantage over Johnny Behan. Ike Clanton's sniveling was an additional irritation that Wyatt could no longer tolerate.

Doc had left town to gamble in Tucson. Impatient for him to return and get Ike off his back, on October 22 Wyatt sent Morgan to fetch Doc. When he got to Tucson, Morgan found Doc reunited with Kate Elder. Kate's boardinghouse in Globe had burned down, so she was going to stay with Doc for a while. Doc always responded to requests from Wyatt. The fact that he was willing to talk with Ike didn't mean he already knew about the plot to trap Leonard, Head, and Crane. Though Doc may have been involved in the scheme from the beginning, it's far more likely Wyatt's message was a simple request that he return to Tombstone and answer honestly when Ike Clanton asked him a question. As an experienced lawman, the always taciturn Wyatt would have known that a key to successfully springing a trap on fugitives was to have as few people aware of the details as possible. Doc, who like Ike Clanton was prone to drinking and talking out of turn, wouldn't have needed to know anything unless he was asked to come and participate in the ambush, and that never happened.

Doc and Kate arrived back in Tombstone late on the night of October 22 and took a room at C. S. Fly's boardinghouse on Fremont Street. But Ike wasn't in town; he spent most of his time on the family ranch on the San Pedro River. The saloons and card games of Tombstone periodically lured him back. Wyatt was certain that Ike would return soon. When he did, Doc would make it clear to Ike that Wyatt hadn't told him anything about any plan to lure the three Benson stage robbery fugitives into an ambush, and that would be the end of it. Even if Ike wasn't convinced, he would surely be intimidated by the hot-tempered dentist. It probably never occurred to Wyatt that Ike might not shut up or back down.

CHAPTER TWELVE:
THE NIGHT BEFORE

In Tombstone, dining out wasn't limited to gourmet cuisine at fancy restaurants. People who wanted to eat cheaply or in a hurry usually visited the town's all-hours "lunch rooms," which offered simple fare like sandwiches and stews. The lunch rooms were especially popular with gamblers trying to snatch a quick bite between hands of cards, so some of Tombstone's saloons built lunch rooms right onto their premises. One was the Alhambra, and late on the night of Tuesday, October 25, its lunch room was crammed with customers. Not all of them were bolting their food. Some, like Wyatt Earp, were lingering over their meals. Wyatt was running card games around town and relaxing until the games broke up and it was time for him to go around and collect money from his dealers. Wyatt's younger brother Morgan was in the Alhambra, too. The atmosphere was congenial as men ate, smoked, and chatted. Then Ike Clanton and Doc Holliday joined the crowd, and the atmosphere took an immediate turn for the worse.

Ike had returned to Tombstone, arriving with Tom McLaury. That morning Ike had met Tom and Frank McLaury riding east of town with Ike's younger brother Billy. The four men ate breakfast at J. J. Chandler's ranch about ten miles from Tombstone and discussed their plans for the day. Frank and Billy had cattle to round up. Tom was going into Tombstone. He needed to buy some supplies, and the McLaurys also had business to transact with town butchers. It was important that Tom run these errands soon — he and Frank were preparing to leave for Iowa to attend a family wedding. Ike decided he'd go to Tombstone with Tom. They'd spend the night in town having a little fun, and Frank and Billy would ride in the next day to join them after getting their herding chores done.

Tom and Ike took a wagon into Tombstone. Both men were armed with pistols and Winchester rifles. It was simple common sense to have weapons with them. There was always danger of attack by renegade Apaches. But on this Tuesday morning everything was peaceful. The air was cold, but Tom had a little extra protection from the chill under his shirt, where he wore a money belt stuffed with cash. Thanks in great part to their business relationships with the cowboys, small ranchers in the area like the McLaurys and

Clantons occasionally handled considerable sums. Conversation during the short trip was probably one-sided. Ike loved the sound of his own voice, and twenty-eight-year-old Tom was the quiet McLaury brother. Frank, five years older, was hot-tempered and argumentative, whereas Tom preferred minding his own business, although like most men on the frontier he was ready to defend himself if honor required it.

Ike and Tom arrived in Tombstone late in the morning. They stabled their team of horses at the West End Corral and then registered at the Grand Hotel, where the cowboys usually stayed when they spent the night in Tombstone. They obeyed town Ordinance Number Nine by checking their guns, either at the corral or the hotel. Ike and Tom may have left their rifles at the stable and worn their gun belts on the walk to the hotel, where they checked their pistols. Then they spent the afternoon and evening enjoying themselves. The two drank and gambled at various establishments, and Tom put off transacting his business until the next day. At some point he and Ike separated, trying their luck in different saloons and card games. Ike's boisterous company probably wore on the milder-mannered Tom.

Sometime around midnight, Ike drifted into the Alhambra's lunch room and ordered a meal. It was probably crowded enough so

356

that he didn't notice that Wyatt was there. If Ike had, he certainly would have taken the opportunity to complain to Wyatt some more about spilling secrets — Ike was never one to exercise restraint, and by the time he got to the Alhambra he had been drinking steadily for at least ten to twelve hours. But Ike sat and ate his food without causing any disturbance until Doc Holliday arrived.

Doc's day had been spent in much the same way as Ike's: He drank and gambled, and by late in the evening he was ready for some food. The Alhambra lunch room was one of his favorite spots to take sustenance. While it's possible that Wyatt had spotted Ike and sent word for Doc to hurry over, it's more likely that Doc simply showed up on his own and discovered Ike sitting there. Doc then had a choice. He could approach Ike calmly, then sit down and rationally discuss what was bothering him. While it would have been difficult for Doc to convince Ike that Wyatt hadn't told him anything about the plot to trap Leonard, Head, and Crane, he could at least have assured the agitated man that the story wasn't going to be spread any further. Or, Doc could stalk over to Ike and threaten him with all kinds of mayhem if Ike didn't stop bothering Doc's friend Wyatt Earp. Predictably, he chose confrontation over conversation.

Later, during legal proceedings concerning the events of the next afternoon, there was conflicting testimony about what happened at the Alhambra lunch room that night. There was general agreement that Doc and Ike engaged in a terrible argument. At one point, Doc shouted that Ike was a damned liar. Then the discrepancies began.

Ike claimed that Doc raised the level of insult by calling him "a son-of-a-bitch cowboy," and then shouting that Ike should "get [his] gun out and get to work." When Ike replied that he didn't have his gun, Doc told him to go and get it. Doc himself, Ike recalled, put his hand on his chest, ready to pull a pistol that Ike suspected Doc carried in a holster under his jacket. As was the case with many gamblers earning their living in Tombstone saloons, Doc certainly had a permit to carry a weapon inside city limits. Ike said his situation became even more perilous when Morgan Earp joined Doc in taunting Ike to retrieve his gun and then come back and fight. Wyatt and Virgil Earp walked up and observed. Wyatt didn't say anything, but Virgil told Doc and Morgan that they should leave Ike alone since town policeman Jim Flynn was on duty and would keep an eye on him. Ike took this as a particularly egregious affront to his manhood. Though he'd been insulted and threatened to the point where any man could have been excused for responding violently, Ike repeated to Doc and the Earps that he wasn't "heeled" and didn't want to fight. Showing great restraint, he then left the lunch room in search of better company, first requesting that Doc and Morgan not shoot him in the back as he walked away.

Wyatt's testimony provided an entirely different account. Yes, Ike and Doc got into an argument in the lunch room over whether Wyatt had told Doc about the ambush plan. Wyatt, who was eating, asked his brother Morgan to break up the dispute since Morgan was still serving as a special deputy appointed by Virgil. So was Wyatt, but he didn't feel the situation was so urgent that he had to interrupt his meal. Morgan grabbed Doc by the arm and pulled him out into the street. Ike Clanton, too drunk or stupid to realize that he'd just been rescued from a very dangerous man, followed them, yelling and threatening Doc. Virgil was nearby in another saloon, trying to enjoy a relaxing night of cards and drinks after unsuccessfully chasing escaped prisoners from the county jail all day with Johnny Behan. Ike and Doc raised such a ruckus in the street that Virgil came out to say that he'd arrest them both if they didn't break it up immediately. At that point, Doc went off to another saloon and Ike headed for the Grand Hotel. It seemed that a potential crisis had been averted — two drunken hotheads were separated and sent on their separate ways by the level-headed Tombstone police chief. Things like that happened all the time.

But according to Wyatt, Ike Clanton didn't let the incident end there. A few minutes after the original squabble was broken up, Wyatt left the Alhambra lunch room to check on a faro game he was running at the Eagle Brewery. Ike approached him in the street and asked to talk. He was still steaming about his confrontation with Doc, and informed Wyatt that he was about to go and get his guns from wherever he had checked them earlier in the day. Since this "fighting talk" had gone on so long, Ike blustered, he guessed "it was about time to fetch it to a close." Wyatt tried to soothe Ike, explaining that all Doc had really meant to do was assure him that Wyatt hadn't talked about the ambush scheme. Ike wouldn't listen. Wyatt walked away and Ike trailed after him, boasting, "I will be ready for all of you in the morning" — effectively expanding his threats to include the Earps as well as Doc. Demonstrating admirable self-control, Wyatt told Ike that he would "fight no one if I could get away from it, because there was no money in it" — an accurate, revealing statement of his personal philosophy, and an unwitting affirmation of what would come later. Ike stuck to Wyatt like a barnacle and followed him into the Oriental Saloon, where Ike ordered a drink and told Wyatt, "You must not think I won't be after you all in the morning." Wyatt reiterated that Doc had only been trying to explain that he knew nothing about any plot to trap the Benson stage robbers. He finally separated himself from Ike and went about his business. After Wyatt retrieved the money from his card games, he bumped into Doc. They walked down Allen Street together, with Wyatt going home to Mattie and Doc returning to Fly's boardinghouse.

In light of what happened the next day, it's obvious that both Ike and Wyatt embroidered their testimony at the hearing several weeks later to make the other side look bad. Certainly Ike must have made all sorts of drunken threats inside the lunch room and out on the street. It would have been typical of him. Doc Holliday and Morgan Earp were also known for short tempers and their readiness to engage in confrontations. Whatever occurred on the night of October 25 wasn't one-sided. Among the acknowledged participants — Ike, Doc, Wyatt, Morgan, and Virgil — only Virgil was willing to diffuse the situation, and, in the hours just past midnight, he tried his best.

After leaving the Alhambra lunch room, and whether he subsequently met with Wyatt in the street or not, Ike didn't return to the

Grand Hotel to sleep. Instead, he resumed barhopping and soon found his way to the Occidental Saloon. Virgil Earp was already there, and so were Tom McLaury and Johnny Behan. It was coincidence that they found themselves in the same place, and Virgil took advantage of it. Virgil, Tom, Johnny, and another man who was never identified were involved in a poker game, and Ike was allowed to join. To Virgil, some convivial hands of cards were just the thing to smooth over personal differences. Hopefully Ike would settle down and concentrate on poker, and if Virgil spent some social time with Tom, maybe the McLaurys would stop threatening the Earps. Johnny Behan was fresh from another humiliation with the recent escape of more prisoners from his jail. That might be good news for Virgil's brother Wyatt, but as a fellow lawman Virgil couldn't help but sympathize with Johnny, who clearly needed to get his mind off his troubles. There was another plus to including Johnny in the game — he was a terrible card player who had lots of disposable income. John Plesent Gray wrote in his Tombstone memoir that gamblers in town "liked to have [Johnny] sit opposite them with his customary canvas sack full of gold and silver."

The game lasted until 6 A.M., indicating that the players got along reasonably well, though Ike was drunk when the first hand was dealt and stayed that way throughout the night. Drinking was part of card playing in frontier saloons — several bottles would have been emptied at their table during the five-hour session. Ike was completely loaded, but the others probably weren't entirely sober either. Finally, with the first streaks of dawn breaking to the east, the game concluded. Everyone but Ike was ready for bed. He had a new reason to be upset, having just noticed that Virgil Earp had played poker all night with a pistol resting under the table in his lap. The Tombstone police chief always wanted to avoid trouble, but after hearing Ike's threats outside the Alhambra lunch room, he was prepared for it all the same.

According to Virgil, after he stuck his gun into the waistband of his pants and bid the other players goodbye, Ike followed him outside the Occidental onto Allen Street and launched into the reasons that he believed Virgil "stood in with those parties that tried to murder me" earlier at the Alhambra lunch room.

Virgil Earp was a man of great but not infinite patience. He was weary and Ike was being foolish. Threats had been exchanged between Ike, Doc, and Morgan, but nobody had tried to murder Ike. Virgil told him he was going to sleep, and suggested that Ike should do the same.

Ike persisted. He wanted Virgil to take a

message to Doc Holliday: "The damned son of a bitch has got to fight." Virgil told Ike he was going home, and Ike was not "to raise any disturbance while I am in bed."

But Ike wouldn't shut up. As Virgil walked away he called out, "You won't carry the message?" Virgil yelled back that of course he wouldn't. Then, according to Virgil's subsequent court testimony, Ike tacked on a menacing coda: "You may have to fight before you know it."

Probably Ike did say that, or something like it. By 6 A.M. on Wednesday he had been drinking steadily for about eighteen to twenty hours, long enough for even the most functional alcoholic to fall into a blackout and lose any sense of inhibition. Even when Ike was sober he was prone to making violent threats. No matter what the circumstances, making such a statement to the Tombstone chief of police was still irrational to the point of lunacy. Virgil would have been fully within his rights to pistol-whip Ike and drag him off to jail. He must have been tempted to do it.

But Virgil was very tired. He'd been out chasing fugitives all day and up calming tempers and playing poker all night. Ike Clanton routinely made threats that he never carried out. Lots of drunks in Tombstone saloons did. If Virgil arrested Ike now it would involve a visit to Tombstone's recorder's court — sometimes called police court

— where suspects accused of violating town ordinances were immediately tried and, if found guilty, fined. Virgil couldn't claim that Ike had attacked anybody. He'd just said that he would. At the moment all Ike could be charged with was being drunk and disturbing the peace. Had Mayor Clum or other town leaders been present, they would have demanded that their police chief arrest Ike anyway — no lawbreaking of any sort was to be tolerated in Tombstone. They had made that very clear. But none of them had heard Ike make his whiskey-soaked threats, so Virgil could use his own discretion. Had Virgil believed that Ike really was prepared to start shooting, he would have taken him into immediate custody. But Virgil didn't, so it just wasn't worth the trouble or the lost sleep.

Without another word, Virgil turned his back on Ike and walked the rest of the way home to bed.

Chapter Thirteen: The Gunfight

At 8 A.M. on Wednesday, October 26, Ned Boyle completed an all-night bartending shift at the Oriental Saloon. It was a cold, nasty morning and on Ned's walk home he encountered Ike Clanton in front of the Tombstone telegraph office near the Grand Hotel. Ned was alarmed to see that Ike was not only drunk, but also armed with a pistol "in sight," which probably meant that the gun was jammed into the waistband of Ike's pants. Concerned for an acquaintance and good customer, Ned pulled Ike's coat closed to cover the illegally carried weapon and told him to go to bed. Ike said he wouldn't. He was waiting for the Earp brothers and Doc Holliday to show themselves on the street; then "the ball would open" and they would fight. Ned had certainly heard Ike blowing off drunken steam before, but this seemed different. He left Ike and hurried over to Wyatt Earp's house. Ned and Wyatt knew each other since Wyatt operated part of the gambling concession in the Oriental. Ned woke Wyatt and told him what Ike had just said, but Wyatt wasn't worried. He went back to sleep, so Ned walked the rest of the way home and did the same.

The Earp brothers craved early morning slumber. Ike felt the same way about whiskey. Within an hour of bumping into Ned Boyle he weaved his way to Kelly's Wine House. Owner Julius Kelly, tending early morning bar there, was called on to serve drinks to Ike and his pal Joe Stump. Kelly heard Ike describing to Stump some kind of problem he'd just had with the Earps and Doc. Concerned with Ike's condition and a rifle that he was now carrying in violation of town law, Kelly asked Ike what had happened. Ike eagerly recounted how, the night before, "the Earp crowd" and Doc insulted him when he wasn't "heeled." Ike said that he was armed now, so he was ready to fight as soon as he saw them again. Kelly suggested to Ike that picking a fight with the Earps and Doc probably wasn't the best idea, since they would undoubtedly fight back, and being outnumbered and outgunned wouldn't work to Ike's advantage. Ike paid no attention.

Word began to spread among Tombstone's morning risers that Ike Clanton was drunk, armed, and promising to commit mayhem on the town police chief, his family, and their friend Doc the moment they showed themselves on the street. Policeman A. G. Bronk, who had to consult Virgil anyway on another matter, hurried to his boss's house around 10 A.M. to warn him that there "was liable to be hell." Virgil may have wondered why his subordinate failed to make an immediate arrest if he was so worried about what Ike might do. He could have ordered Bronk to take Ike into custody right away. Instead, Virgil simply stayed in bed a while longer, finally rising a little before noon. He felt no need to hurry. Policeman Bronk might be spooked by blustering Ike Clanton, but Virgil thought he knew better.

While Virgil and Wyatt dozed, Ike visited yet another saloon. At Hafford's Corner he repeated to the owner the same dire tale he'd told to Julius Kelly: On Tuesday night, the Earps and Doc Holliday had insulted him, taking advantage of Ike because they had guns and he didn't. Now Ike was armed, too, and ready to fight the moment his enemies were out and about. This time Ike added a new, ludicrous detail — they'd already agreed to meet him and fight at noon, and here it was five minutes past. The implication was that the Earps and Doc were cowards. Like Julius Kelly, R. A. Hafford counseled caution. He told Ike it was ten rather than five minutes after twelve, and "there will be nothing of it." But when Ike left Hafford's he resumed stalking his intended victims.

A few minutes later Ike showed up outside photographer C. S. Fly's boardinghouse where Doc and Kate Elder were staying. He apparently knew they had a room there. Ike didn't barge in to confront Doc. Instead he briefly lurked outside and then moved on. Fly's wife, Mollie, saw him. She warned Kate, who was looking at photographs on display in the gallery of Fly's studio behind the boardinghouse, that Ike was armed and waiting for Doc. Like the Earps, Doc was sleeping in that morning. Kate went to their room, woke him, and told Doc that Ike was looking for him. With his usual sardonic humor, Doc replied, "If God lets me live long enough to get my clothes on, he shall see me." Unlike the Earp brothers, Doc seemed to relish the possibility of a showdown with Ike. He didn't hurry out to find him, though. Doc took his time dressing and then went out to enjoy a leisurely breakfast. To him, shouted threats and potential shooting bordered on the routine.

Virgil Earp emerged from his house shortly after noon. Daniel Lynch, a housepainter, rushed over and repeated the warning that Virgil had already heard from A. G. Bronk: Ike Clanton was drunk and armed and threatening to kill the Earps and Doc. It was obvious to Virgil that Ike wasn't going to shut up and stumble off to bed. As he began walking toward the saloon district, Virgil met his brothers Morgan and James. They'd also been alerted about Ike, and wanted to make sure Virgil knew that he was carrying a rifle and handgun. Virgil indicated that he was on his way to find Ike. Morgan went with him, while James went back home or to work. With rare exceptions, James left law enforcement to his brothers. Virgil and Morgan were surely up to the task of getting a single armed, drunken buffoon under control.

Wyatt got up about the same time as Virgil and strolled to the Oriental Saloon. As soon as he arrived, he was accosted by Tombstone attorney and former city council member Harry Jones, who also occasionally served as one of Johnny Behan's deputy sheriffs. "What does all this mean?" Jones asked Wyatt, who replied that he had no idea of what Jones was talking about. "Ike Clanton is hunting you boys with a Winchester rifle and a six-shooter," Jones said. Wyatt was never given to self-criticism, but perhaps he spared a moment to berate himself for trying to cut a secret deal with an idiot like Ike Clanton. Then Wyatt told Jones, "I will go down and find him and see what he wants."

The three Earp brothers briefly met and conferred. Ike had to be disarmed and arrested before the situation got any worse. Police Chief Virgil carried a pistol, and Morgan and Wyatt each had one, too. As special deputies, they were entitled to be armed. Virgil's and Morgan's guns were probably tucked into their belts. All three men wore coats to protect themselves from the chilly wind, and Wyatt's particularly lent itself to armed confrontations. Just the day before, he'd acquired a new coat with a special canvas pocket to carry a handgun — it was less likely to snag the hammer or barrel if the gun had to be drawn in a hurry.

The brothers split up, with Wyatt hunting for Ike on Allen Street and Virgil and Morgan searching for him on Fremont. Within minutes, Virgil and Morgan spotted Ike, but not before the belligerent, drunken Clanton encountered the one man Virgil would have most preferred not to be aware of the tenuous situation.

Tombstone mayor John Clum had just left his office at the *Epitaph* to wander around town looking for material for stories. He wanted some subject of human interest, and he discovered something very interesting indeed. There at the corner of Fourth and Fremont was Ike Clanton, drunk and, as Clum colorfully remembered it years later in his memoir, "holding a Winchester rifle in his arms much after the fashion of a mother holding her child and fondling it accordingly." As a newsman, Clum was pleased with the possibility of "a good story in the making, [but] my conscience as mayor told me that Ike should be arrested." Clum wished Ike a good morning and jokingly inquired, "Any new war on today?" while scanning the street for a police officer. Looking down Fremont, Clum spotted Virgil, who he later recalled seemed to be "sauntering" rather than rushing over to enforce the law.

Virgil certainly saw the mayor, too, and so for him things immediately became more complicated. At this point Virgil certainly regretted not tossing Ike into jail the night before. Now Clum was on the scene; he would expect his police chief to act promptly and in a decisive manner. Ike had to be confronted and subdued in a way that was acceptable to Virgil's boss. Otherwise, Virgil might join Ben Sippy as a former town chief of police. It was a matter of how much force Virgil used to subdue Ike, and one option was to shoot the drunken cowboy where he stood.

Frontier justice traditionally upheld the right to kill in self-defense, and the definition of "self-defense" was elastic. Murder charges were frequently dismissed when defendants claimed they *believed* that the victim intended to assault them. On Wednesday morning, an openly armed Ike Clanton had declared to several witnesses that he intended to gun down the Earps and Doc as soon as he saw them. Virgil could simply walk up to Ike on Fremont Street and shoot him dead, secure in the knowledge that when the matter came to court, Ned Boyle, A. G. Bronk, Daniel Lynch, and Harry Jones — all of whom had warned either Virgil or Wyatt that morning of Ike's threats — would offer testimony that virtually guaranteed Virgil's exoneration.

Virgil had killed before, four years earlier in Prescott when he joined several others in shooting down two felons who initiated a shootout. The episode launched Virgil's subsequent career as a lawman, but he considered shooting to be a last resort. Even with Mayor Clum watching and Ike Clanton brandishing guns and obviously ready to carry out his bloody threats, Virgil still didn't pull a trigger. Instead, he and Morgan drew their guns and walked up behind Ike, who was probably distracted by sighting Wyatt a block away on Allen Street. Ike had his Winchester in his hand; his six-shooter was still stuck in the waist of his pants. Virgil reached out and grasped the rifle. As Ike grabbed for his pistol, Virgil whacked him across the skull with the butt of his own gun, stunning Ike and knocking him flat. It was neatly done, and Mayor Clum, watching from across the street, admired how "Ike stretched his length on the sidewalk."

Virgil later testified that as Ike sprawled on Fremont Street, he asked the battered cowboy if he "was hunting for me." Defiant in spite of his aching head, Ike snarled that he was, and if he'd seen Virgil a second sooner he would have killed him. Once again, Virgil had to make a judgment call. The Tombstone police chief could toss Ike in a cell and let him sleep it off while he decided what to do next. By threatening the life of a deputy U.S. marshal — Virgil still held that office besides serving as Tombstone's top law officer — Ike had made himself liable to federal charges if Virgil wanted to pursue them. But mindful that Mayor Clum was still watching and undoubtedly expecting Ike to suffer immediate consequences for defying town ordinances, Virgil chose to arrest Ike for unlawfully carrying firearms inside city limits. Then he, Morgan, and Wyatt hauled their still dazed prisoner off to recorder's court just a short distance away on the corner of Fourth and Fremont.

If Virgil thought buffaloing, arresting, and arraigning Ike would be the end of it, he was mistaken. When the Earp brothers dragged Ike into the cramped courtroom, there was no judge present to quickly adjudicate the case and send everyone on their way. He was out officiating at a wedding. Virgil went to fetch him, while Morgan and Wyatt remained behind to guard Ike. Virgil should have sent one of his brothers after the judge and remained in the courtroom himself. Townspeople curious about the pistol-whipping jammed inside hoping for further entertainment, and they got it. As soon as Virgil was out the door, Ike and Morgan Earp began squabbling like antagonistic schoolboys while the principal briefly stepped away from his office. In playground terms, Ike probably started it. He couldn't have felt well even before Virgil pounded his skull with a gun butt. At that point Ike had been drinking heavily for more than twenty-four straight hours. Now as he slumped on a chair in recorder's court with Morgan and Wyatt looming over him, blood dripped from a cut on his head. All morning Ike had bragged that he was about to take on the Earps. Then he did, and they subdued him with contemptuous ease. It was embarrassing for Ike, and would be even more humiliating if he waited meekly for whatever punishment the judge chose to mete out and then slunk away. Showing undaunted defiance was necessary to salvage some semblance of pride, and so Ike did. Wyatt was seated on a bench opposite Ike, while Morgan stood beside his brother holding Ike's rifle and pistol. Ike glared at them and snarled that they hadn't given him "any show at all." If he had a six-shooter, Ike said, "I would make a fight with all of you."

If even-tempered Virgil had been present he would have told his brothers to just ignore Ike, but in Virgil's absence hotheaded Morgan took the bait. He offered a six-gun to Ike, saying "Here, take this. You can have all the show you want right now." As gawkers scattered, a court officer grabbed Ike and prevented him from snatching the gun from Morgan. Ike was slammed back into a sitting position, and for a moment it seemed that things might cool down. Ike had demonstrated that despite the beating he'd just suffered on Fremont Street, the Earps didn't scare him. He'd stood up to them just like he said he would. Honor — albeit of a battered variety — was satisfied.

It might have been for Ike, but not for Wyatt. For months, Ike Clanton had badgered him about revealing their secret deal, an agreement Wyatt now devoutly wished he'd never proposed. This man — this *cowboy* — had spent the whole night and morning threatening to kill Wyatt and his brothers, and he was still promising to do it. It had to stop. Wyatt's concern wasn't limited to the safety of the Earps. He wanted to be elected county sheriff, and his best chance was to convince voters that he above all others was best qualified to enforce the law and keep order. Many people in Tombstone were aware of Ike's latest shenanigans — how would it look if he left the courtroom clearly unrepentant and immediately resumed his strutting and threats? Wyatt had to demonstrate that he could master Ike Clanton and any other drunken, gun-toting cowboys who defied the law.

Wyatt fixed his cold blue eyes on Ike Clanton sitting across from him and said, "You damn dirty cow thief, you have been threatening our lives and I know it. I think I would be justified in shooting you down any place I would meet you, but if you are anxious to make a fight I will go anywhere on earth to make a fight with you, even over to San Simon among your own crowd." With those bloodcurdling words, Wyatt called out not only Ike but all of the cowboys. It was the sort of quote that, if anyone heard and repeated it to John Clum, would look impressive in the *Epitaph*. Given Wyatt's menacing glare and hulking physique, most people would have been intimidated — but in his woozy, single-minded condition, Ike Clanton didn't flinch. "Fight is my racket," he replied with more bravado than sense. "All I want is four feet of ground."

Just then Virgil returned with the judge, and order was restored. The hearing concluded in minutes. Since Ike was clearly guilty of the single charge against him — illegally carrying firearms in town — he was fined $25 plus $2.50 in court costs. Ike paid on the spot and was set free by the judge. Ever efficient, Virgil politely asked Ike where he wanted him to leave his rifle and pistol to be picked up when Ike left town. Ike vaguely replied, "Anywhere I can get them," and Virgil took the weapons over to the Grand Hotel, where he checked them at the bar. Ike left to seek medical attention, Morgan apparently went about his early afternoon business, and Wyatt stalked out of the courtroom in a state of absolute rage. For him, there was no satisfaction in Ike's fine. As far as the court was concerned, Ike had been convicted of a minor infraction. After threatening to kill the Earps, after wandering Tombstone with a gun waiting for the chance to shoot them down, after paying his fine Ike was right back on the street like some law-abiding citizen. Soon he'd be hounding Wyatt again about revealing their deal, or, worse, continuing his threats to shoot the Earps and Doc on sight. So long as Ike was on the prowl, Wyatt, his brothers, and Doc remained at risk. Nothing was resolved, and Wyatt was ready to take out his frustration on the next person who crossed him. Within moments of leaving the courtroom he had the opportunity.

Tom McLaury's day was off to a bad start. He'd intended to sleep in, run some errands — settling accounts with a few Tombstone butchers, visiting stores to buy supplies — and then enjoy another hour or two of relaxation with his brother, Frank, and Billy Clanton when they arrived in town before riding back to the McLaurys' ranch. Ike Clanton had acted foolishly the night before, but, so far as Tom knew everything ended well with the all-night poker game. Now on Wednesday Tom had awakened to learn that Ike was at it again, and even worse — apparently he'd armed himself, gone around town threatening to shoot the Earps and Doc Holliday, and been buffaloed and taken to recorder's court because of it. Finding Ike and dealing with the situation had to be added to Tom's list of things to do. He retrieved his pistol from the Grand Hotel bar. It meant there would be one fewer stop to make later in the day. Though there was a city ordinance against carrying a gun unless you were arriving in or leaving town, Tom was at least technically beginning the process of leaving from the moment he got out of bed, and, unlike Ike, he wasn't going to flaunt the weapon. Tom never looked for trouble. He'd find Ike, go about his other business, and hopefully get the chance for a last drink or two before heading home.

As Tom approached the recorder's court he encountered Wyatt. The younger McLaury brother was exactly the wrong person to cross Wyatt's path at that moment. Even in his best moods, Wyatt always saw the world as a place divided into friends and enemies. He had no doubt which side Tom was on. Whatever initial words they exchanged outside recorder's court made Wyatt even more furious. Tom may have asked where he could find Ike, or else said hello. Wyatt's response was so heated that bystander J. H. Batcher recalled that "I thought it was time to get off the [street]" and hurried away, but not before hearing Tom respond that although he had never done anything to Wyatt, he was ready if Wyatt ever wanted to fight. Wyatt then either made a threatening gesture or pulled his gun before asking, "Are you heeled?" Given Wyatt's ferocious mood, it would have been foolish for Tom to admit that he was armed. But Wyatt clearly suspected that he was, and he was not about to take one more gun-toting, ordinance-disdaining cowboy into recorder's court for a slap-on-the-wrist fine. Wyatt's fury boiled over and he slapped Tom with his left hand, smashed his pistol against the young man's head with his right, and left Tom lying in the street. Butcher Apollinar Bauer, another eyewitness to the incident, insisted that Wyatt didn't leave it at that: He hit Tom several more times and walked away snarling, "I could kill the son of a bitch."

Wyatt himself later swore that Tom not only said he wanted to fight, he also carried his pistol "in plain sight on his right hip in his pants." Though onlookers offered different accounts of what Tom and Wyatt said to each other and how many times Wyatt hit Tom, none of them mentioned seeing Tom's pistol. It was in Wyatt's interest later on to make Tom seem as confrontational as possible during their exchange on Allen Street, but anyone acquainted with the younger McLaury brother knew better. Wyatt's uncalled-for manhandling of Tom was a serious loss of self-control. His poor judgment outside the recorder's court contributed greatly to the events that followed.

With the help of an onlooker, Tom slowly picked himself off the ground. True to his nature, he didn't attempt to restore injured pride by calling out insults after Wyatt or threatening revenge. He'd been struck on the head and knocked down. There had already been enough trouble. There was no sense doing something foolish that would make things worse. With his head aching, Tom McLaury visited some Tombstone butcher shops as planned, collecting cash, checks, and letters of bank credit and tucking them in the money belt underneath his shirt. But before Tom went about his business he checked his pistol at the Capitol Saloon. Tom did not intend to give Wyatt or any of the other Earps an excuse to attack him again.

About one in the afternoon Frank McLaury and Billy Clanton rode into Tombstone with their cattleman friend J. R. Frink. Frink was negotiating an agreement to sell beef to a town butcher and the McLaury brothers were involved in the deal. Probably they were to supply some of the cattle. Frank and Billy headed to the Grand Hotel. They hitched their horses outside — the saddles on both animals had rifles in scabbards dangling down their sides. As Frank and Billy dismounted they received a pleasant greeting from a passing Doc Holliday, who shook hands with Billy and politely inquired after his health. Doc and Billy were not well acquainted, if at all, but certainly each would at least have recognized the other. It seemed obvious that at some point Ike and Doc would have it out; neither man was prone to forget disputes. In the meantime, it suited Doc's humor to greet the younger brother of a man he expected to confront sometime soon.

Frank and Billy proceeded to the hotel bar, eager to get out of the cold wind and have a drink. Like his brother, Tom, Frank intended to conduct a little business while he was in Tombstone. Billy was ready to relax for a bit before he, Ike, Frank, and Tom rode out. Town ordinance required that the two newcomers check their guns, and they were probably about to hand them over to the bartender when their friend Billy Allen arrived. He pulled Frank aside and asked if he knew what was going on. Frank didn't, so Allen recounted what had happened to Ike and Tom. Frank was particularly puzzled by Wyatt's assault on his younger brother: "What did he hit Tom for?" he quizzed Allen, who said he didn't know.

The Earps may have considered the cowboys to be menaces, but the feeling was mutual. To Frank McLaury, the Earps were oppressors. Like most of the Cochise County small ranchers dealing in rustled Mexican cattle, Frank in no way considered himself to be a criminal. He was a pragmatic businessman working hard to make a living. Lawmen like the Earps and the government they represented had no right to prevent anyone from earning a few dollars. The McLaurys and other independent-minded men lived out on the Western frontier because they didn't want someone constantly telling them what they could and couldn't do. Tom's pistol-whipping by Wyatt was just one more example of the little man getting pushed around. Even though Frank was extremely protective of his younger brother he realized that in Tombstone, with its policemen and its ordinances favoring the Earps and their friends, it made no sense to hunt Wyatt down and try to even the score. If Frank wanted revenge, it would have to come at another time and in a different place where the odds would be more even. Frank's immediate concern was to get Tom and Ike out of Tombstone before any more disasters could befall them. He and Billy left their drinks untouched at the hotel bar and hurried out to unhitch their horses. "I will get the boys out of town," Frank told Billy Allen, and he and Billy Clanton, still wearing their gun belts, set off to find their battered brothers.

When Ike was set free by the judge in recorder's court, the cut on his head caused by Virgil's pistol-whipping was still bleeding. Just outside the courtroom Ike stumbled upon his friend Billy Claiborne. The twenty-one-year-old Claiborne wanted to be a famous gunslinger — he referred to himself as "Arizona's Billy the Kid" in homage to New Mexico's notorious cowboy who'd been killed just two months before — and would soon be indicted by a Cochise County grand jury for murdering a man in a Charleston saloon. Claiborne escorted Ike to a doctor's office to have his wound patched up. After his head was bandaged, Ike walked with Claiborne down Fourth Street. They separated; Ike went into Spangenberg's, a store selling guns and ammunition. He tried to buy a pistol, but proprietor George Spangenberg knew all about Ike's run-ins with Doc and the Earps and sensibly refused to sell him one. Ike was still feeling shaky from the blow to his skull. Blood from his head wound had seeped through the bandage.

Outside on Fourth Street, Claiborne met Frank McLaury and Billy Clanton. Frank was still leading his horse. Billy had left his at Dexter's Livery and Feed Stable on the corner of Fourth and Allen. Claiborne told them that Ike was nearby, and Billy said that he just wanted to get his older brother "to go out home." Frank and Billy saw Ike in Spangenberg's and went inside. While they were there, they purchased ammunition — it's possible that buying some was one of the reasons they'd come to town. They began pushing bullets into empty loops on their gun belts.

Meanwhile, just a few yards away on Fourth Street, Wyatt Earp glared into Spangenberg's through the store's front window. After pistol-whipping Tom McLaury, Wyatt had gone to Hafford's Saloon on the corner of Fourth and Allen, where he bought a cigar and stood smoking it. He watched Ike Clanton come down the street and go into the gun shop and then saw Frank McLaury and Billy Clanton join Ike there after they met and briefly spoke with Billy Claiborne, who Wyatt must have known had recently killed someone in Charleston. Frank McLaury and Billy Clanton were stuffing bullets in their gun belts. Wyatt could only assume that they were preparing to fight.

Frank had led his horse by the reins as he and Billy walked along Fourth Street looking for Ike. When they went into Spangenberg's Frank tethered the horse too close to the building. It clopped up onto the sidewalk and stuck its head into the door of the gun shop. That provided an excuse for Wyatt to intervene. He stalked over, grabbed the horse's reins and began pulling the animal back onto the street. Frank and the Clanton brothers immediately came outside, and Frank yanked the reins from Wyatt. "You will have to get this horse off the sidewalk," Wyatt told Frank, who tied the horse farther out on Fourth Street and then went back into Spangenberg's without speaking a word. Wyatt was left to watch and seethe as the cowboys continued to put bullets into their gun belts. Wyatt was even more convinced that the cowboys wanted a showdown. As he recalled later, when they briefly left the shop while Wyatt was moving Frank's horse, Billy Clanton clearly "laid his hand on his six-shooter."

The cowboys, Frank in particular, were just as suspicious of Wyatt. It hadn't been necessary for him to barge in and order Frank to move his horse back onto the street. If he wasn't trying to goad them into a battle, then he was at least pushing them around to impress onlookers. The town was still buzzing; everyone was watching the Earps and the cowboys to see what might happen next. Frank McLaury was an especially proud man, as he'd proven fifteen months earlier when Lieutenant Hurst accused him of stealing army mules. Frank cared what people thought about him — about his integrity, his willingness to stand up for himself, his *manhood*. Frank still intended to find his brother

Tom and take him home, but he couldn't leave the impression in Tombstone that Wyatt Earp had scared him into scurrying out of town. Wyatt's actions with the horse had been too public. Prickly Frank McLaury had to make it clear that he wasn't intimidated.

Virgil Earp was just as concerned as Wyatt that more trouble was brewing. As the police chief walked down Allen Street, he was stopped by townspeople alerting him to the cowboys' movements. Somebody reported hearing one of them say, "Now is our time to make a fight." Though Virgil hoped it would be unnecessary, he began preparing for a possible confrontation. He walked to the Wells Fargo office and borrowed a shotgun. It was a significant weapon for Virgil to acquire. Even in a shootout at close range, handguns were notoriously inaccurate. Shotguns with their wide spread of pellets were far more lethal. If the cowboys really intended to fight, perhaps the sight of a shotgun would make them change their minds.

Virgil had just walked out with the shotgun when Bob Hatch, owner of a popular Tombstone saloon and billiards parlor, came running up. "For god's sake, hurry down to the gun shop," Hatch blurted. "They are all down there and Wyatt is all alone. They are liable to kill him before you get there." Virgil hustled down Fourth Street and found Wyatt unscathed but scowling in front of Hafford's Saloon. The two Earp brothers watched as Frank, Ike, and Billy left Spangenberg's and met Tom coming from his stops at the various town butchers. With their friend Billy Claiborne, the cowboys walked down Fourth Street to Dexter's Livery and Feed Stable to get the horse that Billy Clanton had left there earlier. From there they planned to walk two blocks north to the West End Corral on Fremont and Second Street, where they would pick up Ike and Tom's team and wagon. Their route would take them through the back of the O.K. Corral.

It was a little after 1 P.M. on Wednesday when Johnny Behan roused himself from slumber. The controversial Cochise County sheriff dressed and went out to Barron's Barber Shop, where he was lathered up for a shave. Johnny noticed that a crowd was gathered around Fourth and Allen streets, and someone in the shop told him there was trouble between the Earps and the Clantons. Johnny could have ignored the situation. He was the county sheriff; Virgil Earp was town police chief and responsible for keeping the peace in Tombstone. But Virgil had just helped Johnny pursue escapees from county custody. Lawmen were morally obligated to support one another. He told the barber to hurry up with the shave so he could go and disarm or arrest whoever was causing the trouble.

Freshly shaven, Johnny left the barber shop and bumped into Charlie Shibell, the former Pima County sheriff. Shibell said he would come along with Johnny to find Virgil Earp. As they began walking toward Fourth Street, miner R. F. Coleman came up to Johnny and told him that he ought to arrest the Clantons and McLaurys because "they meant mischief." Coleman helpfully added that the cowboys could now be found at the O.K. Corral. Then Coleman hustled ahead of Johnny and Shibell to tell Virgil the same thing.

Johnny and Shibell found Virgil standing outside Hafford's holding the shotgun he had borrowed from Wells Fargo. Doc Holliday, dressed in a long gray overcoat that extended below his knees, was with him. Doc carried a silver-headed cane, an occasional fashion affectation among Tombstone's dandies. Johnny asked Virgil, "What was the excitement?" and Virgil replied that there were "sons of bitches in town looking for a fight." *Son of a bitch* and its plural were apparently favorite epithets among the Earps. Virgil took Johnny's suggestion that they go into Hafford's and discuss it over a drink. According to Virgil, once they got inside he asked Johnny to go down and help him disarm the cowboys, but Johnny refused on the grounds that if Virgil was involved, the Clantons and McLaurys would surely fight rather than surrender their weapons. Johnny said that he told Virgil to go take the guns from the cowboys, but Virgil wouldn't because he wanted "to give them a chance to make a fight." It's possible that both were telling the truth — Johnny believed that the already riled cowboys, who always resented authority, were unlikely to cooperate with a lawman they didn't trust, and Virgil may have been so on edge that he mentioned an extreme course of action as a means of letting off steam rather than expressing his actual intentions.

Whatever they said to each other, Johnny and Virgil were interrupted by businessman William B. Murray, a leader of the Citizens Safety Committee. He asked Virgil to step over to a quiet corner of the bar with him, where Murray offered to bring twenty-five armed men to help the town police chief subdue the cowboys. This was bad news for Virgil in two ways. He still wanted to resolve the situation with the McLaurys and Clantons peacefully, and even the peripheral presence of gun-waving vigilantes would lessen the chances that he could. On a personal level, Virgil must have realized that Murray, speaking on behalf of the Safety Committee, was making it clear that the important people in Tombstone expected Virgil to do something right away.

Virgil offered a reason to delay a little

longer. The cowboys were at the O.K. Corral, he told Murray. So long as they stayed in the corral, it didn't matter if they had their guns. They were either preparing to ride out of town or at least staying away from everybody else. If they came back out onto the Tombstone streets, then Virgil would disarm them. It wasn't the strategy Murray would have preferred, but Virgil's plan seemed plausible. He wasn't refusing to act, just trying to avoid an unnecessary confrontation. "You can count on me if there is any danger," Murray said. Virgil very much hoped he wouldn't have to.

The O.K. Corral wasn't the cowboys' final destination, but they paused there for a few minutes. It wouldn't do to seem in a hurry to get to the West End Corral, where they would collect the buckboard and team and ride out of Tombstone. There were still onlookers to impress. In the worst tradition of overweening male pride, Frank, Tom, Ike, Billy, and Billy Claiborne postured in the O.K. Corral, boasting loudly about what they would do if the Earps were foolish enough to bother them any further. If Virgil Earp showed up, they'd kill him on sight. They'd kill the whole party of Earps if it came to that. The cowboys didn't mind that the people around them could hear every word. They wanted them to.

Among the gawkers outside the corral was

H. F. Sills, a railway worker on job furlough who had arrived in Tombstone a day earlier. Sills didn't know anyone in Tombstone, but it shocked him to hear the cowboys threatening a lawman and his brothers. The one with the bloody bandage on his head was making the most violent comments. Sills asked someone to tell him where he could find Virgil Earp. Directed to Hafford's, Sills identified Virgil and reported what he had heard. After talking to Sills, Virgil agreed that Johnny Behan should go by himself to the O.K. Corral and try to persuade the cowboys to give up their guns. Maybe Johnny was right when he claimed that he stood a better chance than Virgil of bringing about a peaceful resolution.

For Johnny, it was an opportunity to restore his reputation with one heroic act. The Earps and the power elite of Tombstone mocked his sensible law enforcement philosophy of getting along with the cowboys instead of antagonizing them. Now Johnny would demonstrate why his approach had been correct all along by doing what the Earps couldn't — diffusing a dangerous situation with minimal fuss. He'd walk down to the O.K. Corral and talk calmly to the McLaurys and the Clantons, who knew they could trust him. He'd take their guns or shake their hands and watch them ride back to their ranches without any further brawling or gunplay. Either way, his Tombstone critics would be proved wrong. Best of all, the Earps couldn't claim even partial credit. It was Johnny Behan going to the O.K. Corral while the ineffectual Earps skulked at Hafford's. His triumph would be especially galling to Wyatt, who'd caught the eye of Josephine and who planned to wrest away the lucrative job of county sheriff, too. Johnny believed he was a better man than Wyatt, and in another year Cochise County residents would confirm it with their votes. As he walked toward the corral, Johnny would have been less than human if that happy thought didn't cross his mind.

The first sign that things might not go as smoothly as Johnny expected came when he arrived at the O.K. Corral, because the cowboys were no longer there.

Hafford's rocked with the latest rumors. One involved the first sighting that morning of drunken, threat-spewing Ike Clanton. He'd been outside the town telegraph office. Maybe he'd sent a telegram summoning more cowboys to come to his aid in Tombstone, and Frank McLaury and Billy Clanton were only the first arrivals. Apparently no one took the logical step of checking at the telegraph office to see if Ike had sent such a message. It was more exciting to speculate that he had. As anticipation that something bloody and special was about to happen continued to mount among Tombstone's townspeople, so did pressure on Virgil to do something, but he still resisted taking any action. Johnny Behan had gone out to talk to the cowboys. He'd wait a bit longer and give Johnny a chance to resolve the crisis. Wyatt, who waited in Hafford's with Virgil and Morgan, was undoubtedly less inclined to hope that Johnny succeeded. Still in his black mood, Wyatt was prepared to deal with the cowboys himself no matter what that might involve. So was Morgan, who was always ready for a showdown. But Virgil was police chief, and Wyatt and Morgan were special deputies who served at his pleasure and under his command. Like everyone else, Wyatt and Morgan waited and wondered what their older brother would decide to do.

After their pause at the O.K. Corral, the five cowboys walked through the back of the corral and down an alley that opened onto Fremont Street near Union Meat & Poultry Market. Billy Clanton and Frank McLaury were leading their horses. Both animals were still saddled with rifles hanging in scabbards. As they reached Fremont the McLaury brothers stopped outside the market to talk to butcher James Kehoe. There had been what Kehoe would later term a "misunderstanding . . . about some money." While the McLaurys still intended to leave town before

394

there was any more trouble, they paused to resolve their disagreement with Kehoe before riding home. The discussion wasn't heated, and Tom probably joined Ike, Billy, and Billy Claiborne in wandering a bit farther west on Fremont Street while Frank continued talking to the butcher. The four stopped to wait for Frank in an eighteen-foot-wide empty lot on the south side of Fremont between C. S. Fly's boardinghouse and a frame residence owned by William Harwood, who had been Tombstone's first mayor. People watching along Fremont could only see a few feet into the lot unless they were directly across the street from it.

Walking south to Fremont from Allen Street, probably using Fourth Street as his route rather than the alley behind the O.K. Corral, Johnny Behan spotted Frank McLaury talking to James Kehoe. Frank was still holding the reins of his horse. Johnny came up to the cowboy and the butcher, and told Frank that he wanted to disarm him. Johnny added — probably to make certain that always touchy Frank didn't feel unfairly singled out — that he intended to disarm everybody involved. It was one of Johnny's verbal manipulations. As town lawmen, the Earps had every right to carry their guns. By "everyone" Johnny really meant only the cowboys. But Frank replied that he refused to give up his guns "as long as the people in Tombstone act so." People were still watching. He wasn't about to submissively hand over his weapons. Johnny apparently understood that pride was involved, and offered to take Frank to his sheriff's office. The cowboy could surrender his guns in private there. That suited Frank better; he didn't trust the Earps, but he had no reason to doubt Johnny. Frank still had some business to conduct in town. Having made his gestures of defiance at the Earps, with Johnny Behan's help he could save face and then stay in town to complete his errands. But it was important that everyone, including Johnny, understand that Frank was cooperating because he wanted to, not because of any lawman's orders. "You need not take me," Frank told Johnny. "I will go."

Johnny looked west on Fremont and saw for the first time that Tom McLaury and Ike Clanton were loitering on the edge of the vacant lot beyond Fly's boardinghouse. He did not see Billy Clanton or Billy Claiborne because they were farther inside the lot. Johnny told Frank to come along with him while he collected the other cowboys and took everyone over to the sheriff's office to be disarmed. That suited Johnny's purposes even better than relieving the cowboys of their weapons on Fremont Street. If he walked with them to his office and took their guns from them there, it would appear to onlookers as though County Sheriff Behan had made actual arrests, while the cowboys themselves would believe they were going with Johnny of their own volition.

Around 2:30 in the afternoon, Johnny had been gone from Hafford's for about twenty minutes. Virgil had heard nothing from him. John L. Fonck, a furniture dealer, approached Virgil much as William Murray did earlier. He offered Virgil ten men to help disarm and arrest the cowboys. Virgil repeated that if the cowboys stayed at the O.K. Corral he would leave them alone. Fonck said, "Why, they are all down on Fremont Street there now."

Virgil had no choice. Everyone in Tombstone, it seemed, was watching to see how he would respond, and he had promised Murray, a leader of the Safety Committee, that he would disarm the cowboys if they returned to the town streets. The only decision left was whom he would choose to go with him to confront the Clantons and McLaurys. Brave as he was, Virgil wasn't about to face odds of one against four. A. G. Bronk and Jim Flynn, his two policemen, were both off-duty and probably asleep before returning to patrol that night. If he summoned them, there would be more delay before they arrived, and with the cowboys still armed and now on one of Tombstone's main streets Virgil had clearly stalled as long as he could. If he didn't do something promptly, the Safety Committee was prepared to send out vigilantes in his place.

His brothers Wyatt and Morgan were there at Hafford's. Both were experienced lawmen, and they had the added advantage of being family. Neither of his younger brothers had distinguished themselves so far that day in their dealings with Ike Clanton and Tom McLaury, but Virgil could trust them to support him no matter how violently the cowboys responded to an order to give up their guns. He asked Wyatt and Morgan to come and help him disarm the McLaury and Clanton brothers. Doc overheard and invited himself along, both out of friendship to Wyatt and his usual eagerness to fight. Virgil must have recognized the risk of allowing such a volatile character to be involved in what he still hoped would be a peaceful effort, but he had a specific role in mind for him; for a change, Doc could play a part in preventing trouble rather than causing it. Virgil couldn't be certain how many other cowboys might be lurking along Fremont Street. He'd already heard that Billy Claiborne was around. Doc was given the responsibility of standing guard while the Earp brothers relieved the Clantons and McLaurys of their weapons. Virgil handed Doc the Wells Fargo shotgun and took Doc's silver-headed cane in exchange. Until they reached wherever the cowboys were on Fremont Street, Doc was instructed to keep the shotgun under his long coat. Virgil didn't want onlookers becoming any more alarmed than they already were. When the Earps confronted the two sets of brothers, Doc would stand out in the street and, if necessary, brandish the shotgun as a warning to any of their cowboy friends who might be tempted to intervene. He would also be in position to block the Clantons and McLaurys if they tried to run for it across Fremont.

Besides the shotgun, Doc had a pistol in a holster under his coat. Virgil had Doc's cane in his left hand and his right hand on the butt of a pistol stuck in the waist of his pants. Morgan probably had his pistol in his hand, and so did Wyatt. "Come along," Virgil said, and together the three Earp brothers and their tubercular dentist ally left Hafford's and began walking north on Fourth Street toward Fremont, which was only one block away.

When Johnny Behan walked into the vacant lot with Frank McLaury, he was surprised to see Billy Clanton and Billy Claiborne there with Tom and Ike. He asked if they were all together, and Claiborne insisted that he was not "one of the party." Johnny explained to Tom, Ike, and Billy Clanton what he'd just told Frank: The four of them would go with Johnny to his office and he would disarm them there. Ike and Tom protested that they had no weapons for the county sheriff to take. Johnny was skeptical. He frisked Ike by running his hands all around the elder Clanton's waist and found no guns. Tom McLaury pulled open his coat to show that there were no pistols in his waistband. The gesture in itself proved little. Tom could have had a gun pushed in his waistband at the base of his spine, or else had one concealed beneath the untucked shirt that he wore beneath his coat. But Johnny was in a hurry and chose to accept Tom's word. Just as he was ready to lead the cowboys away, Frank balked. He'd had a few moments to think it over, and now said that he would surrender his guns only "after the party that hit [my] brother" was disarmed. It was an obvious deal-breaker. Wyatt Earp was hardly going to give up his six-shooter because Frank McLaury insisted on it. Johnny was stuck. All around, people on the Fremont Street sidewalks were watching and straining to hear what the sheriff and the cowboys were saying. Schieffelin Hall manager William Cuddy testified later that Johnny insisted, "I won't have no fighting. You must give me your firearms or leave town immediately." According to Cuddy, one of the cowboys replied, "They will have no trouble with us, Johnny. We are going to leave town right now."

That was when someone on Fremont shouted, "Here they come!"

Tombstone was built on a low mesa known locally as Goose Flats. Ringed by mines, it grew rapidly into one of the most sophisticated boomtowns on the Western frontier.

Allen Street in Tombstone was lined with restaurants and shops, but its packed-dirt surface was overrun with rats and other pests, and pedestrians were frequently choked by blowing dust.

3

Nicholas Earp, shown here with his second wife, Virginia Cooksey, was a hard man determined to gain prominence and wealth, an obsession he passed on to several of his sons, particularly Wyatt.

Alone among the Earp brothers, Virgil would have been content with a career as a lawman. His poor decisions on the night of October 25, 1881, and on the afternoon of October 26 led directly to the famous gunfight in Tombstone.

4

Handsome, fearless, and absolutely self-assured, Wyatt Earp lacked the political sophistication necessary to reach the positions of wealth and power that he craved. His overweening ambition cost him and his family dearly.

5

Unlike his brother Wyatt, sociable James Earp mingled easily with people of all backgrounds and interests. He rarely worked with his brothers in any aspect of law enforcement and had no part in the renowned shootout.

6

Always a follower of his brothers rather than a leader, Morgan Earp survived the October 1881 gunfight only to die at the hands of assassins months later.

7

Dissolute Warren Earp was kept on the fringe of family activities until he joined his older brother Wyatt on the Vendetta Ride to avenge the crippling of Virgil and the murder of Morgan.

8

Wyatt Earp and Bat Masterson were both gamblers who sometimes served in law enforcement. A magazine article by Masterson in 1907 was the impetus for the resurrection of Wyatt's reputation and the beginning of his one-dimensional modern legend.

9

Knowing he was doomed to die young from tuberculosis, Doc Holliday had a hot temper, no self-discipline, and a devotion to Wyatt Earp that made him willing and even eager to risk his life for his friend.

10

Itinerant prospector Ed Schieffelin struck a silver lode in southeastern Arizona Territory and founded a town named for the tombstone that scoffers had predicted was all he would find there. Put off by the thriving economic hot spot that Tombstone soon became, Schieffelin left about the same time that the Earp brothers arrived.

11

12

A warren of mines soon surrounded Tombstone; part of the town was even built over them. But very few produced enough silver to warrant the considerable investment necessary to construct full extraction facilities.

Newman "Old Man" Clanton and his brood were a typical family wandering the frontier in hopes of striking it rich. His death in an ambush freed his sons, particularly Ike, from their father's rigid control and helped precipitate events that led to the gunfight on October 26, 1881.

13

In 1874 the Clantons successfully petitioned the Pima County Board of Supervisors to establish Clantonville, but the new settlement failed to attract enough investors and settlers to survive. The Clantons moved on to their date with destiny in Tombstone.

14

15

Cowardly, boastful, often drunk, and always belligerent, Ike Clanton represented the worst excesses of men on the Western frontier. His antagonism toward the Earps was based on Ike's fear that his cowboy friends would learn of his failed collaboration with Wyatt.

Soft-spoken and good with a gun, Billy Clanton was the antithesis of his older brother Ike. But it was Billy's fate to die in the gun-fight that Ike's drunken escapades precipitated.

16

Short, feisty Frank McLaury was at odds with Virgil and Wyatt Earp long before he died at their hands during the October 1881 gunfight. Though he was friends with the cowboys and certainly traded in rustled stock, McLaury was never an overt outlaw and was widely considered a respectable citizen.

17

Tom McLaury was quieter than his brother Frank, and more likely to avoid than to seek out arguments. But his one-sided tussle with Wyatt Earp hours before the October 26 gunfight left him dazed, bleeding, and possibly prepared to defend himself at all costs in a subsequent confrontation.

18

19

OFFICERS.

H. B. MAXON, - - - *President.*
CHAS. I. GLOVER, - *Vice-President.*
T. E. NICHOLS, - - - *Secretary.*
J. S. McGINNIS, - - *Treasurer.*
A. G. BRONK, - - *Sergeant-at-Arms.*

COMMITTEE OF ARRANGEMENTS.

A. T. JONES, A. E. FAY,
WARD PRIEST, JAMES VOGAN.
WM. KINSMAN.

RECEPTION COMMITTEE.

H. M. WOODS, B. L. PEEL,
CHAS. I. GLOVER, GEO. A. ATWOOD,
R. F. HAFFORD, W. A. HARWOOD,
H. J. CAMPBELL, B. A. FICKAS,
E. B. GAGE, MARSHAL WILLIAMS.

DIRECTOR.

JOHN S. McGINNIS.

FLOOR MANAGERS.

M. E. JOYCE, WM. HUTCHINSON,
T. E. NICHOLS, D. McCARTY.

THANKSGIVING PARTY

GIVEN UNDER THE AUSPICES OF THE

TOMBSTONE

Social Club,

Thursday Evening, Nov. 26th,

—AT THE—

GRAND HOTEL.

Tombstone's elite enjoyed social seasons that included all manner of sophisticated events. Costume parties featuring dancing and fine dining were the order of the day. As much as they yearned to be included, the Earp brothers and their families were neither among the organizers nor on the invitation lists.

20

KEEP THIS POSTED IN A CONSPICUOUS PLACE.

No. 592 Class 1 $ 4.50

CITY LICENSE.

CITY AUDITOR'S OFFICE,

Tombstone, Cochise Co., A. T. SEP 20 1881 188

Received from Emma Parker
Allen St.

the sum of four Dollars, for License on the
business of House of Ill Fame

Class two for the
term of Thirteen days from Sept 1881.

City Auditor. Mayor.

21

Whorehouse madams in Tombstone paid licensing fees to operate their businesses, which were tolerated and often patronized by civic leaders. As town police chief, Virgil Earp had the job of collecting these fees and dunning those who refused to pay on time.

22

Wyatt Earp owned part of the gambling operations in Tombstone's Oriental Saloon. With its ornate interior and stock of top-line brands of liquor, the Oriental was typical of the town's high-end establishments.

23

Because the railroad had not reached town, the majority of Tombstone's visitors arrived by stage. Townspeople customarily ran out to greet arriving stages, since each passenger was a potential source of revenue.

The *Epitaph* and the *Nugget*, Tombstone's daily newspapers, combined slanted editorial content (the *Epitaph* on behalf of Republicans, the *Nugget* for Democrats) with florid advertisements for the town's many businesses and cultural attractions.

24

25

Johnny Behan's smooth, ingratiating style brought him success as both a politician and a womanizer. His competition with Wyatt Earp for the office of Cochise County sheriff, rather than for the affections of Josephine Marcus, was one of the underlying causes of the October 1881 gunfight.

26

27

While the Earps enjoyed the sophisticated amenities of Tombstone, their rough-and-tumble cowboy adversaries most often made do with cruder establishments like this bar in Charleston.

Enigmatic John Ringo was a leader of the cowboy faction. Though prone to violent mood swings that sometimes incapacitated him, Ringo's skill with a gun was considered virtually unmatched on the frontier.

28

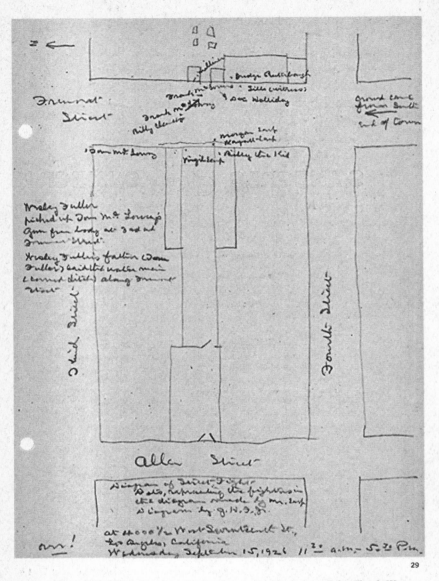

Years afterward while attempting to write a memoir with engineer John Flood, Wyatt Earp made this sketch of the conclusion of the October 26, 1881, gunfight.

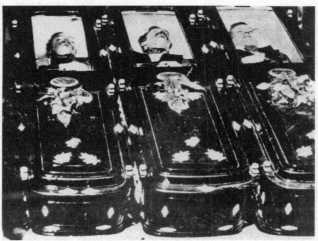

30

Following the gunfight, Texas lawyer Will McLaury was informed by telegram of his brothers' deaths. Hurrying to Tombstone, he came close to convicting Wyatt, Virgil, and Morgan Earp and Doc Holliday of murder.

31

Shortly after the gunfight, the bodies of Tom McLaury (*left*), Frank McLaury (*center*), and Billy Clanton (*right*) were displayed in the front window of a Tombstone funeral parlor. The sight contributed to an unexpected wave of anti-Earp opinion.

After Tombstone, Wyatt and Josephine Marcus lived together as husband and wife. Their later years found them frequently camping in the wilderness as Wyatt continued to pursue the mineral strike that he hoped would make him a wealthy man.

32

33

In his old age, Wyatt Earp remained strikingly handsome and determined to become rich and, if not powerful, at least famous. He did not live to see his dream come true.

34

Bat Masterson's article in the February 1907 edition of *Human Life* was critical in introducing Wyatt Earp as a frontier hero to a new generation of Americans eager to embrace "cowboy" history. The resulting myth of the one-dimensional hero of the Gunfight at the O.K. Corral has little in common with the real man and the actual event.

■ ■ ■ ■

Martha King went to the Union market to buy meat for her family's supper. When she entered the shop the staff was too agitated to wait on her. She was told that there was about to be a fight between the Earp brothers and the cowboys. Martha looked outside and saw four armed men walking west down Fremont Street. She knew the Earps by sight, but not their individual names. Martha didn't recognize Doc Holliday at all. They walked in an almost stately four abreast procession, with Doc on the inside closest to the store and Virgil and Wyatt in the middle, walking slightly ahead of Morgan and Doc. The wind whipped open Doc's long coat, and Martha saw that he was trying to conceal "a gun, not a pistol," beneath it. According to Martha, one of the Earps, probably Morgan, said, "Let them have it," and the man she later learned was Doc Holliday replied, "All right." If Martha heard correctly, it still didn't mean that the Earps and Doc had decided to fight rather than try to peacefully disarm the cowboys. Morgan might have been suggesting a course of action if the cowboys refused to give up their guns and Doc then agreed, but Virgil was the Earp brother who would make such a decision.

The men and their guns frightened Martha. She retreated to the back of the shop and didn't see or hear anything else.

Looking east down Fremont, Johnny saw the Earps and Doc approaching. Morgan and Wyatt had pistols in their hands. Johnny told the four cowboys to stay where they were while he went to head off the police chief and his men.

Virgil, Wyatt, Morgan, and Doc met Johnny on the sidewalk near the butcher shop at about three o'clock. It was still terribly cold. Looking past the county sheriff they could see the cowboys at the front of the empty lot. Doc was probably startled to find them next to the boardinghouse where he was staying with Kate Elder. Johnny, anxious to appear the master of the situation, said formally, "Gentlemen, I am sheriff of this county, and I am not going to allow any trouble if I can help it." Having decided to act, the three brothers and Doc had no patience for one of Johnny Behan's fine speeches. They pushed past him on the sidewalk. Johnny turned and followed. According to Virgil and Wyatt, he called after them that if they kept going they might be murdered. That still didn't stop the Earps and Doc, who were now no more than about a hundred feet from the vacant lot where the cowboys waited. Virgil snapped over his shoulder to Johnny that they were going to disarm them.

According to Johnny, he then informed Virgil that he was in the process of disarming the cowboys, by which Johnny meant that the Earps and Doc should back off and let him collect the weapons. Both Virgil and Wyatt testified later that Johnny told them he had *already* disarmed the Clantons and McLaurys. Hearing that, or at least believing that they had, Virgil and Wyatt slightly relaxed. Virgil pushed the pistol in his belt all the way back to his left hip where it wouldn't be so conspicuous, and switched Doc's cane from his left to his right hand. Wyatt tucked his pistol out of sight in the canvas pocket of his coat. For a very brief moment, it seemed that the risk of a gunfight was averted. But appearances were as important to the Earps as they were to Johnny and the cowboys. Virgil, Wyatt, and Morgan couldn't turn on their heels and abruptly walk away after making such a show of marching down to Fremont Street. As lawmen representing the citizens of Tombstone, they were obligated to see for themselves that the cowboys no longer carried weapons in defiance of city laws. The Earps and Doc kept moving to where the cowboys waited on the edge of the vacant lot, and as they approached they were startled to see that Billy Clanton and Frank McLaury still wore their gun belts, and that the two horses had rifles hanging from their saddles.

Apparently Johnny Behan had lied, and it was still up to Tombstone police chief Virgil Earp, with the assistance of his brothers and Doc Holliday, to disarm the cowboys.

The cowboys watched the Earps and Doc brush past Johnny Behan and continue their resolute march toward them. Billy Claiborne and Billy Clanton stood deepest in the lot and likely had no view of what happened near the Union market. But Ike was only a few feet inside the lot, just off the street, and the McLaury brothers were practically on the sidewalk, with Tom marginally closer to Fremont Street than was Frank. The McLaurys each held a horse; Tom apparently took Billy's when the younger Clanton moved into the narrow lot while he talked with Billy Claiborne.

So far as the cowboys were concerned, the Earps had no business harassing them any further. Johnny Behan was an officer of the law, and they were in the process of negotiating with him to either leave Tombstone or give up their weapons. If Johnny had just explained that to the Earps they evidently didn't care, and it was now up to the cowboys to defend themselves from further insult and, probably, assault. The Clantons and McLaurys had no specific plan for handling a possible confrontation. The cramped lot was a terrible place to be caught in during a fight;

there was no room to maneuver. But they weren't about to retreat. They'd been pushed around enough.

Johnny Behan was never a fighter. If there was to be shooting in the vacant lot, the county sheriff wanted no part of it. As the Earps and Doc reached the east side of the lot, Johnny broke ahead of them, darted into the lot, grabbed Billy Claiborne by the shoulders and began propelling the young cowboy toward a landing that separated Fly's boardinghouse from the photography studio behind it. It demonstrated an admirable sense of duty on Johnny's part to remove Claiborne from the potential line of fire, but he was also interested in saving his own skin now that he believed a gunfight was inevitable.

Up and down Fremont Street, people watched with nervous fascination. Up until this moment the squabbling between the Earps and the cowboys had provided diversion. Now it seemed about to become something more. Since out-and-out gunfights, where opposing parties met publicly and settled their differences with six-shooters while standing face-to-face, were practically unknown, the uniqueness of the moment intensified its ghastly attraction to the citizens of Tombstone. Angles made it impossible for most of them to see all the way into the lot, and even some of those directly across from it had their views partially blocked by Wyatt, Morgan, Doc, Frank, Tom, and the horses held by the McLaurys. Many residents who recognized the Earps collectively couldn't tell the brothers apart since they looked so much alike. The situation was almost as tense and confusing for the onlookers as it was for the eight men they were observing.

Virgil stepped into the lot, pausing a few feet inside it. He still held Doc's silver-headed cane in his right hand. Wyatt, on Virgil's right, stationed himself at the northwest corner of Fly's boardinghouse. Morgan stopped a few feet out on Fremont and Doc was farther out on the street, positioning himself to see all the way into the lot as well as up and down Fremont if any of the cowboys' friends came running to their rescue. Tom McLaury moved toward the horse he held and the rifle in its saddle scabbard. Doc pulled the shotgun from under his coat and Tom froze. For a moment no one spoke. After so many misunderstandings and with so much mistrust between them there was little left to say. During the past thirty hours the final dominoes had tumbled, leading inexorably to this confrontation.

Virgil commanded, "Throw up your hands, boys. I intend to disarm you." Frank McLaury answered, "We will" with the possible intention of adding "not," but even as he uttered the first two words the cowboys began to move. Their friends gaping from the street would testify that Frank and Billy started to raise their hands while Tom threw open his coat to indicate he wasn't armed, but the Earps would recall that they heard instead the sound of pistol hammers being cocked. Everyone's nerves were so overwrought that even the slightest twitch of a hand on either side was instinctively interpreted by the other as initiating an attack. Frank and Wyatt each reached for and cocked his gun, while Billy Clanton, his view of Frank blocked by Frank's horse, could only see Wyatt reaching into his coat pocket and believed that the Earps were starting to shoot and he needed to do the same. The hammers on Frank's, Billy's, and Wyatt's guns all clicked back and Wyatt's gun came out smoothly and fast because it didn't snag on the canvas pocket in his coat. Billy and Frank were known to be fine shots, but that marksmanship hadn't involved quick-drawing from a holster in a real gunfight. Now they had to reach down, cock their guns, pull them into position, aim, and fire while Wyatt, who had never been in a face-to-face gunfight himself but was at least the veteran of actual shooting scrapes in Kansas, cocked and extracted his pistol in one fluid motion. Frank was Wyatt's immediate target and he beat Frank to the draw. Virgil waved the silver-headed cane and shouted, "Hold! I don't mean that," but it no longer mattered what Virgil had meant. Wyatt fired, hitting Frank in the abdomen just to the left of his navel, and as Frank twisted from the impact Billy fired at Wyatt but his shot went wide.

There was a split-second pause as the enormity of what was happening seemed to overwhelm the combatants in the alley and street. Then Virgil, with no option left but to fight, switched Doc's cane back to his left hand and reached across his body with his right for the pistol tucked into the left side of his waistband. As he did Frank McLaury, grievously wounded but game, raised his gun and shot Virgil in the right calf. The Tombstone police chief went down.

Hours earlier, Ike Clanton's big mouth had precipitated these subsequent violent events, and now that he finally had the opportunity to follow through on his threats Ike had neither the guns nor the guts to do so. As Frank shot Virgil and Billy prepared for a second shot at Wyatt, Ike bolted a few feet forward and grabbed Wyatt, not to battle bare-handed but to somehow impress upon Wyatt that he was unarmed and not to shoot him. Though he was engaged in his first actual gunfight, Wyatt still had the presence of mind to remember that Ike probably did not have a gun. He tried to shake the elder

Clanton brother off, not realizing that Ike was inadvertently shielding him from Billy. While Billy hesitated, waiting for a clear shot at Wyatt, Morgan fired at Billy, hitting him in the body and slamming the nineteen-year-old back against the wooden wall of the house on the west side of the lot. Billy managed to keep shooting. One of his bullets probably tore a hole through Wyatt's coat.

Virgil struggled to his feet and aimed at Frank, who instinctively tried to escape from the alley to the street. The horse blocked any opportunity for Virgil to have a clean shot at Frank but he fired anyway. Wyatt still struggled with Ike, and as Ike grabbed at Wyatt's right hand Wyatt's pistol discharged. At the same time Morgan yelled "I am hit" or "I've got it" as he was felled by a bullet that passed through one shoulder and exited out the other. The shot that wounded Morgan could have come from any of several possible sources. He may have been struck by one of Billy Clanton's bullets, or by a shot from Tom McLaury if, as several witnesses later suggested, Tom somehow acquired a pistol just before the gunfight, though none was found on him afterward. But it is also possible that Morgan was hit by friendly fire, either by Virgil's shot at Frank or else by the bullet inadvertently fired from Wyatt's gun as he wrestled with Ike. Morgan tried to get back to his feet but fell again, probably tripping over water pipes being installed along the street. Meanwhile Wyatt finally shook free of Ike. He snapped, "The fight [has] commenced, go to fighting or get away," and Ike got away, scrambling two blocks south to Toughnut Street where he took refuge in an office.

Before the shooting began Doc Holliday waited in the middle of Fremont Street, holding the Wells Fargo shotgun ready and staying alert to any efforts from cowboys in the crowd to jump in and help their friends. Once the fighting started, Doc resisted the impulse to throw himself into the middle of the fray. Instead he left Frank McLaury and the Clantons for the Earps and waited for a clean shot at Tom McLaury, whose horse kept getting between Doc and his intended target. Then Wyatt, free of Ike and once again able to take in what was happening and react, shot at the horse to kill or wound it and get it out of the way. Nicked by Wyatt's bullet, the animal jerked loose and Tom was momentarily in the open. Doc immediately closed on Tom and fired the shotgun. The thick charge of pellets struck Tom under the right armpit. Mortally wounded, he staggered down Fremont Street and collapsed against a telegraph pole near Third Street. Doc threw down the shotgun, drew his pistol from under his coat, and coolly looked for another target.

With Frank staggering onto the street, Tom

down and Ike fleeing, Virgil and Wyatt turned their fire on Billy in the vacant lot. Doc may have sent one or two shots Billy's way as well. The teenager was hit in the abdomen and the right wrist. Billy either sat or squatted in the dirt, his back to the frame house. He gamely transferred his gun from his right to his left hand and fired again, but Billy was too badly hurt to aim accurately. His shot sailed harmlessly up in the air. Billy was effectively out of the battle, leaving only Frank to fight for the cowboys.

Out on Fremont, Frank tried to duck behind his horse, but after he fired a shot at Morgan the animal broke free from his weakened grip and Frank was left crouching and bleeding in the street. Morgan hauled himself up and prepared to shoot, but Frank's attention was captured by Doc Holliday, who, pistol in hand, stalked him in full view of everyone peering from behind cover on the sidewalks or from windows of adjacent buildings. Summoning his last reserves of strength for what he surely knew was a final act of defiance, proud Frank McLaury straightened up, raised his pistol, and cried out to Doc, "I've got you now." Doc, impressed by such feistiness, replied, "Blaze away! You're a daisy if you have," and Frank pulled the trigger. The bullet creased Doc's hip and the dentist yelped, "I'm shot right through." Doc and Morgan fired at the same time. Morgan's bul-

411

let took Frank near the right ear, while Doc's missed. Frank crumpled. Doc stood over the fallen cowboy and declared, "The son of a bitch has shot me and I mean to kill him," but Morgan already had.

About thirty shots and thirty seconds after it commenced, the gunfight was over.

Cautiously, onlookers emerged from where they had taken cover and approached the bloody scene. The silence following the cacophony of gunshots was almost immediately broken by the shrill shriek of a steam whistle at a nearby mine. It was a prearranged signal from the Citizens Safety Committee, meant to indicate that Tombstone was under attack and its vigilantes should arm themselves at once. Men with pistols and rifles began to swarm onto Fremont Street but they slowed at the sight of the carnage. If their purpose had been to prevent trouble they were clearly too late.

Camillus Fly and Bob Hatch gingerly approached Billy as he lay in the vacant lot feebly attempting to eject empty cartridges from his gun. Fly and Hatch briefly argued about who should take the weapon from Billy; Fly finally did, and as he grabbed the gun Billy gasped and begged him for more bullets. Then Billy began writhing in pain, and several men picked him up and took him into a house a few doors down on Fremont,

412

where they laid him on the floor. Frank lay dead on the street, but when Thomas Keefe went over to where Tom sprawled by the telegraph pole he discovered that the younger McLaury brother was still breathing. Keefe and Billy Allen carried Tom into the same house where Billy had been taken. Frank's body was dragged in, too. Billy screamed in agony but Tom made no sound at all. Town doctors Nelson Giberson and William Miller and coroner Henry Matthews were summoned. After cursory examinations, they determined the cowboys were beyond medical help. Billy was shot in the chest, belly, arm, and wrist. Frank had two wounds, one to the abdomen and one to the head under the right ear. Tom had just one, but it was massive — a four-inch-wide cavity gouged by shotgun pellets under his right armpit. He died quietly, but Billy hung on for another fifteen minutes, suffering so long and horribly that Dr. Miller finally gave him two injections of morphine to ease him out of life.

With all three cowboys lying dead, Coroner Matthews examined their bodies. Later he recorded their belongings: "From the body of Frank McLaury one Colts six shooting pistol with belt and cartridges — From the body of William Clanton, one Colts six shooter, with belt and cartridges and one nickel watch and chain." On the body of Tom McLaury, Matthews found no weapon at all, which led to

413

controversy that was never resolved. The cowboys and their supporters declared that it proved Tom was weaponless during the gunfight. The Earps and their adherents insisted that Tom did have a pistol, and that it must have been picked up by one of his cronies in the immediate aftermath of the shootout in an attempt to make the Earps appear to have murdered an unarmed man. Matthews did make one surprising discovery — the money belt under Tom's shirt contained $2,943.45 in cash, checks, and certificates of deposit in the Pima County Bank. The rustling business had been lucrative for the McLaurys. A telegram was sent to Frank and Tom's brother, Will, in Fort Worth, and besides informing him of their deaths it also mentioned the astonishing sum found on Tom's corpse. The three bodies were viewed by a hastily composed coroner's jury and then transported to an undertaker's, where they were prepared for burial. Funerals were always held promptly in Tombstone.

Virgil and Morgan Earp weren't so badly wounded that they required a visit from the coroner, but they still were too hurt to walk. Wyatt, the only participant to escape unscathed from the gunfight, stayed with them on Fremont Street, talking quietly with friends while a wagon was brought to convey the injured men home. As soon as the wagon rolled away Johnny Behan reappeared. He'd watched portions of the gunfight from behind Fly's boardinghouse, and now he informed Wyatt that he was under arrest. Wyatt, still on edge, succinctly replied that he wouldn't be arrested, though he would stay in town "and answer" for what had happened. Tombstone businessman Sylvester Comstock jumped in, telling Johnny that "there is no hurry in arresting this man — he done just right in killing them, and the people will uphold him." Sensing Johnny's hesitation, Wyatt took the offensive: "You bet we did right," he told Johnny. "We had to do it. And you threw us, Johnny. You told us they were disarmed."

Johnny let Wyatt follow after his wounded brothers and set out to find Ike Clanton. He discovered him cowering on Toughnut Street and took him back to the sheriff's office, where he kept Ike in protective custody since rumors were already flying that Safety Committee vigilantes were planning to seize and lynch him. When Ike's brother Phin heard about the gunfight and rode into Tombstone, Johnny placed him in protective custody, too.

Doc Holliday retreated to Fly's boardinghouse, where he went to his room and examined the superficial wound on his hip. After making certain that the graze he had suffered didn't require medical attention, Doc pulled his pants back on and went looking for Wyatt.

He was concerned that the cowboys' friends might seek revenge.

On Wednesday evening, Johnny Behan went to Virgil's house, where the police chief and his brother Morgan had been put to bed. James Earp was there, as well as several of the common-law Earp wives and some friends of the family, including local attorney Winfield Scott Williams, who listened as Johnny spoke to Virgil.

It was a tense conversation, though for the time being Johnny no longer spoke of arresting anyone. The shootout had taken place in Tombstone. The town police chief and his two properly appointed "special deputy" brothers had been involved. Given a few hours to think through the situation, Johnny undoubtedly decided to let the courts determine his next step. If arrest warrants were issued for the Earps, Johnny would again attempt to take them into custody as his role of county sheriff required. The Earps and their supporters would then have to blame the judge, not him. When they spoke on Wednesday night, Virgil repeated Wyatt's earlier accusation that Johnny told the Earps he'd disarmed the cowboys prior to the gunfight. Johnny said to Virgil that he was just trying to perform his duties as county sheriff — he had not been deliberately acting against the Earps in any way. The two lawmen agreed that they were friends. If they meant it at the time, they very soon changed their minds.

Virgil, Wyatt, and Morgan were convinced that public opinion regarding the gunfight would be overwhelmingly in their favor. They represented the law in Tombstone. After giving the cowboys ample opportunity on Wednesday morning and afternoon to either give up their guns or else leave town, they had enforced city ordinances and ensured public safety with the resoluteness demanded on behalf of town residents by civic and political leaders. The Earps believed that they had acted heroically. On Thursday morning, the two daily newspapers reinforced that opinion. The *Epitaph* predictably heaped on the praise, with Clum gracelessly making the point in print that everyone who counted in Tombstone stood with the Earps. He wrote, "The feeling among the best class of our citizens is that the Marshal [Virgil, referred to by his former title] was entirely justified in his efforts to disarm these men, and that being fired upon they had to defend themselves, which they did most bravely." Still, Clum couldn't resist tacking on a reminder that if ever town lawmen failed in their duty, the Safety Committee and its vigilantes remained ready to step in. As though the Clantons and McLaurys had comprised a swarming mob rather than four hardworking men originally in town for errands and a little fun, Clum warned that "if the present lesson is not sufficient to teach the cowboy element that they cannot come into the streets of Tombstone, in broad daylight, armed with six-shooters and Henry rifles to hunt down their victims, then the citizens will most assuredly take such steps to preserve the peace as will be forever a bar to further raids."

The *Nugget* also appeared to take the Earps' side, perhaps because publisher and Behan undersheriff Harry Woods was out of town when the gunfight occurred. According to the *Nugget,* the shooting only started because Frank McLaury tried to draw his gun after Virgil announced to the cowboys that he had come to disarm them. It was more than the Earps could have hoped for, though the *Nugget* report began with the florid observation that "the 26th of October, 1881, will always be marked as one of the crimson days in the annals of Tombstone, a day when blood flowed as water, and human life was held as a shuttlecock."

The Earps' confidence that they would bask in public acclaim lasted only until that afternoon. The bodies of Billy Clanton and Frank and Tom McLaury, restored to reasonable human appearance by undertakers and decked out in finery, were first displayed in a funeral parlor window under a sign declaring "MURDERED IN THE STREETS OF TOMBSTONE." Then, closed in caskets of the finest craftsmanship, the remains of the cowboys were conveyed to the town graveyard in a procession led by the Tombstone Brass Band and including two hearses, surviving Clanton brothers Ike and Phin atop a wagon, three hundred mourners on foot, twenty-two carriages, one stagecoach, and innumerable riders on horseback, with another two thousand or more standing in respectful silence along Tombstone's streets. The attendance was even more impressive because the funeral took place before news of the cowboys' deaths had time to spread throughout the far reaches of Cochise County where many of their friends lived and worked.

The turnout signaled that public opinion regarding the gunfight wasn't overwhelmingly on the side of the Earps after all. "Opinion is pretty fairly divided as to the justification of the killing," Clara Brown informed her San Diego readers. "You may meet one man who will support the Earps, and declare that no other course was possible to save their own lives, and the next man is just as likely to assert that there was no occasion whatever for bloodshed, and that this will be a 'warm place' for the Earps hereafter."

She was right.

Chapter Fourteen:
The Inquest and the Hearing

On Friday morning, October 28, just two days after the gunfight, Cochise County coroner Henry Matthews selected ten jurors and convened a formal inquest into the deaths of Billy Clanton and Tom and Frank McLaury. Under Arizona Territory law, county coroners conducted inquests only when victims died as the result of potentially criminal acts. No judge was involved. Matthews would call witnesses and allow them to testify before his jury. He had the right to call as few or as many as he wanted. There would be no cross-examination, though jurors could ask questions if they wished. After hearing what the witnesses had to say, the jury would then determine whether there were reasonable grounds to believe that the cowboys died "by the act of [others] by criminal means." If that was the jury's finding, warrants would be issued for the arrests of the Earps and Doc and the case would proceed to a higher court. If the jury exonerated Doc and the Earps, finding their killing of Billy and the McLaurys to be "excusable or justifiable by law," then they would escape further prosecution. But from the moment that Matthews's first witness gave his testimony, it was clear that the latter option was unlikely.

Two days before, Johnny Behan had told wounded Virgil Earp that he was his friend. As the inquest began he proved to be anything but that. Johnny informed the coroner's jury that as the Earps approached the vacant lot, one of them shouted, "You sons of bitches, you have been looking for a fight and now you can get it!" about the same time that Virgil instructed the Clantons and McLaurys to throw up their hands. Johnny's expanded memories of the event also included Billy Clanton pleading, "Don't shoot me! I don't want to fight" and Tom McLaury insisting, "I have got nothing" and throwing open his coat to prove he was unarmed — but the Earps and Doc opened fire anyway. That wasn't all; Johnny also stated that the first shot came from a nickel-plated pistol. Though Johnny cagily refused to say which member of the Earp party fired it, Doc was well known to carry a nickel-plated handgun. The clear inference was that the hot-tempered dentist started the fight, and that at the very least Virgil was guilty of terrible judgment by inviting him along.

Billy Claiborne, who had originally joined

the Clantons and McLaurys in the Fremont Street lot, reinforced Johnny's version of events and added a detail of his own: Billy Clanton, Frank McLaury, and Ike Clanton all raised their hands at Virgil's command, while Tom McLaury threw open his coat to indicate that he wasn't armed. Their obedience to Virgil's order didn't matter, because Doc and Morgan Earp began shooting at them anyway. When he stood chatting in the alley with the cowboys prior to the gunfight, Claiborne added, the Clanton and McLaury brothers "were talking about going home and were not talking about fighting."

Ike Clanton, sober and grim-faced, offered an account of provocation and personal forbearance. Doc and the Earps had tormented him all Tuesday night, Ike testified. He ignored the insults as long as he could, but when the poker game ended on Wednesday morning he informed Virgil Earp that he was "in town," meaning that Ike was ready to defend himself if necessary. Ike skipped over most of Wednesday morning's events, mentioning only that Virgil and Morgan knocked him down with a six-shooter. After that Ike and his brother "William" met up with the McLaurys and prepared to ride out of town. They were talking with Johnny Behan when the three Earps and Doc stalked up. One of them called the cowboys sons of bitches. Wyatt personally "stuck his six-shooter" at

Ike, and then Doc and Morgan began firing. Ike, who like Tom was unarmed, grappled briefly with Wyatt and then managed to escape. Ike testified that the Earps didn't like him — "We had a transaction . . . but it had nothing to do with the killing of these three men. There was no threats made by the McLaury boys and Billy Clanton against the Earp boys that day, not that I know of." Yes, Ike admitted, he had himself perhaps said some rude things to the Earps and Doc that day and the previous evening. However, "I made no worse threats against them than they did against me."

Matthews took testimony from five additional witnesses. Three had little of substance to add, but Martha King didn't help the Earp cause by repeating what she had heard discussed between Doc and one of the brothers as they passed the Union butcher shop — "Let them have it!" and "All right." P. H. Fellehy, a Tombstone laundryman, did them even more harm. Fellehy claimed to have heard the conversation between Johnny Behan and Virgil as they met outside Hafford's Saloon prior to the gunfight: "The sheriff says, 'What is the trouble?' The marshal, Virgil Earp, said, 'Those men have made their threats. I will not arrest them, but kill them on sight.' "

The Earps and Holliday were not called to testify. Based on what the jury had already heard, it was obvious legal issues would not be resolved through the inquest. Its members deliberated for about two hours. On Saturday, October 29, Matthews entered into record the most ambiguous verdict possible:

William Clanton, Frank and Thomas McLaury, came to their deaths in the town of Tombstone on October 26, 1881, from the effects of pistol and gunshot wounds inflicted by Virgil Earp, Morgan Earp, Wyatt Earp and one — Holliday, commonly called "Doc" Holliday.

When the inquest nondecision was made public on Saturday, Ike. Clanton marched into the office of Tombstone justice of the peace Wells Spicer, where he filed first-degree murder complaints against Virgil, Wyatt, Morgan, and Doc alleging that they murdered Billy Clanton and Frank and Tom McLaury "with malice aforethought." It was a capital offense — if found guilty, the four men could be sentenced to death. Spicer then issued warrants for their arrests. Under convoluted territorial law, they would be initially held not for trial, but rather for a hearing in Spicer's court. The county district attorney would prosecute them there, the defendants would have legal representation, and ultimately Spicer — not a jury — would decide whether there was sufficient evidence of probable criminal intent to refer the matter to a county grand jury. If he did so, the grand jury would then rule on whether the case would move forward to full-fledged court where an actual trial would take place.

Immediately after Ike filed his complaints with Spicer on Saturday the Tombstone city council met in emergency session. National news coverage of the gunfight had been positive so far — the *San Francisco Exchange* rated it as "among the happiest events Tombstone has witnessed, and especially so as it was attended with so little injury to the law vindicators." But town business leaders were concerned about additional publicity, particularly if it turned out to be true that an unarmed cowboy had been gunned down. Before the shootout, Mayor Clum and the city council believed that Virgil Earp exemplified the hardnosed law enforcement that they wanted. On Wednesday afternoon he had been urged, if not goaded, to make the cowboys obey town ordinances or suffer immediate consequences. But nothing was more important to Tombstone leaders than their town's positive reputation among potential investors. The council cited "grave charges" against Virgil and suspended him from duty. Virgil retained his standing as a deputy U.S. marshal, and responded to all the bad news of the day by formally requesting that a squadron of federal troops be sent to Tombstone to repel an anticipated assault on the town by the cowboys. This undoubtedly was what would become known as spin, an attempt to sway public opinion — Virgil wanted everyone in Tombstone to regard the cowboys as menaces rather than martyrs. But Acting Governor Gosper turned down his request, and many townspeople recognized Virgil's act for what it was, a ploy by a suddenly desperate man.

On the frontier, courts convened as quickly as possible. People routinely moved from one place to another, so it was difficult to keep witnesses available over an extended period. Wells Spicer acted as soon as Ike Clanton filed his murder charges. Virgil and Morgan were excused due to their wounds, but Wyatt and Doc were immediately taken into custody by Johnny Behan. Spicer announced that the hearing would begin on Monday, October 31, and set bail for Wyatt and Doc at $10,000 each. The Earps still had their adherents among Tombstone's rich and powerful — Wyatt's supporters soon raised $27,000 to more than satisfy Spicer's requirement. It was tougher to raise bail money for Doc. As far as the Tombstone establishment was concerned, he was welcome to rot in county jail. Wyatt kicked in $7,000 and with contributions from James Earp, Wells Fargo informant Fred Dodge, and a few others Doc finally made bail, too. He and the Earps had only

426

the weekend to prepare for the hearing, but they made the most of it. Everyone else, including Spicer, expected the hearing to be a quick exercise in observing legal requirements. Spicer needed only to determine if there was sufficient cause to believe "a public offense" had been committed, and if testimony in the coroner's inquest was any indication it would be easy for the district attorney to convince him that there was. Attorneys for the accused typically said very little in such hearings, trying not to reveal their defense strategy until later in an actual trial.

The Earps and Doc agreed on a different approach, beginning with the hiring of Tom Fitch as counsel for Virgil, Wyatt, and Morgan. Fitch was renowned for his courtroom skills; in Cochise County, the Earps could not have been represented by a better-known or more respected attorney. Doc's lawyer was U.S. commissioner T. J. Drum, who allowed Fitch to take the lead. Fitch's strategy was simple — the Earps and Doc had to win the hearing, where it was necessary to convince only Wells Spicer of their innocence. Everything in Spicer's background indicated personal sympathy to the defendants' cause. He was a Republican, and a man who, like the Earps, had followed many frontier paths — lawyer, prospector, land speculator, and journalist, among others. Spicer was a partner in a Tombstone tobacco and stationery shop

427

with Marshall Williams, who had employed
Wyatt and Morgan on behalf of Wells Fargo.
At the very least, Spicer would be easier to
sway than a Cochise County grand jury
whose members might very well include a
majority of cowboy sympathizers. There was
considerable risk to the Earps and Doc by
presenting their full-fledged defense in Spicer's court. If he ruled against them by sending the case forward, prosecutors in a subsequent trial would know exactly what evidence
would be presented on the defendants' behalf
and prepare accordingly. But the Earps and
Doc were veteran gamblers who studied
every possible angle. Their best odds lay with
Spicer, and they knew it.

The opposition had its own problem to
resolve. Ike and the cowboy contingent had
little confidence in Cochise County prosecu-
tor Lyttleton Price. Earlier in the year, Price
had caused Benson stage robbery charges
against Doc Holliday to be dismissed for lack
of evidence. So far as the growing anti-Earp
faction was concerned, that raised the possibility that Price would not aggressively
prosecute the defendants during the hearing.
He'd already gotten one of them off a legal
hook. So the anti-Earps raised money and
hired additional counsel — Ben Goodrich,
Ike Clanton's personal attorney, to serve as
co-prosecutor and several other local lawyers
to help in support roles. Goodrich's politics

were more suited to cowboy philosophy. He was a former officer in the Confederate army and well known for defending cowboys in court. If Price and Goodrich squabbled over strategy for the hearing, it would work to the defense's advantage — but they didn't.

Wells Spicer called the hearing to order on the afternoon of Monday, October 31. Virgil and Morgan remained bedridden throughout the process, but Wyatt and Doc were present with their attorneys. The only witness called on the first day was county coroner Matthews, who simply stated for the record that Billy and Frank died from bullet wounds and Tom from a load of buckshot. But on Tuesday the prosecution's strategy became clear. Ike Clanton had filed first-degree murder complaints, but Spicer had the discretion to reduce the charges against any or all of the four defendants. The Earp brothers were experienced lawmen, and prior to the gunfight Virgil in particular had a reputation for cool-headedness. The justice of the peace might very well be reluctant to send on first-degree cases against the Earps to the grand jury. But if the prosecution made clear at the hearing that Doc Holliday recklessly fired the first shot, then Spicer might be convinced to forward a first-degree charge against Doc and lesser charges, perhaps manslaughter, for Virgil, Wyatt, and Morgan. Though this wouldn't be the complete legal revenge that Ike wanted, it was a more practical approach.

On November 1, the prosecution began introducing a series of witnesses whose collective testimony hammered home several key points: The cowboys were in the process of leaving Tombstone when the gunfight occurred, they raised their hands on Virgil's command, Tom McLaury wasn't even armed, and the Earp posse gunned them down anyway with Doc Holliday firing the first shot. After the first two witnesses, Tom Fitch raised an objection. Wells Spicer, he complained, was a justice of the peace rather than a judge, "in other words . . . a clerk whose only duty [is] to write down such evidence as was offered" and not qualified to rule on what testimony, if any, should be excluded from the record. It seemed like a gratuitous insult, one that easily might offend the very individual Fitch wanted to persuade on behalf of his clients. Spicer immediately ruled in his own favor, but promised he would keep a liberal attitude toward admitting testimony. This would prove critical to the hearing's outcome.

During cross-examination Fitch picked at the virtually identical testimony of Billy Allen and Johnny Behan. The shotgun carried into the gunfight by Doc was one point stressed by Fitch. If the first shot came from a nickel-plated pistol fired by Doc, and, at almost the same moment, Doc also blasted Tom with the shotgun, how was it possible for him to wield the two weapons simultaneously when firing the shotgun accurately required using both hands? Johnny was also forced to offer convoluted reasons for reneging on his agreement to make Wyatt undersheriff, which established that there was animosity between the county sheriff and Wyatt prior to the gunfight. Johnny adamantly denied that he had contributed money to defray Ike's court costs. He also denied telling Virgil that "you did perfectly right" when he visited him on the night of October 26.

Though Fitch had effectively demonstrated that some of Allen's and Johnny's testimony was questionable, at this point in the hearing the prosecution was ahead. Spicer had only to be convinced that there was sufficient cause to suspect that Doc and the Earps murdered the cowboys either with malice aforethought or else by overreacting. Even if witnesses embellished or misrepresented certain facts, the prosecution's basic argument that Doc and the Earps shot the cowboys as they were in the act of obeying Virgil's order to raise their hands was unshaken. At the least, Spicer seemed likely to send forward to the grand jury a murder charge against Doc and manslaughter counts against the Earps, doing so in the belief that evidence strongly indicated Doc deliberately started

431

the killing and the other three joined in "without due cause or circumspection." The pragmatic approach of Lyttleton Price and Ben Goodrich was working well. But then on the night of November 3 Will McLaury arrived in Tombstone.

The McLaurys, like the Earps, were a close-knit family that believed an attack on one member was an assault on them all. A hard-bitten native Iowan who served in the Union army, Will moved to Texas after the Civil War and built a successful law practice in Fort Worth. He came to Tombstone to make certain that all three Earps and Doc were hanged for murdering his two younger brothers. Observing the hearing on the morning of November 4, thirty-six-year-old Will was appalled. Apparently Lyttleton Price lacked the nerve to properly prosecute these cocky killers — in Will's opinion Wyatt Earp and Doc Holliday lolled in the courtroom like they had no cares in the world. Will asked to be admitted to the hearing as an associate counsel for the prosecution, and once he was on the team the moderate strategy of Price and Goodrich was abandoned. Undoubtedly with the full approval of Ike Clanton, who also wanted the killers of his brother to face the death penalty, Will took charge. After several additional prosecution witnesses testified about events leading up to the gunfight and the shootout itself — there was particular emphasis on Tom being unarmed and Doc and Morgan firing first — Will requested that Spicer revoke bail on Wyatt and Doc on the grounds that evidence presented so far strongly suggested that they had committed murder. To the dismay of the defense, Spicer agreed. By territorial law, bail was prohibited in trials for capital offenses "where the proof is evident or the presumption great." Spicer's ruling made clear that, at least so far, he was inclined to agree. Fitch filed an appeal with Tombstone probate judge J. H. Lucas, arguing that once Spicer had granted bail he had no right to revoke it, but the appeal was dismissed and Wyatt and Doc were remanded to the county jail.

Will was pleased with himself. In one of a series of letters sent from Tombstone to a sister and to his law partner back in Texas, he crowed "I think we can hang them." He made plans to stay on in Tombstone through December, when the county grand jury would convene and, Will presumed, rule that the three Earps and Doc would stand trial for murder. For the present, it seemed practically certain that after a few more prosecution witnesses testified and the defense put up some sort of token argument, Spicer would rule for the prosecution and the hearing would conclude.

On November 8, Billy Claiborne took the stand and offered a horrifying new detail. According to Claiborne, in addition to Doc firing first while the cowboys raised their hands, Billy Clanton "was standing [at] one corner [of the lot] and Morgan [stood] at the other corner and put his pistol toward him, right up against him, almost, the pistol was almost a foot from him, and fired." Even worse than hot-tempered, premeditated murder, this bordered on cold-blooded execution. It would have been the perfect scenario with which to conclude the prosecution's presentation. But in a moment of colossal misjudgment, Will McLaury called Ike Clanton to the stand. Will admitted in a November 8 letter to his law partner in Texas that his desire for revenge clouded all his better instincts: "This thing has a tendency to arouse all the devil there is in me. . . . I regard it as my duty to myself and [my] family to see that these brutes do not go unwhipped of justice." He would have better served living and dead McLaurys by keeping Ike far away from the witness stand.

Ike's testimony extended over several days. Never particularly coherent under the best of circumstances, Ike was at least rational when he began testifying on Wednesday, November 9. His account of the gunfight and the events immediately preceding it mirrored those of previous defense witnesses. He and his brother and the McLaurys were trying to leave town. Johnny Behan asked them to give up their weapons. The Earps and Doc appeared, ignored Johnny's efforts to intercept them, and advanced on the four cowboys. He and Tom were unarmed and Billy and Frank raised their hands at Virgil's command, but Doc and Morgan fired and the one-sided slaughter began. Ike briefly struggled with Wyatt, who snarled, "You son of a bitch, you can have a fight," and then Ike escaped with bullets whistling around his head.

At 9 A.M. on Thursday Ike continued his testimony, offering an account of being buffaloed by Virgil and Morgan and dragged into recorder's court where all three Earp brothers tried to goad him into a fight. As he testified, Ike visibly sagged. He was suffering from a terrible headache related to the pistol-whipping two weeks earlier. He may have been concussed. After swearing that prior to the incidents in the lunch room on the night of October 25 he had "never threatened the Earps or Doc Holliday," Ike clearly needed a recess before being cross-examined by the defense. Spicer granted a lengthy one of forty-eight hours.

The hearing resumed at 10 A.M. on Saturday, and when it did Tom Fitch pounced. The opportunity to interrogate Ike was an unexpected gift and he made the most of it. After softening Ike up with questions designed to elicit obvious answers — no, Ike hadn't telegraphed Billy and Frank to ride into

Tombstone on October 26 and yes, he spent that morning drinking, illegally carrying guns ("For self-defense," Ike protested), and threatening the Earps and Doc — Fitch then produced a telegram and asked if Ike had ever seen it before. It was the wire message from Wells Fargo to Marshall Williams specifying that the company would pay its rewards for the Benson stage robbers dead or alive. Ike's greatest pre-gunfight fear had finally come to pass, and his agreement with Wyatt was about to be made public.

Ike did his muddled best to explain away the deal. Wyatt Earp approached him "to help put up a job to kill Crane, Leonard and Head." Besides the already hefty rewards offered by Wells Fargo, Wyatt offered to add his own money and boost the total payout to $6,000 if Ike agreed to betray his cowboy friends. Naturally Ike wanted to know why Wyatt was so anxious to see the cowboys dead. According to him, Wyatt replied that he and Morgan had given the money from the treasure box to Doc and Billy Leonard even before the stage left town, and now they were afraid that Leonard, Crane, and Head might "squeal on [them]" if they were caught. It was a ridiculous claim. The money in the Wells Fargo treasure box was delivered intact, but for the moment Fitch let it pass. He probed further, and Ike denied ever discussing the matter with Wyatt again beyond their original meeting, after which he decided he wanted nothing to do with Wyatt and his offer. Ike finished the cross-examination on a particularly foolish note when Fitch inquired why he hadn't told anyone else about Wyatt's sinister scheme. Ike replied, "[He] made me promise on my honor as a gentleman not to repeat the conversation if I did not like the proposition."

Only Ike's and Will McLaury's obsession with revenge could have blinded them to how Ike's far-fetched claim was damaging the prosecution's case. Instead of getting Ike off the stand the moment Fitch finished his cross-examination, McLaury asked Spicer for permission to redirect more questions. The request was granted; Ike blathered on and made things worse. According to him, there was even more to it than Wyatt's request for help in silencing the three men who helped him rob the Benson stage. A few days after the holdup Doc Holliday asked Ike to chat. Despite Ike's request that Doc "not to take me into his confidence," the tubercular dentist confessed that he'd taken part in the ambush and shot Bud Philpot through the heart. That wasn't all; Ike swore that the day after his conversation with Wyatt, Morgan Earp called him aside and urged Ike to help Wyatt because the Earps had "piped off" treasure box money to Leonard and Doc. Then Ike included the fourth defendant in his round of unlikely confessions: Virgil revealed to Ike that he was not only in league with the Benson stage bandits, he had thrown off the posse chasing them so Leonard, Head, and Crane could escape to New Mexico.

Will McLaury asked Ike why, in light of all the crimes being confessed to him by the defendants, which included robbery, murder, and malfeasance on the part of public officials, he had waited until the hearing to mention them.

"I made a sacred promise not to tell it," Ike replied. "[I] never would have told it had I not been put on the stand." Then Ike tossed in a kicker, probably a closing line that he and Will had planned in advance: "And another reason is, I found out by Wyatt Earp's conversation that he was offering money to kill men that were in the attempted stage robbery, his confederates, for fear that Bill Leonard, Crane and Head would be captured and tell on him, and I knew that after Leonard, Crane and Head was killed that some of them would murder me for what they had told me."

There it was, so far as Ike and Will were concerned — evidence of premeditation on the part of the Earps as well as Doc. They started the gunfight to kill Ike and shut him up, not caring that three other innocent cowboys died in the process. That meant all four were guilty of murder in the first degree. Ike's testimony made it clear that the prosecution would not settle for any lesser charge. Spicer adjourned the hearing until nine on Tuesday morning.

Johnny Behan had anxiously kept track of the proceedings. Except for the Earps and Doc, whose lives were at stake, Johnny had the most to lose depending on Spicer's decision. If he found for the defendants, Johnny's testimony about the gunfight would be repudiated — a terrible blow to someone hoping to turn the lucrative county sheriff's office into a sinecure. Until Ike's testimony veered into the absurd, Johnny had cause to feel confident. Now it was far less certain Spicer would send the case on to the grand jury. But Johnny had chosen his side and had no option other than to support Ike in any way that he could. The hearing had already lurched on much longer than anticipated, and the legal fund raised by friends of the cowboys was probably depleted. Ben Goodrich and other pro-cowboy attorneys helping with the case were not working pro bono. When Ike left the courtroom on Monday, Johnny accompanied him to L. M. Jacobs Mercantile, where he co-signed with Ike on a $500 loan that Ike undoubtedly needed to defray additional legal expenses. Less than two weeks earlier, Johnny had sworn under oath that he "[had] not contributed a cent, nor have I promised to" toward payment to members of the prosecution team. But circumstances had changed.

When court reconvened on Tuesday Fitch openly mocked Ike, asking him whether anyone else besides Virgil, Wyatt, Morgan, and Doc had "confess[ed] to you that they were confederates in stopping the stage and murdering Bud Philpot?" Perhaps, Fitch suggested, Marshall Williams, Wells Fargo's agent in Tombstone, made such a statement to Ike. The prosecution objected. Fitch continued, "Did not James Earp, a brother of Virgil, Morgan and Wyatt, also confess to you that he was [a] murderer and stage robber?" The prosecutors objected again, but Fitch's point had been made. Ike was dismissed, and perhaps was delusional enough to leave the stand believing that he had cinched victory for his side.

The prosecution called several final witnesses who had witnessed Tom McLaury's altercation with Wyatt outside recorder's court. Apollinar Bauer said that Wyatt pistol-whipped Tom on October 26 despite Tom protesting that he was unarmed. J. H. Batcher swore that Wyatt attacked after Tom asked what Wyatt had against him, since Tom "had never done anything against him and was a friend of his." Thomas Keefe recalled seeing Wyatt use his pistol to knock Tom down twice, and added that when he and some others carried the dying Tom away from the scene of the gunfight "we searched the body and did not find any arms on him." Then, after calling more than two dozen witnesses over a period of two weeks, the prosecution rested.

Fitch, Drum, and their clients had a critical decision to make. Perhaps Ike's ridiculous claims had soured Spicer so completely on the prosecution's case that he was ready to set the Earps and Doc free. They could waive presenting their planned defense and hope for that. If Spicer found against them and forwarded the case to the grand jury, at least they would not have given away their trial strategy. But as it had at the beginning of the hearing, the risk of a pro-cowboy grand jury still seemed too daunting. They chose to use every resource at their command on Spicer and the hearing. Tom Fitch had two surprises planned, and as the defense opened on Wednesday, November 16, he revealed the first. In response to an earlier challenge by Fitch, Spicer had promised that he would "exercise a great liberality in accepting testimony." Now Fitch would test whether he really meant it.

Arizona territorial law allowed defendants in preliminary hearings to avoid cross-examination by making "narrative statements." The rule had been in effect for ten years when the Spicer hearing was held in Tombstone. The prosecutors weren't taken off-guard when Fitch announced to Spicer that the defense would begin with a narrative statement by Wyatt. Such statements were traditionally oral. Lyttleton Price, Ben Goodrich, and Will McLaury were outraged when Wyatt began reading from a long, detailed paper that was undoubtedly co-written by the wily Fitch. The prosecution immediately objected, insisting that defendants had no right to use "a manuscript." But Fitch had Spicer boxed in — the justice of the peace had promised to be lenient in allowing testimony. To the fury of the prosecutors, Spicer declared that the statute "was very broad." Wyatt could read a prepared statement without the prosecution being able to cross-examine him about anything in it.

Wyatt gave a masterful performance. Always self-confident, he looked as well as sounded convincing as he offered Spicer an entirely different perspective of what happened on Fremont Street three weeks earlier. It all began, Wyatt explained, in the spring of 1880 (it was actually July) when he and his brothers were part of a posse that tracked six stolen army mules to the McLaury ranch. "Captain Hurst" told the Earps afterward that Frank and Tom "made some threats against our lives," and a month later in Charleston the McLaury brothers made the same threat to Wyatt.

Then Wyatt moved on to the Benson stage

442

robbery. Billy Leonard, Harry Head, and Jim Crane were soon identified as the killers of Bud Philpot. Wyatt "had an ambition" to be Cochise County sheriff and thought if he could capture the three bandits "it would be a great help to me with the people." Since it was "generally understood" that Ike Clanton "was sort of chief among the cowboys" Wyatt asked Ike, Frank McLaury, and Joe Hill for help: "If they would put me on the track of Leonard, Head and Crane, and tell me where those men were hid, I would give them all the [Wells Fargo] reward and would never let anyone know where I got the information." After being shown the telegram from Wells Fargo stating that the company would pay the rewards for the outlaws dead or alive, Ike agreed to the deal, which fell through when two of the felons were killed before Ike, Frank, and Joe Hill could betray them to Wyatt. "After that," Wyatt read solemnly, "Ike Clanton and Frank McLaury claimed I had given them away to Marshall Williams and Doc Holliday, and when they came in town, they shunned us, and Morgan, Virgil Earp, Doc Holliday and myself began to hear their threats against us."

Having neatly joined cowboy "chief" Ike and Frank in a malign partnership out to get the Earps and Doc, Wyatt then explained how their threats against him, his brothers, and their dentist friend escalated. Acquaintances

443

constantly warned the Earps that not only Ike and Frank, but also "Tom McLaury, Joe Hill, and John Ringo" were plotting their murders. Naturally Wyatt was concerned: "[I] did not intend that any of the gang should get the drop on me if I could help it."

When Ike kept haranguing Wyatt about revealing their deal to Doc, Wyatt asked Doc to set him straight. Ike and Doc argued in the Alhambra lunch room on the night of October 25, and by the next morning drunken Ike Clanton had illegally armed himself and stalked the streets of Tombstone waiting to murder the Earp brothers and Doc. The Earps arrested him and took him to recorder's court where, Wyatt admitted, he made threats to Ike because he knew Ike and "his gang" intended "to assassinate me the first chance they had." After Ike was released, Wyatt did pistol-whip Tom McLaury outside the court, but only because Tom was also illegally armed and told Wyatt that he was ready to fight. The gunfight itself erupted when Billy and Frank defied Virgil's order to raise their hands and went for their pistols instead: "The first two shots were fired by Billy Clanton and myself . . . if Tom McLaury was unarmed, I did not know it, I believe he was armed and fired two shots at our party . . . there was nothing . . . in his acts or threats, that would have led me even to suspect his being unarmed." As always, Wyatt

444

swore, "I did not intend to fight unless it became necessary in self-defense and in the performance of official duty. When Billy Clanton and Frank McLaury drew their pistols, I knew it was a fight for life, and I drew in defense of my own life and the lives of my brothers and Doc Holliday."

Wyatt then provided a brief account of his previous career as a lawman, admitting he was only "on the police force" in Wichita but promoting himself to "city marshal" in Dodge. He offered his own version of how Johnny Behan reneged on their deal to make Wyatt undersheriff and told about Billy Clanton stealing his horse, and concluded by stating that Luther King was only captured following the Benson stage robbery because he and Morgan were so alert during the pursuit. Wyatt's reading of his prepared statement, interrupted only by objections from the prosecution that were denied by Spicer, took up the entire day. The hearing was adjourned until the next morning.

Will McLaury did his best to seem unimpressed by Fitch's clever maneuver and Wyatt's prepared statement. He wrote to his sister in Iowa that "this principal witness has been on the stand today and they feel bad his evidence is much stronger for us than it is for them." But he then betrayed his concern by adding, "I do not intend that by perjury these men shall escape. . . . I find a large number of my Texas friends here, who are ready and willing to stand by me and with Winchesters if necessary. . . . I am trying to punish these men through the courts of the country first" but "if that fails — then we may submit."

On Thursday Doc did not follow Wyatt to the stand to deliver a prepared statement of his own. Given Doc's deservedly controversial reputation, the defense wanted him to remain as inconspicuous as possible. During the entire hearing Doc sat quietly at the defense table, often scribbling notes and passing them to the attorneys. It must have been terribly frustrating — Doc always liked to be in on the action. Besides the indignity of spending nights in a cramped, cold cell in the county jail, Doc had an additional aggravation. After he was taken into custody, Kate Elder wanted to leave Tombstone but had no money to pay her way back to Globe. Kate later claimed she was so impoverished because Doc lost all her money playing faro in Tucson just prior to the gunfight. John Ringo, an old acquaintance of Kate's, gave her $50 to make the trip. It might have been a gift, a loan, or payment for sexual services rendered, but one of Doc's foremost cowboy enemies had financed his woman's departure.

Wyatt's statement got the defense off to a good start, and testimony by its next two witnesses was intended to establish Ike's incriminating behavior on October 26 and impeach the accounts of the gunfight offered by Johnny Behan and Billy Claiborne. Neither objective was accomplished. When Ned Boyle began telling about his early morning encounter with Ike, the prosecution objected. Whatever Ike had said then was irrelevant, prosecutors argued, because at the time of the gunfight he was unarmed and not in a position to carry out any previous threats. After lengthy discussion Spicer upheld the objection. Saloonkeeper Robert Hatch told about helping C. S. Fly disarm Billy at the end of the shootout, but admitted that he had his view of the gunfight blocked at certain moments and couldn't say for certain whether Johnny and Claiborne could have seen everything that they claimed. Fitch needed something more impressive if he hoped to maintain any momentum, and so on Saturday, November 19, he called on Virgil Earp to testify. Unlike Wyatt, Virgil waived his right to make an unchallenged statement — there may not have been sufficient time for Fitch to prepare a second carefully crafted, lengthy text. The lead defense attorney had a specific focus for Virgil's testimony; it would emphasize the Earps' responsibility to enforce the laws of Tombstone, and that on the day of the gunfight the defendants were serving loyally as police officers rather than goading cowboy victims into a one-sided fight.

Because Virgil still suffered from his leg

wound, Spicer reconvened the hearing at the Cosmopolitan Hotel, where the suspended chief of police was recuperating. Virgil began by relating that on October 26 both Morgan and Wyatt were serving as special deputies. "John H. Holliday" wasn't, but Virgil "called on him that day for assistance to help disarm the Clantons and McLaurys." From there, Virgil ran through the events leading up to the gunfight — the poker game that broke up early that morning, ignoring Ike's drunken threats and going to bed, awakening late in the morning to discover Ike was illegally armed and still making threats, buffaloing Ike and taking him to recorder's court, and, afterward, seeing "all four; Ike Clanton, Billy Clanton, Frank McLaury and Tom McLaury in the gun shop on Fourth Street." Naturally, Virgil was concerned. When the four cowboys went into the O.K. Corral, Virgil asked Johnny Behan for help in disarming them. Johnny insisted that he try on his own because they wouldn't cooperate with Virgil. When Virgil learned that the cowboys had moved out to Fremont Street, he asked Wyatt, Morgan, and Doc to assist in disarming them. Johnny intercepted the Earp party and warned that the cowboys would murder them, then said that he had disarmed them. Virgil and his three helpers went on to the vacant lot and found that the cowboys were still armed. Virgil ordered them to hold up their hands, "Frank McLaury and Billy Clanton drew their six-shooters," and the unfortunate fight began. During the brief action Tom McLaury fired shots over the back of Billy Clanton's horse.

At this point in his testimony Virgil was too worn out to continue, and Spicer adjourned until Tuesday, November 22. When Fitch resumed gently questioning his client, Virgil recounted all the warnings he received about the cowboys on the day of the shootout, and how both W. B. Murray and J. L. Fonck offered him vigilantes to help subdue the Clantons and McLaurys. Just before the shootout he was approached by a stranger claiming that "four or five men, all armed" in the O.K. Corral were promising to "get Earp, the marshal" and to "kill them all." He didn't know the man who told him that, Virgil concluded, but "his name is Sills, I believe."

The prosecutors had relatively little to attack in Virgil's testimony. Everyone knew Ike had been drunk, illegally armed, and threatening the Earps and Doc prior to the gunfight. They couldn't challenge whether well-known Tombstone residents Murray and Fonck had offered to help Virgil with the cowboys. The defense could simply call them to the stand to verify Virgil's account. But there seemed to be one exploitable detail, and beyond basic questions about Virgil's buffaloing of Ike and where Virgil got the shotgun used in the shootout, the prosecution focused on that. Who was this "Sills"? Where did he live? Did anybody else hear him tell Virgil what the cowboys were allegedly saying at the O.K. Corral? Virgil repeated that he didn't know Sills or anything about him, although he said he'd seen him again just the day before on November 21. That signaled Fitch's second surprise. With Virgil's testimony concluded and the hearing moved back to the courtroom, Fitch called H. F. Sills to the stand. As with Wyatt's previous reading of a prepared statement, Price, Goodrich, and Will McLaury were caught completely off-guard. Until he was mentioned by Virgil, the prosecutors had no idea that Sills even existed, much less that he was going to testify.

H. F. Sills was the perfect witness for the defense. After identifying himself as a resident of Las Vegas, New Mexico, and an engineer for the Atchison, Topeka & Santa Fe Railroad who was currently on furlough and passing through Tombstone, he testified about overhearing the alarming conversation between the cowboys at the O.K. Corral and seeking out Virgil to warn him. Previously, witnesses for the prosecution offered a near-unanimous view of the gunfight as a slaughter initiated by Doc and enthusiastically participated in by the Earps. Sills followed the Earp party to the Fremont Street lot, and his account of the fray exactly paralleled Wyatt's: The

450

marshal (Virgil) spoke to the cowboys — Sills couldn't hear what was said — and they responded by "pull[ing] out their revolvers immediately." Billy Clanton and Wyatt fired first. Sills's description was short and to the point. On cross-examination he explained that he arrived in Tombstone as a Wells Fargo passenger on October 25, stayed in a lodging house for ten days, and then moved to the town hospital where transients sometimes used open beds. The hearing adjourned, and Fitch felt so confident that during the evening he took time away from the case to deliver a public lecture on "Invisible Police." Diarist George Parsons attended and found Fitch to be "good and inimitable," though he omitted any description of what Fitch talked about.

On the morning of the 23rd, prosecutors pressed Sills on his personal background, probably trying to find some previous connection to the Earps or Doc. Sills testified that when he arrived in Tombstone, he didn't know anybody there at all. When he wanted to warn Virgil, he had to ask someone to point him out. He first learned that he "would be wanted here as a witness" a week earlier. The prosecution couldn't shake him. It appeared that Spicer had finally heard the gunfight described by a genuinely unbiased witness.

Fitch still had a few loose ends to tie up. He called Julius Kelly, who told about talking to Ike in his wine shop on the morning of October 26, when the cowboy told him that Doc and the Earps "had to fight on sight." Then the defense recalled Ned Boyle, and this time Spicer overruled objections from the prosecution and allowed him to testify that on October 26 Ike insisted that "the ball would open [and the four defendants] would have to fight." Finally Rezin J. Campbell, clerk of the Cochise County board of supervisors, testified about the McLaury and Clanton reputations for being expert gunfighters and how, in recorder's court on the day of the gunfight, Ike told Morgan that if he and Virgil had been a second later, "I would have furnished a coroner's inquest for the town."

Momentum had clearly swung back to the defense. After Campbell stepped down, Fitch moved for Spicer to once again release Wyatt and Doc on bail. He agreed, though he set the new amounts at $20,000 each. Mining executives E. B. Gage and James Vizina stepped up promptly to pay. Not all the powerful men in Tombstone had abandoned the defendants. Spicer then adjourned the court for a four-day Thanksgiving break.

Fitch did not want to leave any lingering doubts in Spicer's mind about whether Tom McLaury was unarmed during the shootout. On Monday, November 28, he called army surgeon John Gardiner, who said that on the afternoon of October 26, just prior to the gunfight, he saw Tom McLaury leave Everhardy's butcher shop with "the right hand pocket of his pants extending outwards [as though] he had gotten a pistol." Tombstone hotelier Albert Bilicke followed Gardiner to the stand and testified that he'd seen the same thing: "When [Tom] went into [Everhardy's] his right hand pants pocket was flat and appeared as if nothing was in it. When he came out, his pants pocket protruded, as if there was a revolver therein." The testimony of Gardiner and Bilicke was clearly supposition, but to some degree it offset what Spicer had heard earlier from witnesses for the prosecution. When Bilicke was challenged during cross-examination to explain why he'd been watching Tom so closely the witness explained, "Every good citizen in this city was watching all those cowboys very closely on the day the affray occurred." Fitch could not have said it better himself. Then he called his next witness and presented Cochise County district attorney Lyttleton Price with an unwelcome dilemma.

Winfield Scott Williams had been present on the evening of October 26 when Johnny Behan visited wounded Virgil Earp in Virgil's home. One week before the Spicer hearing began, Williams had also been appointed as Cochise County assistant district attorney by Price. After Ike Clanton's ruinous performance on the witness stand, Wyatt's cleverly worded prepared statement, and the unexpected testimony of H. F. Sills, the prosecution's most effective remaining evidence was Johnny Behan's description of the gunfight — that Virgil told the cowboys to raise their hands, they did, and Doc Holliday began shooting anyway. But when the Cochise County assistant district attorney, Price's own newly appointed right-hand man, took the stand, he contradicted everything that Johnny had said. First Williams testified that, despite Johnny's denial three weeks previously under oath, he did tell Virgil, "You did perfectly right." According to Williams, Johnny's recollection of how the gunfight began was completely different when he described it to Virgil that night. The county sheriff told the town police chief that "I heard you say, 'Boys, throw up your hands, I have come to disarm you.' One of the McLaury boys said, 'We will,' and drew his gun and shooting then commenced." There was nothing the prosecution could do. If they disputed Williams's testimony, they would essentially be attacking the integrity of the district attorney's office.

The next defense witness was dressmaker Addie Borland, who during the gunfight could see clearly into the vacant lot from the window of her home across Fremont Street. She testified that five men she "supposed . . . to be cowboys" loitered there when four other men came down the street toward them. "A

454

man with a long coat" — Doc Holliday — walked up to a cowboy holding a horse, put a gun to his stomach, "stepped back two or three feet, and then the firing seemed to be general." When the shooting started, Borland wisely backed away from the window and saw nothing more. Coaxed by Fitch, she added two critical details. She did not see any of the cowboys throw up their hands, and although "it looked to me" like both sides were firing, she saw "no parties fall" before she retreated from the window. That contradicted testimony from prosecution witnesses that Doc and the Earps fired a fusillade that felled Billy Clanton and Tom McLaury before the cowboys could even draw their guns to defend themselves.

Wells Spicer wasn't quite satisfied with Borland's testimony. He thought there were several more details the dressmaker might have added had she been asked the right questions. During the noon lunch break, Spicer left the courtroom and called on Borland in her home. When he reconvened the hearing that afternoon, Spicer infuriated the prosecution by announcing his visit to Borland and recalling her to the witness stand "for the purpose of further examination without the solicitation of either the prosecution or the defense." The prosecutors objected. Spicer ruled against them, and asked Borland to "state the position in which the party called the cowboys held their hands at the time the firing commenced; that is, were they holding up their hands, or were they firing back at the other party?" Borland replied, "I didn't see anyone holding up their hands; they all seemed to be firing in general, on both sides."

Fitch's final witness was Cochise County probate judge J. H. Lucas, whose testimony about seeing Billy Clanton still firing his gun late in the shootout had little to offer in the way of critical information. Fitch just wanted another government law official besides Winfield Scott Williams testifying for the defense. Then Fitch rested the defense's case and Spicer offered prosecutors the opportunity to call rebuttal witnesses before he rendered his decision. Ernest Storm, an employee at Everhardy's butcher shop, took the stand the next day on November 29 and testified that Tom McLaury came into his store between 2 P.M. and 3 P.M. on October 26 and "had no arms on his person and did not get any in there that I saw." The prosecution had no more rebuttals, and Spicer adjourned the hearing while he made his decision.

It took a month and thirty witnesses for the prosecution and defense to make their cases. Wells Spicer made up his mind in a single day. At 2 P.M. on November 30 he called the hearing to order for the final time and rendered his verdict.

Spicer began by reiterating the earlier events of October 26 — Ike's drunken threats, his buffaloing by Virgil, the scene in recorder's court — and then gave the prosecution hope by describing Virgil's decision to ask his brothers and Doc for help disarming the Clantons and McLaurys as "an injudicious and censurable act" committed by Virgil "incautiously and without due circumspection." But, Spicer emphasized, "I can attach no criminality to his unwise act. In fact, as the result plainly proves, he needed the assistance and support of staunch and true friends upon whose courage, coolness and fidelity he could depend, in case of an emergency." The cowboys were violating town ordinances. Virgil, Wyatt, Morgan, and Doc "were doing what it was their right and duty to do."

Spicer conceded that "witnesses of credibility" offered conflicting accounts of how the gunfight began, and whether Tom McLaury was armed. But he ruled it did not matter whether Tom had a gun or not, because he was "one of a party . . . making felonious resistance to an arrest," and if he was shot "in the melee" then it was his own fault and not the defendants'. Prosecution witnesses who claimed Morgan shot Billy Clanton at point-blank range were wrong, because there were no powder burns on Billy's clothes. Then, citing the testimony of H. F. Sills and Addie Borland, Spicer declared that "I am of the opinion that the weight of the evidence sustains and corroborates the testimony of Wyatt Earp, that their demand for surrender was met by William Clanton and Frank McLaury drawing or making motions to draw their pistols."

Spicer politely ridiculed Ike's claim that the gunfight was staged by the Earps and Doc to kill him, ruling that it "[fell] short of being sound theory" since it would have been easy for them to kill Ike during the shootout if that had been their intention. He offered a sop to Johnny Behan, noting that he gave "great weight in this matter to [Johnny's] testimony," but said that "I cannot resist the conclusion that the defendants were fully justified in committing these homicides — that it [was] a necessary act, done in the discharge of an official duty." He noted that if the grand jury disagreed with his decision, it had the authority to consider indictments against the defendants anyway. Meanwhile, "there being no sufficient cause to believe the within named Wyatt S. Earp and John H. Holliday guilty of the offense mentioned within, I order them to be released."

On December 16, the Cochise County grand jury voted not to consider indictments against the Earps and Doc. In the eyes of the law they were cleared of any wrongdoing in the gunfight, but the cowboys had other ideas.

CHAPTER FIFTEEN: "BLOOD WILL SURELY COME"

By the time Wells Spicer rendered his verdict it was almost superfluous. With the possible exception of Ike Clanton, everyone in Tombstone already knew that the Earps and Doc were going to be released. But the end of the hearing didn't affect the ongoing controversy. Opinion remained sharply, irrevocably divided. The Earps either acted in justified self-defense or else cold-bloodedly murdered three innocent men. There was no middle ground.

The cowboy faction accepted Ike's version of events. It didn't matter that some of his claims were preposterous. Belief is frequently a matter of convenience rather than the result of objectively weighing evidence. Even before the gunfight the cowboys considered the Earps to be their enemies. Billy Clanton and the McLaury brothers were their friends, and the Earps and Doc could not be allowed to get away with murdering them. Spicer and his court, representing the government that the cowboys loathed anyway, had failed to deliver justice — now the cowboys would.

Almost as soon as Spicer gaveled the hearing to a close, pledges of retaliation began to circulate. Eight names were mentioned — besides Virgil, Wyatt, Morgan, and Doc, the supposed hit list included Tombstone mayor John Clum, Wells Spicer, Earp defense attorney Tom Fitch, and Wells Fargo town agent Marshall Williams. (James Earp was apparently never threatened because the cowboys considered him to be a noncombatant.) Bizarre details added color to the basic threat. Clum wrote in his memoir that rumor had it that "the death-list had been prepared with most spectacular and dramatic ceremonials, enacted at midnight within the recesses of a deep canyon, during which the names of the elect had been written in blood drawn from the veins of a murderer. Not one of those whose names appeared on this blood-red death-list would be permitted to escape from Tombstone alive."

The cowboys didn't need bizarre ceremonies to adopt their simple strategy. In the time-honored tradition of alienated men in Texas and the South, they would isolate their intended victims and ambush them, choosing settings where they held the advantage in numbers as well as through surprise. To the cowboys, there was no dishonor in such skulduggery. They believed themselves to be

461

targets of a government bent on destroying them, with Spicer's verdict providing legal sanction for its minions like the Earps to commit murder. The oppressed had to strike back at their more numerous and powerful oppressors through surprise and stealth. It was not a matter of if and how, but of when and where. The Earps never doubted that the cowboys would come after them — Wyatt especially was familiar with their bushwhacking tactics from his law enforcement experiences in Kansas. But the Earps also had another concern. Although the brothers may have suspected that rural Cochise County dwellers would be outraged by Spicer's decision, they were taken off-guard when many of Tombstone's leaders and rank-and-file citizens turned on them, too. Virgil, Wyatt, and Morgan believed they had acted appropriately, even heroically, but after the hearings were concluded and he was exonerated, the Tombstone town council did not reinstate Virgil as chief of police. The business community was appalled by all the negative national publicity that had been generated. A dismayed Clara Brown complained to her San Diego readers that "an incalculable amount of injury must have been wrought by the exaggerated reports [broadcast] over the land until many . . . believe that Tombstone is appropriately named, and dare not venture into so . . . criminal infested a locality."

Months later in an interview with the *San Francisco Daily Examiner,* Virgil recalled the Earps' frustration with what they considered civic ingratitude. "The greatest object with [leadership there] is to have as much money as possible spent in the town and to get as much of it as they can," he told the reporter, and the Earps' apparent surprise at that realization is the best proof of their collective naïveté regarding politics and power brokers. Virgil added, "An officer [in Tombstone] must rely almost entirely upon his own conscience for encouragement. The sympathy of the respectable portion of the community may be with him, but it is not openly expressed."

Town and territorial leaders expressed plenty of public concern, just none for the Earp brothers' feelings. Mayor Clum petitioned Acting Governor Gosper to send the guns he'd promised to the Safety Committee without further delay. Gosper forwarded Clum's message to President Arthur as proof that federal intercession was necessary to keep the U.S.-Mexican border from going up in flames. Arthur in turn began petitioning Congress to amend or at least temporarily suspend the *Posse Comitatus* Act so army troops could get Cochise County back under control. All the while the Earps stayed in town, oblivious to any greater issues. Clara Brown wrote that "if the Earps were not men

463

of great courage, they would hardly dare remain in Tombstone," but she had mistaken stubborn pride for bravery.

Two years earlier, the Earp brothers arrived in Tombstone seeking the prominence and wealth they had failed to attain anywhere else. At times they felt tantalizingly close to achieving some of their lifelong dreams of wealth and power — when Virgil was named town marshal, and when Wyatt expected to be appointed county sheriff — but after the gunfight and the Spicer hearing there was no longer any possibility of that. They had become pariahs to many town residents and targets of the cowboys. In every way it was in their best interests to move on. Even their crusty father, Nicholas, urged them to return to California, where at least they would be safe. But like the Clantons and McLaurys on October 26, Virgil, Wyatt, and Morgan were not about to give the impression that their enemies could run them out of Tombstone. Risking their lives was preferable to being perceived as cowards. Wyatt went so far as to finally register to vote in Cochise County, publicly demonstrating that he had no intention of going anywhere.

John Clum chose not to seek a second term as Tombstone's mayor. In his memoir he cited a desire to focus on his duties as town postmaster, and also a growing sense that his

Epitaph was a financial sinkhole. Clum and a handful of other prominent town leaders — William Harwood, George Spangenberg, and Marshall Williams among them — prevailed on businessman L. W. Blinn to run in his place. Then Clum, worn down by the gunfight controversy and certainly ready to escape the reach of the cowboys, left town on the night of December 14 for an extended trip to Washington, D.C., that he intended would keep him away from Tombstone for almost two months. He left town on the stage to Benson, but the conveyance was only four miles out of town when masked men leaped out into the road, shouted "Halt," and began firing. Clum and four other passengers were rocked inside the carriage as the driver first stopped, then allowed the stage to lurch forward as the horses panicked and ran. The attackers were left behind, but it wasn't certain whether they might mount horses and continue in pursuit.

After careening forward a mile or two, the stage team stumbled to a stop. One of the lead horses had been shot and was bleeding to death. Clum, certain that the attack was an attempt to assassinate him and not a robbery, chose to leave the stage and walk several miles to a mill on the San Pedro. He borrowed a horse there and rode to the railway station in Benson, where he resumed his eastbound journey. A witness described Clum as "the most scared man I have ever seen for some time," and back in Tombstone the *Nugget* ridiculed the lame-duck mayor for fleeing from what many believed was a simple roadside holdup. The anti-Earp faction speculated that Clum had stage-managed the whole thing to convince doubters of the cowboys' murderous intentions. But the Earps and their remaining adherents believed that Clum had escaped the cowboys' opening salvo.

The Clum incident triggered more near-violence. Milton Joyce, Doc Holliday's old adversary and one of Tombstone's leading Democrats, met Virgil at the Oriental Saloon the night after the news of the alleged attack on the mayor reached Tombstone. Joyce told Virgil that he'd been expecting a stage to be held up "ever since [the Earps and Doc] had been liberated from jail," a none-too-subtle reminder that some people in town still believed they were participants in the March 15 Benson stage robbery and killings. Virgil, understandably on edge, slapped Joyce's face. Noticing that Virgil was with several friends, probably including Wyatt and Doc, the hot-tempered Joyce chose not to fight for the moment. He backed out of the saloon taunting that "Your favorite method is to shoot a man in the back, but if you murder me you will be compelled to shoot me in front." The next night, a pistol-packing Joyce confronted Wyatt and Doc in the Alhambra Saloon and challenged them to fight if they were in the same mood as the night before. Johnny Behan pulled Joyce away before the confrontation could escalate, and Joyce was subsequently fined $15 for illegally carrying a concealed weapon. The *Nugget* made much of the episode, praising Joyce for not fighting Virgil to begin with, and praising his "coolness and good judgment [that] undoubtedly saved Tombstone from the disgrace of another bloody tragedy, all who are cognizant of the peculiar characteristics of the Earp party will readily admit."

On December 18, the *Epitaph* reprinted a threatening letter addressed to Wells Spicer. It advised him to "take your departure for a more genial clime, as I don't think this One Healthy for you much longer. . . . And the community at large you may make light of this But it is only a matter of time you will get it sooner or later." The missive was signed "A MINER." Spicer's response, also printed by the *Epitaph,* was defiant. After denying he had favored the Earps during the hearing, Spicer denounced "low-bred, arrant cowards" and concluded, "I will say that I will be here just where they can find me should they want me."

The threats weren't all directed toward the Earps and their supporters — the *Nugget* reported that ominous messages had been "communicated by words, letters and postal cards" to "many others who have denounced the murder of the McLaurys." But Virgil, Wyatt, and Morgan moved with their families into the Cosmopolitan Hotel on Allen Street so they could better watch over and protect each other. The lone holdout was Mattie Earp, who for two more months remained in the house she had shared with Wyatt. Their relationship had clearly become tenuous, probably because Mattie was aware of the strong attraction between Wyatt and Josephine Marcus. The cowboys established a hotel base, too, in the Grand directly across the street from the Cosmopolitan. Local gossip had it that at least one of them was always there keeping a sharp eye on the comings and goings of the Earps. Only Doc Holliday carried on as usual. The threat of a cowboy ambush didn't intimidate Doc in the least. He thrived on tension.

As Christmas approached, Tombstone's holiday spirit was dampened by a growing sense that more awful events were about to occur. But the town tried. In late December the new Bird Cage Variety Theater opened on the corner of Sixth and Allen streets. Famous performers appeared onstage, but the real lure at the Bird Cage was a bevy of scantily clad women who were available to dance with any male patrons who bought them drinks, Mexicans excepted. A writer from the *Tucson Star* came to cover the opening and reported, "a dizzy dame came along and seated herself alongside of me and playfully threw her arms around my neck. . . . Her bosom was so painfully close to my cheeks that I believed I had again returned to my infantile period." This was the sort of publicity guaranteed to make the Bird Cage a popular spot.

On Christmas Eve, Republicans dissatisfied with Clum and his chosen successor, L. W. Blinn, met at the Mining Exchange Building to form a new cadre in time to contest the January 3 mayoral election. Dubbing themselves "the People's Independent Ticket," they selected as their candidate a blacksmith named John Carr. The race for Tombstone chief of police was discussed, too. Virgil Earp wisely chose not to run, but current chief James Flynn, promoted from patrolman by the town council when Virgil was suspended, was already a candidate. Participants at the December 24 meeting considered supporting Flynn but ended up choosing as their nominee Dave Neagle, one of Johnny Behan's county deputy sheriffs. The Carr-Neagle ticket had the instant support of the anti-Earps, and the *Nugget* reported that Flynn had promised, if elected, to immediately step down in favor of Virgil. The hapless Flynn took out an ad in the *Nugget* protesting that he wasn't part of any political faction, but the damage was done.

469

On Christmas, diarist George Parsons celebrated with a dinner of "imported oysters and imported claret." Johnny Behan graciously accepted two diamond studs and a quartz scarf pin as holiday gifts from his deputies and left for a few days to race his horse Little Nell in Tucson. Will McLaury finished disposing of his late brothers' affairs and prepared to leave the next day for his home in Fort Worth. Josephine Marcus began her own preparations to return to her family in San Francisco — she left Tombstone either around Christmas or early in the new year, undoubtedly with Wyatt's blessing and promise that they would see each other again. The Earp brothers huddled in the Cosmopolitan Hotel, wondering what havoc the cowboys would attempt to perpetrate next. Around midnight, revelers at the Crystal Palace Saloon began whooping it up and firing their pistols into the ceiling, much to the discomfort of Parsons, who was living in the room above. "A circus till early morning which seemed to terminate in a free fight," he wrote. "Expected a bullet to come up every minute for awhile but was spared." None of the Christmas night shooting involved any of the Earps, Doc, or their cowboy nemeses, but if there had been an unspoken holiday truce in place it would soon be over.

Virgil, Wyatt, and Morgan couldn't remain

cooped up in the Cosmopolitan all of the time. They still had livings to make, which required taking part in card games at night and negotiating minor land and water rights deals during the day. Together and individually, the three Earps would venture out on Tombstone's streets, not always as watchful as they should have been for potential ambush.

Just before midnight on December 28, Virgil ended a congenial evening at the Oriental Saloon. Wyatt stayed behind there, keeping an eye on the gambling concession that furnished the bulk of his income. Virgil walked toward the Cosmopolitan, which was just a block west from the Oriental on Allen Street. As Virgil reached the northwest corner of the intersection of Allen and Fifth a series of shotgun blasts erupted from a building under construction on the southeast corner. The pellets hit Virgil in the back and thigh and left arm. He was staggered, but found the strength to lurch toward the Oriental for help. Wyatt heard the gunfire and raced out into the street. He and several onlookers carried Virgil to the Cosmopolitan, where town doctors treated his wounds and wondered whether to amputate his shredded arm. George Parsons was sent to the town hospital by the physicians to fetch supplies, and on returning to the hotel took the opportunity to tell pain-racked Virgil that he was sorry about what had happened. "It's hell, isn't it?" Virgil replied. Then the wounded man tried to comfort his horrified wife, Allie, by remarking, "Never mind, I've got one arm left to hug you with." After Virgil refused to allow them to amputate, the doctors removed more than five inches of shattered bone from around his left elbow. Afterward the arm was essentially useless for anything other than partially filling a shirt sleeve. Virgil's would-be assassins had failed to kill him, but they left him crippled for life.

Witnesses claimed to have seen two or three men fleeing past the ice house on Toughnut Street and down a gulch toward the Vizina hoisting works, where they apparently had tethered their horses. There was considerable speculation about their identities. Parsons guessed that "Ike Clanton, Curly Bill and [lawyer Will] McLaury" did the shooting. Curly Bill could have, and Ike was almost certainly involved — his hat with his name proudly written inside it was found behind the building where the bushwhackers opened fire — but Will McLaury had left for Texas two days earlier. John Ringo and Pony Deal were mentioned — they always were when cowboys were suspected of Cochise County crimes — and so was Ike's older brother Phin. Virgil expanded the list of suspects to include Frank Stilwell. Just before he was shot, Virgil swore, he'd seen Stilwell entering the empty building on the corner of Allen and Fifth.

On the afternoon of December 29, still not certain that Virgil would survive his wounds, Wyatt determined that the Earps would no longer wait for the cowboys to strike first. Despite being removed as Tombstone's chief of police, Virgil was still a deputy U.S. marshal, so Wyatt telegraphed Virgil's boss in Prescott. In the aftermath of the October 26 gunfight, U.S. marshal Crawley Dake had been perhaps the most outspoken supporter of the Earps. Contacted then by acting territorial governor Gosper with the strong suggestion to appoint new deputy marshals "of cool sound judgment," Dake praised Virgil in his reply and pledged that "my deputies will not be interfered with in hunting down stage Robbers, Mail Robbers, Train Robbers, Cattle thieves and all that class of murdering banditti on the border."

Now Wyatt's telegram pleaded with Dake for authority to take the offensive: "Virgil was shot by concealed assassins last night. His wounds are fatal. Telegraph me appointment [as U.S. deputy marshal] with power to appoint deputies. Local authorities are doing nothing. The lives of other citizens are threatened." Dake made the appointment by return telegram, and Wyatt began recruiting a posse to pursue Virgil's alleged attackers. He deputized men chosen for their fighting skills

— Morgan and Doc, and several others who were often sought by the law rather than representing it, including "Turkey Creek" Jack Johnson, "Texas Jack" Vermillion, and Sherman McMasters. A few weeks later when Warren Earp arrived in Tombstone, Wyatt added his hard-drinking younger brother to the band. There was no pretense concerning the intent of the new U.S. deputy marshal. He and his battle-ready troops would make arrests if possible, but they were prepared to shoot at the slightest provocation.

It took Wyatt a while to organize his deputies, and they could not be outfitted and pursuit begun until Crawley Dake provided money for expenses. Meanwhile, all Wyatt's time and attention were focused on avenging Virgil. He even gave up his lucrative interest in the gambling operations of the Oriental Saloon, selling out to his frequent business partner Lou Rickabaugh. Wyatt needed the money to live on while he pursued Virgil's attackers.

If Virgil, Wyatt, and Morgan held out any hope that the attack on Virgil might swing public opinion back in their favor, it was dashed by the city election results on January 3. Fueled by heated editorials in the *Nugget* and the *Epitaph,* the race for mayor became a referendum on the gunfight and the Earps: L. W. Blinn on the Citizens Party ticket was their supposed advocate, and John Carr of the People's Independent Ticket had the support of their opponents. On the morning of the election, the *Nugget* declared that "the election will to-day decide whether Tombstone is to be dominated for another year by the Earps and their [allies]," and voters responded by sweeping Carr into office by a landslide. The final tally was 830–298. Further insult to the Earps was added when Dave Neagle defeated James Flynn for chief of police, though the 590–434 margin in that race was more respectable. On January 4 the *Nugget* exulted, *"Exeunt Earps!"* The brothers no longer had any semblance of political clout in Tombstone. Their repudiation there was complete.

On January 6, the stage from Tombstone was robbed eight miles west of Bisbee. Three armed bandits stole $6,500 from a Wells Fargo treasure box guarded by company messenger Charlie Bartholomew. The thieves also made off with Bartholomew's company shotgun. Wyatt claimed later that Curly Bill Brocius ended up with the stolen weapon. James Hume, Wells Fargo's chief detective, set out to Cochise County to investigate, only to have his stage stopped and robbed between Contention City and Tombstone. There was no treasure box to pillage, but the bandits took cash from the other passengers and two fine revolvers from Hume. The company detective had never cared for Tombstone, and this personal humiliation did not improve his opinion of the town or of the cowboys, who were blamed for the two incidents. After Hume discussed the situation with Marshall Williams, Wells Fargo took the drastic step of shutting down its office in Bisbee — the fees received for transporting cash and bullion to and from the picturesque border town were not worth potential losses through holdups. Tombstone's office remained open, and Hume spent at least some of his time there conferring privately with Wyatt Earp. Wells Fargo wanted the Cochise County stage robbers shut down permanently, and if that could come about through Wyatt's successful pursuit of his brother's attackers, so much the better. Within two weeks U.S. marshal Crawley Dake secured a loan of $3,000 from Wells Fargo to pay the expenses of Wyatt's posse. Dake promised that the loan would be repaid "as soon as the [posse's] vouchers could be approved at Washington and the money could be gotten in return."

While Dake was en route to San Francisco to request the loan, there was another near-bloodbath in Tombstone. On January 17 John Ringo and Doc Holliday crossed paths on Allen Street; witnesses were unable to agree later on who challenged whom first, only that both men seemed eager to fight. Wyatt was involved, too; a version of the story told later by county deputy sheriff Billy Breakenridge had Ringo suggesting to Wyatt that the two of them conclude the Earp-cowboy feud with a one-on-one gun duel, which Wyatt refused. James Flynn, who had not yet turned over his duties as police chief to Dave Neagle, arrested Wyatt, Doc, and Ringo and hauled all three to recorder's court. Judge Wallace fined Doc and Ringo $32 each. Wyatt escaped a fine because he was a federal law officer.

After using some of the Wells Fargo loan to pay for salaries ($5 a day), rations, ammunition and rental of six-guns, rifles, saddle tack, and horses, Wyatt and his men finally rode out of Tombstone on January 23. They had warrants issued by First Judicial District judge William H. Stilwell (no relation to Frank Stilwell, suspected in the attack on Virgil) for Ike Clanton, his older brother, Phin, and Pony Deal. Wyatt and his men were joined part of the time by a second unofficial posse led by Wells Fargo guard Charlie Bartholomew. Wyatt was determined to capture the Clantons and Deal; at one point he and his men surrounded the cowboy hangout of Charleston and infuriated residents by conducting — unsuccessfully — a house-to-house search for their quarry. Some anonymous Charlestonians fired off an angry telegram to county sheriff Johnny Behan protesting that "Doc Holliday, the Earps and about forty or fifty more of the filth of Tombstone are here. . . . Last night and today they have been stopping good, peaceable citizens on all the roads leading to our town, nearly paralyzing the business of our place." Johnny was urged to "come here and take them where they belong," but chose not to respond.

Ike and Phin Clanton had no intention of falling into Wyatt's hands. Since arrest seemed inevitable — clearly, Wyatt was prepared to stalk them indefinitely — on January 30 the Clanton brothers surrendered to the rump posse led by Charlie Bartholomew. When Ike and Phin arrived in Tombstone and appeared in Judge Stilwell's court they were surprised to learn the charge against them. They thought they'd been accused of one of the stage holdups. Instead, they faced a hearing for the attempted murder of Virgil Earp. Stilwell set bail at $1,500 each and assigned the Clantons a court date of February 2. By then, Virgil's and Wyatt's already shaky standing in the community had taken another direct hit.

While Wyatt's posse made its unsuccessful pursuit of the Clantons, terrorizing Charleston in the process, Crawley Dake was summoned to Tombstone for a private meeting with the town's leading Republicans. They feared that a party split over the Earps might tip political power toward the Democrats, and strongly urged fellow Republican Dake to appoint as his area deputies "men who [are] not allied with either faction . . . who are now distracting our community." The group helpfully formed a five-member sub-committee chaired by Mayor Carr to suggest suitable candidates, and quickly put forward John Henry Jackson and Silas Bryant, both prominent in the mining community.

Fully expecting Dake to cave in to political pressure, Virgil and Wyatt chose to quit before they were fired. Their letter to Dake, reprinted in the February 2 issue of the *Epitaph,* thanked "the citizens for their hearty co-operation in aiding us to suppress lawlessness, and their faith in our honesty of purpose" before acknowledging that "there has arisen so much harsh criticism in relation to our operations" due to "efforts . . . to misrepresent or misinterpret our acts" that they had no choice other than to resign. But Dake surprised them. Bowing to the wishes of the Tombstone Republicans, he named Jackson as a new U.S. deputy marshal, but he did not accept the Earps' resignations. They continued to hold their badges, and with them the authority as federal law officers to carry weapons, deputize whoever they chose for posses, and aggressively pursue lawbreakers.

On February 2, Ike Clanton appeared for his hearing in Judge Stilwell's court. Unlike the

Spicer hearing three months earlier, this was an abbreviated affair. Sherman McMasters, one of Wyatt's deputies, testified that after Virgil's shooting he spoke to Ike in Charleston, and Ike complained that since Virgil had survived he "would have to go back and do the job over." But the defense then paraded six witnesses to the stand, all of whom swore under oath that they'd seen Ike in Charleston at the time of the attack. Sticking to the script for once, Ike testified that he'd lost his hat and had no idea why it had been found near the ambush spot. Citing a lack of evidence, Stilwell set Ike free. Charges against Phin Clanton and Pony Deal were also dismissed. According to Wyatt, after the hearing Judge Stilwell told him privately that, no matter how openly they attacked the Earps, the cowboys could never be convicted. They would always produce lying witnesses to claim they'd been far from the scene of the crime. The only way for Wyatt to see that the brigands were punished, Stilwell allegedly urged, was to shoot them himself.

Briefly, Wyatt tried an entirely different tack. The February 2 edition of the *Nugget* reported that Wyatt contacted Ike "with a view of reconciling their differences and obliterating the animosity that now exists between them." It was an uncharacteristic gesture on Wyatt's part, demonstrating not only pragmatism but perhaps a sense that both he and Ike had lost more than enough already without attempting to inflict further damage on each other. But Ike refused to speak with Wyatt, and what proved to be the last chance for a peaceful settlement of their differences was lost.

Marshall Williams skipped town on February 3 after Wells Fargo discovered significant discrepancies in its Tombstone office's account ledgers. Initial newspaper reports had Williams headed "toward the Orient" with a "sport" or prostitute, but he eventually surfaced in Brooklyn. Williams used $4,000 from the sale of his tobacco and stationery store to pay back Wells Fargo. J. M. Seibert took over Tombstone operations for the company. The Earps had lost one of their remaining friends, but Wells Fargo remained committed to Wyatt in his feud with the cowboys.

On February 6, Republican Frederick Tritle was sworn in as governor of Arizona Territory. One of his immediate concerns was the deteriorating situation in and around Tombstone. Tritle knew the town well — he'd opened a stock and mining brokerage office there in February 1881. Soon after his inauguration Tritle visited Tombstone, where town leaders and residents harangued him about the Earps and the cowboys and the townspeople's ongoing fear of attack by renegade Apaches. Like Acting Governor

John Gosper, Tritle had little respect for the ability of incumbent county and town lawmen to maintain order. He petitioned President Arthur and the U.S. Congress for a $150,000 appropriation to "secure law and order in [Arizona] Territory," especially along the U.S.-Mexican border in Cochise County. Tritle also authorized newly appointed U.S. deputy marshal John Henry Jackson to form a new militia company "of not less than thirty men, at least ten of whom will be mounted and held in constant readiness to respond to the call of the Sheriff for a posse." The new troop was officially named the Arizona Rangers, but in their hometown they were proudly referred to as the Tombstone Rangers. When the funds Tritle requested from Washington were not immediately provided, Tombstone leaders raised operating funds themselves.

Ike Clanton made a second attempt to avenge the death of his brother Billy through the courts. On February 9 he appeared in the court of justice of the peace J. P. Smith in Contention and once again swore out murder complaints against Virgil, Wyatt, Morgan, and Doc, alleging that they "willfully, feloniously, premeditatedly and of their malice aforethought, kill[ed] and murder[ed] . . . William Clanton, Thomas McLaury and Frank McLaury." Tom Fitch had moved to Tucson, so the Earps hired another prominent Tombstone lawyer, William Herring, to represent them. Wyatt and Mattie had to mortgage their house for $365 to pay his fee. Mattie finally moved to the Cosmopolitan Hotel, and Morgan Earp's young wife, Louisa, went to stay with his parents in California.

Wyatt, Morgan, and Doc were taken into custody by Johnny Behan (Virgil was still recovering from his wounds) and escorted by him to Smith's court. The Earps were convinced that the new accusations were a ruse by the cowboys, who planned to ambush them on the road between Tombstone and Contention. They arranged for some of their friends — undoubtedly, the members of Wyatt's posse — to ride with them, armed to the teeth and watching carefully for potential attack. But no bushwhackers appeared; once again Ike hoped to see the brothers and Doc ignominiously hanged in public, not shot down from cover.

After several days of legal maneuvering, Herring managed to get the case transferred from Smith's court in Contention to that of Judge J. H. Lucas in Tombstone. Lucas ruled that since no new evidence against the Earps and Doc had come to light since the Spicer hearing, and since the Cochise County grand jury had chosen not to consider the case, "it is apparent to any reasonable being" that the defendants must be set free. Ike was not reasonable. He believed that for a second time justice had been subverted by the courts. It was once again left to him and his cowboy friends to punish the Earps and Doc for killing Billy Clanton and the McLaurys. No one in Tombstone doubted that Ike and the cowboys intended to continue their crusade until all four were dead, or that the Earp brothers and Doc remained ready to fight. On the day that Lucas rendered his decision, George Parsons wrote in his diary that "a bad time is expected again in town at any time. Earps on one side of the street with their friends and Ike Clanton and Ringo with theirs on the other side — watching each other. Blood will surely come."

Wells Spicer had issued arrest warrants related to the January 6 robbery of the Bisbee stage for cowboys Pony Deal, Al Tiebot, and Charles Hawes. As soon as he was released by Judge Lucas, Wyatt gathered his posse, which included Morgan and Doc, and rode out in pursuit of the three cowboys. He remained convinced that Deal was involved in the ambush of Virgil. If Wyatt couldn't get him convicted of that, a robbery charge would have to do. For several weeks the posse was gone from Tombstone. Besides fruitlessly chasing Deal, Tiebot, and Hawes, Wyatt and his men were rumored to be patrolling the Mexican border, on the lookout for renegade Apaches before they finally returned to town sometime in early March. Their absence gave Tombstone some respite from the tension. Clara Brown noted in a San Diego newspaper dispatch that "the turbulent condition of affairs which was prevailing . . . has been for some time subdued." Townspeople were concerned instead about a sudden smallpox epidemic. Tombstone schools were closed for two weeks, and sufferers were confined in a "pest house" supplied with food and a stove. A city committee began studying the possible installation of a sewer system; it would be built within a year. Meanwhile, Mayor Carr ordered a massive street cleanup. It remained unseasonably cold; on March 6, temperatures plummeted to thirteen degrees. The Tombstone Literary Society tried to divert townspeople's minds from the Earp-Cowboy feud, smallpox scare, and icy streets by performing readings from the works of Sir Walter Scott. Parsons grumbled in his diary, " 'Literary' tonight didn't amount to much."

On Saturday, March 18, in Tombstone, Wyatt encountered lawyer Briggs Goodrich, the brother of Ike Clanton's attorney, Ben Goodrich. Wyatt told Briggs that he suspected the cowboys had been stalking the Earps on the night before, and wondered if Briggs knew anything about it. He did: Frank Stilwell of the cowboys "seemed to expect that there would be a fight." Briggs warned Wyatt that he and his brothers "were liable to get it in the neck anytime." Meanwhile, Briggs added, John Ringo had asked him to tell the Earps that "if any fight came up between you all, that he wanted you to understand that he would have nothing to do with it." Ringo intended to take care of himself and suggested that everyone else do the same.

The message could not have been plainer: The cowboys were about to resume their attack, and the Earps needed to be on their guard. But Morgan wanted a few hours of recreation; he was always the impulsive Earp brother who rarely considered possible consequences. A new comedy, *Stolen Kisses,* was opening at Schieffelin Hall that night, and even though it was raining and cold Morgan and Doc Holliday decided to go. They were accompanied by Dan Tipton, another member of Wyatt's posse. After the show was over, Doc went home to bed and Morgan and Tipton walked on to Campbell & Hatch's Saloon and Billiard Parlor, which was only a few doors east on Allen Street from the Cosmopolitan Hotel. Campbell & Hatch's was one of Tombstone's showplaces. The *Nugget* described it as "the pleasantest place in town for billiard players and a quiet game of cards, not taking into consideration the fine liquors and cigars to be had." It had become an unofficial headquarters for the Earps and their allies. Co-owner Robert Hatch was a good friend of the brothers. When Morgan and

Tipton arrived just before 11 P.M., Hatch and Morgan began playing pool on a table near the back entrance of the saloon. The door behind them had four large panes of glass that looked out onto passageways to several shops and restaurants. Tipton sat down and watched the game. Wyatt and Sherman Mc-Masters were nearby talking.

Morgan and Hatch finished their first game and began another. As they did, two rifle shots rang out and the bullets smashed through the windowpanes of the saloon's back door. One hit the wall just above Wyatt's head and the other tore into Morgan's right side, where it ripped through his spine, exited and lodged in the thigh of a man standing across the room. McMasters and Hatch raced into the back alley but weren't able to spot the fleeing shooters. Wyatt and others carried Morgan to a couch. Doctors were summoned, but Morgan's wounds were too severe for him to be saved. He died about forty minutes later, surrounded by his grieving family.

On Tuesday, March 21, Dr. Henry Matthews convened another coroner's inquest. It didn't take long to identify Morgan's probable killers. Marietta Spencer testified that her husband, Pete, along with Frank Stilwell, a man called Indian Charlie, and another assassin eventually identified as Frederick Bode had planned and carried out the fatal ambush. She testified against her husband and his partners in retaliation for him beating her and threatening to kill her if she told anyone what they had done. The jury took Mrs. Spencer at her word and ruled that Spencer, Stilwell, Indian Charlie, and Bode were responsible for the death of Morgan Earp. By law, the next step would be for a judge to issue warrants for their arrest, and for authorized lawmen to capture and remand them for trial. As a deputy U.S. marshal, Wyatt Earp had the authority to do so, but now, exactly like Ike Clanton, he no longer believed that the courts were capable of providing justice. Even before the coroner's jury met three days after Morgan's murder, Wyatt had already spurned the law and begun avenging his younger brother.

CHAPTER SIXTEEN:
THE VENDETTA RIDE

Wyatt Earp marked his thirty-fourth birthday on Sunday, March 19, by sending his brother Morgan's body home to their parents in Colton, California. The sealed casket was placed in a wagon about 12:30 in the afternoon; Wyatt, his brothers James and Warren, and a few friends — probably Doc and one or two more deputized members of Wyatt's posse — escorted the remains from Tombstone to the new railway station in Contention City. All of them except James returned that afternoon to Tombstone; he took the coffin the rest of the way to California by train, with a connection in Tucson. On Monday, Wyatt, Warren, Doc, Sherman McMasters, and Turkey Creek Jack Johnson made the trip to Contention again, this time escorting Virgil and his wife, Allie. Wyatt planned to hunt down Morgan's killers, and didn't want the distraction of a crippled brother virtually defenseless against further attack back in

Tombstone. So Virgil was going to Colton, too.

As he had on Sunday with James, Wyatt originally intended that he and his men would accompany Virgil and Allie only as far as the Contention depot. But either on the ride there or soon after arrival, he received messages indicating that several cowboys, having learned of Virgil's travel plans, might be staking out the Tucson railway station in hopes of killing him along with any other Earp brother or ally that they could ambush there. Leaving their horses in Contention, Wyatt and his posse took the train all the way into Tucson, ready to attack would-be assassins on sight if any of the cowboys did turn out to be lurking around the station. When they arrived in the early evening, Doc checked two shotguns at the depot office and the entire Earp party went to eat dinner at a hotel just across the railroad tracks. Virgil and Allie's train was scheduled to depart about 7:15 P.M.

Frank Stilwell had been in Tucson since early Sunday. He needed to be there later in the week to appear in court and face federal charges of mail robbery related to the Bisbee stage holdup back on September 8. If, as the Earps believed and Marietta Spencer's inquest testimony alleged, Stilwell had been one of Morgan's assassins in Tombstone on

Saturday night, he would have had to ride hard to be in Tucson by Sunday morning. But it was possible for a good rider like Stilwell. Once well away from the crime scene, secure in the knowledge that if he was accused of Morgan's murder he could produce cowboy friends to swear he was elsewhere, it was an unexpected bonus for Stilwell to learn that Virgil and perhaps other Earps would be passing through the Tucson railway station on Monday. There would be an excellent chance to pick someone else off.

Ike Clanton was in Tucson, too. He and Stilwell met at least briefly near the depot on Monday. Ike said later that when he saw the Earps arrive, he warned Stilwell to leave before they attacked him. They agreed to meet soon afterward at a nearby stable and walked off in opposite directions. According to Ike, that was the last time he saw his friend Frank Stilwell alive.

Shortly after seven the Earp party emerged from the hotel restaurant and walked to the train that would take Virgil and Allie west. Either Doc or Sherman McMasters retrieved the shotguns that had been checked earlier at the depot office. Wyatt took one, and Warren probably got the other. As he settled his older brother and sister-in-law on the train, Wyatt spotted Frank Stilwell loitering alongside the tracks. Pima County sheriff Bob Paul later told a reporter that Stilwell was actually balancing himself on an adjacent gravel car, peering into the window of the passenger car to see if Virgil was inside.

Wyatt bolted out and chased Stilwell down the tracks alongside the train. Doc, Warren, Johnson, and McMasters followed. Several railroad workers saw the men running, and then heard a series of shots followed by cheering. According to Wyatt and Virgil later, when Stilwell was cornered he confessed to killing Morgan and named several others involved in plotting and carrying out the ambush; they allegedly included Curly Bill, John Ringo, and Hank Swilling, another cowboy. Given Wyatt's furious pursuit and the burst of gunfire that immediately followed, it's unlikely that Stilwell had time to blurt anything beyond a plea for mercy, which he did not receive. Despite the shotgun and pistol blasts and cheering, no one immediately ran to the scene. Tucson was illuminated that night for the first time by gas lights, and these had been turned on just as the shooting began. It was apparently assumed that the shooting and cheering were part of an impromptu celebration of that momentous occasion. Stilwell's body wasn't discovered alongside the Tucson tracks until the next morning, but someone among the Earp party of executioners sent word back to Tombstone prior to that. George Parsons noted in his March 20 diary entry that "tonight came news of Frank Stilwell's body being found riddled with bullets and buckshot. A quick vengeance, and a bad character sent to Hell."

With Stilwell dead and Virgil and Allie safely on their way to California, Wyatt and his men walked eight miles east of Tucson to a small station where they flagged down an eastbound freight to Benson. From there they either took another train or a stage to Contention City, where they picked up their horses and rode the rest of the way back to Tombstone. They arrived early on the afternoon of Tuesday, March 21, and began gathering belongings in preparation for leaving again almost immediately. Frank Stilwell was just one of Morgan's killers; Wyatt meant to eliminate more of them as soon as possible, though he may have found time during the afternoon to consult with J. M. Seibert at the Wells Fargo office and E. B. Gage, the most powerful mine owner in town. Any discussions in which Wyatt may have solicited their help were brief — there was another reason that Wyatt and the others had to be on their way. Back in Tucson, they were wanted for murder.

Even as Marietta Spencer gave her testimony regarding Morgan's murder at the inquest in Tombstone on Tuesday morning, a hastily convened coroner's jury in Tucson found

493

Wyatt, Warren, Doc, McMasters, and Johnson responsible for the death of Frank Stilwell. The town was outraged by the shooting. The *Tucson Star* described Wyatt and his deputies as "a roving band [whose] path is strewn with blood," and declared that "wherever they halt in a settlement . . . human life ceases to be sacred." A Pima County justice of the peace issued warrants for their arrests, and a telegram was sent to Cochise County sheriff Johnny Behan in Tombstone asking him to apprehend the alleged killers if he encountered them. The message arrived at the Tombstone telegraph office not long after Wyatt and his party returned to town. But the office manager was a friend of the Earps' and didn't deliver the telegram to Johnny immediately upon receipt, hoping that the delay would give the fugitives time to get away. But when he finally gave the message to Johnny around eight that evening, Wyatt and the others were still at the Cosmopolitan Hotel.

At this point, Johnny Behan must have detested Wyatt Earp. Though much of Tombstone had turned against Wyatt, there had been no corresponding uptick in public opinion regarding Johnny. In town he was still largely seen as an ineffectual lawman with inappropriate ties to the cowboys. His prospects for reelection as county sheriff in November were negligible, particularly after the disastrous Spicer hearing that exonerated the Earps and Doc despite Johnny's testimony against them. Wyatt himself still seemed determined to run for sheriff in November, and there was also the matter of Josephine. Even if the rest of Tombstone was oblivious, Johnny was too skilled at reading other people to have missed the strong attraction between his glamorous former lover and Wyatt. Although there were potential legal complications involved — did a county sheriff have the authority to arrest a U.S. deputy marshal? A canny defense attorney like Tom Fitch might raise the issue — Johnny would take great satisfaction in hauling Wyatt and his cronies off to jail on murder charges. Maybe this time they'd hang.

Johnny certainly knew that Wyatt and his men had returned to town. When he received the long-delayed telegram about 8 P.M. he knew where to find them. As a career politician, Johnny understood the potential impact of a splashy public act. Arresting Wyatt Earp for murder in the heart of Tombstone's business district might yet salvage enough of Johnny's reputation to give him some hope of reelection. Failing that, at least it would humiliate Wyatt. Eager to place his rival in custody, Johnny summoned county deputies Billy Breakenridge and Dave Neagle (also serving as Tombstone chief of police), ordered them to get their shotguns, and hurried to head off the Earp party at the Cosmopolitan.

To Wyatt, Johnny Behan had become more of an annoyance than a real enemy. Compared to his burning desire for revenge on Morgan's killers, Wyatt's issues with Johnny paled. When the Cochise County sheriff approached him outside the Cosmopolitan Hotel and announced, "Wyatt, I want to see you," Wyatt brushed him off like a pesky fly. Though witnesses clustered on the street differed over a word or two, they generally agreed Wyatt responded that Johnny might someday see him once too often. Wyatt added that "I will see Paul," an apparent promise to eventually turn himself in to the Pima County sheriff, Bob Paul. Then Wyatt and his party, which now included at least two more friends — Dan Tipton and Charlie Smith — mounted their horses and rode out of town, leaving Johnny red-faced and fuming in their wake. Since it was already so late, they camped just a few miles north of town. Someone may have delivered a copy of that morning's coroner's inquest report to Wyatt. Reading Marietta Spencer's testimony by the light of a campfire, Wyatt added the names of Pete Spencer, Frederick Bode, and Indian Charlie to his hit list if they weren't already on it. He now knew where he and his friends would go in the morning.

Except for co-signing Ike Clanton's $500 loan during the Spicer hearing, Johnny Behan had never openly sided with the cowboys against the Earps. At least technically, Johnny had acted as an impartial lawman — his testimony could have been the basis for convicting Virgil, Wyatt, Morgan, and Doc of murder, but he was recounting the gunfight and events before and following it from his personal perspective. He'd taken Wyatt, Morgan, and Doc into custody when Ike filed new complaints against them in the Contention court, but that was his responsibility as county sheriff. He'd been requested by authorities in Tucson to arrest Wyatt and his partners in front of the Cosmopolitan Hotel. In all these instances he could claim to be simply doing his job.

But in the wake of his latest public humiliation at the hands of Wyatt Earp, Johnny abandoned any pretense of objectivity. On Tuesday night, he began forming a posse to pursue Wyatt, Warren, Doc, McMasters, and Johnson, who were all wanted for Stilwell's murder. But the makeup of Johnny's posse reflected his intention to force a bloody showdown rather than seek peaceful surrender. Though Johnny himself was no fighter, his recruits were comprised of Earp-hating cowboys, some of whom, including John Ringo and Phin Clanton, were at least rumored to be involved in the attacks on Virgil and Morgan. Pima County sheriff Bob Paul was so appalled at the collection of thugs assembled by Johnny that he refused to ride with them. Paul believed that at some point Wyatt's respect for the law would prevail; he told the *Epitaph,* "I'll let Wyatt know I want him, and he'll come in."

On Wednesday morning Wyatt had no intention of coming in. Instead, he led his men to a wood-cutting camp operated by Pete Spencer in the Dragoon Mountains. Wyatt questioned workers there regarding their boss's whereabouts, and learned that Spencer had just ridden into Tombstone for a hearing on charges unrelated to the Earps. Alerted in town that Wyatt was on his trail, Spencer prudently asked Johnny Behan for sanctuary and took refuge in the county jail. About the same time, alleged assassin Frederick Bode was also taken into custody.

Deprived of Spencer, their original target, the Earp forces fixed on another. Florentino Cruz, suspected by them of being the Indian Charlie named by Marietta Spencer as one of Morgan's assassins, worked for Spencer and was rounding up stray stock, probably mules, just east of the main camp. The visitors rode off in that direction. A few minutes later, camp workers heard a series of shots. They found Cruz's body sprawled under a tree. He had been shot several times by different weapons. When his body was taken into Tombstone for examination, the doctor speculated that at least one of the bullets struck Cruz after he was dead. Yet another coroner's jury convened, and it quickly reported that Cruz died from "gunshot wounds inflicted by Wyatt Earp, Warren Earp, J. H. Holliday, Sherman McMasters, Texas Jack [Vermillion], [Turkey Creek Jack] Johnson, and two men whose names are unknown to the jury" — probably Tipton and Smith.

Wyatt later claimed that, before he died, Florentino Cruz supplied him with specifics about the plot to kill Morgan. Curly Bill, John Ringo, Frank Stilwell, and Ike Clanton supposedly met at Clanton's ranch to plot the murders of Morgan and Wyatt. Pete Spencer, Hank Swilling, Frederick Bode (whom Cruz couldn't properly identify by name), and Cruz were accomplices. Stilwell, Curly Bill, and Swilling fired the shots that killed Morgan and missed Wyatt. Cruz's role was simply to stand watch while the assassins carried out their mission. According to Wyatt, once he had this information he was ready to let Cruz go, but before he did he could not resist asking what the Earps had ever done to him personally. Cruz replied that Curly Bill, Ringo, Ike, and Stilwell were his friends and, besides, Curly Bill paid him $25 for his help. At that point, Wyatt recalled, he lost his temper and killed Cruz. It probably didn't happen exactly that way, given the multiple wounds suffered by the dead man, but it's likely that Wyatt did at least briefly interrogate him before carrying out what amounted to an execution. Based on Wyatt's later conversations and correspondence with biographer Stuart Lake, from that point forward he no longer believed that Pete Spencer was a major player in Morgan's ambush.

Killing Cruz inarguably put Wyatt Earp beyond the pale of the law. In court, he could have claimed that Frank Stilwell was actively attempting to kill Virgil at the Tucson train station. But at Spencer's wood camp, Florentino Cruz wasn't threatening anyone except for some stray mules. Wyatt carried out the same brand of violent vigilante justice that he had previously deplored, and was so gratified by doing it that he immediately rode on to mete out more.

On Thursday, March 23, Earp posse members Dan Tipton and Charlie Smith rode back into Tombstone. Wyatt needed money to continue his vendetta and had instructed Smith to secure a $1,000 loan from mining executive E. B. Gage. Smith probably had a message to be delivered to the Wells Fargo office as well. But when Tipton and Smith arrived in town they were taken into custody by Johnny Behan, who charged them with resisting arrest on Tuesday night when Wyatt's party rode past Johnny on its way out of town. The charge didn't stick; Tipton and Smith were immediately released by the courts on a legal technicality — Johnny had only a telegram and no official arrest warrant on Tuesday. George Parsons wrote gleefully in his diary, "Much excitement. False charges. Behan will get it yet," but the arrest and court hearing delayed Wyatt receiving the money he needed for supplies and to pay his men.

National coverage of the most recent spate of southeast Arizona Territory killings was as negative as Tombstone leaders feared. The Earps and the cowboys were mostly presented as interchangeable frontier gunslingers who would only stop murdering when they were killed themselves. The *San Francisco Exchange* opined that "it may fortunately happen that the slaughter on both sides will leave but a few survivors, and a big funeral, with the Earps and cowboys to furnish the remains, would be the lifting of a great weight from the minds of the citizens of Tombstone."

But not all the press was antagonistic toward Wyatt and his posse. Wells Fargo, which had a company policy of not publicly commenting on most issues, took the nearly unprecedented step of speaking on Wyatt's behalf to the *San Francisco Examiner*. An unidentified executive, probably James Hume, described the majority of the cowboys as "cattle thieves, and for a change [they] will occasionally rob a stage." An unspecified "leading official" — Johnny Behan, who Hume loathed — was accused of "stand[ing] in with them whenever occasion arises." And

Wells Fargo had more than moral support to offer Wyatt. Company officials certainly regretted the death of Morgan Earp, who had served them well as a shotgun messenger, but their main concern was the permanent elimination of those cowboys they believed were the instigators of, if not always participants in, stage robberies in Cochise County. Wells Fargo could not be seen openly participating in vigilante justice that the courts might eventually rule to be murder, but there were ways to help Wyatt behind the scenes. If he had promised to keep their involvement a secret, company leaders could count on Wyatt to keep his word.

Johnny Behan's posse grew to more than a dozen members. There were many cowboys anxious to be deputized and have the opportunity to kill Earps under the aegis of the law. Their initial efforts to corner their quarry were unsuccessful — the *Epitaph* provided sarcastic reports. Wyatt and his men never seemed to be anywhere the posse was looking for them, but Johnny was not about to give up. The killing of Florentino Cruz strongly suggested that Wyatt intended to stay in the area and pick off Morgan's alleged killers one by one. Every additional death underscored Johnny's inability as county sheriff to enforce the law.

Besides Johnny's group, another even more

dubious posse may have been searching for Wyatt's party. After several months of apparent inactivity, Curly Bill Brocius was back on the scene and eager to settle the score with his longtime adversary. Despite Curly Bill's own current troubles with the law — he was still under indictment from the Cochise County grand jury for the theft of nineteen head of cattle — Johnny may have deputized him to help run down Wyatt. Curly Bill was described as a deputy in the *Nugget*'s coverage of the pursuit. With several cowboys joining him — the number was variously described between four and nine — Curly Bill began scouring the area for his quarry.

When Wyatt sent two of his men back to Tombstone for money, he instructed them to meet him at some springs near the Whetstone Mountains about twenty miles west of town. The rendezvous point may have been selected for convenience; it was a place where Wyatt and his friends could rest and keep their horses well watered while they waited for an infusion of funds before hunting down more of Morgan's alleged killers. But the cowboys often camped in the area, too. Wyatt traditionally made frequent use of informants; for a time, current Earp cohort Sherman McMasters had ridden with the cowboys and reported back to Wyatt on their activities. Wyatt may have had informants serving in the Be-

503

han and Curly Bill posses, sending messages to him about where they would be and when. That would have allowed Wyatt to easily elude them, or, if he preferred a fight, to catch them off-guard at a place of his own choosing. Whether by chance or design, on the morning of Friday, March 24, Wyatt's band and Curly Bill's cowboy posse found themselves in the same place by the springs west of Tombstone.

Wyatt always insisted that the violent encounter came as a complete surprise. After sending his younger brother Warren out to meet his friends returning from Tombstone with money from E. B. Gage, Wyatt and his reduced force — Doc, Sherman McMasters, Texas Jack Vermillion, and Turkey Creek Jack Johnson — made their way to the springs. The ride was long; to stay comfortable in the saddle, Wyatt loosened his gun belt a little. The Earp group was exceptionally well armed, with shotguns and rifles as well as six-shooters. This was fortunate, because by Wyatt's account as they trotted up "nine cowboys sprang up from the bank where the spring was and began firing at us" from about thirty yards away. Wyatt jumped from his horse and returned fire, but to his consternation his men were more interested in retreating than in fighting. Texas Jack's horse was hit in the first barrage, and a cowboy named Johnny Barnes went down; he later died of his wounds. Then Wyatt spotted Curly Bill among the assailants. He aimed his shotgun at the cowboy and blew a huge hole in his chest.

Their leader had fallen, but the remaining cowboys kept shooting. Since the rest of the Earp party had given ground, Wyatt was their prime target. His horse panicked and began to buck, making it hard to draw his rifle from its saddle scabbard. With bullets flying around him, Wyatt's next thought was to mount and retreat himself, but couldn't because his loosened gun belt had fallen "down over my thighs, keeping my legs together" and prevented him from climbing into the saddle. As Wyatt frantically tried to yank the gun belt back up around his waist, a cowboy slug tore off his saddle horn, making it even harder to get astride his horse. Finally he did, and rode back to where the other posse members had taken refuge among some nearby trees. The remaining cowboys by the spring were ready to continue the fight, but Wyatt led his men away. He told a reporter years later that "I did not care to go back" at the cowboys, "so we sought out another water hole for camp. The skirt of my overcoat was shot to pieces on both sides, but not a bullet had touched me."

Word of the confrontation began to filter back to Tombstone on Saturday morning. The first rumors indicated that four of the Earp party had died, but soon it was widely known that Curly Bill had been killed instead. The *Epitaph* reported that "friends of Curly Bill went out with a wagon and took the body back to Charleston," but then the local grapevine began buzzing with testimony from several cowboys that Curly Bill not only hadn't died, he hadn't even been at the springs on Friday morning. Curly Bill's possible demise was the talk of Tombstone, with opinion divided as to whether Wyatt had really killed him. On April 1, the *Nugget* took the position that "Curly William is alive" and offered $1,000 to anyone who could prove that he wasn't. Not to be outdone, the *Epitaph* responded with an offer to pay $2,000 "to any worthy charity provided that Curly Bill [will] put in an appearance alive and well." Neither bounty was ever paid. Though in the years to come there would be reports of various sightings or even encounters with Curly Bill, the outgoing cowboy never definitively reemerged in southeastern Arizona or anywhere else. Given his previous near-insatiable desire for attention, it seems highly unlikely Curly Bill would have passed up such an unparalleled opportunity for a dramatic reappearance if he had, in fact, survived the March 24 encounter with Wyatt. Still, debate over whether Curly Bill did or didn't die at the springs continues among historians.

On the same day as the battle at the springs The *Epitaph* reported that "Mrs. James Earp and Mrs. Wyatt Earp left to-day for Colton, California, the residence of their husbands' parents. These ladies have the sympathy of all who know them, and for that matter the entire community. Their trials for the last six months have been of the most severe nature." Bessie Earp would soon be reunited with her husband, James, but Mattie Earp's trials were only beginning.

Wyatt and his followers — Warren, Doc, McMasters, Vermillion and Johnson, probably rejoined by Charlie Smith — spent the night of March 25 outside Tombstone. If they had hoped to actually sneak into town, probably to finally get money from E. B. Gage, they were thwarted by cowboy patrols on the lookout for them. Tombstone visitor George Hand wrote in his diary that "the cowboys, 20 or more, have been prowling. . . . They are well mounted, well armed and seem intent on biz. They are in search for the Earp party, who took breakfast two miles above here this morning." Wyatt desperately needed some respite. Beyond practical considerations — Wyatt and his men needed supplies and fresh horses to replace their worn-down mounts (Texas Jack's horse had been killed at the springs, so he was probably riding double with someone else) — Wyatt must have been emotionally drained. In a single week he had lost his brother Morgan and killed three men. He was wanted for murder and Johnny Behan's large posse gave every indication of being willing to hunt him indefinitely. Money he'd expected to receive from Gage hadn't been delivered. Wyatt had to find a place where he and the others could at least briefly rest and resupply. Thankfully, he still had one friend he felt certain would help, someone so self-sufficient and powerful that he wouldn't be daunted by Behan's posse or packs of revenge-minded cowboys. After undoubtedly sending word of his destination to the remaining friends he had in Tombstone, Wyatt led his men about fifty miles northeast toward the upper end of the sprawling Sulphur Springs Valley.

Henry Clay Hooker was a colossus among Arizona Territory cattlemen. Though he engaged in a variety of businesses, he initially made his mark supplying beef to army forts and Indian reservations. While rivals dealt in stringy Texan and Mexican beef, Hooker imported top stock from California and New Mexico and bred top-quality cattle. He established his base eight miles from Fort Grant between foothills and mountains and around a confluence of rivers and creeks that kept vast grazing lands well watered; eventually the aptly named Sierra Bonita (Beautiful Mountain) Ranch spread out over more than

250,000 scenic acres. The main house was constructed in the shadows of eleven-thousand-foot high Mount Graham, whose slopes in the spring were thick with colorful flowers. Hooker built that house and barracks for his men inside fortresslike walls; he and the ranch hands were always ready to defend the property against attacks by Indians, and because of the location they could see riders coming from miles away in almost every direction. They were also on constant guard against rustlers — Hooker abhorred the presence of the cowboys in Arizona, and as head of the region's Stockgrowers Association he supported all efforts to exterminate or drive them away. That meant he greatly admired Wyatt Earp, and undoubtedly believed that whatever cowboys might have died at his hand richly deserved their grisly fate. Hooker welcomed Wyatt's seven-member band when they appeared at the Sierra Bonita on Monday, March 27, with Dan Tipton arriving soon afterward. That murder warrants had been issued for them meant nothing so far as Hooker was concerned; his personal wealth was matched by his political influence, and Hooker promised to intercede with Governor Tritle on everyone's behalf. In the meantime, he placed all the resources of the Sierra Bonita at their disposal.

Wyatt was gratified by the warm reception. He uncharacteristically took a drink — possibly his first since the dark period following his first wife, Aurilla's, death in Missouri just over eleven years earlier. He and the others enjoyed a meal, and may have picked horses out of Hooker's herd to replace the animals they had ridden so far and hard. But their respite was brief. About twelve hours after they arrived, lookouts at the Sierra Bonita spotted a dust cloud indicating riders from the west. There was no doubt who they were.

Johnny Behan was tired of his posse being mocked for its failure to capture Wyatt and his men. Outfitting and paying such a large group had already run into considerable expense — the bill would ultimately come to a staggering $2,593.65, and Johnny had to justify costs when presenting invoices and receipts to his supervisors. His political future hung in the balance — if Wyatt escaped, Johnny would have an even harder time in November convincing voters that his record in law enforcement justified a second term as county sheriff. News that Wyatt was heading to Henry Hooker's ranch was unsettling; the Sierra Bonita was within about fifty miles of the New Mexico border. Perhaps Wyatt intended to ride out of the territory, placing himself beyond Johnny's jurisdiction. Even if he was eventually captured by someone else and extradited back to Arizona, Johnny couldn't claim any of the credit. He needed to catch Wyatt now. It might be his last chance.

So on Monday morning, March 27, Johnny led his posse northeast. The group included county undersheriff Harry Woods; it was almost one year to the day since Woods had allowed Benson stage robber Luther King to escape from Tombstone's county jail. The ensuing twelve months had been mostly bad ones for Johnny. As he and the posse approached the walls surrounding the Sierra Bonita compound at dawn on Tuesday, he had reason to hope that his luck was about to change for the better.

Before the posse arrived, Wyatt discussed his options with Henry Hooker. The most obvious was to immediately ride on into Mexico or New Mexico; the Earp band could easily reach either of those borders ahead of their pursuers. But ignominious retreat wasn't acceptable. Even with his own freedom and that of his friends at stake, pride was still an issue with Wyatt. He couldn't allow Johnny Behan and his cowboy henchmen to brag that they'd run Wyatt Earp out of Arizona Territory — better instead to make a courageous stand.

Since Wyatt was determined to fight, Hooker suggested that he do so from the ranch compound. Johnny and the posse would have a hard time breaching its walls. It was a risky offer for Hooker to make. Even with his political connections he would clearly be abetting fugitives and exposing himself to criminal charges. Perhaps he expected to make the case that as a county sheriff Johnny had no authority to arrest deputy U.S. marshal Wyatt. But Wyatt turned down the offer. Instead, he and his seven men — Warren, Doc, McMasters, Turkey Creek Jack Johnson, Texas Jack Vermillion, Dan Tipton, and Charlie Smith — rode about three miles from the compound and took up defensive positions on a hill. If Johnny tracked them there — easy enough to do — and attacked, the Earp party would have the advantage of higher ground. Despite being outnumbered by about two to one, they were all well armed and had already survived kill-or-be-killed gunplay against Curly Bill and his cowboys four days earlier. It remained to be seen whether Johnny and his sinister crew would have the stomach for a fight to the death.

About 7 A.M. the Behan posse clattered into the Sierra Bonita compound and received a chilly welcome. Johnny asked Hooker where the fugitives were, and the cattle baron replied that he didn't know and wouldn't tell the Cochise County sheriff even if he did. Johnny, offended, snapped that Hooker was "upholding" murderers. Hooker said that he'd always known the Earps to be gentlemen, unlike the horse thieves and outlaws comprising Johnny's posse. Frontier hospitality required Hooker to feed his latest guests, but he made a point of having his hands set out two tables, one for Johnny and Harry Woods as duly elected lawmen and another for their disreputable hirelings. After breakfast, Johnny tried again to convince Hooker to help him, admitting that "If I can catch the Earp party it will help me at the next election." The crusty cattleman had no interest in keeping Johnny in office. He'd fed the posse; now he wanted them to leave.

From their vantage point atop the hill, the Earp band prepared to fight as they watched the posse depart the compound. It would be no special feat for their pursuers to track them to the hill. It was an obvious place to look. Perhaps Johnny or some of his more experienced cowboy companions suspected where they were, but for the moment they chose not to approach. Instead, Johnny rode on to Fort Grant, where Major James Biddle, the commanding officer, refused Johnny's offer of $500 for the use of his Indian scouts. Stymied again, certain that the Earps were nearby, Johnny and his men camped for the night and returned to the Sierra Bonita on Wednesday. This time Henry Hooker was glad to tell them where the Earp band was waiting on the hill. He added that they were better armed than Johnny's posse and would defeat them if there was a fight.

Johnny had recruited and deputized the cowboys specifically for combat. If he hadn't earlier, he now knew exactly where Wyatt and his companions could be found. All he had to do was lead his men three miles to the hill where Wyatt waited and give the order to attack. The Cochise County sheriff had spent more than a week and thousands of dollars trying to bring about this moment when the fugitives were cornered, or at least stopped running. But at the top of the hill Wyatt Earp was prepared to risk death and, despite the potential consequences to his political future, at the foot of the hill Johnny Behan decided that he wasn't. The eight fugitives watched as the Behan posse spent a few face-saving hours seeking out their quarry everywhere in the vicinity but on the hill where Wyatt waited, and then wheeled their horses to begin the long ride west back to Tombstone.

After the posse returned to town empty-handed on March 30, county undersheriff Harry Woods granted an interview about the fruitless pursuit to his old newspaper. On March 31 the *Nugget* dutifully reported that "Under-Sheriff Woods speaks in the highest terms of the treatment of the posse by the citizens of both Cochise and Graham counties, with the single exception . . . [of] Mr.

514

H. C. Hooker, of the Sierra Bonita Ranch, a man whom, from the large property interest he has in the country, would naturally be supposed to be in favor of upholding the constituted authorities and the preservation of law and order." The *Nugget* reported that, ignoring their crimes and subsequent flight from justice, Hooker had supplied the fugitives with supplies and horses.

The clumsy attempt at spin control was foiled five days later when the *Epitaph* printed a letter received from an anonymous member of the Earp party, probably Doc Holliday given the flowery, formal text. Postmarked from Wilcox near the New Mexico border, the missive denied Hooker had done anything more than supply "refreshments for ourselves and stock, which he kindly granted us. . . . As regards to Mr. Hooker outfitting us with supplies and fresh horses as mentioned in the *Nugget,* it is false and without foundation as we are riding the same horses we left Tombstone on." This latter claim was probably not true.

Then the writer deftly skewered Johnny for his perceived lack of nerve and questionable choice of deputies. He described the hilltop where the fugitives waited in anticipation of an attack, and "not being in a hurry to break camp, our stay was long enough to notice the movements of Sheriff Behan and his posse of honest ranchers, with whom, had they possessed the trailing abilities of the average Arizona ranchman, we might have had trouble." The letter was snarkily signed, "One of them."

The note also promised that Wyatt's band would use its own "trailing abilities" to run down more cowboys, undoubtedly others that Wyatt associated with Morgan's assassination and the crippling of Virgil. But days passed, and there was no further word from or of the Earp party. Rumors began to circulate that Wyatt and his men had left the territory. On the same day that Johnny's posse straggled back to Tombstone, George Parsons wrote in his diary, "What and when the end will be — God only knows." Back at the Sierra Bonita compound, Wyatt was trying to decide.

It was clear that the retreat of the Behan posse was only a temporary reprieve for Wyatt, Doc, and the other fugitives. Despite their host's generosity, they couldn't remain as guests at Hooker's ranch indefinitely. Surrendering to Pima County sheriff Bob Paul was not a palatable option, even though he was Wyatt's firm friend. Paul would still have to hold his prisoners for trial, and Wyatt had learned the hard way that the cowboys excelled at assassination. They would descend on Tucson as soon as they heard that the Earp party was in custody.

If Wyatt remained determined to avenge himself on everyone involved in Morgan's murder, there were still cowboys left to pursue — certainly key plotters John Ringo and Ike Clanton, and perhaps Hank Swilling, Pete Spencer, and Frederick Bode. But Wyatt had already killed three men in the past eight days; he was surely sick of slaughter. The immediate emotional devastation caused by his brother's death must have lessened at least a little, and it was time to think about himself and the seven men riding with him. So long as they remained in Arizona Territory they could expect to be dogged by posses and packs of cowboys. There was no sense in Wyatt holding out hope that if he stayed, at least he would have the satisfaction of seeing the courts punish Morgan's surviving assailants. On April 4 in Tombstone, murder charges against Pete Spencer and Frederick Bode were dismissed for lack of evidence. And, finally, financial considerations dictated that it was time to move on.

During what the *Los Angeles Express* described in its ongoing coverage as "the Earp vendetta," money had been a constant concern, not only for expenses incurred during the killing spree but to provide getaway money for Wyatt's men afterward. They would all have to go to ground somewhere, and that meant transportation costs and outfitting themselves in their new surroundings. But as Wyatt rested at the Sierra Bonita Ranch and pondered his next move, he found himself suddenly flush with funds. Dan Tipton finally delivered the $1,000 from E. B. Gage, and there was another thousand dollars conveyed by a Tombstone stage driver named Lou Cooley. That money came from Wells Fargo, and, more than anything else, it signaled the end of Wyatt's bloody spree.

On the night of October 25, Wyatt told Ike Clanton that he "would not fight no one if [he] could get away from it, because there was no money in it." It was true. To a limited extent, Wells Fargo was willing to underwrite Wyatt and his men on the Vendetta Ride. The deaths of Frank Stilwell and Curly Bill Brocius benefited the company even as the killings helped satisfy Wyatt's thirst for revenge. They eliminated two men that Wells Fargo considered key conspirators in the spate of Cochise County stage robberies. Perhaps it would be enough to discourage future hold-ups; meanwhile, the company was not about to pay out any more money than necessary. A year earlier, Wells Fargo authorized dead-or-alive individual rewards of $1,200 for the three alleged Benson stage bandits, considerable sums designed to motivate area lawmen into dogged pursuit. Wyatt Earp, on the run himself and desperate for money, had to settle for lesser amounts — $500 each for Stilwell and Curly Bill. Because Wells Fargo couldn't be seen to subsidize men who were wanted by the law themselves, that money was paid off the books, but in April a company ledger noted under the heading "Loss and Damage" that it paid "Earp & posse a/c Stilwell & Curly Bill $150.00," plus $34 for "extra EX's Jany, Feby" and "Mch & Apl $80.00" — reimbursement for posse salaries and expenses beyond the $1,000 under-the-table bounty paid to Wyatt for killing Stilwell and Curly Bill.

But Wells Fargo was not willing to make further payments for any additional cowboys Wyatt and his men might kill. Its $1,000, plus the $1,000 from Gage, was all the money that Wyatt was going to get. He could roam the territory hoping for further opportunities to administer violent vigilante justice while his bankroll gradually dwindled to nothing, or else, satisfied that he had at least partially avenged Morgan and defended Earp family honor, he could pay off his companions and lead them out of Arizona Territory. The decision may have been made easier when Wyatt learned that Jack Stilwell, Frank's brother who was a famed scout and Indian fighter, had arrived in Tombstone and organized a new posse — it included Ike Clanton, John Ringo, and as many as thirty others. Like Wyatt, Jack Stilwell was determined to avenge a murdered brother. Unlike Johnny Behan, Stilwell was a formidable leader who wouldn't rest until his quarry was either in custody or dead. Wyatt and his band would be hard-pressed to elude him.

Wyatt made a quick trip to Fort Grant to have documents notarized and mailed to his family in California. Major Biddle formally told Wyatt that he would have to arrest him and then conveniently stayed out of sight until the Earp party had left. Around the middle of April, regional newspapers reported that Wyatt and his seven companions had crossed over the territorial border into New Mexico, where, with help from Wells Fargo in arranging transportation, they made their way to Albuquerque and then on into Colorado. From there, Wyatt divided his remaining money with everyone and the party split up. McMasters, Johnson, Vermillion, Tipton, and Smith probably returned to New Mexico, where it was relatively easy to hide from the law. Doc went to Pueblo and Denver to gamble, while Wyatt and Warren stopped in Gunnison, where Wyatt began operating a faro bank. It wasn't a permanent relocation — Wyatt was marking time because he expected that Arizona governor Tritle would soon pardon him.

Tritle had no such intention. He used the Vendetta Ride as further proof that southeastern Arizona Territory was beyond control by civilian lawmen. In one letter to President Arthur he asked permission from Congress to "remove from office any county officer . . .

found to be corrupt, inefficient, and incompetent." Johnny Behan's job was saved when Congress refused. Congress also turned down the president's request to amend the *Posse Comitatus* Act so federal troops could move in to combat the outlaw threat. Undaunted, on May 3 Arthur issued a proclamation threatening to impose martial law at noon on May 15 if "unlawful combinations of evil disposed persons, who are banded together to oppose and obstruct the execution of the laws of the United States" did not "disperse and retire peaceably to their respective abodes." The edict was generally ignored, and martial law was not imposed as Arthur had threatened.

Though no pardon for Wyatt was forthcoming from Tritle, authorities in Arizona hadn't forgotten him or Doc Holliday. While the others in Wyatt's vendetta band were allowed to avoid prosecution, Wyatt and Doc remained targets for extradition. As the best known of the fugitives, their capture and trial might serve as deterrents to other lawbreakers in the territory. In mid-May Doc was arrested in Denver. Within a week Pima County sheriff Bob Paul arrived in Colorado with extradition papers, but by then Doc had cagily granted several interviews to local newspapers and gained considerable local sympathy. Acting more out of friendship toward Wyatt than any affection for Doc, Bat Masterson — recently elected marshal in Trinidad — helped convince Colorado governor Frederick Pitkin to refuse extradition. Bob Paul returned to Arizona without a prisoner and told the *Tucson Star* that Pitkin "had been informed by prominent citizens of Denver that if Holliday was placed in my custody he would be murdered by cowboys before reaching Tucson." Doc was eventually freed in Colorado, and with that any active efforts to bring him and Wyatt back to Arizona for trial ended. In Tucson and in Tombstone, leaders had other matters requiring their full attention.

On May 26 Tombstone was ravaged by fire for the second time, and the resulting destruction was even worse than what the town had suffered during the blaze of June 1881. All the major hotels burned, including the Grand and the Cosmopolitan. Most saloons, restaurants, and dry goods stores were also lost. Once again, Tombstone had to rebuild, but now fire damage was only one civic and economic problem. Several major mining operations were in trouble, either from exhausting ore deposits or else flooding. The Tombstone Gold and Silver Mill and Mining Company stopped paying dividends, and the Grand Central Mine was at least temporarily closed because of water. The Earps were relegated to a painful, if recent, past that was best shunted aside in order to concentrate on overcoming these new challenges. Despite all his dreams of gaining wealth and influence, of becoming *important* in Tombstone, Wyatt's immediate legacy was limited to uncomfortable memories of a minor functionary who ultimately overstepped himself in particularly violent, regrettable ways.

In Colorado, Wyatt was slow to realize that any realistic hopes of exoneration and a triumphant return to Tombstone were gone. In a June 4 interview with the Gunnison newspaper, he claimed that he "look[ed] for a pardon in a few weeks, and when it comes I'll go back [to Tombstone]." Once he returned he planned "to run for sheriff . . . Behan knows he can't get it again." If no pardon was forthcoming, Wyatt promised, "I'll go back in the fall anyway and stand trial." But at some point Wyatt accepted the obvious, because he never returned to Tombstone.

Chapter Seventeen:
Legends

Tombstone's decline was precipitous in the aftermath of the Vendetta Ride. Above all else the community depended on its mines, and when they were in trouble so was the town. In 1882 mine flooding became a serious problem, necessitating the installation of massive pumps to expel water. The pumps were expensive and balky. Profits were further reduced by an extended miners' strike in 1884. Superintendents of the major Tombstone mines — the Contention, the Grand Central, the Tombstone Gold and Silver Mill and Mining Company — cut wages from $4 to $3 a day. Workers formed the Tombstone Miners' Union and walked out. Mine officials immediately shut down operations, gambling that the miners would return to work after missing a few weeks of pay. But the miners proved more stubborn than expected, and the general Tombstone economy began to crumble. Hudson & Company, a major bank, closed and in the process cost its customers

$130,000 in deposits.

In July and August 1884 some of the striking miners gave up and returned to work at the reduced daily rate. The holdout miners skirmished with mine guards; federal troops helped quell the disturbance. On August 25, the Miners' Union disbanded and its members went back to work for $3 a day, too. The strike was over, but the flooding problems were not. Profits were devastated by falling prices for silver — from a high of $1.15–$1.20 per troy ounce, by 1886 they had dropped to 63 cents. Smaller mines shut down. The Contention closed in 1886, followed by the Grand Central. The Tombstone Gold and Silver Mill and Mining Company hung on until 1896. Though there would be sporadic attempts to reestablish mining operations in and around town, these met with such limited success that they, too, eventually closed.

For a while, people hung on and hoped. Railroad grading came within two and a half miles of town, but didn't reach the city limits until 1903. New amusements offered temporary respite from civic troubles — a Tombstone baseball team battled other "nines" from Tucson, a public swimming pool opened, and George Parsons noted in his diary entry of November 11, 1882, that "roller skating [is] all the go now." But three days later Clara Brown informed her San Diego readers that "quite a number of people are leaving this Fall. . . . Tombstone has been a good place in which to make money, probably will be for some time to come, but — *Voil! Voil!*" Clara concluded by informing her readers that the November 14 column was the last that "I shall ever [write] from so gloomily named a town. . . . In a few days more I shall be on the wing."

Other prominent Tombstoners joined the exodus. In the spring of 1882 John Clum sold the *Epitaph;* he moved to Washington, D.C., and remarried. Even in its early death throes Tombstone still appealed to its former mayor. He returned in 1885 after being reappointed as town postmaster, but within a year Clum realized the town was on a permanent downward spiral and moved west to California. He spent years working for the Postal Service in far-flung posts that included stops in Washington state, Colorado, and Alaska. Late in life he enjoyed giving lectures about his adventures on the frontier. Clum died in 1932.

George Parsons remained in Tombstone until January 1887. He wrote in his diary, "Town going," and then he did, too, moving to Los Angeles. He was much more successful there, dabbling in real estate and devoting much of his energies to civic endeavors. After Parsons's death in 1933, his voluminous diaries became the property of the Arizona

Pioneers' Historical Society, and during the Depression the Works Project Administration hired out-of-work historians to transcribe the entries made by Parsons during his seven years in Tombstone. As a result, Parsons became justly revered by subsequent generations of frontier historians. Philosophically attuned to the town elite, Parsons was rarely an objective observer, but he was a faithful one.

When his term as a territorial district judge expired in 1882, Wells Spicer turned his attention from the law to prospecting. In 1884 there were rumors of silver strikes in the Quijotoa Mountains southwest of Tucson, and Spicer joined other investors in a mine operation there. It showed the potential of being a rich strike — the *Arizona Daily Star* reported that "the claim is universally spoken of as being one of great promise." But there ultimately wasn't enough ore to turn a profit, and Spicer lost everything. By early 1887 he had made two failed attempts at suicide, then wandered off by himself into the desert. Spicer was never seen again.

Johnny Behan's once promising political career in Cochise County sputtered out. In September 1882 the loyal Democrat failed to even gain his party's nomination for county sheriff, and in November voters elected Republican Jerome Ward to succeed him. Johnny tried to stay in office and siphon off

10 percent of collected tax monies as long as he could; in May 1883 he was indicted by a county grand jury for failing to turn over tax rolls to Ward. But the district attorney dismissed the case, and from then until his death in 1912 Johnny held a number of appointed political jobs including warden of Yuma Territorial Prison. He became one of the country's earliest bicycle enthusiasts — while working as a customs inspector in Texas he helped organize the El Paso Cycle Track Association. With the notable exception of Wyatt Earp, almost everyone liked Johnny and proved willing to overlook his shortcomings as a lawman. After his death at age sixty seven, a statement from the Arizona Pioneers' Historical Society declared, "He was first Sheriff of Cochise County, appointed by General Fremont and was a terror to the evil disposed in those stirring time[s]."

Billy Breakenridge, who served as one of Johnny's deputies, was fired by him in August 1882 and ran against his former boss for the Democratic nomination for county sheriff. He didn't get it, either — Larkin Carr was the eventual nominee. Breakenridge worked for a while as a U.S. deputy marshal, then as a surveyor, and eventually became a private detective. He collaborated with writer William MacLeod Raine on a memoir of his days on the frontier and in Tombstone, and in the process inadvertently became one of the initiators of the town's unexpected revival. Breakenridge's *Helldorado* would not see print until 1928, though, and in the interim Tombstone continued to dwindle in population and significance.

In 1886, Geronimo finally surrendered to the army; before he did, Camillus Fly hauled his bulky camera equipment out and snapped the Apache renegade's photo. But that didn't end Indian raids in the area; Cochise County suffered them into the early twentieth century.

In the late 1890s, writer Owen Wister, a Harvard graduate and friend of Theodore Roosevelt's, traveled to Tombstone; he was considering writing a book about the Earps and the 1881 gunfight. But he was too repulsed by the dying town to tackle the project, reporting on his return east that "Tombstone is quite the most depressing town I have ever seen. 'The glory is departed' is written on every street and building." But, like Breakenridge, Wister would write a book that directly contributed to Tombstone's curious future. Published in 1902, *The Virginian* was a novel set in 1890s Wyoming, and its colorful dialogue ("When you call me that, smile!") and rousing scenes of cattle rustling and a final epic gunfight captured the imaginations of Americans; the book went through fourteen printings in just eight months. To readers, rustlers became stock characters in frontier entertainment. Back in Tombstone and Cochise County, they remained part of real life — though the nature of the rustling and the men stealing stock had changed.

In the wake of the gunfight and the Vendetta Ride, the core of the Texas cowboys operating in and around Cochise County broke apart. Curly Bill was dead, and so was Frank Stilwell. By the middle of July 1882 John Ringo was, too, and under the most mysterious circumstances. On the 11th or 12th of the month, Billy Breakenridge encountered Ringo near the south pass of the Dragoon Mountains. Though it was only noon, Ringo was drunk. He told Breakenridge that he was on his way to Galeyville, but on the afternoon of July 14 his body was discovered in a remote canyon. There was a bullet hole in Ringo's right temple, and his .45 Colt revolver was still clutched in his right hand. Ringo's rifle was propped against a tree, and his boots were missing. Torn strips of cloth were wrapped around his feet. His saddled horse was found wandering about two miles away. A coroner's jury ruled that Ringo committed suicide, but rumors spread that he had been gunned down by one of several possible assailants including Doc Holliday, Buckskin Frank Leslie, Johnny Behind-the-Deuce, and Wyatt Earp, with Wyatt himself eventually claiming credit for the shooting.

As with many of Wyatt's tales of his life on the frontier, it is marginally possible but not probable. After leaving Arizona Territory for Colorado at the end of the Vendetta Ride, he was trying to get on with his life rather than seeking additional revenge. The circumstances of John Ringo's death will probably never be known, and continue to provide grist for vigorous debate among frontier historians.

In late 1882 Ike and Phin Clanton moved two hundred miles north of Tombstone to Apache County, where their sister Mary had settled with her husband. The brothers acquired land there, but couldn't stay out of trouble with the law. They were suspected of rustling and robbery; several times charges against them were filed and subsequently dropped for lack of evidence. But in June 1887 Ike and Phin were accused of stealing cattle and were pursued by J. V. Brighton, who'd been hired by officials in Apache and Cochise counties to chase down rustlers. Brighton and his posse cornered the brothers, who were ordered to surrender. Phin did; Ike either tried to escape or went for his gun — given his past habit of preferring to run than fight, it was probably the former — and Brighton shot and killed him. Phin was sentenced to ten years in Yuma Territorial Prison.

The remaining Cochise County cowboys

who'd feuded with the Earps drifted away, but there were plenty of other stock thieves to replace them. Cattle rustling faded as an illicit means of making money, not because of decreasing demands for beef but thanks in part to the advent of refrigerated railroad cars, which began being used to transport perishable foods (initially fruit) in 1867 and proliferated by the early 1880s. Not long after Wyatt concluded the Vendetta Ride, butchers in Cochise County no longer had to buy cattle that were obviously stolen. Now fresh meat could be shipped in as the market required. But rustlers continued to plague southeastern Arizona ranchers; their focus simply shifted from stealing cattle, which was no longer as profitable, to horses and mules, which were in great demand. Federal forces on both sides of the border were kept busy chasing brigands, and also the bands of renegade Apaches who continued to raid with near-impunity.

Doc Holliday had been controversial long before the Fremont Street gunfight, and he didn't change his ways or reputation after leaving Arizona Territory. Stories persist that at the end of the Vendetta Ride he quarreled with Wyatt, perhaps about Josephine — as with many Southern gentlemen of his time, Doc probably had no fondness for Jews — and they separated in anger. While Wyatt dithered in Gunnison, waiting for a pardon that never came, Doc resumed rambling and gambling in Colorado. Almost immediately, his health began to deteriorate. The Arizona desert had apparently been good for Doc; during his time in Tombstone there is no record of him having been debilitated. But certainly the physical demands and the emotional stress of the Vendetta Ride took their toll. He lost a disturbing amount of weight — one report had him at 122 pounds — and was in constant trouble with the law for fighting. As usual he drank far too much, which didn't improve his temper. Doc mostly haunted saloons in Leadville and Denver, and his luck at the tables turned sour. Denver police even arrested him for vagrancy. Bit by bit, Doc withered away. In May 1885, Wyatt and Josephine encountered him at Denver's Windsor Hotel. Josephine recalled in her memoir that they were appalled by his "thinner, more delicate" appearance and constant racking cough. Whatever disagreement Wyatt and Doc might have had three years earlier was forgotten. They talked quietly together, and the habitually taciturn Wyatt had tears in his eyes when they said goodbye for what both men knew would be the last time.

Doc continued to eke out a marginal living as a gambler until his health finally broke completely. Somehow he must have saved a little to subsidize his final days, because in

October 1887 Doc moved to a hotel in Glenwood Springs, 180 miles west of Denver. Bellboys there would recall bringing the terminally ill man his room-service breakfast every day — a bottle of whiskey, for which he generously tipped a dollar. A few weeks after he arrived, Doc slipped into a coma. He died on November 8 at the age of thirty-six. Kate Elder claimed later that Doc contacted her when he knew his death was imminent, and the two had a brief, final reunion. According to the *Aspen Daily Times,* when Doc was buried on November 9 his coffin "was followed to the cemetery by a large number of kindred spirits," but none of them was named Earp. All of the surviving brothers were preoccupied with their own post-Tombstone lives, though in some cases their luck was not much better than Doc's.

Warren Earp, the youngest and wildest of the brothers, found it impossible to settle down after leaving Arizona with Wyatt in April 1882. He did some prospecting and made small mine investments with his brothers, but much of the time he stayed on his own. Like Doc Holliday, he kept getting into trouble, and because of his now notorious last name his misadventures were considered news. In May 1883 the *Los Angeles Herald* reported that Warren reportedly killed "a Mexican" in San Bernardino, then "declined to be arrested as he acted in self-defense." In 1891 the *Riverside Morning Enterprise* informed readers that Warren Earp "had shot and killed the City Marshal of San Jacinto," and only after offering that exciting tidbit did the story mention that "the report was a canard." A year later a San Bernardino newspaper reported that "Juan Bustamente and Warren Earp engaged in the pleasant pastime of cracking each other's heads," and a year after that Warren was back in the news for "cut[ting] [Charles] Steele with a pocket-knife. . . . At the trial there being no prosecuting witnesses Earp was discharged." Warren then returned to Arizona Territory, where the eleven-year-old Stilwell murder warrant against him had either been forgotten or was deliberately ignored. But he still couldn't stay out of trouble. In Yuma he was accused of attacking and then extorting money from a "Professor Behrens," who had Warren arrested. But the alleged crime was committed on a bridge that crossed the California-Arizona line, and it was impossible for the prosecution to prove Warren had done the deeds on the Arizona side. The Yuma court released Warren after he promised to leave town, but he didn't go far enough to save his life. On July 6, 1900, he got into an argument with John Boyett in a bar in Willcox, Arizona. According to a witness, Warren dared Boyett, who was unarmed, to go and get his gun. Boyett fetched two, returned, and shot forty-five-year-old Warren to death. Because Warren was an Earp, the incident made national headlines, though the *Seattle Post-Intelligencer* mistakenly identified Virgil as the victim.

James was the Earp brother with the fewest ambitions and the most friends, and for him life after Tombstone remained pretty much the same. He stayed married to former prostitute Bessie until her death in 1887, ran a boardinghouse, drove a hack, and ended up tending bar in San Bernardino. Late in life the arm injury he suffered in the Civil War gave him problems, and he became a semi-invalid. James died in Los Angeles in 1926 at the age of eighty-four.

Virgil Earp was already crippled when he left Tombstone for Colton just before Wyatt embarked on the Vendetta Ride. He gradually regained his health; when George Parsons departed from Tombstone in 1887, he made Colton his first California stop and recorded in his diary that he "met Virgil Earp who looks well and seems to be doing well. Can use his arm some." There was one early blip on Virgil's new life: In July 1882 he was arrested in San Francisco for participating in an illegal card game. Except for the embarrassment involved, the incident had no lasting consequences. Virgil and his wife, Allie, moved around the West; he operated a detective agency, managed a burlesque theater, and briefly served as Colton's city marshal. Wanderlust and an unshakable belief that better things were just ahead continued to consume Virgil. He resigned as Colton's marshal in 1889 and entered into a series of relatively unsuccessful business ventures in California, Colorado, Arizona, and Nevada.

In 1898, a letter reached Virgil from a woman in Portland, Oregon, named Janie Law. She wrote that during the past seventeen years she had read occasional newspaper and magazine articles mentioning the role played by Virgil Earp in a Tombstone gunfight. By any chance, she wondered, might he be the same Virgil Earp who was briefly married to Ellen Rysdam in Illinois just prior to the Civil War? If so, then Janie was his daughter. Virgil was thrilled to learn that he had a child, and a year later he traveled to Portland to meet her. Janie and her father formed an immediate bond and remained in touch.

For a time it seemed that Virgil and Allie might end their days in Prescott, the same town where Virgil got his start in law enforcement nearly a quarter-century earlier. Virgil even took preliminary steps toward running on the Republican ticket for Johnny Behan's old job of Yavapai County sheriff, but illness forced him to abandon the race. When word reached him via Wyatt about mineral strikes in western Nevada, the old lure of possible quick riches overcame Virgil again. He and Allie moved to the boomtown of Goldfield, which for a few years seemed likely to become another Tombstone or even Virginia City before its ore deposits petered out. The Earps had no money to invest, so Virgil tried an old tactic to establish himself with local leaders: In January 1905 he was sworn in as a county deputy sheriff. But sixty-two-year-old Virgil no longer had much stamina to carry out his official duties. In October a pneumonia epidemic swept through the area, and Virgil was one of eleven who died. At his daughter, Janie's, request, Allie Earp had her husband's remains buried in Portland; she took her own comfort from remembering the years she had spent at Virgil's side.

After Tombstone, Mattie Blaylock Earp wanted very much to stay at Wyatt's side, but that didn't happen. Mattie had gone ahead to wait for Wyatt at his parents' home in Colton while he avenged his brother Morgan on the Vendetta Ride, but when Wyatt finally returned to California sometime in late 1882 he went to San Francisco and Josephine Marcus instead. Mattie was typical among common-law wives in the West for more than just being deserted by her husband. As so many others did, Mattie turned to prostitution to support herself. She returned to Arizona, ending up in Pinal near the San Carlos Indian Reservation. It was a horrible existence, and Mattie dulled her pain with liquor and laudanum, both frequent vices of frontier prostitutes. In July 1888 thirty-eight-year-old Mattie told a friend that Wyatt "had wrecked her life by deserting her and she didn't want to live." The next day she was discovered dead on her bed, with empty whiskey and laudanum bottles scattered around her body. The coroner ruled it an overdose; common sense indicated suicide. If Wyatt had any regrets about his treatment of Mattie or the deplorable circumstances of her death, there is no record of them. Besides, he was with Josephine Marcus by then, and she demanded a man's complete attention.

Based on their personalities and past romantic histories, the odds were against Wyatt and Josephine lasting very long as a couple. At twenty-one or twenty-two (her exact date of birth remains in question) Josephine loved luxury, and thirty-four-year-old Wyatt's penchant for prospecting and frontier boomtown life virtually guaranteed the opposite. Yet once they reunited in San Francisco in late 1882 they stayed together for forty-six years, and theirs was a genuine, if occasionally tumultuous, love story. Josephine in particular had to change and did. She endured the hardships of remote mining camps, and even when life with Wyatt took her to the big cities she loved — San Francisco, San Diego, Los Angeles — difficult financial circumstances often forced them to scrape by. Wyatt never gave up trying to get rich, but he was generally unsuccessful. There were two significant changes in his life after Tombstone. Being with Josephine was one, and being famous was the other.

National publicity about the gunfight on Fremont Street and the subsequent Vendetta Ride had been pervasive enough to make Wyatt's name widely known. His celebrity status guaranteed news coverage, which in turn extended his reputation further. Wherever he and Josephine traveled, local newspapers would note their arrival and always mention the Arizona incidents or at least attribute to him a highly exaggerated kill count. When Wyatt refereed an 1888 prizefight in Tijuana, the story about the contest mentioned that "Earp has a cemetery which he has stocked with over 30 men."

Wyatt and Josephine headed to the Northwest and opened a saloon in Eagle City, Idaho. Whatever they earned from it was invested in mining claims that didn't pay off. From there Wyatt and his fourth wife — it was probably Wyatt's third common-law relationship, though Josephine would claim that they officially married — drifted a bit more and then settled for a while in San Diego, where Wyatt did well with property investments, enough so that he could afford to buy several racehorses. Then and later, Wyatt picked up additional income with occasional stints guarding money shipments for his old patrons at Wells Fargo. All the while, he remained a controversial public figure. During his San Diego sojourn, the popular *Police Gazette* declared to its readers that "probably no man has a wider reputation throughout the Western territories than Wyatt S. Earp, of the famous Earp Brothers, who created such a sensation a few years since at Tombstone, Arizona, by completely exterminating a whole band of outlawed cutthroats." Identifying Wyatt as the most famous figure in the West was a stretch. He certainly ranked behind Wild Bill Hickok, Buffalo Bill Cody, and George Armstrong Custer, but there was no denying that his name was generally well known.

In 1888 Wyatt suffered business reversals in San Diego and was wiped out. He and Josephine moved north to San Francisco — her family still lived there — and Wyatt rebuilt his fortunes. He took a job managing a horse stable, made the acquaintance of important players in local racing, and began placing bets. He made good picks frequently enough to travel in style with Josephine, including to Chicago in 1893 to attend the World's Fair.

When Wyatt and Josephine stopped in Denver on the Chicago trip, a local paper noted that "he wore, while here, a neat gray tailor-made suit, immaculate linen and fashionable neckware. With a derby hat and a pair of tan shoes he was a figure to catch a lady's eye and to make the companions of his old, wild days at Tombstone and Dodge, who died with their boots on and their jeans pants tucked down in them, turn in their graves."

Wyatt couldn't escape his past, so in 1896 he tried to at least take control of his reputation. He allowed the *San Francisco Examiner* to run a three-part, first-person account of his frontier adventures; the editor assigned an overenthusiastic ghostwriter to help him. The stories appeared on successive Sundays in August, and their prose was as purple as the Arizona desert sage. On August 2 the first installment, "How Wyatt Earp Routed a Gang of Arizona Outlaws," began:

It may be that the trail of blood will seem to lie too thickly over the pages that I write. If I had it in me to invent a tale I would fain lighten the crimson stain so that it would glow no deeper than demure pink. But half a lifetime on the frontier attunes a man's hand to the six-shooter rather than the pen, and it is lucky that I am asked only for the facts, for more than facts I could not give.

The three stories were virtually devoid of facts; Wyatt completely indulged in the frontier tradition of exaggerating his adventures and achievements to the very brink of complete fabrication. *Examiner* readers were told that Wyatt was city marshal in Dodge, that bumbling Ike Clanton was "sort of a leader" among the southeast Arizona Territory rustlers, and that at the Tucson train depot Wyatt "was forced to fight Ike Clanton and four or five of his friends who had followed us to do murder." Wyatt's other stretchers included elevating hapless cowboy George Hoyt to the status of a veteran assassin hired by Texas cattlemen to kill Wyatt in Dodge, and an outrageous account of backing down Clay Allison despite "ten or a dozen of the worst Texans" armed with Winchesters lurking nearby to help Allison "in the killing." At the end of August 9's second installment Wyatt and his ghostwriter wondered "who would ever have expected such garrulity from an old frontiersman! I actually astonish myself."

San Francisco readers were astonished — and delighted. Wyatt's local prominence increased to the point that a month after the series appeared in print he was hired to referee one of the most important prizefights ever staged in San Francisco, a heavyweight match on December 3 between title contenders "Sailor" Tom Sharkey and Bob Fitzsimmons. Refereeing the Sharkey-Fitzsimmons bout was the perfect means for Wyatt to further extend his fame in a positive way; a flood of additional good publicity might gain him entrée to the city's highest business circles and most lucrative investment opportunities.

But for Wyatt, the fight was a public relations disaster. A crowd of ten thousand jammed shoulder to shoulder in San Francisco's Mechanic's Pavilion was unexpectedly entertained before the bout even began; upon entering the ring and removing his coat, Wyatt revealed a pistol stuck in his pants. Carrying a concealed weapon was just as illegal in 1896 San Francisco as it had been in 1881 Tombstone. Police confiscated the weapon and Wyatt was later fined $50. That misstep was nothing compared to what happened next. Fitzsimmons was winning easily until the eighth round, when Sharkey was floored by a low blow that was observed only by the fallen fighter and referee Wyatt, who disqualified Fitzsimmons and declared Sharkey the winner. Fans were outraged, and stories about the fight speculated that the bout had been fixed in Sharkey's favor. Wyatt was suddenly a pariah in San Francisco, and he and Josephine had no choice but to move on.

For a few months they stopped in Yuma; Wyatt was apparently in no danger of arrest in Arizona from the old 1882 warrants, and the isolated town was a good place to stay out of sight for a while. But he and Josephine had a more far-flung destination in mind; gold had been discovered in remote sections of Alaska, and on August 7, 1897, the *Arizona Sentinel* reported that "Wyatt Earp, who has lived a greater portion of his life in a surrounding of mining districts and gold, has . . . left for San Francisco Thurs[day], from which point he will board a San Francisco steamer, as he 'has become imbued with the Alaskan fever and started for Klondyke country.' "

Wyatt and Josephine opened another saloon in Nome, and over the next few years it became a stopping place for many old frontier friends who were passing through, including John Clum and George Parsons. On August 30, 1900, Parsons noted in his diary that he, Wyatt, and Clum had enjoyed "a regular old Arizona time, and Wyatt unlimbered for several hours and seemed glad to talk to us who knew the past." Wyatt was in a sad, contemplative mood that night; he'd recently received word about his brother Warren's death in Willcox. Whatever the usually reticent Wyatt shared with his Tombstone pals that night must have been interesting. Parsons didn't offer specifics, but guessed that sitting in on the conversation "would have been worth $1,000 to the newspapers."

Wyatt and Josephine returned to the States

in 1901, gladly abandoning Alaska's snowy climes for the more familiar dry heat of the Southwest. Western Nevada had become the latest region where gold was discovered, and for a change the couple had some money to invest — about $80,000 according to the recollections of family members. The amount is probably exaggerated, but certainly they came to Nevada with a larger than usual grubstake. The Nome saloon had been a moneymaker, and according to Earp family gossip some of the profits came from running prostitutes there. Once again, the Earps opened a saloon, this time in Goldfield, Nevada, though a partner ran it on a day-to-day basis while Wyatt did some prospecting on his own. Sometimes he stayed away for significant periods — on November 23, 1904, the *Arizona Sentinel* reported that "A vote count for the November election shows that Wyatt Earpe ran for constable in Cibola [in western Arizona near the California border] against Leo Frankenburg, and won by 9 to 1," and on November 30 Wyatt's name was listed among elected officials. He never entirely lost the urge to wear a badge. But soon he was back in Goldfield; Virgil and Allie Earp joined them there until Virgil's death in October 1905.

Soon afterward, Wyatt and Josephine departed Goldfield for Los Angeles; from then on they lived there part of the year and spent the other months at a desert camp in the Mojave Desert. Wyatt never quite gave up on the dream of striking it rich as a prospector. But whatever funds the Earps had when they departed Alaska were soon depleted. In Los Angeles they settled into genteel poverty, sometimes depending on the charity of relatives. In July 1911 sixty-three-year-old Wyatt hit an all-time low when he was arrested for participating in a crooked card game. According to the *Los Angeles Herald,* Wyatt was one of four connivers who tempted a sucker into playing fixed hands of faro with them in a hotel owned by Wyatt's former Tombstone supporter Albert Bilicke. The charges were dismissed due to lack of evidence, but clearly Wyatt was desperate for money. He'd been unsuccessful as a prospector, unlucky as an investor, and even unable to turn a profit from gambling shenanigans. But during those dark Los Angeles days, the old desert dog decided to attempt a new trick. So far, fame hadn't brought the aging man fortune, but perhaps there was still time. Wyatt pinned his last hopes for striking it rich on a book about his life on the frontier.

As early as 1900 in Nome, John Clum urged Wyatt to write a memoir. According to Clum, "the plan was discussed but never carried out." The potential for profit was there. Ever since the mid-1860s, when *Harper's* published a biography of Wild Bill Hickok and Ned Buntline's *Buffalo Bill, King of the Border Men* was serialized in Street and Smith's *New York Weekly,* readers had demonstrated eagerness for tales of the Western frontier. Gunslingers on horseback replaced woodsmen like Crockett and Boone as cultural icons, most often through exaggerated or entirely fictitious adventures recounted in dime novels. Cody, a master marketer, took the concept further with his cartoonish but popular Wild West Shows, which for decades sold out arenas in the United States as well as in England and Europe. Americans wanted to believe that life on the frontier was a series of death-defying adventures; as Cody biographer Louis S. Warren noted, "Audience expectations of frontier stories were so powerful that they could look past the blatant fiction . . . and embrace the 'real' frontier heroes as proof that their expectations and assumptions about the frontier were mostly true." In 1874 Colonel George Armstrong Custer's memoir, *My Life on the Plains, or, Personal Experiences with Indians* was a sensation, and his final personal experiences with Native Americans at the Little Big Horn two years later didn't dim the luster of his reputation. As with David Crockett, readers were willing to forgive their hero for dying because he did it fighting the forces of evil in such dramatic fashion.

Until Wister's *The Virginian* in 1902, frontier

fandom was widespread but in some ways considered juvenile. The elegant, if factually challenged, novel by the Harvard alumnus made it convenient for even cultural snobs to indulge themselves in Wild West fantasy. More novels and magazine articles resulted, and one of the writers profiting from the expanding market was Bat Masterson, who reinvented himself on the East Coast as a journalist. Next to Cody, Masterson may have been the frontier veteran who best understood how to craft, then profit, from personal legend. He strutted the streets of New York dining out on tales of his experiences, and wrote a series of widely read stories about frontier gunmen for *Human Life* magazine. One published in 1907 deified Wyatt Earp: "[He] is one of the few men I personally knew in the West in the early days, whom I regarded as absolutely destitute of physical fear. . . . I have known Wyatt Earp since early in the [eighteen] seventies, and have seen him tried out under circumstances which made the test of manhood supreme." Bat even had a reason for the occasional negative stories about Wyatt that had dogged him since Tombstone: "[B]y his display of great courage and nerve under trying conditions, [he attracted] the envy and hatred of those small-minded creatures with which the world seems to be abundantly peopled, and whose sole delight seems to be in fly-specking the reputations of real men."

Wyatt certainly didn't mind the encomiums from his old pal Bat, but he continued to fume about stories that painted him in a less saintly light. These contributed to his decision to tell his own story in his own way. The final straw was probably a series of stories by Frederick Bechdolt in 1919 that appeared in *The Saturday Evening Post*. Unlike many journalists who simply made up stories to suit the market, Bechdolt traveled to the West and interviewed people there, including former Cochise County deputy Billy Breakenridge. The second story in the series was titled "Tombstone's Wild Oats," and it included a description of the Earps' questionable methods of law enforcement, which Bechdolt compared to the bloody misdeeds of the Apaches.

Wyatt was prepared to tell his story but needed a collaborator. His first choice was writer Forrestine Hooker, cattle baron Henry Hooker's daughter-in-law. Wyatt told her some of his life story, not concerning himself as much with fact as with melodrama, and Forrestine dutifully wrote it all down. The project was never completed. Wyatt may have quarreled with Forrestine; in any event her manuscript was put aside and forgotten until it was eventually discovered by Earp historian Jeff Morey in Los Angeles's Southwest Museum. In it, Wyatt claimed among other improbable things that he had killed John Ringo at the conclusion of the Vendetta Ride.

Wyatt needed another ghostwriter. He might have asked Bat Masterson, but Bat died in New York in 1921. So Wyatt next turned to John Flood, an engineer who had befriended the Earps. Flood had no experience as an author, but he could take accurate notes — Wyatt was less interested in credentials than a willingness to copy down his story exactly as he told it. Flood began interviewing Wyatt and sometimes found it hard going. The book was to be written in the third rather than the first person — Wyatt didn't want to seem to be bragging about himself. Flood's private notes indicate ongoing frustration — sometimes Wyatt explained one thing in a way that didn't jibe with something else he'd talked about earlier. Flood did get Wyatt to draw several diagrams of the street fight, as well as of the Stilwell shooting at the Tucson railway station and the gunfight with Curly Bill.

Due to Flood's inexperience as a writer it was slow going and Wyatt, now in his seventies, grew impatient. It didn't help his mood that *When the West Was Young,* a collection of Bechdolt's stories, was a great success when it was published in 1922. Wyatt began entertaining another means of telling his story. While living in Los Angeles he had made friends in the burgeoning movie community, particularly among actors in western films. John Ford, Tom Mix, and Charlie Chaplin were all among his acquaintances. William S. Hart became a particular pal, and they often exchanged letters when one or the other was out of town. In July 1923 Wyatt wrote Hart with a suggestion:

During the past few years, many wrong impressions of the early days of Tombstone and myself have been created by writers who are not informed correctly, and this has caused me a concern which I feel deeply. You know, I realize that I am not going to live to the age of Methuselah, and any wrong impression, I want made right before I go away. The screen could do all this, I know, with yourself as the mastermind.

Hart didn't bite on the idea of a film about Wyatt, but he did become involved in the Flood book project, encouraging Wyatt to proceed with it. In April 1925 Wyatt wrote Hart that "My friend has the story completed," but it was another ten months before the collaborators sent off the manuscript to *The Saturday Evening Post,* where it was immediately rejected. Flood tried hard, but based on almost any page of the manuscript he would have been hard-pressed to write a coherent postcard. Everything was long-winded and presented Wyatt as virtually superhuman, with one example being Flood's description of Wyatt's supposed heroics protecting Johnny Behind-the-Deuce as the lynch mob approached Vogan's Bowling Alley in Tombstone:

The gaze of the mob shot forth in a hard, defiant glitter against the blank walls. . . . The venom of reptiles, the malice and envy of bitter men, the wild, delirious frenzy of fanatics, the will of hate and vengeance fixed itself in the faces, almost adamantine, of the standing horde. . . . Suddenly, there was a shifting in the ranks, and then some one caught sight of Earp standing in the road. . . . The sun shone down upon him in a great circle of light almost like an apparition. Across the street, the mob faced him in awe; they were stupified. As if it were a great mass of humanity banked against an imaginary dead line they pressed forward, but they had no power to cross.

Wyatt and Hart surely realized that Flood was no master wordsmith, but they were convinced that Wyatt's name would sell the book where the quality of the writing might not. After the *Saturday Evening Post* rejection, they began sending the manuscript off to one prominent publisher after another — Bobbs-Merrill, Houghton Mifflin, Thomas Y. Crowell. The turn-downs continued, and as they did another potential collaborator approached Wyatt.

In 1926 Chicago journalist Walter Noble Burns made his first mark as a Western historian with *The Saga of Billy the Kid,* written with an eye more for drama than for accuracy but evincing the kind of storytelling skills that publishers found lacking in Flood's manuscript. Burns was anxious to write another gunslinger bestseller and approached Wyatt to suggest that they work on an Earp memoir. Wyatt, always loyal to his friends, said he was committed to John Flood on a similar project and so had to turn Burns down. But their Los Angeles meeting in July 1926 went so well that Burns thought he'd try another Tombstone–Fremont Street gunfight-related topic, a biography of Doc Holliday. But after visiting Tombstone and doing some preliminary research, Burns decided the story was too good to limit to Doc. Instead he wrote *Tombstone: An Iliad of the Southwest,* which was published in 1927 to wide acclaim. Burns presented Wyatt as "the Lion of Tombstone," but Wyatt was still furious. Someone else was telling his story and making money from it.

Nine months before Burns's *Tombstone* was published, Hart counseled Wyatt that it was time to rethink working with John Flood: "Ordinarily I would not accept the verdicts that have been thrown at us by [the publishers], but there seems to be such a ring of sincerity in their letters of refusal — after their eagerness to read the story when it is first received and their disappointment seems to be so honest that I believe we should sort of hold a council of war before sending the manuscript out any more." Flood generously offered to step aside and give all his notes to another author. Wyatt and Hart went back to Burns, but by that time he was already deep into writing *Tombstone* and had no further interest in collaboration.

Stuart Lake was a colorful character in his own right. Besides writing for magazines he had been Teddy Roosevelt's press aide during the former president's failed Bull Moose campaign in 1912, and then fought and suffered serious wounds in World War I. In New York, Lake became friendly with Bat Masterson, who told him rollicking stories about Wyatt Earp in Dodge City and Tombstone. About the same time that Burns's *Tombstone* reached bookstores, Lake began writing to Wyatt and suggesting that they discuss working together on Wyatt's autobiography. It took almost six months but finally Wyatt, frustrated by lack of success with Flood, agreed to meet Lake in Los Angeles. Josephine came along; she took a keen interest in the tale that Lake proposed to tell. At one point in the negotiations she insisted to Lake that "It must be a nice clean story." After eliciting his promise to write a positive book, the Earps agreed to work with him. As he had promised, John Flood handed over all his notes and the unpublished manuscript; Lake judged them completely useless and decided to start from scratch. But when he attempted to interview Wyatt, he experienced the same frustration that Flood had before him — the old man simply wasn't talkative. Lake later wrote to a friend that "Wyatt never 'dictated' a word to me. I spent hours and days and weeks with him — and I wish you could see my notes! They consist entirely of the barest facts." In truth, Wyatt's energy was fading along with his health. He had suffered for some time from chronic cystitis, a bladder infection with the potential to be terminal. Wyatt and Lake discussed traveling together to places in his past to help refresh the aged frontiersman's memory, but decided to postpone the trips until Wyatt felt better.

In 1928 Houghton Mifflin published *Helldorado* by Billy Breakenridge. Assisted by his own ghostwriter, the former Cochise County deputy included long sections about Tombstone in his memoir, and though he didn't entirely paint Wyatt and the other Earps as villains he didn't go out of his way to praise them. *Helldorado* bothered Wyatt more than anything else in print that had made mention of him, both because Breakenridge, a minor figure in Tombstone events, presented himself as a key player and because Wyatt had recently helped Breakenridge, now a private detective, with information on a case. Wyatt told Lake that Breakenridge was "a sly fox of the worst kind" who resented Wyatt for refusing to be arrested by him and Johnny Behan in Tombstone on the night following the shooting of Frank Stilwell in Tucson. Lake might have used Wyatt's resentment as a means of loosening his tongue, but in December Lake fell ill with the flu and couldn't work on their book for the rest of the year. In January Lake was ready to resume; then Wyatt took to his bed in Los Angeles. He had dodged bullets and murder warrants, but couldn't escape cystitis. He died on January 13 from his bladder infection. Josephine, who was at his bedside, claimed that her husband's last words were, "Suppose, suppose" — she had no idea what he meant. Wyatt was eighty years old and had spent his last days in near-poverty. It was an ignominious end for a man who always sought fortune and, later in life, glory rather than notoriety. It was ironic that soon after Wyatt was no longer alive to enjoy it, he finally began to achieve the widespread acclaim and even hero worship that he had come to yearn for.

Stuart Lake knew that Wyatt Earp's exploits, if described adroitly, had all the elements of a bestseller. Wyatt's death was a problem, but not an insurmountable one. Lake and Josephine agreed to continue with the project. They would split any profits equally, and Josephine would have approval of the text. The combination of Wyatt's reputation and Lake's credentials as an established writer impressed Boston-based Houghton Mifflin enough to offer a contract. Now all Lake had to do was research the book, write it, and get Josephine to approve it. All three tasks proved far more difficult than he anticipated.

Lake had some scant material directly from Wyatt, the Flood notes that he had disparaged, and newspaper and magazine clippings whose accuracy was highly suspect. Lake traveled west and interviewed old-timers who had known Wyatt. Their veracity was suspect, but the tall tales suited Lake's purposes in presenting Wyatt as a powerful force for frontier justice. Lake made a point of insisting that he double-checked everything he was told, writing to a friend that "I took no man's unsupported word for anything, not even Wyatt's." If that was true, then Lake either didn't try very hard or else he was one of the worst fact-checkers ever.

Once Lake assembled his information, the challenge was to do what John Flood could not — turn it into a compelling story. Wyatt was dead, so Lake didn't have the option of writing in the first person. But third person

— Wyatt Earp did this, then he did that — would be too dry for the thrill-seeking audience Lake wanted to reach. Lake's compromise was to write as an omniscient narrator who frequently quoted Wyatt and others as though he was standing next to them listening to the conversations. "Possibly it was a form of 'cheating,' " he admitted later. "I've often wondered if I did not overdo in this respect." As the book began to take shape, it was promising enough for *The Saturday Evening Post* to agree to run excerpts. Everything was in place to virtually guarantee success, and then Josephine began meddling. She'd been difficult to deal with all her life, and now she dedicated herself to ensuring that Wyatt's story was told exactly as she wanted — the tale of a true gentleman whose distinguished life only occasionally involved distasteful episodes with guns and frontier riffraff. When Lake demurred, Josephine took her case directly to editor Ira Rich Kent at Houghton Mifflin, barging into his office and sobbing as she pleaded with him to make Lake write the book her way. Kent, whose only previous problem with the material Lake had turned in was curiosity whether Wyatt really talked in "this rather literary and polysyllabic style (Lake swore that he did)," pleaded with Lake to calm Josephine down. "She sat at my desk for the better part of an hour, tears rolling down her cheeks in her emotion," Kent wrote to Lake. "She would much prefer that her husband's memory be left in as quiet a state as possible. I tried to show her that if there were to be any book at all, it must deal with the exciting episodes in which Earp played so important a part. It is obviously a situation calling for great tact, patience, kindliness and forbearance on your part."

Lake tried, but Josephine couldn't be dissuaded. Under the terms of their agreement she had the right to veto anything he wrote. Even the book's proposed title infuriated her: *Wyatt Earp: Gunfighter* hardly fit the image of her late husband that she preferred. She reluctantly compromised on *Wyatt Earp: Frontier Marshal* even though Wyatt had never been a full-blown U.S. marshal. A completed draft of the book appalled her; she informed Lake that "what I have read of the story impressed me more as that of a blood and thunder type than a biography. . . . I can say now that some changes will be necessary."

In November 1930, as the squabbling between Lake and Josephine continued, excerpts of the forthcoming book appeared in *The Saturday Evening Post*. Josephine may have abhorred their content, but she didn't try to block their publication. America was in the depths of the Depression, and in bad times as well as good Josephine was extravagant and always needed money. When the magazine articles were a huge hit with readers, it was obvious even to her that the most financially expedient thing to do was to get out of the way and let Houghton Mifflin place the book in stores as quickly as possible. In February 1931 she informed Lake that "while, as you know, there are parts of your manuscript that are not what I would like to have, I have concluded to make no further objection to it, and you may consider this as my approval."

October 1931 wasn't the best time to publish a book; people had little money to spend on food, let alone reading material. But *Wyatt Earp: Frontier Marshal* struck a chord. Americans wanted to get their minds off their troubles with colorful stories providing both entertainment and the simplistic but comforting theme that good eventually wins out over evil. The book initially sold seven thousand copies, an astounding number considering the dreadful economic conditions. Lake began shopping film rights, and in 1932 he struck a deal with Twentieth Century-Fox for $7,500. Josephine tried to exert the same control on the filmmakers that she attempted with Lake, but it didn't work with movies any better than it had with the book. When she threatened to sue Fox if it used Wyatt's name in the film — a hypocritical act since she had accepted half of what the studio paid for the rights to the book —

the studio simply changed the title from *Wyatt Earp: Frontier Marshal* to *Frontier Marshal,* went ahead with a story featuring lawman "Michael Wyatt," and got the film into theaters. The producers of *Frontier Marshal* and several other subsequent films clearly based on Wyatt's exploits were far more interested in the town where many of his highly fictionalized adventures took place. Tombstone was the magic name, not Wyatt Earp, and the real Tombstone took full advantage.

Nineteen twenty-nine should have marked Tombstone's final demise. The Cochise County seat was moved thirty miles southeast to the thriving community of Bisbee, taking Tombstone's apparent last economic prop away. But the books by Walter Noble Burns and Billy Breakenridge, plus the popular magazine articles by Frederick Bechdolt, had rekindled national interest in the frontier outpost with the memorable name. Americans were now driving cars instead of riding horses, and Arizona State Highway 80 ran right through Tombstone — it was relatively easy to get there. Nineteen twenty-nine marked the town's official fiftieth birthday, and it celebrated in October with a "Helldorado" festival meant to lure tourists with parades, pageants, and a reenactment of the Fremont Street gunfight. Burns and Breakenridge served as consultants, and John Clum led the main parade. Some old-timers, including Clum, felt there was too much emphasis on the town's history of violence rather than culture — besides the gunfight, actors participated in a mock lynching and stage robbery. It almost didn't matter — on the same day that Helldorado commenced, the stock market crashed.

But Tombstone struggled on. Some area mines went back into operation and for a time turned modest profits. Studios kept churning out Tombstone-themed movies, and, when television eventually followed suit with a flood of Western-themed series set in or around the town, tourism replaced ore as the basis of Tombstone's economy. In their struggle to hang on, most of the remaining residents didn't mind that visitors were only interested in the bloody aspects of Tombstone's history. The town population gradually settled at around 1,500; many made their livings from tourism-related business. Helldorado is still staged every October, and the town is open for business throughout the year. During 2009, an estimated 400,000 visitors flocked to Tombstone to ride around in stagecoaches, visit a refurbished Boot Hill, test their marksmanship in a shooting gallery, enjoy lunches of buffalo burgers and T-bone steaks, and, above all, to pay $10 each to attend a reenactment of the gunfight where Wyatt, his brothers, and Doc blast Billy Clanton and the McLaurys into smithereens.

Wyatt Earp: Frontier Marshal continued to sell steadily for the rest of Stuart Lake's life and beyond. He went on to a successful career writing movie and television scripts and died in San Diego in 1964 at the age of seventy-four. But Josephine Earp's later years were less fulfilling. The book royalties she split with Lake should have been sufficient to support her in reasonable comfort if not style, but Josephine was never satisfied with just getting by. She complained to relatives that Lake was cheating her, railed about movies clearly based on Wyatt that didn't tell *nice* stories, and finally decided that she needed to write a book herself — that way, she could control every word. Josephine recruited two sisters from the Earp branch of the family to help — Mabel Earp Cason and Vinnolia Earp Ackerman. They were initially excited by the project, and put together outlines of a book they believed might sell as well as Lake's. Vinnolia took notes in shorthand as she and Mabel quizzed their subject about her life. Josephine concocted a charmed childhood in San Francisco that was probably as much imagination as fact, went into near-excruciating detail about post-Tombstone life with Wyatt in mining camps and big cities, and refused to talk about Tombstone at all. But Tombstone yarns were what readers would want and a publisher would pay for; Mabel and Vinnolia pleaded with Josephine to come up with some. Josephine wanted a book that presented herself as well as Wyatt above any form of questionable behavior, and that meant no mention of Tombstone so far as she was concerned. Finally she capitulated just a little, admitting she came to town believing that Johnny Behan would marry her, then became increasingly disillusioned as he put off the wedding. In Josephine's sanitized retelling, she lived chastely with chaperones until finally breaking up with Johnny. That was it; from there she insisted on taking up the story again after she and Wyatt got together in San Francisco. Mabel and Vinnolia gave up. Mabel explained later that "we finally abandoned work on the manuscript because she would not clear up the Tombstone sequence where it pertained to her and Wyatt."

Josephine continued to carp about movies that she believed demeaned Wyatt's memory until she died in December 1944, never knowing that the resurrection of Wyatt Earp had barely begun. The breadth and cultural impact of what was yet to come would have amazed even her.

The initial films set in Tombstone weren't distinguished, but in 1946 John Ford's *My Darling Clementine*'s taut storytelling and memorable performances by a talented cast (Henry Fonda as Wyatt, Victor Mature as Doc, Walter Brennan as Old Man Clanton, Ike's father) made a lasting impression on audiences. The plot exaggerated the criminality of the Clantons, and Wyatt's love interest was named Clementine rather than Josephine, but its effect was to introduce Wyatt as an authentic frontier hero to countless Americans who had never previously heard of him. The public wanted more cinematic Wyatt, and over the next decade filmmakers obliged with another half-dozen movies that varied in quality but never in presenting Wyatt as a gallant lawman whose goal in life was to rid his town, his territory, and his West of bad men.

In the process of whitewashing Wyatt, the most storied incident in his life was rechristened. The 1881 shootout with the Clantons and the McLaurys was sufficiently dramatic, especially if creative license was exercised — in *My Darling Clementine,* Doc died in the battle. But "Gunfight in the Empty Lot on Fremont Street" didn't lend itself well to legend. This was recognized early on by Billy Breakenridge and Stuart Lake. In *Helldorado,* Breakenridge described "The Incident Near the O.K. Corral." Lake's chapter on the battle was titled "At the O.K. Corral." The combination of *K* and a hard *C* offered an ear-pleasing concussive resonance that complemented gunfire. But no book could match the cultural influence of a popular movie, and in 1957 *Gunfight at the O.K. Corral* starring Burt Lancaster and Kirk Douglas permanently established the term. Like David Crockett at the Alamo and Colonel Custer at the Little Big Horn, Wyatt Earp was now remembered for his brave stand against overwhelming odds at a very specific location — and, unlike Crockett and Custer, he survived.

As Americans embraced Wild West mythology by ignoring inconvenient facts and exaggerating or inventing more palatable ones, they also altered the meaning of a traditionally negative term. In Wyatt's real West, anyone referred to as a cowboy was most likely a criminal. But in movies the word was used first to describe hardworking ranch hands and then, generically, those who rode horses, toted six-guns, and, when necessary (and it always became necessary) fought to uphold justice at the risk of their own lives. Cowboys were heroes, and their enemies were outlaws. So far as his growing legion of fans was concerned, Wyatt Earp was a cowboy in the new, best sense of the word.

Books planted the seeds of Wyatt's historical reemergence, and movies expanded his new appeal. But it was television that completed his rehabilitation and guaranteed his eternal celebrity. Everything about a mythologized

Wyatt, from the magnificently named town where he performed his most notable heroics to the long-barreled Buntline Special he supposedly carried, lent itself perfectly to the medium that took the country by storm.

Television was introduced at the 1939 World's Fair, but it was only after World War II that manufacturers began mass-producing the bulky sets that quickly found their way into American living rooms. Commercial broadcasting commenced in 1948; the first popular programming included variety shows and professional wrestling. But in an increasingly complex world dominated by the Cold War and fears of nuclear attack, Americans yearned for simpler times when there was no doubt that the good guys were going to win. Shows about cowboys and the Old West offered the right kind of nostalgic entertainment — they were widely accepted as factually accurate because viewers wanted them to be. This was especially the case with Wyatt Earp and Tombstone. In 1959 at the height of the TV Western craze, when more than two dozen "cowboy" programs were broadcast every week, at least six were in some way connected with Wyatt or places and people prominent in his career: *The Life and Legend of Wyatt Earp, Bat Masterson, Tombstone Territory, Broken Arrow, Johnny Ringo,* and *Gunsmoke.* The *Wyatt Earp* series ran six seasons;

in it, Wyatt was portrayed first as marshal of Dodge City and then of Tombstone. In real life he was hulking, blond, and mustached; TV Wyatt was played by slender, dark-haired, clean-shaven Hugh O'Brian. But Stuart Lake, serving as a consultant to the show, was pleased with O'Brian's portrayal, believing that the actor captured Wyatt's "spring in his step, the firm slant of his jaw and those narrow hips." The show's theme song hammered home the image of Wyatt that viewers gladly bought into: The West was wild, Wyatt was saintly, and tales of his historic exploits should be told forever. In the years since, there have been occasional attempts by writers, historians, and filmmakers to present a more balanced view of Wyatt — the movies *Tombstone* in 1993 and *Wyatt Earp* in 1994 contained some basic elements of history. A few debunkers have argued in books and magazine articles that Wyatt was worse than any of the criminals he ever fought. It's made little difference. For most, Wyatt remains a hero.

Had Wyatt never lived, or if there had never been a gunfight on Tombstone's Fremont Street and Wyatt accordingly faded into obscurity, the TV cowboy craze would still have swept America. But viewers could not as easily have convinced themselves that there was some foundation of fact even in the adventures of the Lone Ranger and Matt Dillon. Maybe they were the creations of script-writers, but they were still fighting for right and justice in the spirit and tradition of real-life Wyatt Earp. Like audiences at Buffalo Bill's Wild West Shows decades earlier, TV viewers willingly accepted fantasy as proof that the frontier was just the way they liked to imagine it.

Because of that willingness, and because of Wyatt's emergence as an icon, the so-called Gunfight at the O.K. Corral is a key element in general, modern-day interpretations of frontier history. Historian John E. Ferling has observed that "events by themselves are unimportant; it is the perception of events that is crucial," and Earp mythology may be the best proof of how perception trumps fact and history is subsequently distorted. The October 26, 1881, shootout on Tombstone's Fremont Street was an arrest gone wrong and the result of complicated social, economic, and political issues that left eight men danger-ously mistrustful of each other. In a very real sense, the confrontation did change the West; because of national publicity regarding the subsequent trial, it became clear that, in the future, on the remaining frontier the rule of law would ultimately be enforced by the courts rather than gunplay, Wyatt's subse-quent actions on the Vendetta Ride notwith-standing. But many have come to consider it an ultimate showdown between clear-cut forces of good and evil, when Wyatt Earp and Doc Holliday defined the best of the wonderful Old West — and America — by shooting down the Clantons (Virgil, Morgan, and the McLaurys have faded into supporting roles). Modern-day soldiers, athletes, and politicians routinely compare their victories to surviving the O.K. Corral. The image is rampant in our culture, and indelible.

As for Wyatt Earp, who was both more and less than his legend insists, we can feel certain of this: He would be pleased by the way everything turned out, except for the fact that he never made any money from it.

NOTE ON SOURCES

There will never be a definitive book on any nonfiction subject because there is always new information not only to be discovered, but interpreted. In the 130 years since the most famous gunfight in Western history, there have been consistent cycles of breakthrough research and resulting books claiming to finally tell the *real* story of what happened in Tombstone on the afternoon of October 26, 1881. It began in the 1920s with *Tombstone: An Iliad of the Southwest* by Walter Noble Burns and *Helldorado* by Billy Breakenridge, followed in 1931 by *Wyatt Earp: Frontier Marshal,* Stuart Lake's smash bestseller that gave readers Wyatt Earp's posthumous version of events. There it stood for a while, until further research first suggested, then proved, that Wyatt had the frontier oldtimer's habit of embellishing his accomplishments and glossing over or completely leaving out anything that might place him in the slightest of bad lights.

Dozens of books and thousands of magazine articles followed, many the products of honest, extensive research, some relying on long-accepted fable, too many crafted to prove the writer's one-sided opinions. The best of the printed lot, judged collectively, prove one thing — even the most talented, best-intentioned researchers and writers can look at the same information and then arrive at radically different conclusions about what it all means.

The 1980s and 1990s produced some fine, thought-provoking books about the life and times of Wyatt Earp, including Casey Tefertiller's *Wyatt Earp: The Life Behind the Legend,* Allen Barra's *Inventing Wyatt Earp: His Life and Many Legends,* and Paula Mitchell Marks's *And Die in the West: The Story of the O.K. Corral Gunfight.* It in no way disparages their work to say that material subsequently discovered by other researcher-writers — Ray Madzia, Anne E. Collier, Lynn Bailey, Jeff Morey, Bob Palmquist, Tom Gaumer, Robert J. Chandler, Kevin J. Mulkins, Gary L. Roberts, Mark Dworkin, Jane Lee, Ben Traywick, Steve Gatto, Roger Jay, Pam Potter, Paul Cool, Nancy Sosa, Steven Lubet, Dan Chaput, Ann Kirschner, and others — proves there was still more to the story, and in a few cases their finds have been nothing less than revelatory. Several have written or are writing

574

their own books about some aspect of the American West, or the lives of the Earps, or the history of southeast Arizona and Tombstone. It's typical of the generosity among many writers and researchers that they were so willing to share their discoveries and opinions with me for *The Last Gunfight.* Collectors Bob McCubbin, Kevin and Bev Mulkins, Mark Ragsdale, Glenn Boyer, Scott Dyke, and others have graciously shared access to documents, letters, photos, and other material that continues to vastly expand the records available for study. The hardiest enthusiasts have spent long, sweaty days hiking through the prickly snake-and-scorpion-infested underbrush of southeastern Arizona's San Pedro Valley to puzzle out the precise spot of the Benson stage robbery on March 15, 1881, and exactly where Wyatt Earp culminated the so-called Vendetta Ride approximately one year later by blasting away Curly Bill Brocius — if, in fact, Curly Bill died that day at all. No one agrees about everything, some agree on virtually nothing, and in a few cases mutual dislike and mistrust have festered into outright hostility. I've chosen not to become embroiled in any quarrels, and can honestly state that everyone involved has, at the very least, been reasonably friendly and open with me. My rule, always, is to talk to anyone who may have helpful information to share.

The Last Gunfight isn't an attempt to write yet another biography of Wyatt Earp. Instead, I want to blend all the best information available — old, new, incontrovertible, or destined for eternal debate — into a fresh storytelling approach that provides readers with greater context. To understand what motivated the Earps and the Clantons and the McLaurys and Doc Holliday to blunder into a gunfight near, but not in, Tombstone's O.K. Corral, it's first necessary to understand the lure of the American West, and why Arizona Territory, Tombstone, and Cochise County in particular attracted so many disparate people who inevitably couldn't coexist. It's a much more complicated topic than we've been led to believe by books and magazines and movies and TV shows that reduce the ever-evolving frontier into a series of scrubby, primitive outposts where six-gun-toting cowpokes routinely gathered on Main Street for that day's shootout. We know more now than we ever have, and one thing, at least, is inarguable: The real story of the American West — and of the Earps, and of Tombstone — is far more fascinating than mythology.

NOTES

PROLOGUE: TOMBSTONE THAT MORNING

Christine Rhodes's generous sharing of material compiled by the late historian Carl Chafin provided essential information. With permission from Glenn Boyer, the Ford County Historical Association of Dodge City, Kansas, allowed me access to original letters written by Louisa Earp (common-law wife of Morgan Earp).

Dawn on that Wednesday morning: William B. Shillingberg, "Wyatt Earp and the 'Buntline Special' Myth," *Kansas Historical Quarterlies,* Summer 1976.

Yet as Virgil Earp fell asleep: Odie B. Faulk, *Tombstone: Myth and Reality* (Oxford University Press, 1972), pp. 121–23; Christine Rhodes interview; John Plesent Gray manuscript, University of Arizona Special Collections.

the town was well known throughout the country: Faulk, p. 67; George Whitwell Parsons,

A Tenderfoot in Tombstone: The Private Journal of George Whitwell Parsons — The Turbulent Years: 1880–82, edited by Lynn R. Bailey (Westernlore Press, 1996); Gray manuscript; Bob Boze Bell interview.

Yet it was also unique: Ray Madzia, Christine Rhodes, Lynn Bailey, and Anne E. Collier interviews.

a place soon to be described: Allen Barra, *Inventing Wyatt Earp: His Life and Many Legends* (Carroll & Graf, 1998), pp. 94–95.

Tombstone was mostly a safe place: Gray manuscript; William M. Breakenridge, *Helldorado: Bringing the Law to the Mesquite* (University of Nebraska Press, 1992; originally published, 1928), p. 162; Steve Gatto, *The Real Wyatt Earp: A Documentary Biography* (High Lonesome Books, 2000), pp. 69–71; Paula Mitchell Marks, *And Die in the West: The Story of the O.K. Corral Gunfight* (William Morrow, 1989), p. 197; Ray Madzia and Paula Mitchell Marks interviews.

Billy Breakenridge, who served: Breakenridge, pp. 165–66.

The cowboys were menaces: Steven Lubet, *Murder in Tombstone: The Forgotten Trial of Wyatt Earp* (Yale University Press, 2004), pp. 23–24; Alford E. Turner, ed., *The O.K. Corral Inquest* (Creative Publishing, 1981), p. 13; Art Austin, Ray Madzia, Jim Turner, and Lynn Bailey interviews.

an equally blunt warning: Jeff Morey interview. In November 1880, John Clum and the *Epitaph* endorsed Ben Sippy rather than Virgil Earp in the election for Tombstone town marshal (the title was later changed to chief of police), and Sippy won. Virgil became acting sheriff in early June 1881 after Sippy skipped town amid rumors of shady financial dealings, and was named permanently to the post after he performed heroically during the terrible fire that destroyed much of Tombstone's business district on June 22. But the formation of the Tombstone Citizens Safety Committee is a clear indication that, besides disdaining Cochise County sheriff Johnny Behan, Clum and his powerful friends harbored significant doubts about their town officers' abilities to handle the cowboys, too. Virgil, no fool, would have gotten the unsubtle message in the *Epitaph*'s August editorial. This undoubtedly affected his judgment during the fatal events of October 26.

CHAPTER ONE: THE WEST

Those who want the whole, fascinating story of America's expansion west — and ongoing American fascination with the "wild frontier" — can find it in two books that have been invaluable to me in my own research: Michael L. Johnson's *Hunger for the Wild: Ameri-*

ca's Obsession with the Untamed West and Richard White's *"It's Your Misfortune and None of My Own": A New History of the American West.* These aren't the only two available books on the subject, of course, but they are the ones I've learned from and enjoyed the most among those I've read. They're not specifically cited in every Chapter One footnote, but they inform each page.

Boonesborough didn't work out: Things didn't work out badly for Richard Henderson. As a very hefty consolation prize, Congress awarded him 200,000 acres of public land for his trouble. Boone apparently got a firm handshake and best wishes in future endeavors.

Its goal, until 1890: Bob Palmquist interview.

One, with a clear lust for wealth: Richard White, *"It's Your Misfortune and None of My Own": A New History of the American West* (University of Oklahoma Press, 1991), pp. 215–16.

a man needed his wife and children: Anne E. Collier interview.

As decades passed: Michael L. Johnson, *Hunger for the Wild: America's Obsession with the Untamed West* (University Press of Kansas, 2007), p. 112; Michael L. Johnson interview.

The vastness of the frontier: Cissy Stewart Lale and Frederick Nolan interviews.

A popular territorial folksong inquired: David McCullough, *Mornings on Horseback: The Story of an Extraordinary Family, a Vanished Way of Life, and the Unique Child Who Became Theodore Roosevelt* (Simon & Schuster, 1981), p. 331.

Except in times of physical danger: Archie McDonald interview; White, pp. 57, 168–69.

One thing the army didn't do: Roy Morris Jr., *Lighting Out for the Territory: How Samuel Clemens Became Mark Twain* (Simon & Schuster, 2010), p. 43.

One of the most attractive aspects about mining: White, p. 185.

the most certain way to escape: Ibid., p. 209.

After the California Gold Rush the West became: Cissy Stewart Lale interview.

One passenger wrote: Morris, p. 44.

Comstock acquired much of the massive claim: Ibid., p. 69.

From the early days of American self-rule: Archie McDonald and Cissy Stewart Lale interviews.

the southerners now coming west wanted to retain: Richard Slotkin, *Gunfighter Nation: The Myth of the Frontier in Twentieth-Century America* (Atheneum, 1992), p. 129.

Buffalo hunting was initially seasonal work: William B. Shillingberg, *Dodge City: The Early Years, 1872–1886* (Arthur H. Clark Company/University of Oklahoma Press,

2009), pp. 75–91; George Laughead interview.

Tourists from as far away as Britain: Eric Jay Dolin, *Fur, Fortune, and Empire: The Epic History of the Fur Trade in America* (W. W. Norton, 2010), p. 312.

while the Civil War shut down traditional markets: Robert M. Utley, *Lone Star Justice: The First Century of the Texas Rangers* (Oxford University Press, 2002), pp. 1, 139–40; George Laughead and Dave Webb interviews.

These longhorns weren't the choicest beef: White, p. 221.

Herding cattle was a chore: Frederick Nolan and Bob McCubbin interviews.

The goal of the cow towns: Casey Tefertiller and Craig T. Miner interviews.

If word spread: Lubet, p. 3.

there were very few face-to-face gunfights: Archie McDonald, Ben Traywick, Craig T. Miner, Dave Webb, and George Laughead interviews.

Pistols were notoriously inaccurate: Joseph C. Rosa, *Wild Bill Hickok: The Man and His Myth* (University Press of Kansas, 1996), p. 65–71.

most ambitious men who came west to Kansas: Cissy Stewart Lale and Lynn Bailey interviews.

For them, life's choices: Anne E. Collier, Cissy

Stewart Lale, Pam Potter, and Archie Mc-
Donald interviews.

*the American frontier was dramatically shrink-
ing:* Cissy Stewart Lale, Bruce Dinges, and
Jim Turner interviews; White, p. 186.

The Desert Land Act of 1877: Bob Palmquist
interview; White, pp. 151–52.

*what remained unlimited in the remaining
Western frontier:* Cissy Stewart Lale and
Frederick Nolan interviews. Fred Nolan
expressed to me that on the American
frontier everyone was in the process of *becoming.* It's the perfect description.

CHAPTER TWO: THE EARPS

Nicholas found it intolerable: Barra, pp. 20–23;
interviews with Allen Barra, Scott Dyke,
Paula Mitchell Marks, and Glenn Boyer.

He may have left town: Barra, p. 23.

his light blue eyes glared: Glenn Boyer interview.

All of Nicholas's boys learned from their father:
Scott Dyke interview.

When Virgil enlisted: Casey Tefertiller, *Wyatt
Earp: The Life Behind the Legend* (Wiley &
Sons, 1997), p. 3; Don Chaput, *Virgil Earp:
Western Peace Officer* (Affiliated Writers of
America, 1994), pp. 8, 9–11.

For seven months Nicholas was in charge:
Gatto, *The Real Wyatt Earp,* p. 7; Barra, p.
23; Don Chaput, *The Earp Papers: In a*

Brother's Image (Affiliated Writers of America 1994), p. 14.

Wyatt told biographer Stuart Lake: Stuart N. Lake Collection, Huntington Library, San Marino, California.

Wyatt was slow to trust anyone: Chaput, *The Earp Papers,* p. 16; Glenn Boyer interview.

Wyatt's wedding to Aurilla Sutherland: Anne E. Collier interview. Many historians identify Wyatt's first wife as "Urilla" or "Rilla," but those apparently were nicknames.

At some point soon after: Cason manuscript; Tefertiller, pp. 4–5.

In the spring of 1871: Until recently, most researchers assumed Wyatt Earp posted bail after his arrest in Arkansas and then skipped town. But Gary L. Roberts has discovered an issue of the Van Buren newspaper that includes a story about Wyatt and several other prisoners breaking out of jail. It's a significant find, and I'm immensely grateful to Dr. Roberts for allowing me to include the information here.

For about a year beginning in February 1872: Roger Jay, "Wyatt Earp's Lost Year," *Wild West,* August 2003. This disclosure was a bombshell among Earp researchers. Anti-Earps among them use the information as a basis for portraying Wyatt as a lifelong ne'er-do-well: witness Steve Gatto, "Wyatt Earp Was a Pimp," *True West,* July 2003.

Upper-class men, even on the frontier: Cissy Stewart Lale, Archie McDonald, and Anne E. Collier interviews.

it's important to place his problems: Jeff Morey, Craig Miner, and Michelle Emke interviews.

Wyatt claimed that in August 1873 he found himself: Lake Collection, Huntington Library; Ragsdale Collection, Shrewsbury, Massachusetts; Cason manuscript; interviews with Jeff Morey and Casey Tefertiller; Barra, pp. 43–45; Shillingberg, *Dodge City,* p. 148; Gatto, *The Real Wyatt Earp,* pp. 2–3; Nyle H. Miller and Joseph W. Snell, *Why the West Was Wild* (University of Oklahoma Press, 2003), pp. 635–36.

It's a fine story: Stuart N. Lake, a journalist and former press agent for Theodore Roosevelt, became interested in helping Wyatt Earp write his memoirs after hearing about Earp from Bat Masterson. He and Wyatt began meeting in June 1928, and *Wyatt Earp: Frontier Marshal,* published in 1931, became a smash bestseller and initiated the explosion of Wyatt's reputation as a frontier lawman. Wyatt died in January 1929, long before Lake finished writing the book. He based much of it on Wyatt's testimony, and Wyatt did not always stick to the facts. Lake assured friends that he personally checked every claim made by Wyatt, traveling all over the country and seeking out facts wherever he went. If so, he didn't do a very good job of it. Lake's version of the supposed confrontation between Wyatt and Ben Thompson in Ellsworth offers a good example. Lake relied on Wyatt's testimony, plus a notebook of Bat Masterson's (discovered after Bat had died) and what he himself could learn on an Ellsworth visit. In an October 19, 1928, letter to Wyatt, Lake noted that an account of Whitney's murder in the Ellsworth newspaper was "exactly in accordance with your memory." It wasn't. In the same letter, Lake pointed out that Cad Pierce, whom Wyatt claimed to have disarmed in Wichita months after facing down Thompson in Ellsworth, had in fact died just two days after Whitney was murdered. "Don't let this little slip in memory disturb you," Lake wrote Wyatt. "We all get 'em, and I'll catch most of them, all of any importance."

After Lake's account of Wyatt's Ellsworth gallantry was published, researchers were puzzled by a lack of supporting evidence. An article in the *Ellsworth Reporter* on August 21, 1873, credited town deputy sheriff Edward Hogue with arresting Ben Thompson, and didn't mention Wyatt Earp at all. But Wyatt wasn't the only one telling the story his way. Lake said Wyatt's version was confirmed by an account in an old copybook of Bat Masterson's that Lake read after Wyatt and Masterson were both dead: "I used it, verbatim." In her aborted memoir, Josephine Earp said she was not only told about Wyatt's heroics in Ellsworth by Masterson, Ben Thompson himself confirmed the details when she and Wyatt crossed his path years later. It's a given that Josephine and Bat would be willing to believe whatever Wyatt told them; both, in their own writing, would prove to be embellishers themselves. But Stuart Lake wasn't the only potential biographer who heard the self-serving Ellsworth tale from Wyatt. Twenty years before Wyatt met Stuart Lake, he told John Flood that he "arrested Ben Thompson . . . having taken him from a crowd with his friends."

In this and many other instances, it's apparent Wyatt Earp had the frontier knack of not letting too many facts interfere with a good story; when he wanted to seem heroic, he added whatever extra details were necessary, even if he had to make them up. In Wyatt's version of his life in the West, Ellsworth was only the first time he faced down a dangerous mob all by himself. It was a scenario he liked enough to recycle. According to Wyatt, strikingly similar showdowns later played out in Dodge City and Tombstone. But it is also true that, except in one later instance involving John Ringo,

Wyatt never seems to have made something up completely. If he didn't do all the things he claimed, he was still involved to some extent in the incidents. Wyatt was possibly in Ellsworth on the day Billy Thompson shot Sheriff Whitney, maybe playing cards in the same saloon where the deadly argument broke out. Perhaps he knew the Thompson brothers well enough to suggest to Ben that it would be smarter to give himself up than to shoot it out with the local law. Billy was the one who blasted Whitney; Ben wouldn't be charged with murder. Even if Deputy Hogue rather than Wyatt escorted Ben to the local courthouse, Wyatt could have played a critical role in bringing things to a satisfactory conclusion, or at least believed that he did. Afterward, he would not have seen any harm in giving himself all the credit. After telling the same exaggerated story long enough — twenty years, at least — he might even have convinced himself that it happened exactly as he told Stuart Lake.

There is no sense noting every discrepancy between what Lake wrote in *Wyatt Earp: Frontier Marshal* and facts that have since come to light. The list would take up an entire volume. In fairness to Stuart Lake, he had to write much of his book after Wyatt died. That left Josephine, Wyatt's widow, in the position of overseeing what

Lake wrote, and, in accordance with a publisher's contract, having to give her consent before the book could go into print. A more difficult woman may never have lived. It's amazing that Lake completed the book instead of going to prison for murder.

Wichita extolled itself: Michelle Emke, Casey Tefertiller, and Craig T. Miner interviews.

Wichita was the first major cow town: Rosa, pp. 143–44.

James had just married: Anne E. Collier, "Harriet 'Hattie' Catchim: A Controversial Earp Family Member," *Western Outlaw-Lawman History Association (WOLA) Journal* 16, no. 2 (Summer 2007).

That concern dated back to May: Michelle Emke and Craig T. Miner interviews; Tefertiller, pp. 10–11.

Texans had well-deserved reputations: Cissy Stewart Lale and Craig T. Miner interviews.

the idea was that men who'd broken laws: Michelle Emke interview.

New deputy Earp spent most of his time: Craig T. Miner interview.

Despite Wyatt later telling John Flood: Flood notes, the Ragsdale Collection. Before he began telling "stretchers" to Stuart Lake, Wyatt did the same beginning in 1906 to engineer John Flood, who interviewed Wyatt at length and unsuccessfully attempted to publish Wyatt's autobiography. The so-called Flood manuscript is included in the Stuart Lake collection at the Huntington Library, but other copies exist, including one I studied courtesy of the Ford County Historical Society and Glenn Boyer. But beyond concocting a nearly unreadable manuscript, Flood took copious notes during the Earp interviews. These are often amazing; Wyatt would contradict himself, Flood would push for more details, and, in the end, they may offer information that's as close to the truth as Wyatt's memory and imagination ever allowed. I was given access to these notes in the private Ragsdale Collection; I'm grateful to Mark Ragsdale for the opportunity.

The atmosphere on Front Street: George Laughead and Dave Webb interviews; Barra, pp. 55–56; Cason manuscript; Miller and Snell, pp. 10, 19–20.

It took more courage: Cason manuscript.

some of the Texas trail bosses offered: Ibid.

They demonstrated their professional skills: Gary L. Roberts, *Doc Holliday: The Life and Legend* (Wiley & Sons, 2006), p. 68.

he was often traveling in company with Kate Elder: Anne E. Collier interview; documents, Kevin J. and Bev Mulkins Collection.

With so few women on the frontier: Ibid.

Wyatt told Stuart Lake: Documents, Lake Collection, Huntington Library.

Their arrival had nothing to do: Gary L. Roberts interview.

Initially, Doc and Kate didn't see Wyatt: Documents, Mulkins Collection.

Eddie Foy stood onstage: Flood notes, Ragsdale Collection; Marks, pp. 86–87; Barra, pp. 77–78; Shillingberg, *Dodge City,* pp. 219–20; Cason manuscript.

Historians have long wondered: Flood notes, Ragsdale Collection. Stuart Lake went out of his way to denigrate Flood's work with Wyatt, writing in one letter dated January 1941 that "John Flood's so-called manuscript contributed exactly nothing to my job. . . . Wyatt never dictated anything of his career to him, [Wyatt] told me." My guess is that Lake saw the Flood manuscript, but never the interview notes on which Flood based it. Lake is correct that the manuscript is poorly written, but the notes themselves are fascinating and in many cases contradict versions of events as Lake wrote about them. Historian Anne E. Collier suggests that, over time, Wyatt honed the stories he told about his career, eliminating some things and embellishing others as he tried to craft tales that would present him in the best possible light. I think she's right.

Wyatt Earp was not a saint: Jeff Morey interview.

Doc Holliday returned that absolute loyalty: Gary L. Roberts interview.

Clay Allison was legendary: Casey Tefertiller interview; Tefertiller, pp. 26–27; Marks, p. 87; Barra, pp. 78–82; documents, Kansas Heritage Center; Miller and Snell, pp. 25–26.

Long-barreled pistols were occasionally used: Jeff Morey interview; Cason manuscript; Shillingberg, "Wyatt Earp and the 'Buntline Special' Myth."

Lee Silva, an exhaustive researcher who devoted 150 pages of a self-published book to Wyatt and the Buntline Special, believes Wyatt did own such a gun (with a ten-inch barrel) that was, in fact, given to him by Ned Buntline. In Silva's view, Buntline had plans for a Western-themed stage production that originally involved cooperation with Buffalo Bill Cody. After he and Cody had a falling-out, Buntline tried to entice Wyatt Earp, Bat Masterson, and a few other veteran buffalo hunters and lawmen into taking part in the show. He gave them long-barreled pistols as an inducement. For unknown reasons, Buntline's plans for the show fizzled. Silva was interviewed on the telephone by Andrea Ahles Koos, my research assistant.

James Kenedy was a Dodge lawman's worst nightmare: Robert K. DeArment, *Bat Masterson: The Man and His Legend* (University of Oklahoma Press, 1979), pp. 117, 123; White, p. 330; Marks, pp. 87–88;

Barra, p. 86.

It didn't help that soon after: Tefertiller, pp. 29–30.

Wyatt hadn't stopped wanting to be the boss: Ben Traywick interview.

when Virgil and his new wife, Allie: Bob Palmquist interview.

In early October 1877, two drifters: Ibid.; Chaput, *The Earp Papers,* pp. 35–41.

It was the kind of powerful political connection: Bruce Dinges interview.

Newspapers across America: Ibid.; Flood notes, Ragsdale Collection.

No one is certain which Earp brother: Barra, pp. 95–96; Marks, p. 89; Chaput, *The Earp Papers,* pp. 50–51.

CHAPTER THREE: TOMBSTONE

twenty-nine-year-old Ed Schieffelin: Marilyn F. Butler, ed., *Destination Tombstone: Adventures of a Prospector* (Royal Spectrum, 1996), pp. 80–84; Lynn R. Bailey, *Too Tough to Die: The Rise, Fall and Resurrection of a Silver Camp, 1878 to 1990* (Westernlore Press, 2004), pp. 4–10.

no one believed an itinerant like Ed: Bob McCubbin and Lynn Bailey interviews; *Tombstone,* Faulk, p. 33.

Since the sixteenth century: Lynn R. Bailey interview; Faulk, pp. 5–6.

There was briefly an exception: Lynn R. Bailey

interview; Bailey, *Too Tough to Die,* pp. 1–3; Faulk, p. 24.

The author gave a series of East Coast lectures: Breakenridge, *Helldorado,* p. 115.

Among the ambitious small-timers: Documents, Mulkins Collection; Kevin J. Mulkins, Lynn R. Bailey, and Ben Traywick interviews.

This was what many observers: Lynn R. Bailey interview.

For a few days, Ed did his prospecting: Paul Hutton, Bob McCubbin, and Art Austin interviews; Butler, pp. 77–78, 80–81; Bailey, *Too Tough to Die,* p. 5; Faulk, p. 28.

Like any experienced prospector: Lynn R. Bailey and Jim Turner interviews; Butler, pp. 67–68; Faulk, p. 24.

DeLong took a cursory look: Bailey, *Too Tough to Die,* pp. 4–10; Butler, pp. 83–84.

The mines in Prescott: Faulk, p. 22.

when Ed arrived he learned: Lynn R. Bailey and Art Austin interviews; Bailey, *Too Tough to Die,* pp. 10–13.

ore so soft and pure: Nancy Sosa and Jim Nelson, *Tombstone: A Quick History* (Blue Chicken Publishing, 2009), pp. 60–62.

The bonanza was so overwhelming: Butler, pp. 86–88. Here, Ed Schieffelin misstates Oliver Boyer's name as Jack Oliver.

It always galled Ed Schieffelin: William B. Shillingberg, *Tombstone, A.T.: A History of Early*

Mining, Milling, and Mayhem (Arthur H. Clark Company, 1999), p. 40.

rank amateurs who had no real idea: Lynn R. Bailey interview; Joseph Conlin, "Beans, Bacon and Galantine Truffles: The Food of the Western Miners," *Arizona and the West* 33 (Spring 1981).

Most came on foot: Shillingberg, *Tombstone, A.T.,* p. 81.

There was nothing particularly sophisticated: Ray Madzia, Kevin J. Mulkins, Bob Palmquist, and Lynn R. Bailey interviews.

A broad band of mineral-laden rock: Sosa and Nelson, p. 46.

Although there eventually were more than three thousand mines: Faulk, p. 69.

But gold comprised only: Chaput, *The Earp Papers,* pp. 62–63.

One they accepted: Bailey, *Too Tough to Die,* p. 13.

the equivalent of California's Silicon Valley: Bob Boze Bell interview. I think he captured the essence of the San Pedro Valley silver rush perfectly with this apt comparison.

Many of them had no intention: Cissy Stewart Lale, Paul Hutton, Bob Boze Bell, and Lynn R. Bailey interviews; White, pp. 204–5; Slotkin, pp. 17–18; Shillingberg, *Tombstone, A.T.,* pp. 56–57.

Most of all, the miners wanted food: Bruce Dinges interview; Joseph R. Conlin, *Bacon,*

Beans and Galantines: Food and Foodways of the Western Mining Frontier (University of Nevada Press, 1986), pp. 132–54. I had absolutely no idea about this fascinating by-product of working in an underground mine until it was brought to my attention during an interview with Bruce Dinges, publications director of the Arizona Historical Society in Tucson. Bruce suggested I read Joseph Conlin's magazine articles and book on the subject, and they are wonderful.

The company sent veteran lawman Bob Paul: Interview with Robert J. Chandler; Robert J. Chandler, "Under Cover for Wells Fargo: A Review Essay," *Journal of Arizona History* 41 (Spring 2000).

Speculators began vying: Bob Palmquist, Ray Madzia, Lynn R. Bailey, and Art Austin interviews; Sosa and Nelson, pp. 72–74; Bailey, *Too Tough to Die,* pp. 42–43; Faulk, pp. 72–79; Shillingberg, *Tombstone, A.T.,* pp. 66–79, 92. Entire books could and probably should be written about Tombstone and its town site controversy. It's a complicated mess, and delving too deeply into the details would bog down the larger story I'm trying to tell here. As the situation affects other events in Tombstone, there will be some subsequent referrals to it, but I don't claim to be presenting anything other than the few most basic facts.

By then, the whole country was reading and talking: Flood notes, Ragsdale Collection; Lynn R. Bailey, Jim Turner, Bruce Dinges, and Kevin J. Mulkins interviews; Faulk, p. 67.

But with an exploding, hungry population: Marks, pp. 27–28; Gatto, *The Real Wyatt Earp,* p. 84; Ben Traywick, Jim Turner, Bob McCubbin, Frederick Nolan, Pam Potter, Christine Rhodes, Lynn R. Bailey, and Bruce Dinges interviews.

The Clantons weren't the only family hoping: Pam Potter interview.

It happened very occasionally: Ray Madzia interview; Conlan, *Arizona and the West;* Morris, pp. 101, 110.

But the indications were there: Faulk, pp. 79–80.

he and Dick Gird had been quarreling: Shillingberg, *Tombstone, A.T.,* p. 108.

CHAPTER FOUR: THE EARPS ARRIVE

For eyewitness accounts of the early days in Tombstone when the Earps were first in town, there are two indispensable sources of printed information — the *San Diego Daily Union* dispatches of Clara Spalding Brown and the diaries of George Whitwell Parsons. (The memoir of John Clum is rife with exaggerations. Clara and Parsons stick more to the facts, or at least the facts as they perceived them.) In researching *The Last Gunfight,* I was fortunate enough to have two separate versions of the Parsons diaries. Historians have long been grateful to Lynn R. Bailey for initially publishing Parsons's reminiscences in 1996. Lynn did this after losing patience with lifelong Tombstone-Earpian scholar Carl Chafin, who for decades swore he was about to publish his own edition of the Parsons diary with exhaustive annotations that would much more clearly identify whom Parsons might be writing about, and offer considerably more context than the frontier prospector–business speculator did in his original writings. Carl never forgave Lynn, and died before publishing his version of the diaries concerning the years in which the Earps lived in Tombstone and the events involving their gunfight with the Clantons and McLaurys. (Carl did publish an annotated version of the Parsons diaries covering the post-1882 period.)

But just prior to his death, Carl Chafin delivered his nearly completed work in progress to Cochise County recorder Christine Rhodes, who generously made the material available to me. It's enlightening stuff — Carl's notations about relationships between individuals cited by Parsons allow much more understanding of local friendships, business connections, and resentments during Tombstone's so-called Earp era.

I cite both versions of Parsons in this chapter and throughout the rest of the book. Notes will indicate Bailey/Parsons and Chafin/Parsons to differentiate between them. There are no page numbers to cite on the Chafin material provided to me by Christine Rhodes — who, by the way, continues to be an invaluable resource for all would-be Cochise County scholars who visit her office in Bisbee. The fact that Carl Chafin trusted her with his prized manuscript is a testament to Christine's own great gifts as a researcher-historian.

traveling in three wagons: Chaput, *The Earp Papers,* p. 57; Collier, *"Harriet 'Hattie' Catchim."* Some historians believe Virgil Earp arrived in Tombstone ahead of the rest of the family, but it seems more likely he would have come with everyone else. Whenever possible, the Earps always liked to be together.

Dake had appointed Virgil: Chaput, *The Earp Papers,* p. 52; Barra, p. 97. Wyatt Earp later told Stuart Lake that Dake offered *him* the job of U.S. deputy marshal; Wyatt turned it down in favor of Virgil. But at this point, Dake knew Virgil well, and Wyatt not at all. True, Wyatt had been a lawman in Kansas, but Virgil had served as an officer in Prescott. Wyatt was probably just doing a bit more embellishing to his co-author, and, besides, Virgil by that point was dead. What was the harm? Virgil's appointment was originally as a U.S. deputy marshal serving in Yavapai County. When the Earp party passed through Tucson, Virgil had the document certifying his appointment changed to reflect his new residence in Pima County.

the deputy job might lead to something better: Jim Turner interview.

Like Virgil, he arrived with big plans: Marks, p. 33; Tefertiller, pp. 36–37; Robert J. Chandler interview. It's strange that Wyatt didn't at least check whether Tombstone already had stage lines before investing in a wagon and planning to start one there himself.

Like other area prospectors: Chaput, *The Earp Papers,* p. 63; Paula Mitchell Marks, Kevin J. Mulkins, and Lynn R. Bailey interviews.

The Earp women: Chaput, *The Earp Papers,* pp. 63–64; Shillingberg, *Tombstone A.T.,* p. 105.

Perhaps a few people in town had heard of him: Paul Hutton and Kevin J. Mulkins interviews. In his memoir, John Clum claimed that when Wyatt arrived in Tombstone almost everyone there had already heard of him, but Clum was, as usual, exaggerating.

At first, all the Earps lived together: Ray Madzia interview. If ever you visit Tombstone, ask Ray Madzia to show you the sites where the various Earps lived, and to tell the stories about how the properties frequently changed hands afterward. You won't be sorry.

They were not socially acceptable: Cissy Stewart Lale interview.

There were perhaps nine hundred residents: Tefertiller, p. 37; Gatto, *The Real Wyatt Earp*, p. 29; Chaput, *The Earp Papers*, pp. 40–42.

Tombstone residents established the custom: John Plesent Gray, *Tombstone's Violent Years, 1880–1882*, edited by Neil B. Carmony (Trail to Yesterday Books, 1999), p. 7.

the flood of arrivals featured: Lynn R. Bailey interview.

For the first time, Tombstone looked *sophisticated:* Bob McCubbin interview.

He read about Tombstone in the San Francisco papers: Bailey/Parsons, pp. 18–19.

But after walking around a bit: Chafin/Parsons, pp. 30–31.

As a result, packs of rats joined: Bailey/Parsons, pp. 21–26.

But Clara's initial description of Tombstone: Clara Spalding Brown, *Tombstone from a Woman's Point of View: The Correspondence of Clara Spalding Brown July 7, 1880 to November 14, 1882,* compiled and edited by

Lynn R. Bailey (Westernlore Press, 2003), p. 17.

The digestive systems of the entire community: Chafin/Parsons, p. 108.

But most Tombstone residents lived in dread: Ray Madzia and Lynn R. Bailey interviews.

When visitors came to town: Sosa and Nelson, pp. 192–97.

When Wells Fargo opened an office: Robert J. Chandler interview. From May 1880 through February 1881, Wells Fargo paid Howard C. Walker amounts ranging from $500 to $750 a month to lease space for its deliveries on his stage routes between Tucson and Tombstone. After February 1881, Wells Fargo leased space on John D. Kinnear's Arizona Mail & Stage Co., paying between $700 and $950 each month. Beyond a lengthy phone interview and an extensive e-mail exchange with Bob Chandler, various facts in this chapter about Wells Fargo operations come from three magazine articles he wrote: "Wells Fargo: 'We Never Forget!' " *Western Outlaw-Lawman History Association (WOLA) Journal* 2, no. 3 (Winter 1987); "Wells Fargo and the Earp Brothers: The Cash Books Talk," *California Historical Quarterly,* Summer 2009; and "Wells Fargo Never Forgets," *California Historical Quarterly,* Summer 2009.

He reported that six mules had been stolen:

Barra, pp. 109–10; Tefertiller, pp. 43–44; Gatto, *The Real Wyatt Earp,* pp. 33–35; Lubet, pp. 27–28.

Frank and Tom McLaury weren't there: In his letter published in the *Nugget,* Frank McLaury claimed that he personally met with Lieutenant Hurst when the posse arrived on the ranch, but every other version has Hurst dealing directly with Frank Patterson. Based on what we know about Frank McLaury and his hot temper, it doesn't seem very likely that he would have calmly chatted with an army officer who was essentially accusing him of rustling government stock.

Virgil Earp claimed later: Lubet, p. 28.

U.S. marshals and their deputies: Jim Turner interview; Marks, p. 65; Tefertiller, p. 45; Gatto, *The Real Wyatt Earp,* pp. 35–36; Chaput, *The Earp Papers,* p. 43.

Many of the remaining 1,900: Ray Madzia, Lynn R. Bailey, Craig T. Miner, Paul Hutton, Michael Johnson, Archie McDonald, and Bruce Dinges interviews.

they were in far more danger from cave-ins: Christine Rhodes interview.

Western judges and juries: Jeff Morey interview.

A good example occurred: Shillingberg, *Tombstone, A.T.,* pp. 125–28.

On July 24, Parsons wrote: Bailey/Parsons, p. 66.

But Wyatt was also inflexible: Gary L. Roberts, Jim Turner, and Jeff Morey interviews.
This aspect of Wyatt's personality is key to
everything that happened later in Tombstone.

John Plesent Gray described his pals: Gray,
Tombstone's Violent Years, 1880–1882, Carmony, ed. p. 35.

CHAPTER FIVE: THE COMING OF THE COWBOYS

Psychoanalysis is always tricky territory, but
it seems to me that truly informative nonfiction has to at least attempt to explain why
people did things rather than just list what
they did and when. That's a special challenge
when writing about Curly Bill Brocius, John
Ringo, and their cowboy company, because,
as Arizona historian Lynn R. Bailey likes to
point out, there's very little known for certain
about any of them. Record keeping on the
American frontier was notoriously erratic
under the best of circumstances. The cowboys
frequently changed their names, making it
even harder to pinpoint their background
and, often, their criminal career. I've tried to
make clear in this chapter what facts are actually documented, and when I'm instead offering informed conjecture based on studying
documents and interviewing experts on
frontier history. Of particular note is a caveat

from Lynn Bailey: The earliest herds driven to Arizona Territory came from California; the Texas cowboys weren't the first to arrive. But the troublemakers in what would become Cochise County were mostly of Texas lineage, at least in the sense that they cut their lawbreaking teeth there.

Researching this chapter was especially tough, yet enjoyable — if there's one thing everyone agrees about concerning the cowboys, it's that they were a colorful, rambunctious bunch. It's always fun to write about such fascinating characters.

For almost three decades: Much of my information about the history of the Texas Rangers is drawn from two impeccable sources. The first is *The Portable Handbook of Texas,* edited by Roy R. Barkley and Mark E. Odintz, published in 2000 by the Texas State Historical Association. If you are at all interested in Texas history, you must own this massive, fact-crammed book. The second is a series of interviews and conversations with my good friend Ben Procter, professor emeritus of history at Texas Christian University in Fort Worth, past president of the Texas State Historical Association, and longtime chronicler of the Texas Rangers. Ben is currently in poor health, and was able to grant only one interview for this project. But we'd had plenty of in-depth discussions on the subject of the Rangers for two of my previous books, *Our Land Before We Die* (Jeremy Tarcher, 2002) and *Go Down Together* (Simon & Schuster, 2009). Accordingly, I also relied on notes from those interviews. With every other source cited in these notes, all interviews were exclusively conducted during research for *The Last Gunfight.*

Texas became a magnet: William C. Davis, *Three Roads to the Alamo: The Lives and Fortunes of David Crockett, James Bowie and William Barrett Travis* (HarperCollins, 1998), p. 205.

A Code of Conduct was instituted: Documents, Texas Rangers Hall of Fame, Waco, Texas.

His monthly field reports: Ibid.

In the border town of Brownsville: Roy R. Barkley and Mark E. Odintz, eds., *The Portable Handbook of Texas* (Texas State Historical Association, 2000), p. 862.

Wherever they relocated: Ben E. Procter, Frederick Nolan, and Paul Hutton interviews.

There was plenty of room: Paul Cool, "Bob Martin: A Rustler in Paradise," *WOLA Online Journal,* 2003. This article is one of the most distinguished examples of scholarly yet informative writing that I've ever learned from and enjoyed. You'd be well advised to look it up and read it in its entirety.

Often, the rustlers conducted their illegal ar-rangements: Breakenridge, pp. 165–66; Barra, pp. 102–3; Bruce Dinges, Frederick Nolan, Paula Mitchell Marks, and Paul Hutton interviews.

Outlaws were nothing new: Wagoner, p. 105.

Wells Fargo began leasing space: Chandler, "Wells Fargo: 'We Never Forget!' "

Wells Fargo itself opposed the governor: Ibid.

thieves from Mexico never stopped coming north: Lynn R. Bailey interview.

For American rustlers: Cool, "Bob Martin"; Scott Dyke interview.

The army was always desperate for beef: Ben Traywick interview.

The small ranchers got more than money: Allen A. Erwin, *The Southwest of John H. Slaughter, 1841–1922* (Arthur H. Clark Company, 1965), p. 188; Pam Potter inter-view.

They did not belong to a single: A vociferous segment among Tombstone historians would strongly disagree, led by retired town historian Ben Traywick. Ben believes that Newman "Old Man" Clanton was a "godfather-like" criminal kingpin who for a time controlled most illicit goings-on in the Tombstone area. I found no evidence of this. I respect Ben's research efforts without agreeing with some of his conclusions.

"Curly Bill" Brocius came to Arizona: The best

607

book about this colorful cowboy is Steve Gatto's *Curly Bill* (Protar House, 2003). Gatto is an indefatigable researcher, and all of us who attempt to write about Tombstone and the cowboys should feel grateful to him. As with Ben Traywick, I often disagree with Gatto's conclusions, but when it comes to sniffing out obscure documents in public archives, the man is a bloodhound.

he and his sidekick Curly Bill: Bob Alexander, *Desert Desperadoes: The Banditti of Southwestern New Mexico* (Gila Books, 2006), pp. 124–29.

Martin was part of a group: Cool, "Bob Martin."

One of the few cowboys whose background: Steve Gatto, *Johnny Ringo* (Protar House Books, 2002), pp. 7–12; Jack Burrows, *John Ringo: The Gunfighter Who Never Was* (University of Arizona Press, 1987), pp. 106–31.

He and a friend named George Gladden: Burrows, p. 135.

Ringo appealed his conviction: Gatto, *Johnny Ringo,* pp. 49–50.

Ringo celebrated regaining his freedom: Burrows, p. 135.

Perhaps alone among the outlaws: Marks, p. 38.

A. M. Franklin, a shopkeeper: Gatto, *Johnny Ringo,* p. 62.

A widespread story at the time: Alexander, *Desert Desperadoes,* p. 154.

They considered themselves to be lawbreakers: Ben E. Procter and Bob Boze Bell interviews.

they brought with them to Arizona Territory: Ibid.; Breakenridge, p. 169.

In a pragmatic if not legal sense: Paula Mitchell Marks and Lynn R. Bailey interviews.

he underestimated his current antagonists: Jim Turner interview.

CHAPTER SIX: DOC, JOHNNY, AND JOSEPHINE

Doc Holliday never stayed: Gary L. Roberts interview.

Kate could only imagine: Documents, Kevin J. and Bev Mulkins Collection.

Years later, she told a journalist: Ibid.

Doc apparently felt better: Gary L. Roberts interview.

It was a heady time in Tombstone: Bailey/Parsons, pp. 62, 88–89.

Local leaders organized: Shillingberg, *Tombstone,* pp. 154–55.

On the night of October 10: Gary L. Roberts interview; Roberts, pp. 128–29; Gatto, *The Real Wyatt Earp,* pp. 42–44.

Among them was the bar at the newly opened Grand Hotel: Sosa and Nelson, pp. 192–95.

Famous frontier figures passed through: Bob

Alexander, *John H. Behan: Sacrificed Sheriff* (High-Lonesome Books, 2002), pp. 23–24. Alexander, a retired lawman living in Maypearl, Texas, may be Johnny Behan's most enthusiastic advocate among historians. That places him in the minority, which he acknowledges with good humor and absolutely no malice toward the majority, who think Behan was a conniving lightweight. My own position is somewhere in between.

This worked well for Johnny: Bob Alexander interview; Alexander, *John H. Behan: Sacrificed Sheriff,* pp. 30–32; Bailey, *Too Tough to Die,* p. 60.

Johnny's annual income: There's no way to be certain of the amount. I base this estimate on the number of taxable businesses operating in Prescott about this time. The Yavapai County sheriff in 1871 would make far less from 10 percent of the taxes collected than whoever became Cochise County sheriff ten years later, because Tombstone mining operations were far more profitable than those a decade earlier in northern Arizona Territory.

his wife, Victoria, filed for divorce: Alexander, *John H. Behan: Sacrificed Sheriff,* p. 42; Anne E. Collier and Glenn Boyer interviews. The mention of sixteen-year-old prostitute Sadie Mansfield in the Behan divorce petition has caused some historians to believe that she later identified herself as

Josephine Sarah "Sadie" Marcus in Tombstone, particularly since there is evidence that Sadie Mansfield came to Arizona Territory from San Francisco. That would mean Josephine completely fabricated rather than exaggerated her tales of early life, and of joining the Pauline Markham troupe in its frontier performances of *H.M.S. Pinafore.* Considering Josephine's talent and propensity for reinventing her past, it's possible, though to me it seems unlikely. Among other things, in her very old age Josephine astonished young relatives by dancing an agile hornpipe she said she once had to master for her role in *Pinafore.* There is always the chance that at some point new evidence will be unearthed to prove Josephine Marcus was — or wasn't — Sadie Mansfield. That's part of the allure of history. It's never definitive.

Johnny used the same persuasive skills: There's no doubt that Johnny Behan knew how to sweep women off their feet, including plenty who should have known better. For an entertaining few hours, visit the University of Arizona's Special Collections on the school's Tucson campus. Ask to see the folders containing love letters to Johnny, including some particularly explicit missives from a married paramour calling herself "Bert."

The strategy would probably have worked: Bob

611

Alexander interview; Alexander, *John H. Behan: Sacrificed Sheriff,* pp. 49–50.

Common-law wives were not: Cissy Stewart Lale interview.

The San Francisco performances: Cason manuscript.

Bat Masterson, who didn't like her personally: Paul Hutton interview; Paul Hutton, "Showdown at the Hollywood Corral: Wyatt Earp and the Movies," *Montana: The Magazine of Western History,* Summer 1995.

When a friend urged her: Cason manuscript.

one place must have been Tucson: Clum manuscript, University of Arizona Special Collections.

It was probably there or in the wild outskirts: Tefertiller, p. 69; Marks, p. 38.

Not long afterward Josephine became ill: Glenn Boyer interview.

Whatever the reason, Johnny pursued her: Cason manuscript. As indicated, I think Josephine was exaggerating — but not completely making up — Johnny's pursuit of her. For a Casanova like Johnny, pursuit was part of the fun.

Around the end of September 1880: The Cosmopolitan Hotel in Tombstone's guest book for the week of May 12–18, 1880, includes the name "J. Marcus." Some researchers think this may be proof Josephine arrived in Tombstone well ahead of Johnny Behan

612

moving there in the fall — which in turn lends itself to the theory that she originally came to town as a high-end prostitute rather than Johnny's fiancée. With Josephine, anything is possible, but after extensive research and interviews I don't think she ever sold her favors professionally, though she certainly knew how to use her considerable charms to her best personal advantage. There was a substantial Jewish population in Arizona Territory in 1880, including droves of traveling salesmen who visited Tombstone occasionally or even on a regular basis. "Marcus" was not an unusual last name. I don't think the Cosmopolitan guest was Josephine.

The most energetic advocate of Josephine-as-Tombstone-prostitute/dance-hall-girl was Stuart Lake, who understandably loathed her after attempting to work with Josephine on Wyatt's memoir after his death. In 1930, an exasperated Lake wrote to Houghton Mifflin's Ira Rich Kent that "Mrs. Earp went to Tombstone from [San Francisco] with the first rush, to work the dancehalls of that camp. Bat Masterson and a score of old timers have told me that she was the belle of the honkytonks, the prettiest dame in 300 or so of her kind. Johnny Behan was a notorious 'chaser' and a free spender making lots of money. He persuaded the beautiful Sadie to leave the honkytonk and set her up as his 'girl,' after which she was known in Tombstone as Sadie Behan."

She said she was persuaded: Cason manuscript.

In fact, she moved in with him: Barra, pp. 112–14.

Johnny and Josephine may have tried to explain: Tefertiller, pp. 68–72.

She was flashy and seductive: Jane Candia Coleman and Anne E. Collier interviews.

Being shacked up long term: Pam Potter and Cissy Stewart Lale interviews. Potter, a McLaury family descendant who has researched supposed romantic relationships in Earp-era Tombstone, rightly points out that young women as well as young men went to the frontier in hopes of great adventure. For the women, that often meant spicy romances that would have been impossible back in more civilized climes.

Then and forever, Josephine Sarah Marcus: Stuart Lake's anguished notes in the Huntington Library collection bearing his name are ample proof that even in her dotage Josephine would alternately resort to tears and threats to get what she wanted; Anne E. Collier interview.

Bob Boze Bell suggested to me that, if he were alive today, Wyatt Earp would be happily employed as a dealer in a Las Vegas casino — he loved saloons and gambling that much. I think that a modern-day John Clum would be an executive at Fox News, figuring out just the right hot-button issues to exploit and engage the unwavering loyalty of a substantial portion of the public who prefer satisfactory results to due process. Just my opinion.

On October 23, he arrested Pete Spencer: Ray Madzia interview; Chaput, *The Earp Papers,* p. 56. Pete Spencer's first interactions with the Earps are important because of what came later.

Earlier that evening: Marks, pp. 103–6; Gatto, *Curly Bill,* pp. 34–35; Gatto, *The Real Wyatt Earp,* pp. 46–56; Barra, p. 117; Shillingberg, *Tombstone, A.T.,* pp. 158–61.

The group included: Wyatt Earp told Stuart Lake that those present in the cowboy contingent included Pony Diehl (one of the most notorious rustlers), Frank McLaury, and Billy Clanton. Court records make clear they were not — otherwise, like the rest, they would at least have been fined for their actions. Wyatt added their names after the fact to try and establish that McLaury and Clanton were regular participants in outlaw activities. They weren't.

When the cowboys got into mischief: Paula Mitchell Marks interview.

Fred Dodge did: Dodge is an interesting if marginal character in Tombstone history. Ostensibly a dealer in saloon card games, he claimed much later to have been a secret agent in place for Wells Fargo. The company already had Marshall Williams as its Tombstone representative. There was no need for a full-time spy who would report (I guess) on rumors of plans to rob stages, which mining companies were in financial trouble, and other local gossip. My best guess is that Wells Fargo occasionally paid Dodge if he had some interesting tidbit to report. He might have considered himself a company employee because of that.

But it had never been Wyatt's custom: Craig T. Miner and Art Austin interviews.

John Clum's main marketing strategy: Shillingberg, *Tombstone, A.T.,* pp. 130–31, 180.

the two Earp brothers controlled: Lubet, p. 31.

On the way, Curly Bill asked: Gatto, *Curly Bill,* p. 39. This is ludicrous. The last thing Curly Bill would have done would be to gratuitously confess that he'd once been arrested for another murder.

Tension between Republicans: Archie McDonald interview.

John Ringo was in no sense: Gatto, *Johnny Ringo,* pp. 69–70.

In Tombstone, avowed Republican George Parsons: Parsons, pp. 156, 162.

Pima County voters cast their ballots: Ben Traywick, *The Clantons of Tombstone* (Red Marie's Books, 2006), p. 53; Alexander, *John H. Behan,* p. 67; Gatto, *Johnny Ringo,* p. 72; above all, Tefertiller, pp. 52–55.

He had a plan to make certain: Lake Collection documents, Huntington Library.

Tombstone voters chose Ben Sippy: Marks, p. 114; Barra, p. 125.

Wyatt met with Curly Bill: Flood notes, Ragsdale Collection; Lake notes, Huntington Library.

He proudly related: Flood notes, Ragsdale Collection.

According to Johnson, he had been ordered: A great deal of behind-the-scenes bargaining took place. Apparently, Bob Paul "loaned" Johnson $250 in return for his court appearance and helpful testimony. Ike Clanton may have brokered the deal. Bob Palmquist, *Election Fraud 1880: The Case of Paul v Shibell,* Arizona Historical Society Archives.

The list of his enemies was growing: Barra, p. 127. Allen also discussed this with me in person. It's an excellent point.

Later, each would offer a different version: Tefertiller, pp. 55–56; Barra, p. 126. I personally don't think either Johnny or Wyatt was telling the truth. They each wanted to make the other one look bad.

Hattie, James's stepdaughter, became en-gaged: Anne E. Collier interview; Collier, "Harriet 'Hattie' Catchim." One of the ongoing fables about Tombstone is that the O.K. Corral gunfight happened in part because Hattie was romantically involved with one of the cowboys, or perhaps Tom McLaury. In fact, she was married to someone else. Stuart Lake later mistakenly identified Louisa (Morgan's common-law wife) and Mattie (Wyatt's) as James's step-daughters.

Perhaps the happiest Earp of all: Boyer Collection, Ford County Historical Society.

the town still did its best to celebrate: Gatto, *The Real Wyatt Earp,* p. 44; Parsons, pp. 105–6.

Viewed from a modern perspective: Bob Palmquist interview.

John Clum already wielded considerable power: Clum manuscript, University of Arizona Special Collections.

Curly Bill had nothing to do with: Casey Tefertiller interview; Tefertiller, pp. 56–58; Marks, pp. 122–24; Parsons, p. 120. My personal opinion is that Wyatt was there and assisted Virgil, Johnny Behan, and Ben Sippy in keeping the mob away and later escorting Johnny Behind-the-Deuce to jail in Tucson. He did not play a leading role, or protect the prisoner all by himself.

618

The other consequence was more immediate: Bailey/Parsons, p. 118.

Chapter Eight: Cochise County Sheriff

The most obvious drawback: Frederick Nolan and Bruce Dinges interviews; Marks, p. 118. Over the course of writing fifteen books, I've driven around much of the continental United States. In these travels, I have rarely seen more rugged, spectacular scenery than can be found in the San Pedro Valley and the surrounding area, particularly a stretch of Arizona State Highway 16 that cuts through the Mule Mountains between Tombstone and Bisbee.

The potential for violence: Paul Hutton and Cissy Stewart Lale interviews.

And the sheriff couldn't expect appreciation: Archie McDonald interview.

This caused rank-and-file citizens: White, pp. 176–77.

the primary duty of a county sheriff: Christine Rhodes interview; Alexander, *John H. Behan,* pp. 63–64; John Plesent Gray manuscript, University of Arizona Special Collections.

a monthly stipend of $150: Art Austin interview.

could anticipate a substantial income: Cochise County Recorder Christine Rhodes estimates $25,000. Bill Breakenridge suggested $40,000 in *Helldorado.*

They would still consider him an employee: Bruce Dinges interview.

Wyatt expected the system to work: Gary L. Roberts and Bob Boze Bell interviews.

By 1881, the federal government allowed: White, p. 172.

Johnny offered Wyatt a deal: Marks, pp. 119–20; Tefertiller, p. 55; Shillingberg, *Tombstone, A.T.,* p. 189.

Wyatt, who always kept his word: Ben Traywick interview.

Johnny reneged on his promise: Bob Alexander interview. I disagree with Bob's belief that Johnny Behan was an upstanding martyr in much of what occurred in Tombstone during 1881. Like everyone else involved, Johnny was a hustler on the make who sometimes placed his own ambitions ahead of the public's well-being. But Bob's theory about why Johnny went back on his word to make Wyatt undersheriff seems valid to me.

Harry Woods as undersheriff: Marks, pp. 119–20; Breakenridge, p. 162.

opened his sheriff's office: Shillingberg, *Tombstone, A.T.,* p. 190. Some historians believe the Cochise County sheriff's office was in the back of a Tombstone tobacco shop, but I think they're mixing its location up with

620

that of the town library.

the legislature in Prescott debated: Sherry Monahan, *Taste of Tombstone: A Hearty Helping of History* (Royal Spectrum, 1998), p. 42; Marks, pp. 131–33; Wagoner, *Arizona Territory,* p. 175.

Billy Breakenridge had a tough time: This section is based almost entirely on *Helldorado: Bringing the Law to the Mesquite,* Bill Breakenridge's memoir that was originally published in 1928. He describes his curious tax collecting alliance with Curly Bill on pages 225–28.

Wyatt Earp never seemed to have any problems with Breakenridge while they both were in Tombstone, but much later in life Wyatt felt betrayed when *Helldorado* was published. He complained that the book made him look bad — which it didn't, though it also did not portray Wyatt as the shining hero he liked to say that he'd been. (Breakenridge even credited Wyatt with single-handedly holding off the mob that wanted to lynch Johnny Behind-the-Deuce.)

Acting on Johnny's instructions: In *Helldorado,* Breakenridge presents Curly Bill's recruitment as his own idea, but as a deputy he didn't have the authority to make such a decision himself. He was following Johnny Behan's orders.

Tombstone continued to grow: Lynn Bailey interview; Bailey, *Town Too Tough to Die,* pp. 88–97. I think it is absolutely impossible to understand Tombstone circa 1881 without reading this book. I also recommend William Shillingberg's *Tombstone, A.T.*

Parties hosted and attended: Brown, pp. 24, 27.

Few career gamblers: Letter, F. B. Streeter to W. S. Campbell, Kansas Heritage Collection; Barra, p. 53.

Charley Storms, another veteran: Marks, p. 131; Bell, p. 52; Bailey/Parsons, p. 129.

a man known as One-Armed Kelly: Bailey/Parsons, p. 130.

Appalled at the reputation: Bailey, *Town Too Tough to Die,* p. 125.

essentially left Wyatt broke: Art Austin interview.

There were, in Tombstone, three ways: Paula Mitchell Marks interview. This concept is absolutely critical to understanding Wyatt's subsequent plans and actions, and full credit for it must go to Paula Marks.

Citizens Safety Committee members convinced themselves: Chafin/Parsons, p. 20.

If Wyatt could make the right people believe: Christine Rhodes interview.

CHAPTER NINE: THE BENSON STAGE ROBBERY

In November 2009, Scott Dyke arranged a hike across part of the San Pedro Valley that included the site of the Benson stage robbery. He and I were accompanied by my assistant, Andrea Ahles Koos, two U.S. park rangers, and several members of the Friends of the San Pedro, a nonprofit organization devoted to preserving the history of the area. It was a *long* day. Be assured that when I describe various draws that the stage had to go up and then down, it's from sweat-drenched personal experience. Even though hiking through the area is arduous, I would urge anyone interested in Tombstone–Earp–Southeast Arizona history to do it with the help of qualified guides — it would be very easy to get lost if you tried getting there on your own. Slogging through sand on foot, blinking through clouds of blowing dust, having to keep a watchful eye out for snakes and scorpions and pointed ends of plants — these experiences really give a sense of how hardy the early Cochise County denizens had to be.

Students of the Benson robbery frequently argue about whether the holdup occurred before or after the stage could stop at Drew's Station. After walking the ground myself, I'm in the "before" camp.

it had snowed lightly: Bailey/Parsons, p. 134.

The stage carried: Chandler, *"Wells Fargo: 'We Never Forget!' "*; Gatto, *The Real Wyatt Earp,* p. 66; Chandler, "Under Cover for Wells Fargo."

two more got on in Watervale: Shillingberg, *Tombstone, A.T.,* p. 193.

Philpot complained of stomach cramps: Marks, p. 135; Barra, p. 139.

a masked man stepped out into the road: Marks, pp. 134–38; Tefertiller, pp. 76–79; Shillingberg, *Tombstone, A.T.,* pp. 193–94.

A search of the spot: Terfertiller, p. 76.

Cowen had to ride to Tombstone: Shillingberg, *Tombstone, A.T.,* p. 194.

lawmen and citizens alike were galvanized: Parsons, p. 134.

There had been stage robberies: Lynn Bailey interview; Marks, p. 133.

even Doc Holliday was relieved: Roberts, p. 80.

If the delivery of mail was constantly disrupted: Art Austin interview.

According to Parsons, on the night: Bailey/Parsons, pp. 134–35.

The hybrid posse galloped out of town: Barra, p. 140; DeArment, *Bat Masterson,* pp. 201–3; Shillingberg, *Tombstone, A.T.,* pp. 195–96; Tefertiller, p. 77.

Johnny Behan took custody of King: Tefertiller, p. 77.

On the night of March 28: Marks, p. 144; Chafin/Parsons, p. 41.

Though there has been considerable speculation: Luther King is one of the black holes of Tombstone history. Depending on whose best guess you choose to believe, he either fled to Lake City in Colorado Territory or else reinvented himself as Sandy King in New Mexico. On November 9, 1881, Sandy King was lynched by an angry mob in the New Mexico town of Shakespeare. The most far-fetched suggestion is that King's real name was Luther Woods, and that he was the brother of Cochise County under-sheriff Harry Woods, the man who allowed him to escape from the county jail in Tombstone. It is odd that Wells Fargo placed $1,200 bounties on the heads of Billy Leonard, Harry Head, and Jim Crane but didn't offer a reward for King. Perhaps they wanted Cochise County lawmen to concentrate their efforts on apprehending those three, who King swore fired the shots that killed Bud Philpot and Peter Roerig. Luther King was himself quite capable of murder — his role in the killing of Bob Martin proves that.

Parsons, ever their spokesman: Parsons, p. 137.

Tombstone almost immediately buzzed: Barra, pp. 141–44.

Doc Holliday had rented a horse: Roberts, p. 140.

But it was well known that: Ibid., p. 139.

Perhaps Doc participated: Marks, pp. 137–38; Lubet, p. 38.

Writing many years later: John Plesent Gray manuscript, University of Arizona Special Collections.

John Clum, trying to whitewash: John Clum manuscript, University of Arizona Special Collections.

he soon took another opportunity to thwart Wyatt: Lubet, p. 38; Tefertiller, p. 80.

Virgil was particularly annoyed: Tefertiller, p. 80.

Company records show: Robert J. Chandler, historian of Wells Fargo in San Francisco, is a "treasure box" of information. In phone interviews with Bob, and through his willingness to share notes and copies of documents, I was able to piece together key elements of the Earp family's often tangled connections to the company. Regarding payments to Wyatt, Virgil, and Morgan for their roles in the Benson stage robbery posse, I used figures provided by Bob in the draft of an article he submitted in February 2001 to *True West* magazine. *True West* published a much edited, much abbreviated version. For this chapter and others, I used Bob's complete original.

Reputation meant everything to Wells Fargo: Robert J. Chandler interview; Chandler, "Wells Fargo: 'We Never Forget!' "; Chandler, "Wells Fargo and the Earp Brothers: The Cash Books Talk"; Chandler, "Wells Fargo Never Forgets"; Chandler, "Under Cover for Wells Fargo: A Review Essay"; Cissy Stewart Lale interview.

instructions to Bob Paul for alerting: Taylor, p. 9.

Mayor Clum and the Tombstone city council: Bailey, *Too Tough to Die,* pp. 123–25.

Doc Holliday certainly had a permit: Gary L. Roberts interview.

CHAPTER TEN: PLANS GO AWRY

Details of Wyatt Earp's proposed deal with Ike Clanton, Tom McLaury, and Joe Hill come directly from testimony by Wyatt and Ike at the hearing following the October 26, 1881, gunfight to determine whether the Earp brothers and Doc Holliday should be tried for murder. Original hearing transcripts were recently recovered and are being prepared for Internet display. Meanwhile, everything is readily available to researchers in Alford E. Turner's *The O.K. Corral Inquest.* Steven Lubet's exceptional *Murder in Tombstone: The Forgotten Trial of Wyatt Earp* is also recommended to anyone who wants to know more about Wyatt's proposition to Ike, Tom McLaury, and Joe Hill.

The average lifespan of frontier boomtowns: Faulk, p. 73.

If nobody yet realized: Ray Madzia interview.

Tombstone's best defense: Lynn Bailey interview; Monahan, pp. 52–53.

in 1881 the broiling temperatures didn't wait: Parsons, pp. 142–43; Brown, pp. 32–33.

Sometime during that stifling afternoon: Bob Palmquist interview; Tefertiller, p. 89; Brown, pp. 29–31; Marks, pp. 156–59; Bailey, *Too Tough To Die,* pp. 98–100; Chaput, *Virgil Earp: Western Peace Officer,* p. 97; Parsons, pp. 236–44.

Ben Sippy's brief tenure: Tefertiller, p. 86; Alexander, *John H. Behan: Sacrificed Sheriff,* p. 86. One of the lingering Tombstone mysteries is, What happened to Ben Sippy? He disappeared forever, at least until his name was resurrected for a lead character in Larry McMurtry's novel *Anything for Billy.*

To Wyatt Earp, working as a lawman: Craig T. Miner interview.

Being an officer meant more than that to Virgil: Paula Marks interview.

Six days after the fire: Marks, p. 159; Bailey, *Too Tough To Die,* p. 127.

Authorities argued about how many cowboys: Faulk, p. 133.

In early July 1881, Kate Elder: Documents, Kevin J. and Bev Mulkins Collection; Roberts, p. 154, p. 156; Marks, pp. 162–63; Anne E. Collier interview; Barra, pp. 144–45; Tefertiller, pp. 87–88; Alexander, *John H. Behan: Sacrificed Sheriff,* p. 89; Lubet, p. 39. Some versions have Kate recanting her testimony against Doc. I'm not certain whether she did or didn't.

More than half a century later: Cason manuscript, Ford County Historical Society Collection; Tefertiller, pp. 71–72, 100.

Wyatt was big and good-looking: Clum manuscript, University of Arizona Special Collections.

She stood out: Jane Candia Coleman interview.

There is no way to be certain what relationship blossomed: Anne E. Collier and Pam Potter interviews.

there seemed to be little Johnny could do: Bob Alexander interview.

In early June, Wyatt asked: Marks, pp. 151–52; Tefertiller, pp. 83–84; Bailey, *Too Tough To Die,* p. 132.

So if Hill, McLaury, and Clanton would help him do it: Turner, p. 158.

Soon Ike was back: Jeff Morey and Robert J. Chandler interviews. Jeff Morey makes the excellent point that Wells Fargo took upon itself the right to sentence the three suspects to death for their alleged crimes.

Wyatt's motive for making the offer: Gary L. Roberts interview.

Ike got into a brawl: Tefertiller, p. 93; Gatto, *The Real Wyatt Earp,* p. 85.

Joe Hill returned with practically the worst news: Bell, *Classic Gunfights,* p. 70; Tefertiller, pp. 84–85; Breakenridge, p. 211; Bailey, *Too*

Tough To Die, pp. 132–33.

Marshall Williams got drunk: Gary L. Roberts interview.

On July 4, 1881, Cochise County residents gathered: Brown, p. 33; Bailey/Parsons, p. 159.

CHAPTER ELEVEN: ESCALATION

Galeyville butcher Al McAlister: Gatto, *Curly Bill,* p. 81; Lynn Bailey interview.

Border crime wasn't one-sided: Lynn Bailey interview.

the Mexican government's high taxes: Tefertiller, pp. 91–92.

In late July, a particularly well-laden pack train: Traywick, *The Clantons of Tombstone,* p. 64; Marks, p. 170; Tefertiller, pp. 97–98; Bell, *Classic Gunfights,* p. 67; Bailey/Parsons, p. 167.

The incident escalated from a regional clash: Paul Hutton interview.

The weather had everyone living there: Bailey/Parsons, p. 168; Marks, p. 170.

Old Man Clanton and several other men: Traywick, *The Clantons of Tombstone,* pp. 67–69; Gray manuscript, University of Arizona Special Collections; Marks, pp. 170–73; Tefertiller, pp. 97–98; Gray, *Tombstone's Violent Years, 1880–1882,* Carmony, ed., p. 30; Bailey/Parsons, pp. 166–67. Ben Traywick insists that a posse led by the Earps rather than Mexican troops perpetrated the attack, but I respectfully disagree. As they proved throughout their years in law enforcement, the Earps were not cold-blooded killers.

There was another critical consequence: Gary L. Roberts interview.

Well-to-do citizens stepped up their dabbling: Chafin/Parsons, p. 98; Brown, p. 41.

a town meeting was convened: Bailey, *Too Tough To Die,* pp. 130–31; Bailey/Parsons, p. 171; Chafin/Parsons, p. 110.

The acting territorial governor: Marks, pp. 174–75.

Frank McLaury felt threatened enough: Tefertiller, p. 110; Marks, p. 181.

On September 9, Virgil received a telegram: Bell, *Classic Gunfights,* p. 82; Gatto, *Johnny Ringo,* pp. 90–92; Tefertiller, p. 102.

Wyatt and Morgan were busy pursuing: Gatto, *The Real Wyatt Earp,* pp. 93–95; Bailey, *Too Tough To Die,* pp. 128–29; Barra, pp. 159–60; Marks, pp. 171–81; Alexander, *John H. Behan,* p. 108; Lubet, p. 42. Pete Spencer's real name was Elliott Larkin Ferguson and, like so many of the cowboys, he fled to southeast Arizona from Texas.

Wyatt claimed that Frank McLaury: Turner, *The O.K. Corral Inquest,* p. 159.

He warned Billy Breakenridge: Breakenridge, p. 237.

631

If the ensuing adventures of the Tombstone militia: Bailey, *Too Tough To Die,* p. 131; Parsons, pp. 180–82; Chafin/Parsons, p. 127.

In all, the posse traveled: Marks, p. 187.

The long ride home took them: Gatto, *The Real Wyatt Earp,* p. 79; Tefertiller, pp. 105–6; Parsons, p. 182; Chafin/Parsons, p. 129.

A preliminary hearing on the federal mail robbery charges: Marks, p. 189; Alexander, *John H. Behan,* pp. 111–12.

Before Virgil left: Shillingberg, *Tombstone, A.T.,* p. 240.

Ike Clanton continued accusing Wyatt: Documents, Mulkins Collection; Tefertiller, p. 114; Roberts, p. 182. According to Wyatt's testimony at the Spicer hearing, Ike claimed that Doc himself swore Wyatt told him about the failed plot.

CHAPTER TWELVE: THE NIGHT BEFORE

When faced with contradictory descriptions of events by participants and eyewitnesses, I think that in most cases it's the writer's responsibility to study everything and then make a case for what most likely happened rather than fall back on "one said this and the other said that." But regarding the events on the night of October 25, 1881, in Tombstone, it's important to see how Ike Clanton's, Wyatt Earp's, and Virgil Earp's versions diverged. Almost every quote or instance of paraphrasing here is based on testimony from the three at the November hearing in U.S. commissioner/probate judge Wells Spicer's court to determine if the Earp brothers and Doc Holliday should be remanded to a grand jury that would consider bringing charges of murder against them. All three embellished their testimony to a certain extent. As will be seen, Ike fell into an embellishing frenzy that ultimately cast doubt on his ability to tell any semblance of the truth — that probably saved the Earps from further legal peril.

Interpretation of events by the writer calls for studying those involved and trying, based on their past and future actions, to decide what they were most likely to have thought and done in specific instances. A good example in this chapter is the infamous poker game played by Virgil, Ike, Tom McLaury, and Johnny Behan in the Occidental Saloon. There's been endless debate among Tombstone scholars about it — how did these four ever manage to put aside their differences and play cards? It seems to me that Virgil Earp, who always tried to head off trouble by keeping things friendly rather than confrontational, must have seen an opportunity to diffuse Ike-Earp and McLaury-Earp tensions while also offering some diversion to a fellow lawman who'd just suffered professional humiliation when prisoners escaped his jail.

It fits what we know about Virgil. The same goes for whether Ike or Doc and Morgan were responsible for the confrontation in the Alhambra lunch room. All three were hot-heads and they all clearly were contributors. Wyatt should have known better than to ask Doc to *talk* to Ike. Any interaction between those two was not going to end well.

Ike had returned to Tombstone: Marks, p. 194; Gatto, *The Real Wyatt Earp,* p. 99.

Both men were armed: On October 26, Ike's pistol and rifle and Tom's pistol figured in the events of the day. Ike Clanton testified at the Spicer hearing that Tom had a rifle, too.

Tom had a little extra protection: Bailey, *Too Tough To Die,* p. 132; Marks, pp. 235–36.

They stabled their team of horses: Lubet, p. 50; Alexander, *John H. Behan,* p. 113.

They obeyed town Ordinance Number Nine: There is some question regarding when Ike Clanton reclaimed his weapons. At the coroner's inquest immediately following the gunfight, Ike testified that he retrieved his pistol after confronting Doc Holliday in the Alhambra lunch room on the night of Tuesday, October 25. According to Ike, he was armed for the rest of the night.

Wyatt Earp testified during the Spicer hearing in November that, when Ike stalked him in the Tombstone streets following the lunch room squabble, he had "his six-shooter in plain sight." This would mean Ike was also openly armed during his marathon poker game with Virgil Earp. Virgil was town police chief, and on the night of October 25 Wyatt still retained the authority of a special deputy. Neither arrested Ike for violating Ordinance Number Nine.

About noon on October 26 Virgil Earp pistol-whipped and arrested Ike Clanton, who was publicly drunk and making threats against the Earps and Doc Holliday — the same situation as the previous night. The difference was that Ike was now armed with his pistol and Winchester rifle. It was one thing for him to spew alcoholic threats of violence, and very much another for Ike to do so with weapons in hand. For that reason, I don't believe Ike got his pistol and rifle back until after the all-night poker game. Either Virgil or Wyatt would have arrested him the moment that they saw that he was armed.

It's legitimate to ask why, then, both Ike and Wyatt would testify that Ike had his pistol on the night of October 25. It's one of the few things they agreed on regarding the events leading up to the gunfight. My interpretation is this: At the coroner's inquest, Ike Clanton wanted to make a case that the Earps and Doc Holliday were actively seeking an armed confrontation.

He testified that he defied a well-known city ordinance to arm himself in order to demonstrate just how certain he was that he might have to defend himself against the gun-toting Earps and Doc. It was a lie, and not the only one Ike told under oath that day.

In preparing their defense at the Spicer hearing, Wyatt Earp and his defense attorney, Tom Fitch, would have carefully studied Ike's testimony at the inquest. Seeing Ike's foolish claim that he'd retrieved his gun after the incident at the Alhambra, they seized upon it to demonstrate just how seriously the Earps had to take Ike's drunken promises to shoot them in the morning. Wyatt didn't see Ike Clanton with a gun "in plain sight" when Ike followed him into the Alhambra because Ike didn't have one. Wyatt could testify that he did because Ike said so earlier while he was under oath at the inquest.

Ike and Tom may have left their rifles: Gary L. Roberts interview via e-mail. The possibility that Ike and Tom checked their rifles at the West End Corral and their handguns at the Grand Hotel lends itself to how Tom McLaury briefly armed himself with his pistol on October 26. I had not considered this until Gary Roberts suggested it to me, and the more I considered it, the more sense it made. I can't say this is definitely what they did, but I believe it to be true.

Tom put off transacting his business: I base this on the amount of money found on Tom's body the next day. If he'd already bought supplies it's unlikely he would still have had almost $3,000.

Sometime around midnight, Ike drifted into: Turner, *The O.K. Corral Inquest,* p. 32; Marks, pp. 194–96; Lubet, pp. 45–46. There is disagreement about whether Ike or Doc got to the lunch room first. Ike makes the most sense. If Doc had already been there when Ike arrived, Ike might very well have decided to eat somewhere else. Ike liked to make threats, but he was also a coward.

There was general agreement that Doc and Ike: Tefertiller, pp. 114–15; Marks, pp. 196–97.

Ike claimed that Doc: Turner, *The O.K. Corral Inquest,* pp. 97–98.

As was the case with many gamblers: Gary L. Roberts interview.

Wyatt's testimony provided: Turner, *The O.K. Corral Inquest,* pp. 159–60.

over whether Wyatt had told Doc: On the night of October 25, the plot was still not public knowledge. Both Ike and Wyatt testified about it at the Spicer hearing. We don't know, and can't be certain, whether Doc was told about the plan by Wyatt as Ike Clanton believed. I don't think Wyatt did.

Doc had a habit of talking too much, and if Wyatt really did want to keep his agreement with Ike secret, he would have realized that Doc shouldn't know about it.

Ike and Doc raised such a ruckus: Roberts, p. 184.

"fight no one if I could get away from it": Marks, p. 198; Tefertiller, p. 115. Truer words were never spoken, as Wells Fargo records supplied by Robert B. Chandler will prove in Chapter Sixteen.

he was a terrible card player: John Plesent Gray manuscript, University of Arizona Special Collections.

He had a new reason to be upset: Turner, *The O.K. Corral Inquest,* p. 98.

According to Virgil: Barra, pp. 164–66.

Virgil told him he was going to sleep: Turner, *The O.K. Corral Inquest,* pp. 191–92.

Ike Clanton routinely made threats: Lynn Bailey interview.

Had Virgil believed that Ike: Virgil Earp was an excellent lawman. He would not have avoided arresting someone he considered dangerous just because he was tired and wanted to go home to bed. Virgil really believed that Ike Clanton was a harmless blowhard. It was, in more than one way, a fatal error in judgment.

Above all else, this should be made clear: No one living knows exactly what happened during the fabled Tombstone gunfight on October 26, 1881, and probably those participants who survived it really didn't either. The best we can do is to piece together the most likely scenarios based on testimony by shootout survivors who made court statements (Virgil, Wyatt, and Ike) and witnesses, many of whom were demonstrably prejudiced in favor of one side or the other.

Beyond the books, magazine articles, and documents cited here, I based much of my interpretations on extended interviews — in person, by telephone, and through e-mail — with historian Jeff Morey. Devotees of Tombstone and frontier history argue about almost everything, but reach near-consensus on Morey being the best-informed scholar of the gunfight. I cannot stress enough his complete cooperation and amazing generosity in sharing with me all the details he has painstakingly researched for decades, as well as good-humoredly debating me when my conclusions sometimes didn't mesh with his. (One example: Morey tends to believe that Tom McLaury was armed during the shootout and I don't.) Ideally, researchers and writers should work together in a mutual effort to advance understanding of overall history and specific events, but instead there are all too often proprietary issues and resulting hard feelings. Morey has proven over and over that he is above that, and if he never writes a book of his own I hope he gains considerable satisfaction from knowing his excellent work is reflected in books by so many others, including this one.

Sharp-eyed readers will note that in this chapter I do not cite Billy Breakenridge's *Helldorado* or the Tombstone memoir of John Plesent Gray, even though both include descriptions of the gunfight. My reason is simple: They weren't there to see any of it. They base their first-person versions of this event completely on hearsay, much of it negative regarding the Earps.

In Tombstone, I twice walked through the bloody events of October 26, 1881, with the alternating help of two research assistants, Andrea Ahles Koos and Patrick Andro. Let the record show that ten-year-old Patrick was much more enthusiastic about pretending to be various dead bodies.

Ned Boyle completed an all-night bartending shift: Turner, *The O.K. Corral Inquest,* pp. 173–75.

he weaved his way to Kelly's Wine House: Ibid., p. 203.

At Hafford's Corner he repeated: Ibid., pp. 61–63.

With his usual sardonic humor: Documents,

Mulkins Collection.

He didn't hurry out to find him: Roberts, p. 190.

Just the day before, he'd acquired a new coat: Shillingberg, "Wyatt Earp and the 'Buntline Special' Myth." According to his story notes, Shillingberg learned this from a conversation with now deceased Earp scholar-collector John Gilchriese. I am generally skeptical of secondhand information, but the practice of fitting an overcoat with a canvas gun pocket was not uncommon on the frontier. It would have made sense for Wyatt Earp to do so. Political backstabbing may have been beyond his ken, but he was the most pragmatic of street fighters.

Tombstone mayor John Clum: Clum manuscript, University of Arizona Special Collections.

Frontier justice traditionally upheld the right: Jeff Morey interview.

When the Earp brothers dragged Ike: There is some disagreement whether Ike first clashed with Morgan or with Wyatt while waiting for the judge to return to the courtroom. To me, the best description of this incident can be found in Paula Mitchell Marks's *And Die in the West.*

Tom McLaury's day was off to a bad start: Turner, *Inquest,* p. 75. Gary L. Roberts, Jeff Morey, and Pam Potter interviews. Where Tom checked his guns and when he reclaimed them is a topic of ongoing debate among Tombstone scholars. After listening to and reading all the different opinions, my own conclusion is this: Tom checked his rifle at the West End Corral and his pistol at the Grand Hotel. He retrieved his pistol before leaving the hotel on Wednesday morning and was, in fact, armed when he was buffaloed by Wyatt Earp outside recorder's court. Afterward Tom checked his pistol at the Capitol Saloon. Despite the persuasive arguments of several people whom I very much respect, I don't think Tom had a handgun during the gunfight.

The Earps may have considered the cowboys to be menaces: Cissy Stewart Lale and Bruce Dinges interviews.

When Ike was set free: Marks, p. 209; Turner, *The O.K. Corral Inquest,* p. 114.

It hadn't been necessary for him: Pam Potter interview.

he couldn't leave the impression: Paul Hutton and Cissy Stewart Lale interviews.

It was a significant weapon: Jeff Morey interview.

Frank, Ike, and Billy left Spangenberg's and met Tom: Afterward, Wyatt insisted that Tom was also in the gun shop, but timing clearly proves he could not have been. Wyatt placed him there to support his assertion that all four cowboys were preparing for a showdown by purchasing ammunition.

This was bad news for Virgil: Jeff Morey interview. James Earp later said that pressure from leading town citizens really was the basis for the gunfight.

The O.K. Corral wasn't the cowboys' final destination: Marks, pp. 211–12. R. F. Coleman would later testify that Billy Clanton asked him for directions to the West End Corral.

In the worst tradition of overweening male pride: Anne E. Collier, Pam Potter, and Cissy Stewart Lale interviews.

Among the gawkers outside the corral: Jane Matson Lee and Mark Dworkin, "H. F. Sills: Mystery Man of the O.K. Corral Shootout," *Western Outlaw-Lawman History Association (WOLA) Journal* 12, no. 4 (Spring 2004). This seminal work by Lee and Dworkin provides the basis for pretty much all any of us know about Sills. Titles often exaggerate, but in this case "Mystery Man" is absolutely appropriate.

the McLaury brothers stopped outside the market: Jeff Morey correctly points out that there is an excellent chance Tom was not part of this conversation at all.

The four stopped to wait for Frank: Traditional gunfight lore has the cowboys loitering near Fly's so they can kill Doc when he returns to the boardinghouse. I disagree. They were on their way to the West End Corral and paused in the vacant lot while Frank had his conversation with James Kehoe.

That suited Johnny's purposes even better: Behan biographer Bob Alexander captured it perfectly in a conversation with me at the Wild West History Association annual meeting in the summer of 2010: "Johnny was like everybody else out there. He was constantly trying to get himself ahead in every situation."

Virgil could trust them to support him: Bruce Dinges interview.

Virgil must have recognized the risk: Jeff Morey interview; Jeff Morey, " 'Blaze Away': Doc Holliday's Role in the West's Most Famous Gunfight," *B.J.'s Tombstone History Forum,* disc.yourwebapps.com/Indices/39627.htmil. I rarely recommend Internet discussion sites, but if you are at all interested in Tombstone history this one usually offers lively, informed discussion by participants such as Jeff Morey, Gary L. Roberts, Anne E. Collier, Tom Gaumer, and Paul Cool — they don't come any more expert than that bunch.

Tom McLaury pulled open his coat: Some observers said Tom was wearing a vest rather than a coat. It's possible. His shirt was certainly untucked, probably because he'd been taking off and putting back on his money belt so often that afternoon.

She knew the Earps by sight: Turner, *The O.K. Corral Inquest,* p. 66. I believe at least some of the conflicting testimony in the subsequent Spicer hearing was caused not by intent to lie, but by some observers not being able to tell the Earp brothers apart. Virgil, Wyatt, and Morgan all looked very much alike and things were happening fast. It would have been easy for onlookers to become confused concerning who was doing what.

Billy Claiborne and Billy Clanton stood deepest: Jeff Morey interview. Nobody alive knows more about participant positioning during the gunfight than Morey.

Johnny broke ahead of them: Jeff Morey interview. Afterward it was understandable that Johnny, among others, had sketchy and occasionally contradictory memories of when and where he ran as well as the order of events during the gunfight. Bullets were flying everywhere.

even as he uttered the first two words: My interpretation of the gunfight is based on interviews, reading of books, articles, and court transcripts, and, in the words of the late historian Stephen Ambrose, "walking the battleground." Surviving participants left conflicting testimony, so we're left with informed modern-day conjecture as the best option. In writing this scene I relied on interviews with Jeff Morey, Michael Johnson, and Gary L. Roberts; Marks, pp. 219–36; Tefertiller, p. 157; Barra, pp. 174–

75, 180–82; Roberts, p. 221; Lubet, pp. 154–55; Turner, *The O.K. Corral Inquest,* pp. 155–71; Gatto, *The Real Wyatt Earp,* p. 102; documents from the Ragsdale Collection, the Lake Collection at the Huntington Library, and the Clum manuscript from the University of Arizona Special Collections; Casey Tefertiller, "O.K. Corral: A Gunfight Shrouded in Mystery," *Wild West,* October 2001; and Jeff Morey, " 'Blaze Away!' " *Wild West,* October 2001.

It was a prearranged signal: Tefertiller, *Wyatt Earp,* p. 124.

Keefe and Billy Allen carried Tom: Barra, pp. 181–82.

With all three cowboys lying dead: Marks, pp. 235–36.

As soon as the wagon rolled away: Ibid., pp. 238–39.

Johnny Behan went to Virgil's house: Barra, pp. 182–83; Turner, *The O.K. Corral Inquest,* p. 151.

The Earps' confidence that they would bask: Marks, pp. 254–55; Roberts, p. 202; Tefertiller, *Wyatt Earp,* p. 126; Barra, pp. 186–87.

The turnout signaled that public opinion: Brown, p. 43.

Chapter Fourteen: The Inquest and the Hearing

Entire books have been written about the inquest and the Spicer hearing. I relied on and recommend Steven Lubet's *Murder in Tombstone* and Alford E. Turner's *The O.K. Corral Inquest,* though Turner gets witnesses out of order. As I was writing this book the original handwritten inquest and hearing transcripts were discovered in Cochise County. They are now available to be viewed online at http://azmemorylib.az.us/cdm4/browse.php?CISOROOT=/ccolch.

The intricacies of the hearing procedures and witness testimonies are condensed to the essentials in this chapter. Controversies continue, and I expect they always will. For instance, Addie Borland's testimony about Doc wielding a "bronze-colored gun" and whether certain witnesses were actually in position to see what they claimed provide ongoing arguments for Earpophiles who love to debate every detail. That's part of the fun of history — there's always something more to figure out.

In trying to understand all the territorial legalities, I relied on the expertise of Bob Palmquist, a Tucson lawyer-historian with a knack for untangling complex courtroom issues so the rest of us can understand them. *Two days before, Johnny Behan had told:*

Marks, pp. 257–58; Turner, *The O.K. Corral Inquest,* pp. 25–36.

Billy Claiborne, who had originally joined: Lubet, pp. 62–63.

Ike Clanton, sober and grim-faced: Turner, *The O.K. Corral Inquest,* pp. 33–35.

ultimately Spicer — not a jury — would decide: Bob Palmquist and Lynn Bailey interviews. It was suggested then and is still suspected by some historians that Spicer planned to find in favor of the Earps all along, and that Ike erred in swearing out his complaint with Spicer (he could have gone through another Tombstone justice of the peace — there were as many as three according to Bob Palmquist). But Spicer was the jurist who in September had dismissed stage theft charges against Frank Stilwell and Pete Spencer, citing lack of evidence. There is no proof that Spicer ever let his personal politics influence his decisions on the bench.

Lynn Bailey believes that the case went to Spicer's court because in addition to being a justice of the peace Spicer was also a U.S. commissioner, and since Virgil Earp was a deputy U.S. marshal anything involving him fell under Spicer's jurisdiction.

the Tombstone city council met: Tefertiller, p. 129; Gatto, *The Real Wyatt Earp,* p. 104.

On the frontier, courts convened: Lubet, p. 74.

The opposition had its own problem: Ibid., pp. 69, 83; Tefertiller, p. 131; Alexander, *John H. Behan: Sacrificed Sheriff,* p. 125.

the prosecution's strategy became clear: Steven Lubet makes this point frequently in *Murder in Tombstone,* and I think he's right.

how was it possible for him to wield: Jeff Morey interview.

Will took charge: Pam Potter interview. The moment Will McLaury was allowed to join the prosecution, the tenor of the hearing changed completely.

Will was pleased with himself: McLaury letters, New-York Historical Society.

a horrifying new detail: Turner, *The O.K. Corral Inquest,* pp. 76–87; Lubet, pp. 114–15.

Will McLaury called Ike Clanton: The original hearing transcripts don't indicate which lawyers questioned which witnesses. I'm certain Will McLaury did most of the examinations and cross-examinations for the prosecution once he became part of the team, just as Tom Fitch handled witnesses for the defense.

Will admitted in a November 8 letter: McLaury letters, New-York Historical Society.

Ike's testimony extended: Turner, *The O.K. Corral Inquest,* pp. 91–120; Marks, pp. 271–74; Barra, pp. 201–3.

Ike clearly needed a recess: Casey Tefertiller believes that during this two-day break Ike's headache may have been treated with cocaine, a frequent frontier headache remedy. This might be why Ike's subsequent testimony was so foolish and out of control. Still, Will McLaury must have encouraged him.

Johnny accompanied him to L. M. Jacobs Mercantile: Documents, University of Arizona Special Collections; Tefertiller, p. 141. Ike paid back this loan on November 25.

Fitch, Drum, and their clients: Lubet, pp. 135–36.

Arizona territorial law allowed: Bob Palmquist interview; Barra, p. 229; Tefertiller, p. 142.

Wyatt then provided a brief account: The defense entered into evidence affidavits from city officials in Dodge City and Wichita praising Wyatt for his services as a lawman.

He wrote to his sister: McLaury letters, New-York Historical Society.

Doc had an additional aggravation: Documents, Mulkins Collection.

H. F. Sills was the perfect witness: Jeff Morey, Mark Dworkin, and Casey Tefertiller interviews. No aspect of the Spicer hearing continues to be more controversial than the testimony of H. F. Sills. He's a mystery man in history; besides his brief time in Tombstone, researchers haven't been able to find much else out about him, though Jane Matson Lee and Mark Dworkin have at least established some strong possibilities in a Spring 2004 article in the *WOLA History Journal.* Anti-Earpists argue that Sills must have been hired by the defense to testify as a supposedly neutral observer of the gunfight, and it could be true — but, as Jeff Morey noted to me, no one has been able to find any proof of that, either.

My best guess is that Sills was, in fact, a stranger passing through town who saw the gunfight, and afterward was recruited and coached by Tom Fitch so that his description of it on the stand exactly matched Wyatt's.

Fitch felt so confident: Chafin/Parsons, p. 153.

on November 30 he called the hearing to order: Marks, pp. 292–95, Lubet, pp. 184–202, Turner, *The O.K. Corral Inquest,* pp. 220–23.

the Cochise County grand jury voted: Despite fears that the grand jury would be stacked with cowboy sympathizers, its makeup turned out to be ideal for the Earps and Doc. Members included former Tombstone mayor William Harwood, saloon-keeper-gambler Sylvester Comstock, and Marshall Williams, head of the Wells Fargo office in Tombstone.

everyone in Tombstone already knew: Lubet,
p. 204.

The cowboy faction accepted: Gatto, *Johnny
Ringo,* p. 97.

Eight names were mentioned: Clum manuscript, University of Arizona Special Collections; Lubet, pp. 205–7; Shillingberg,
Tombstone, A.T., p. 286.

In the time-honored tradition: Cissy Stewart
Lale and Archie McDonald interviews.

they were taken off-guard: Tefertiller, pp. 155–
59; Shillingberg, *Tombstone, A.T.,* p. 285;
Barra, p. 214; Gatto, *The Real Wyatt Earp,*
p. 136; Marks, p. 390; Brown, p. 49.

Even their crusty father, Nicholas: Shillingberg,
Tombstone, A.T., p. 294.

*Clum and a handful of other prominent town
leaders:* Ibid., p. 290.

He left town on the stage: Clum manuscript;
Lubet, p. 205; Shillingberg, *Tombstone, A.T.,*
pp. 285–86.

The Clum incident triggered: Gatto, *The Real
Wyatt Earp,* p. 138; Marks, p. 317; Tefertiller, p. 167.

On December 18, the Epitaph *reprinted:* Tefertiller, p. 170; Marks, pp. 312–13.

But Virgil, Wyatt, and Morgan moved: Marks,
p. 316; Tefertiller, pp. 163, 173.

As Christmas approached: Faulk, pp. 116–17;

Chafin/Parsons, p. 162; Marks, p. 316.

Just before midnight on December 28: Marks, pp. 318–19; Tefertiller, pp. 174–76; Gatto, *The Real Wyatt Earp,* pp. 129–40; Parsons, pp. 198–99; Cissy Stewart Lale and Pam Potter interviews. There is some disagreement whether this occurred just before or after midnight.

He even gave up his lucrative interest: Barra, p. 239; Shillingberg, *Tombstone, A.T.,* p. 297.

Fueled by heated editorials: Lubet, p. 208; Shillingberg, *Tombstone, A.T.,* pp. 290–91; Tefertiller, p. 178.

the stage from Tombstone was robbed: Roberts, p. 235; Robert J. Chandler interview; Marks, pp. 324–27; Barra, pp. 240–41; Shillingberg, *Tombstone, A.T.,* p. 303; Tefertiller, p. 183.

Curly Bill Brocius ended up with the stolen weapon: Gatto, *Curly Bill,* p. 130. This apparently was one of Wyatt's embellishments; on March 14, just over two months after the stage robbery but before the Vendetta Ride, the *Nugget* reported that Bartholomew's shotgun had been recovered from a Mexican who claimed his cousin found it near the robbery site.

there was another near-bloodbath: Roberts, pp. 236–38; Tefertiller, p. 184; Marks, pp. 327–28.

After using some of the Wells Fargo loan: Shillingberg, *Tombstone, A.T.,* p. 303. Bob

653

Chandler does not believe Wells Fargo would have made this loan to Dake, or later sent $1,000 in cash to Wyatt, because it wasn't ordinary company policy. With all respect to him, I disagree. Above all else, Wells Fargo was pragmatic. If their best means of avoiding future Cochise County robberies was to send a few thousand dollars to fund Wyatt's pursuit of the cowboys that company officials believed were masterminding and carrying out the thefts — Curly Bill and Frank Stilwell above all others — then the unique loan and payout would make sense from the Wells Fargo perspective.

Wyatt and his men finally rode out of Tombstone: Marks, pp. 331–33, Tefertiller, pp. 187–90, Gatto, *The Real Wyatt Earp,* pp. 149–51. Pete Spencer volunteered to bring the Bartholomew posse to the Clantons so Ike and Phin could give themselves up. It's another example of how the cowboy network operated against the Earps.

Crawley Dake was summoned to Tombstone: Bailey, *Too Tough to Die,* p. 139; Tefertiller, pp. 189–90; Shillingberg, *Tombstone, A.T.,* pp. 302–3; Barra, pp. 243, 246.

Ike Clanton appeared for his hearing: Gatto, *The Real Wyatt Earp,* pp. 160–61; Lubet, p. 209; Tefertiller, p. 191; Shillingberg, *Tombstone, A.T.,* p. 301.

Briefly, Wyatt tried: Barra, p. 244. There was

another important event on February 3, the day after the *Nugget* published this story; the paper was sold to a Prescott investor who replaced Harry Woods as editor with a more experienced, objective journalist. The *Nugget* immediately toned down its one-sided Tombstone news coverage, but the damage had already been done to the Earps.

Marshall Williams skipped town: Robert C. Chandler interview.

Frederick Tritle was sworn in: Bailey, *Too Tough to Die,* p. 146; Tefertiller, p. 197.

Ike Clanton made a second attempt: Lubet, pp. 210–11; Bailey/Parsons, p. 206; Marks, p. 336; Tefertiller, pp. 196–97; Barra, p. 246.

Morgan Earp's young wife, Louisa: Tefertiller, p. 198.

Wells Spicer had issued arrest warrants: Gatto, *The Real Wyatt Earp,* p. 163; Tefertiller, pp. 198–99.

Their absence gave Tombstone: Chafin/Parsons, p. 18; Brown, pp. 52–53; Bailey, *Too Tough to Die,* pp. 114–15; Bailey/Parsons, p. 210.

Wyatt encountered lawyer Briggs Goodrich: Lubet, p. 211; Shillingberg, *Tombstone, A.T.,* p. 307.

But Morgan wanted a few hours: Ray Madzia interview; Marks, pp. 339–40.

Dr. Henry Matthews convened: Lubet, p. 213; Bailey, *Too Tough to Die,* p. 140.

Chapter Sixteen: The Vendetta Ride

Wyatt Earp marked his thirty-fourth birthday: Shillingberg, *Tombstone, A.T.,* p. 311. Some historians place James Earp in Tucson on March 20 returning to Colton with Morgan and Allie.

Wyatt originally intended that he and his men: Lubet, p. 212; Chaput, *Virgil Earp: Western Peace Officer,* pp. 240–41.

Frank Stilwell had been in Tucson: Kevin J. Mulkins interview; Breakenridge, pp. 286–87; Lubet, p. 213; Shillingberg, *Tombstone, A.T.,* p. 312; Roberts, p. 246; Chaput, *Virgil Earp: Western Peace Officer,* p. 154.

Shortly after seven the Earp party: Jeff Morey interview; Marks, pp. 343–48; Tefertiller, pp. 226–29; Shillingberg, *Tombstone, A.T.,* p. 313; Chaput, *Virgil Earp: Western Peace Officer,* pp. 240–41; Parsons, p. 212.

Wyatt and his men walked eight miles: Shillingberg, Tombstone, *A.T.,* pp. 313–14.

The town was outraged by the shooting: Roberts, p. 247.

At this point, Johnny Behan must have detested Wyatt Earp: Jeff Morey interview; Lubet, p. 214; Marks, pp. 349–50; Tefertiller, pp. 232–33.

But in the wake of his latest public humiliation: Lubet, p. 215; Marks, p. 354; Barra, pp. 259–60; Shillingberg, *Tombstone, A.T.,* p. 317.

Florentino Cruz, suspected by them: Shillingberg, *Tombstone, A.T.,* pp. 315–16; Marks, pp. 352–54. It is far from certain that Florentino Cruz was "Indian Charlie."

Wyatt later claimed: Jeff Morey interview; Barra, p. 256.

Killing Cruz inarguably put Wyatt Earp: Allen Barra interview; Barra, p. 258.

Dan Tipton and Charlie Smith rode back into Tombstone: Parsons, p. 213; Shillingberg, *Tombstone, A.T.,* pp. 316–17; Marks, p. 355.

But not all the press was antagonistic: Robert J. Chandler interview; Roberts, pp. 262–63; Tefertiller, p. 235.

Johnny Behan's posse grew: Bailey, *Too Tough to Die,* p. 141; Shillingberg, *Tombstone, A.T.,* p. 317.

another even more dubious posse: Tefertiller, p. 238.

he instructed them to meet him at some springs: The site of the Wyatt–Curly Bill throwdown is almost as controversial as whether or not Curly Bill died that day. The location has variously been identified as Burleigh, Iron Springs, Mescal Springs, and Cottonwood Springs. Earp enthusiasts roam these spots and debate what happened where. To save pages of detailed and ultimately futile speculation, in this chapter I simply identify the general area.

Wyatt always insisted: Documents, Lake Collection, Huntington Library; Flood manuscript notes, Ragsdale Collection; Paul Hutton, Tom Gaumer, and Jeff Morey interviews; Lubet, pp. 215–16; Marks, pp. 358–60; Tefertiller, pp. 237–41; Barra, pp. 260–68; Shillingberg, *Tombstone, A.T.,* pp. 317–18.

On the same day as the battle: Shillingberg, *Tombstone, A.T.,* p. 318.

Henry Clay Hooker was a colossus: Lynn Bailey and Scott Dyke interviews; Marks, pp. 367–68.

Wyatt was gratified: Tefertiller, pp. 244–45.

the Behan posse clattered into the Sierra Bonita compound: Barra, p. 270; Marks, pp. 369–72; Shillingberg, *Tombstone, A.T.,* p. 319.

On the same day that Johnny's posse straggled back: Bailey/Parsons, p. 216.

financial considerations dictated: Bob Chandler, Cissy Stewart Lale, and Jeff Morey interviews; Chandler unpublished full manuscript informally labeled "Wyatt Earp/Cashbook"; Tefertiller, pp. 244–45. Bob Chandler does not believe Wells Fargo would send Wyatt Earp $1,000 in cash because that was not typical of the company. I very much respect Bob, but in this case I disagree with him. Wells Fargo was always willing to pay to see stage robbers eliminated, and throughout the Vendetta Ride company officials made other exceptions for Wyatt, particularly in granting an interview on his behalf to a major news-paper.

Bob submitted a long article about the Wells Fargo ledger notations regarding "Stilwell & Curly Bill" to *True West* magazine, which chose to print an extremely truncated version. As one of his many contributions to this book, Bob sent me the story as he had originally written it, and much of the information is used in this chapter.

The decision may have been made easier: Roberts, p. 264; Tefertiller, p. 247.

Wyatt made a quick trip: Barra, pp. 271–73.

with help from Wells Fargo: Roberts, pp. 268–69.

the party split up: Marks, p. 379.

Tritle had no such intention: Ibid., pp. 376–77.

authorities in Arizona hadn't forgotten him: Paul Hutton interview; Marks, pp. 379–80; Roberts, p. 267; Tefertiller, p. 247.

leaders had other matters requiring their full attention: Bailey, *Too Tough to Die,* pp. 146–48; Marks, pp. 390–91.

Wyatt's immediate legacy was limited: Michael Johnson and Lynn Bailey interviews.

Wyatt was slow to realize: Tefertiller, p. 262.

he never returned to Tombstone: Mark Dworkin interview. Wyatt did come back to Arizona Territory on several occasions, but not to the dying town where he had been the center of so much controversy. In *Tomb-*

stone, A.T., William Shillingberg writes that
Wyatt made a late-life visit to Tombstone
with John Flood. While it's possible, in an
April 10, 1928, letter to Billy Breakenridge,
Wyatt wrote that he'd had "in his mind" a
visit to Tombstone, but poor health
wouldn't permit it. Since he died the following January, that wouldn't leave much
of a travel window for a very sick elderly
man.

CHAPTER SEVENTEEN: LEGENDS

Tombstone's decline was precipitous: Marks,
pp. 398–401; Carl Chafin, ed., *The Private
Journal of George Whitwell Parsons: The
Tombstone Years,* Vol. II: *Post-Earp Era*
(Cochise Classics, 1997), pp. 64-69; Bailey,
Too Tough to Die, p. 117.

Clara concluded by informing her readers:
Brown, pp. 73–76.

John Clum sold the Epitaph: Clum manuscript, University of Arizona Special Collections.

George Parsons remained: Lynn R. Bailey and
Don Chaput, *Cochise County Stalwarts: A
Who's Who of the Territorial Years,* Vol. I
(Westernlore Press, 2008), pp. 67–70.

Wells Spicer turned his attention: Ibid., Vol. II,
pp. 128–36.

Johnny Behan's once promising political career:
Marks, p. 400; Alexander, *John H. Behan,*

pp. 205–6; Bailey and Chaput, *Cochise County Stalwarts,* Vol. I, pp. 20–23.

By the middle of July 1882 John Ringo: Burrows, p. 178, p. 197; Breakenridge, p. 313; Marks, pp. 391–98; Jeff Morey interview.

Ike and Phin Clanton moved two hundred miles north: Traywick, *The Clantons of Tombstone,* pp. 129, 133; Bailey and Chaput, *Cochise County Stalwarts,* Vol. I, pp. 63–64.

But rustlers continued to plague: Lynn Bailey interview.

Doc Holliday had been controversial: Marks, pp. 406–7; Roberts, pp. 350–51, 354–55, 360, 362–72; Cason manuscript, Ford County Historical Society.

Warren Earp, the youngest and wildest: Tefertiller, pp. 307–8; Shillingberg, *Tombstone, A.T.,* p. 357; Marks, p. 421.

Virgil Earp was already crippled: Chaput, *Virgil Earp, Western Peace Officer,* p. 160; Shillingberg, *Tombstone, A.T.,* pp. 355–56; Chafin/Parsons, Vol. II, p. 415; Barra, p. 336; Marks, p. 416.

Virgil was thrilled to learn: There remains a reasonable possibility that Virgil did know he had a daughter at the time he returned from the Civil War to find his first wife gone. But he may not have felt parenthood to be an issue of great importance until, in his middle age, he had a chance to reunite with her.

Mattie Blaylock Earp wanted: Anne E. Collier and Cissy Stewart Lale interviews; Marks, p. 410; Tefertiller, pp. 232, 280.

His celebrity status guaranteed: Tefertiller, p. 282.

For a few months they stopped in Yuma: Mark Dworkin, "Wyatt Earp's 1897 Yuma and Cibola Sojourns," *Western Outlaw-Lawman History Association (WOLA) Journal* 14, no. 1 (Spring 2005).

Wyatt was one of four connivers: Barra, pp. 338–40.

Wyatt pinned his last hopes: Anne E. Collier interview.

As early as 1900: Clum manuscript, University of Arizona Special Collections.

Americans wanted to believe: Warren, p. 177.

The final straw was probably: Bailey, *Too Tough to Die,* p. 282.

Flood began interviewing Wyatt: Flood notes, Ragsdale Collection.

Wyatt wrote Hart with a suggestion: Documents, Arizona Historical Society.

Hart counseled Wyatt: Ibid.

Stuart Lake was a colorful character: Tefertiller, pp. 325–28; Hutton, "Showdown at the Hollywood Corral"; Documents, Lake Collection, Huntington Library.

Stuart Lake knew: Documents, Lake Collection, Huntington Library.

as the squabbling between Lake and Josephine

continued: Tefertiller, p. 330.

The book initially sold: Ibid., p. 332.

Lake began shopping film rights: Hutton, "Showdown at the Hollywood Corral."

Nineteen twenty-nine should have marked: Bailey, *Too Tough to Die,* pp. 292–94; Marks, pp. 422–23.

But Josephine Earp's later years: Cason manuscript, Ford County Historical Society; Ann Kirschner interview; Barra, p. 385.

The initial films set in Tombstone: Hutton, "Showdown at the Hollywood Corral."

In the process of whitewashing Wyatt: Jim Turner and Bruce Dinges interviews; Barra, p. 399.

But Stuart Lake, serving as a consultant: Hutton, "Showdown at the Hollywood Corral."

A few debunkers have argued: The most effective may have been respected Western historian/novelist Frank Waters, who in 1960 published *The Earp Brothers of Tombstone: The Story of Mrs. Virgil Earp.* Waters and Allie had collaborated on a book prior to her death in 1947, but Allie didn't like the result. Thirteen years later, Waters went forward with the project, which referred to Lake's *Wyatt Earp: Frontier Marshal* as an "assiduously concocted blood-and-thunder piece of fiction" and, often based on supposed testimony from Allie, depicted Wyatt as an amoral con man and philanderer. Allie Earp did not care for her brother-in-law, and doubtless had hard things to say about him to Waters. But Allie's refusal to allow publication seems to be solid evidence that book should not and could not be used by me as source material. Stuart Lake wasn't objective about Wyatt, either, but at least he had firsthand dealings with him in writing *Frontier Marshal.*

BIBLIOGRAPHY

CITED INTERVIEWS

Bob Alexander is a retired Texas lawman who has written numerous books about the American West, including a biography of Cochise County sheriff Johnny Behan.

Art Austin is the former manager of the Tombstone Courthouse State Historic Park.

Lynn R. Bailey is the author of numerous books about the history of southeast Arizona.

Allen Barra is the author of *Inventing Wyatt Earp: His Life and Many Legends*.

Bob Boze Bell is executive editor of *True West* magazine and the author of several books about Tombstone and Arizona history.

Glenn G. Boyer is an author whose collection of Earp-related memorabilia includes the original Cason manuscript.

Dr. Robert J. Chandler recently retired as

senior research historian for Wells Fargo Bank.

Jane Candia Coleman is a prolific author-historian whose best-known novel may be *Doc Holliday's Woman.*

Anne E. Collier is a researcher-writer in California who focuses on frontier history.

Paul Cool is the author of *Salt Warriors: Insurgency on the Rio Grande* and numerous articles about the American West.

Bruce Dinges is director of publications for the Arizona Historical Society.

Mark Dworkin is an author-historian who specializes in the study of the American West.

Scott Dyke is a historian-researcher who focuses on Tombstone and Wyatt Earp.

Michelle Emke is the local history librarian for the Wichita Public Library.

Tom Gaumer is a historian-researcher based in Tucson. Keep laughing.

Paul Hutton is a professor of history at the University of New Mexico in Albuquerque and a frequent writer and television commentator on subjects involving frontier history.

Michael L. Johnson is a professor of English at the University of Kansas in Lawrence and the author of *Hunger for the Wild: America's Obsession with the Untamed West.*

Cissy Stewart Lale is a past president of

the Texas State Historical Association; her area of expertise is the lives of women on the American frontier.

George Laughead is president of the Ford County Historical Society in Dodge City, Kansas.

Ray Madzia is a Tombstone historian.

Paula Mitchell Marks is a professor of history at St. Edwards University in Austin and the author of *And Die in the West: The Story of the O.K. Corral Gunfight.*

Robert G. McCubbin is a historian, a collector of frontier memorabilia, and a founder of the Wild West History Association.

Archie McDonald is a past president of the Texas State Historical Association, a former history professor at Stephen F. Austin University, and the author of many articles and several books on Texas history.

Craig T. Miner is a professor of history at Wichita State University and the author of many books and articles about Kansas history.

Jeff Morey is an author-historian who is widely acknowledged as *the* expert on the gunfight at the O.K. Corral.

Kevin J. and Bev Mulkins are historians who also own a collection of key Tombstone and Earp memorabilia.

Frederick Nolan is a British historian whose books include *The Lincoln County War: A*

Documentary History.

Bob Palmquist is a Tucson attorney and expert in frontier law.

Pam Potter is a McLaury family descendant, a researcher-writer, and current president of the Wild West History Association.

Ben Procter is a past president of the Texas State Historical Association and the author of several books on the history of the Texas Rangers.

Mark Ragsdale owns a large collection of Tombstone and Earp memorabilia.

Christine Rhodes is the longtime Cochise County recorder and a gifted researcher in her own right.

Gary L. Roberts is a professor emeritus at Abraham Baldwin College in Georgia and the author of *Doc Holliday: The Life and Legend.*

Lee Silva has written voluminous histories of Wyatt Earp. His interview was conducted by Andrea Ahles Koos.

Casey Tefertiller is the author of *Wyatt Earp: The Life Behind the Legend.*

Ben Traywick is historian emeritus of Tombstone and the author of innumerable books on town history.

Jim Turner is an author-lecturer who recently retired from the Arizona Historical Society.

Dave Webb is assistant director of the Kansas Heritage Center in Dodge City.

BOOKS

Alexander, Bob. *Desert Desperadoes: The Banditti of Southwestern New Mexico.* Gila Books, 2006.

————. *John H. Behan: Sacrificed Sheriff.* High-Lonesome Books, 2002.

————. *Lawmen, Outlaws, and S.O.B.s,* Vol. II. High-Lonesome Books, 2007.

————. *Winchester Warriors: Texas Rangers of Company D, 1874–1901.* University of North Texas Press, 2009.

Anderson, Oscar. *Refrigerated America: A History of a New Technology and Its Impact.* Princeton University Press, 1953.

Bailey, Lynn R. *Mines, Camps, Ranches, and Characters of the Dragoon Mountains.* Westernlore Press, 2008.

————. *The Life, Times and Writings of Wells W. Spicer.* Westernlore Press, 1999.

————. *"Too Tough to Die": The Rise, Fall, and Resurrection of a Silver Camp, 1878 to 1990.* Westernlore Press, 2004.

————. *The Valiants: The Tombstone Rangers and Apache War Frivolities.* Westernlore Press, 1999.

Bailey, Lynn R., and Don Chaput. *Cochise County Stalwarts: A Who's Who of the Territorial Years,* Vols. I–II. Westernlore

Press, 2000.

Ball, Larry D. *The United States Marshals of New Mexico and Arizona Territories: 1846–1912.* University of New Mexico Press, 1999.

Barkley, Roy R., and Mark E. Odintz, eds. *The Portable Handbook of Texas.* Texas State Historical Association, 2000.

Barra, Allen. *Inventing Wyatt Earp: His Life and Many Legends.* Carroll & Graf, 1998.

Bell, Bob Boze. *Classic Gunfights,* Vol. II: *The 25 Gunfights Behind the O.K. Corral.* Tri Star–Boze Publications, 2005.

Breakenridge, William M. *Helldorado: Bringing the Law to the Mesquite.* University of Nebraska Press, 1992; originally published 1928.

Brown, Clara Spalding. *Tombstone from a Woman's Point of View: The Correspondence of Clara Spalding Brown, July 7, 1880 to November 14, 1882.* Compiled and edited by Lynn R. Bailey. Westernlore Press, 2003.

Brown, Meredith Mason. *Frontiersman: Daniel Boone and the Making of America.* Louisiana State University Press, 2008.

Burns, Walter Noble. *Tombstone: An Iliad of the Southwest.* Grosset & Dunlap, 1927.

Burrows, Jack. *John Ringo: The Gunfighter Who Never Was.* University of Arizona Press, 1987.

Cataldo, Nicholas R. *The Earp Clan: The*

Southern California Years. Back Roads Press, 2006.

Chafin, Carl, ed. *The Private Journal of George Whitwell Parsons,* Vol. II: *Post-Earp Era.* Cochise Classics, 1997.

Chaput, Don. *"Buckskin Frank" Leslie.* Westernlore Press, 1999.

————. *The Earp Papers: In a Brother's Image.* Affiliated Writers of America, 1994.

————. *Virgil Earp: Western Peace Officer.* Affiliated Writers of America, 1994.

Clifford, Howard. *Wyatt Earp and Friends: Alaska Adventures.* Gorham Printing, 2000.

Conlin, Joseph R. *Bacon, Beans, and Galantines: Food and Foodways on the Western Mining Frontier.* University of Nevada Press, 1986.

Davis, William C. *Three Roads to the Alamo: The Lives and Fortunes of David Crockett, James Bowie and William Barret Travis.* HarperCollins, 1998.

DeArment, Robert K. *Bat Masterson: The Man and His Legend.* University of Oklahoma Press, 1979.

Devere, Burton Jr., *Bonanzas to Borrascas: The Mines of Tombstone, Arizona.* Rosetree Museum, 2010.

Devereaux, Jan. *Petticoats, Pistols and Poker: The Real Lottie Deno.* High-Lonesome Press, 2009.

Dolin, Eric Jay. *Fur, Fortune and Empire:*

The Epic History of the Fur Trade in America. W.W. Norton, 2010.

Dugger, Ronnie. *The Politician: The Life and Times of Lyndon Johnson.* W. W. Norton, 1982.

Eppinga, Jane. *Images of America: Tombstone.* Arcadia Publishing, 2003.

Erwin, Allen A. *The Southwest of John H. Slaughter, 1841–1922.* Arthur H. Clark Company, 1965.

Faulk, Odie B. *Tombstone: Myth and Reality.* Oxford University Press, 1972.

Garavaglia, Louis A. and Charles Worman. *Firearms of the American West, 1866–1894.* University Press of Colorado, 1997.

Gatto, Steve. *Curly Bill.* Protar House Books, 2003.

———. *Johnny Ringo.* Protar House Books, 2002.

———. *The Real Wyatt Earp: A Documentary Biography.* High-Lonesome Books, 2000.

Goodwyn, Lawrence. *Democratic Promise: The Populist Movement in America.* Oxford University Press, 1976.

Gray, John Plesent. *Tombstone's Violent Years, 1880–1882: As Remembered by John Plesent Gray.* Edited by Neil B. Carmony. Trail to Yesterday Books, 1999.

———. *When All Roads Led to Tombstone: A Memoir.* Edited and annotated by W. Lane Rogers. Tamarack Books, 1998.

Grimsted, David. *American Mobbing, 1828–1861: Toward Civil War.* Oxford University Press, 1998.

Hand, George. *Next Stop: Tombstone: George Hand's Contention City Diary, 1882.* Edited by Neil B. Carmony. Trail to Yesterday Books, 1995.

Howe, Hubert. *History of Arizona and New Mexico, 1530–1888.* Bancroft, Horn & Wallace, 1962.

Jent, Steven A. *A Browser's Book of Texas History.* Republic of Texas Press, 2000.

Johnson, Michael L. *Hunger for the Wild: America's Obsession with the Untamed West.* University Press of Kansas, 2007.

Lake, Stuart N. *Wyatt Earp: Frontier Marshal.* Houghton Mifflin, 1931.

Lubet, Steven. *Murder in Tombstone: The Forgotten Trial of Wyatt Earp.* Yale University Press, 2004.

Marks, Paula Mitchell. *And Die in the West: The Story of the O.K. Corral Gunfight.* William Morrow, 1989.

Martin, Douglas D. *Tombstone's Epitaph: The Truth About the Town Too Tough to Die.* University of New Mexico Press, 1951.

McCullough, David. *Mornings on Horseback: The Story of an Extraordinary Family, a Vanished Way of Life, and the Unique Child Who Became Theodore Roosevelt.* Simon & Schuster, 1981.

Miller, Nyle H., and Joseph W. Snell. *Why the West Was Wild: A Contemporary Look at the Antics of Some Highly Publicized Kansas Cowtown Personalities.* University of Oklahoma Press, 2003; originally published by the Kansas State Historical Society, 1963.

Miner, Craig T. *Wichita: The Early Years, 1865–80.* University of Nebraska Press, 1982.

— — — . *Wichita: The Magic City — An Illustrated History.* Wichita-Sedgwick County Historical Museum Association, 1988.

Monahan, Sherry. *Taste of Tombstone: A Hearty Helping of History.* Royal Spectrum, 1998.

Morris Jr., Roy. *Lighting Out for the Territory: How Samuel Clemens Became Mark Twain.* Simon & Schuster, 2010.

Parsons, George Whitwell. *A Tenderfoot in Tombstone: The Private Journal of George Whitwell Parsons — The Turbulent Years: 1880–82.* Edited by Lynn R. Bailey. Westernlore Press, 1996.

Rappleye, Charles. *Robert Morris: Financier of the American Revolution.* Simon & Schuster, 2010.

Rath, Ida Ellen. *The Rath Trail.* McCormick-Armstrong Company, 1961.

Reynolds, David S. *John Brown, Abolitionist: The Man Who Killed Slavery, Sparked the Civil War, and Seeded Civil Rights.* Alfred A.

Knopf, 2005.

Roberts, Gary L. *Doc Holliday: The Life and Legend.* Wiley & Sons, 2006.

Rosa, Joseph C. *Wild Bill Hickok: The Man and His Myth.* University Press of Kansas, 1996.

Schieffelin, Edward. *Destination Tombstone: Adventures of a Prospector.* Edited by Marilyn F. Butler. Royal Spectrum, 1996.

Shachtman, Tom. *Absolute Zero and the Conquest of Cold.* Houghton Mifflin, 1999.

Shelton, Richard. *Going Back to Bisbee.* University of Arizona Press, 1992.

Shillingberg, William B. *Dodge City: The Early Years, 1872–1886.* Arthur H. Clark Company/University of Oklahoma Press, 2009.

———. *Tombstone, A.T.: A History of Early Mining, Milling, and Mayhem.* Arthur H. Clark Company, 1999.

Slotkin, Richard. *Gunfighter Nation: The Myth of the Frontier in Twentieth-Century America.* Atheneum, 1992.

Smith, Hedrick. *The Power Game: How Washington Works.* Random House, 1988.

Sonnichsen, C. L. *I'll Die Before I Run: The Story of the Great Feuds of Texas.* Harper & Brothers, 1951.

Sosa, Nancy, and Jim Nelson. *Tombstone: A Quick History.* Blue Chicken Publishing, 2009.

Stone, Ron. *The Book of Texas Days.* Eakin Press, 1997.

Suagee, E. Kathy. *Around Benson.* Arcadia Publishing, 2009.

Tate, Michael L. *The Frontier Army Settlement of the West.* University of Oklahoma Press, 1999.

Taylor, Don. *The United States of America v. The "Cowboys."* Old West Research & Publishing, 2006.

Tefertiller, Casey. *Wyatt Earp: The Life Behind the Legend.* Wiley & Sons, 1997.

Traywick, Ben T. *The Clantons of Tombstone.* Red Marie's Books, 2006.

Traywick, Ben T., ed. *Death's Doings in Tombstone.* Red Marie's Books, 2002.

————. *Minute Book — Common Council, Village of Tombstone: September 10, 1880 thru January 16, 1882.* Self-published, 1999.

————. *Tombstone Paper Trails.* Red Marie's Books, 1999.

Trimble, Marshall. *Roadside History of Arizona.* Mountain Press Publishing, 1986.

Turner, Alford E., ed. *The Earps Talk.* Creative Publishing Company, 1980.

————. *The O.K. Corral Inquest.* Creative Publishing Company, 1981.

Utley, Robert M. *Lone Star Justice: The First Century of the Texas Rangers.* Oxford University Press, 2002.

————. *Lone Star Lawmen: The Second*

Century of the Texas Rangers. Oxford University Press, 2007.

Wagoner, Jay J. *Arizona Territory, 1863–1912: A Political History.* University of Arizona Press, 1970.

Warren, Louis S. *Buffalo Bill's America: William Cody and the Wild West Show.* Alfred A. Knopf, 2005.

Waters, Frank. *The Earp Brothers of Tombstone: The Story of Mrs. Virgil Earp.* University of Nebraska Press, 1976; first published 1960.

Weir, William. *Written with Lead: Legendary American Gunfights and Gunfighters.* Archon Books, 1992.

Wert, Jeffry. *Custer: The Controversial Life of George Armstrong Custer.* Simon & Schuster, 1996.

White, Richard. *"It's Your Misfortune and None of My Own": A New History of the American West.* University of Oklahoma Press, 1991.

Woodworth, Steven A. *Manifest Destinies: America's Westward Expansion and the Road to the Civil War.* Alfred A. Knopf, 2010.

Young, Frederic R. *Dodge City: Up Through a Century in Story and Pictures.* Boot Hill Museum, 1972.

Young, Frederic R. The Delectable Burg: An Irreverent History of Dodge City — 1872 to 1886. Boot Hill Museum/Kansas

Heritage Center, 2009.

Young, Roy B. *Cochise County Cowboy War: A Cast of Characters.* Young & Sons Enterprises, 1999.

MAGAZINES AND PUBLICATIONS
(INCLUDING ONLINE)

Bell, Bob Boze. "Shootout at Cottonwood Springs? Wyatt Earp vs. Curly Bill Brocius." *True West,* May 2009.

Britz, Kevin. "Boot Hill Burlesque." *Journal of Arizona History,* Autumn 2003.

———. "A True Life Reproduction: The Origins of Tombstone's Helldorado Celebration." *Journal of Arizona History,* Winter 2001.

Chandler, Robert J. "A Smoking Gun? Did Wells Fargo Pay Wyatt Earp to Kill Curly Bill and Frank Stilwell? New Evidence Seems to Indicate — Yes." *True West,* July 2001.

———. "Under Cover for Wells Fargo: A Review Essay." *Journal of Arizona History* 41 (Spring 2000).

"Wells Fargo and the Earp Brothers: The Cash Books Talk." *California Historical Quarterly,* Summer 2009.

———. "Wells Fargo Never Forgets." *California Historical Quarterly,* Summer 2009.

———. "Wells Fargo: 'We Never Forget!' " *Western Outlaw-Lawman History Association*

(WOLA) Journal 3, no. 3 (Winter 1987).

Collier, Anne E. "Harriet 'Hattie' Catchim: A Controversial Earp Family Member." *Western Outlaw-Lawman History Association (WOLA) Journal* 16, no. 2 (Summer 2007).

Conlin, Joseph. "Beans, Bacon and Galantine Truffles: The Food of the Western Miners." *Arizona and the West* 33 (Spring 1981).

Cool, Paul. "Bob Martin: A Rustler in Paradise." *WOLA Journal Online,* 2003.

DeArment, R. K. "Wyatt Whoppers." *Wild West History Association Journal,* October 2009.

Dworkin, Mark. "Wyatt Earp's 1897 Yuma and Cibola Sojourns: Wyatt Earp Returned to Arizona Numerous Times After 1882 Despite Stilwell and Cruz Murder Warrants." *Western Outlaw-Lawman History Association (WOLA) Journal* 14, no. 1 (Spring 2005).

Gatto, Steve. "Wyatt Earp Was a Pimp." *True West,* July 2003.

Hitt, Jack. "Big Brother at the O.K. Corral: A Frontier Fable of Gun Control and Federal Justice." *Harper's,* September 2002.

Hutton, Paul. "Showdown at the Hollywood Corral: Wyatt Earp and the Movies." *Montana: The Magazine of Western History,* Summer 1995.

Isenberg, Andrew C. "The Code of the West: Sexuality, Homosociality, and Wyatt

Earp." *Western Historical Quarterly,* Summer 2009.

Jay, Roger. "Wyatt Earp's Lost Year." *Wild West,* August 2003.

Johnson, David. "The Fifth Ace: H. F. Sills and His Testimony." *Quarterly of the National Association for Outlaw and Lawman History,* 31, no. 2 (2007).

Lee, Jane Matson, and Mark Dworkin. "H. F. Sills, Mystery Man of the O.K. Corral Shootout." *Western Outlaw-Lawman History Association (WOLA) Journal* 12, no. 4 (Spring 2004).

Morey, Jeff. " 'Blaze Away!' Doc Holliday's Role in the West's Most Famous Gunfight." *B.J.'s Tombstone History Forum.*

————. "Wyatt Earp's Buntline Special." *Guns & Ammo,* December 1997.

Raymond, H. H. "Diary of a Dodge City Buffalo Hunter." *Kansas Historical Quarterly,* Winter 1965.

Sanders, John R. "Faro: Favorite Gambling Game of the Frontier." *Wild West,* October 1996.

Shillingberg, William B. "Wyatt Earp and the 'Buntline Special' Myth." *Kansas Historical Quarterlies,* Summer 1976.

Steinfield, Joseph D. "After the Guns Stopped Blazing." *Legal Times,* January 2005.

St. Johns, Adela Rogers. "I Knew Wyatt

Earp." *American Weekly,* May 22, 1960.

Tefertiller, Casey, and Jeff Morey. "O.K. Corral: A Gunfight Shrouded in Mystery." *Wild West,* October 2001.

Traywick, Ben. "Tombstone's Cemetery: Boothill." *Wild West,* October 2006.

Wagoner, J. J. "History of the Cattle Industry in Southern Arizona, 1540–1940." *University of Arizona Social Science Bulletin,* No. 20, April 1952.

GOVERNMENT DOCUMENTS AND REPORTS

Tombstone Census 1879 (with notes by Ben Traywick)

MANUSCRIPTS AND COLLECTIONS

Various documents, Special Collections, University of Arizona.

Various documents, Glenn Boyer Collection, Tucson, Arizona.

Cason manuscript (original), Special Collections, Ford County Historical Society. Made available by permission of Glenn Boyer.

John Clum manuscript, Special Collections, University of Arizona.

Various documents, Scott Dyke Collection.

Louisa Houston Earp letters (original), Special Collections, Ford County Historical Society. Made available by permission of Glenn Boyer.

Drafts of the John Flood manuscript and various documents, Ragsdale Collection, Shrewsbury, Massachusetts.

Letters from the collection of Tom Gaumer, Tucson, Arizona.

John Plesent Gray manuscript, Special Collections, University of Arizona.

Letters and documents from the Kansas Heritage Center, Dodge City, Kansas.

Various documents, Stuart N. Lake Collection, Huntington Library, San Marino, California.

Will McLaury letters, New-York Historical Society.

Various documents, Kevin J. and Bev Mulkins Collection, Tucson, Arizona.

Various documents, Special Collections, University of Oklahoma.

"The Private Journal of George Whitwell Parsons, January 1, 1880–June 28, 1882." Edited by Carl Chafin. Made available from the private collection of Christine Rhodes.

Various Documents, Texas Rangers Hall of Fame, Waco.

PAPERS, PRESENTATIONS, PRIVATE STUDIES

"Mary Katherine Cummings: A Survivor in an Era of Limitations." Presented by Anne E. Collier, Arizona Historical Society

Annual Meeting, Prescott, Arizona, March 2009.

Helldorado: Bringing the Law to the Mesquite by William M. Breakenridge: A Publication History of the Influential and Controversial Autobiography of a Tombstone Lawman and Wyatt Earp Contemporary, by Mark Dworkin, 2005.

"A History of the Land, Owners and Historic Home Situated on Block 29, Lots 20–22, Tombstone, Arizona," by Ray Madzia. *History, Indeed!*, 2008.

" 'Blaze Away!' Doc Holliday's Role in the West's Most Famous Gunfight," by Jeff Morey, 2008.

"Tombstone 2001." The Arizona Territorial Justice Forum at Tombstone Courthouse State Historic Park, Tombstone, Arizona.

RECORDINGS

John Gilchriese taped interviews from the collection of Kevin and Bev Mulkins.

WEB SITES AND CHAT ROOMS

B.J.'s Tombstone History Discussion Forum: http://disc.yourwebapps.com/Indices/396.27.html.

Cochise County Records (Earp Inquest and Spicer Hearing Transcripts): http://azmemory.lib.us/cdm4/browse.php?CISOROOT=/ccolch.

http://library.Stanford.edu/depts/dp/pennies/
time.html.

www.wyattearp.net (hosted by historian-
author Steve Gatto).

www.newmexicohistory.org (official state
site).

ACKNOWLEDGMENTS

I'm grateful as always to Andrea Ahles Koos, my researcher/right hand; Roger Labrie of Simon & Schuster, an editor with a keen eye and tactful manner; and Jim Donovan, the kind of dedicated, plainspoken literary agent that every writer should have.

Kelly Welsh is one of the best young publicists in the business and will someday run Simon & Schuster. You heard it here. I send best wishes to Victoria Meyer, who over the years did so much for me.

Special thanks to my readers who helped me through this complex project. In Arizona they were Lynn Bailey and Bruce Dinges; in New York, Christopher Radko; and in Texas, Mike Blackman, Carlton Stowers, and James Ward Lee.

Ann Kirschner was an invaluable comrade and confidante. I look forward to her new book about Josephine Earp.

No one knows more possible sources of information than Tucson's Bob Pugh, who in addition to operating Trail to Yesterday Books is always ready to help out any writer trying to research a book involving Western history.

Everything I write is always for Nora, Adam, and Grant.

ILLUSTRATION CREDITS

Courtesy of the Arizona Historical Society / Tucson: 1 (#42005), 2 (#14835), 3 (#27242), 4 (#1444), 5 (#11374), 6 (#1441), 7 (#91370), 8 (#1442), 9 (#76636), 11 (#26483), 16 (#91376), 22 (#18346), 26 (24740), 27 (91848), 31 (#17483), 32 (#76627), 33 (#76620)

From the Robert G. McCubbin Collection: 10, 13, 28

From the Kevin & Bev Mulkins Collection: 12, 14, 19, 20, 21, 24, 25, 34

Collection of The New-York Historical Society: 15 (#40746), 17 (#40745), 18 (#40747), 30 (#83285d)

Arizona State Library, Archives and Public Records, History and Archives Division, Phoenix: 23 (#97-2856)

Courtesy of the Ragsdale Collection: 29

ABOUT THE AUTHOR

Jeff Guinn is the bestselling author of numerous books of fiction and nonfiction, including *Go Down Together: The True, Untold Story of Bonnie and Clyde*. An award-winning former investigative journalist and a member of the Texas Literary Hall of Fame, he lives in Fort Worth, Texas.

The employees of Thorndike Press hope you have enjoyed this Large Print book. All our Thorndike, Wheeler, and Kennebec Large Print titles are designed for easy reading, and all our books are made to last. Other Thorndike Press Large Print books are available at your library, through selected bookstores, or directly from us.

For information about titles, please call:

(800) 223-1244

or visit our Web site at:

http://gale.cengage.com/thorndike

To share your comments, please write:

Publisher
Thorndike Press
10 Water St., Suite 310
Waterville, ME 04901